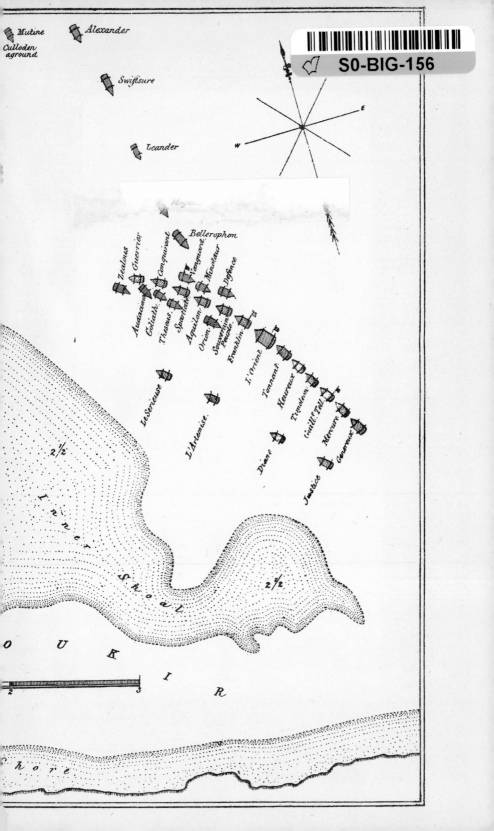

A PORTRAIT OF
LORD NELSON

CAPTAIN HORATIO NELSON, R.N.

by J. F. Rigaud, R.A.

The earliest portrait, begun in 1777; altered in 1781 to show
the insignia of a post-captain. The fort in the background is
that of San Juan, Nicaragua

A PORTRAIT OF
LORD NELSON

Oliver Warner

19
223

1958

CHATTO & WINDUS

LONDON

Published by
Chatto and Windus Ltd
42 William IV Street
London W.C.2

✷

Clarke, Irwin & Co Ltd
Toronto

Printed in Great Britain
© Oliver Warner 1958

To
ELIZABETH

CONTENTS

ILLUSTRATIONS

NOTE.—*Plates II, III, VIa, VII, X, XI and XIIa have*
not been reproduced in any earlier biography of Nelson,
and the Beechey portrait, Plate IX, has been re-
photographed to show its elaborate contemporary frame.

LETTERS & SIGNATURES

BATTLE PLANS

NELSON'S RANKS

c. 1st January 1771	Midshipman	Aged 12
24th September 1776	Acting Lieutenant	Aged 17
9th April 1777	Lieutenant	Aged 18
8th December 1778	Commander	Aged 20
11th June 1779	Captain	Aged 20
4th April 1796	Acting Commodore: 2nd class	Aged 37
11th August 1796	Commodore: first class	Aged 37
20th February 1797	Rear-Admiral of the Blue	Aged 38
17th May 1797	Knight of the Bath	Aged 38
6th November 1798	Peer of the Realm	Aged 40
14th February 1799	Rear-Admiral of the Red	Aged 40
13th August 1799	Duke of Brontë, Sicily	Aged 40
1st January 1801	Vice-Admiral of the Blue	Aged 42
22nd May 1801	Viscount	Aged 42
23rd April 1804	Vice-Admiral of the White	Aged 45
	—Nelson died in this rank, 1805	Aged 47

ACKNOWLEDGEMENTS

I

WITH a work protracted over several years, it is easier to assemble an intricate scaffolding of acknowledgements and notes than to reduce it: but many kindnesses call for thanks.

First I should like to make clear my debt to the Trustees and staff of the National Maritime Museum, for tireless courtesy in helping my researches and for leave to publish material in their care. I was fortunate in working at Greenwich when the Monmouth Manuscripts were being calendared there, and I am grateful to the Trustees of the Monmouth Museum of Nelson relics for allowing me to publish my gleanings, particularly from Nelson's letters to his wife. Great help has also been afforded me by the British Museum, the Bodleian, the Public Record Office, the Admiralty Library and other places I have haunted; while colleagues in the British Council, especially Mr L. Brander and those with whom I arranged an exhibition in honour of the 150th Anniversary of Trafalgar, have given me much cause to thank them.

Among others to whom this book owes a debt are: the Society for Nautical Research; Mr James Champion and Mr Stephen Notcutt; Captain D. H. C. Cooper, R.N.; Lord Cottesloe; Mr Wilfred Granville; Mr Rupert Gunnis, who kindly lent me a transcript of a letter from Captain Harvey of the *Temeraire*; Sir William Halliday; Mr P. Hepworth, City Librarian of Norwich, who, abetted by Messrs R. H. Mottram, W. O. Copeman and T. D. Copeman, persuaded me to attempt my first and last public speech; Mr F. W. Hawcroft; my kinsman Commander Edward Lee, R.N.; Commander H. P. Mead, R.N., Hon. Librarian of Lloyds; Sir Bruce Ingram; Mr Ruari McLean, with whom I descended into the strongholds of Somerset House to see the script of Nelson's prayer before Trafalgar; Mr Charles Mitchell, who cheered me by saying that nobody ever wrote badly about Nelson; Colonel J. Norton; Miss Carola Oman, author of the most attractive Nelson tapestry of modern times; Sir William Parker; the Rev. S. H. Heaton-Renshaw, for courteously giving information about Merton; Mr J. C. Sharp; Mr John Skidmore and the Society for Promoting Christian Knowledge; Mrs K. Suckling of

Roos Hall, Beccles; Mr Peter Smithers, M.P., Mr Maurice and Miss Rose Nelson Ward, for an entrancing glimpse of relics of Emma Hamilton, and Mr F. Y. Thompson. My dedication gives only a faint indication of what I owe to my wife.

II

I am spared a survey of manuscript sources by Miss K. F. Lindsay-MacDougall's authoritative article in the *Mariner's Mirror* (1955), pp. 227-32. One or two later references amplify the field. The principal Nelson literature is already listed and annotated in my *Lord Nelson: a Guide to Reading* (Caravel Press, 1955). Where sources are not given in the text, all my information derives from (1) *The Life and Services of Horatio Viscount Nelson*, by James Clarke and John M'Arthur, 2 vols. (1809); (2) *The Dispatches and Letters*, edited by Sir Harris Nicolas, 7 vols. (1844-46), and the many documents quoted therein; and (3) the second volume of *The Nelson and Hamilton Papers*, Morrison MSS. (1893-94). My notes indicate the principal references *other* than these, and earlier volumes of the *Naval Chronicle*.

Nelson rarely punctuated, and his spelling was not faultless. Having experienced the drawbacks of at least one important volume where Nelson documents are printed exactly as they were written, I have followed Sir Harris Nicolas and made use either of his sensible punctuation or, where I have worked from original MS., my own. Nelson wrote a clear hand, left and right: guesswork is seldom necessary.

ABBREVIATIONS

Add. MSS.	British Museum: Additional Manuscripts.
H.M.C.	Historical Manuscripts Commission Reports.
M.M.	*Mariner's Mirror*: the Journal of the Society for Nautical Research.
Mon. MSS.	Monmouth Museum Manuscripts.
N.M.M.	National Maritime Museum, Greenwich.
N. & Q.	Notes and Queries.
N.R.S.	Navy Records Society Publications.
P.R.O.	Public Record Office documents.

I. LEGACY

The Mirror of the Sea, Joseph Conrad (1903), XLVII.
Memoirs, Sir Edward Codrington, 2 vols. (1873). A copy annotated by his daughter, Lady Bouchier, British Museum, C. 45, f. 12.

2. PRELUDE

I First Ordnance Survey: Sheets 68 and 69. Information for this survey was gathered in Nelson's lifetime. I have consulted the Admiralty copy of the first printing. *United Services Journal* (1841), Pt. I, p. 560.

II The Rev. Edmund Nelson's family notes are among *N.M.M.* manuscripts.

III *A Voyage Towards the North Pole*, Constantine Phipps (1773).

IV *M.M.* (1948), p. 121. Contains Cdr. G. Rawson's valuable summary of the logs of H.M.S. *Seahorse*, etc., in the East Indies.

VI *A Brief History of the Late Expedition against Fort St Juan*, Thomas Dancer, Kingston, Jamaica (1792). *M.M.*, (1924) p. 78, (1942) pp. 213-21.

VII *N. & Q.*, 8th Series, XI (1897), p. 201. Includes Nelson's letter from New York.

IX *Letters and Papers of Sir Thomas Byam Martin*, ed. Sir R. Hamilton (1905), N.R.S. Includes glimpses of Nelson in the West Indies.

X *Nelson's Letters from the Leeward Islands*, ed. G. Rawson (1953). Includes notes by Prof. Michael Lewis and is valuable for letters and documents previously unpublished.

XI *Mon. MSS.*, Nelson Papers, Vol. I. Includes Nelson's letters to his wife, 1785-94, which have not been published *in extenso*, though I understand that the Navy Records Society have an edition in preparation. The extracts in this and later sections are from this source.
Add. MSS. 28, 333. Includes Lady Nelson's marriage certificate and other personal documents.
N. & Q., Vol. 150, p. 55.
P.R.O. Adm. 1/5325. Contains details of William Clark's court-martial.
Nelson's first statement of his services is quoted in *M.M.* (1944), pp. 18-21, from an MS. now in *N.M.M.* (Nelson-Ward MS.).

XII *Naval Miscellany*, Vol. IV, ed. C. Lloyd (1952), N.R.S. Includes the full story of the Prince and Lieut. Schomberg.

3. Partisan

I *P.R.O.* Adm. 36/11358 (*Agamemnon's* Muster Book), Society for Promoting Christian Knowledge, General Board Minutes, 5.3.1793. I am obliged to Mr John Skidmore for the transcription of items in the Society's Minutes which refer to Nelson, and for the Society's kind permission to reproduce them.

II Nelson's Journal, 27.6.1793 to 24.3.1794. Phillipps MS. 89/14 (Nel/1), *N.M.M.* I am grateful to Mr Peter Smithers, author of the *Life of Joseph Addison* (1954), for clarifying Nelson's reference to the *Spectator*.
Freshly Remembered: the Story of Thomas Graham, Lord Lynedoch, Cecil Aspinall-Oglander (1956), p. 60.

IV Francis Drake's Papers are now *Add. MSS.* 46822-38. An important series of letters from Nelson to Prince William Henry, 1795-1805, are now *Add. MSS.* 46356.
Diary of Sir John Moore, ed. Sir F. Maurice, 2 vols. (1904).
Life of Viscount Nelson, James Harrison, 2 vols. (1806).
The relevant sentences by Captain Thomas Fremantle are quoted from Chapter 19 of the enchanting selection from the *Wynne Diaries* made by Anne Fremantle for the Worlds Classics (1952). Captain Fremantle's Diary is not printed in the original 3 vol. edition (1935, 1937 and 1940).

VI *Tomlinson Papers*, ed. J. G. Bullocke (1935), N.R.S. Includes Miller's letter on Nelson's kindness to him.

4. The Year of Fame

I *A Narrative of the Battle of St Vincent with Anecdotes of Nelson*, Col. K. Drinkwater Bethune (2nd Ed. 1840). First published anonymously in 1797. Additional material was added to the 1840 edition by Admiral Sir George Cockburn.
M.M. (1954), pp. 228-30. Includes a valuable summary of Spanish accounts by Rear-Admiral A. H. Taylor. I have also examined the unpublished Private Journals and Memoranda Books of Lieut. W. B. Wyke, R.N., No. 35/36 in the Library of the Royal United Services Institution.

II *Add. MS.* 37, 877, ff. 5, 29, 30. Includes details of the presentation of the Spanish sword to Norwich. It is now in the mediaeval Guildhall, part of a trophy-memorial of great interest, designed by Jeremiah Freeman.

IV *N. & Q.*, 12th Series, XI, p. 321. Includes details of Nelson's wound, from the Surgeon's Journal.

5. THE NILE

I S.P.C.K. General Board Minutes, 6.2.1798. *The Diary of Lady Francis Shelley*, ed. R. Edgcumbe (1912).
Cop/2e, *N.M.M.* Nelson's letter to Baldwin.

II *An Authentic Narrative of the Proceedings of H.M. Squadron under the command of Sir H. Nelson* . . . (1798). The most immediate and authentic account of the Nile is this, by Sir Edward Berry, originally published anonymously.
The Friend, Samuel Taylor Coleridge (ed. H. Coleridge 1837). Essay IV contains Ball's anecdote of the Nile.
Add. MS. 34, 974. *Vanguard's* log covering the Battle of the Nile.

III *P.R.O.* Adm. Med. Journal 124 (1). Includes details of the Nile wound.
Minto and Fitzharris details quoted in A. T. Mahan, *Life of Nelson*, 2 vols. (1897).

IV *Add. MSS.* 34, 989. Contains Emma Hamilton's letter on hearing news of the Nile.

6. NAPLES AND SICILY

I *Italienische Reise*, Goethe (16th March 1787).
The Letters of Lord Nelson to Lady Hamilton (1814), Vol. II, p. 173. Contains Hamilton's expression of his philosophy.
A friend, Mr J. Tipping, long in service at Up Park, tells me that the servants knew a very large silver dish as one in which Emma was brought into the dining-room to dance on the table for the edification of Sir Harry Featherstonehaugh and his friends.

II *Mon. MSS.*, Nelson Papers, Vol. I. Includes Nelson's letter to Fanny on the Naples festivities; Edmund Nelson's letter to the Rev. B. Allott is quoted in *Nelson's Friendships*, H. Gamlin, 2 vols. (1899).

III *Nelson and the Neapolitan Jacobins*, H. Gutteridge (1903), N.R.S. Invaluable for the Naples period.

VII Cop/2a, *N.M.M.* Nelson's letter urging the presence of the King at Naples.

VIII *Praeterita*, John Ruskin (1893), Chap. III.

X *Keith Papers*, Vol. I, ed. W. G. Perrin (1927), N.R.S.; Vol. II, ed. C. Lloyd (1950), N.R.S.; Vol. III, ed. C. Lloyd (1955), N.R.S.
Nelsonian Reminiscences, G. S. Parsons, ed. W. H. Long (Reprint of 1905).

7. HOMECOMING

I James Harrison's *Life* of 1806 is valuable for this and all sections which concern Nelson's life in England.
M.M. (1935), pp. 153-7. Contains a digest of accounts of Nelson's Continental journey.
N. & Q., 12a, Series IV, p. 129 (Collenbach).

II Through the kindness of Miss Rose Nelson Ward, I have been able to examine pieces of the actual dress worn by Emma at Palermo, and Yarmouth.
Autobiography, Cornelia Knight, 2 vols. (1861).
Dearest Bess: the Life and Times of Lady Elizabeth Foster, D. M. Stuart (1955). Contains vivid glimpses of Nelson in the years immediately before Trafalgar, based on the MSS. of Lord Dormer.
Add. MSS. 37, 076, f. 49, shows what is probably the last signature of Nelson and his wife to occur on the same document. It relates to the release of Ipswich property.
Farington's Diary. Entry for 13.12.1805 (B.M. transcript 2878/3140).
H.M.C. Var. Coll. vi, p. 339 (Cornwallis Wykeham-Martin MS.). Containing reference to Lady Nelson at Bath.

8. The Baltic

I S.P.C.K. General Board Minutes, 13.1.1801.
Letters of Lord St Vincent: 1801-1804, ed. D. Bonner Smith, Vol. I (1922), Vol. II (1927), N.R.S.
Naval Miscellany, Vol. II, ed. J. K. Laughton (1912), N.R.S. Valuable for St Vincent's letters about Nelson.
Naval Miscellany, Vol. I, ed. J. K. Laughton (1902), N.R.S. Contains letters from Nelson to Troubridge on the Baltic expedition.
Add. MSS. 28, 333. Includes what remains of the original of Nelson's last letter to Fanny.

II *Cumloden Papers* (1871). Include details of Col. Stewart's Baltic service.
Nelson's Baltic Journal, 12.3.1801 to 13.5.1801. Phillipps MS. (Nel/30), *N.M.M.*

IV *Add. MS.* 30, 927. Southey's letters to his naval brother Tom, extending over many years, include evidence of how much he relied on Tom for details of the Baltic campaign. "I believe I am making a most impressive narrative of the battle with your help," he wrote in 1812: and later: "You have made me glad that I have written."
Add. MS. 46, 119. Includes Nelson's letters to Captain Thomas Thompson of the *Bellone*.
Three Dorset Captains at Trafalgar, A. M. Broadley and R. G. Bartelot (1906). Including original letters from Captain Hardy covering events from the Baltic to the end of Nelson's life.

VI *Add. MS.* 34, 274, f. 61. Contains Nelson's important letter of 24th May to Emma Hamilton from the Baltic.

9. England, Home and Beauty

I *Sir William Beechey*, W. Roberts (1907).
John Hoppner, W. Mackay and W. Roberts, 2 vols. (1909, 1914).

II *Add. MS.* 30, 182. Contains material relating to the attack on
the Boulogne flotilla.

I was lately enthralled by a conversation in Merton churchyard
where an inhabitant, tending the grave of her father,
offered to show the exact spot on which Nelson and Emma
emerged from the "Merton tunnel" to attend divine service.
Nel/37, *N.M.M.*

IV Expense item inserted in A. M. Broadley's extra-illustrated
and documented copy of Clarke and M'Arthur. *B.M.* 556
g. 1, Vol. VI, p. 312.

10. THE LONG WATCH

I *The Friend*, S. T. Coleridge (Ed. of 1837), Essay VI.
Observations upon Military and Political Affairs, George Monck
(1671).
Vigée Le Brun, W. H. Helm (1915).

II *The Influence of Sea Power upon the French Revolution*, A. T.
Mahan.

IV *Add.* 34966/8. Nelson's notebook series.

V *P.R.O.*, C.O. 300/6. Quoted in *N. & Q.*, Vol. 159, p. 272.
B.M. Egerton MS. 2240. Contains letters on the failure of the
West Indian foray.

11. FAREWELL TO ENGLAND

I *The Friend*, S. T. Coleridge, Essay VI.

II *The Nelsons of Burnham Thorpe*, M. Eyre Matcham (1911).
Correspondence and Diaries of J. W. Croker, ed. L. Jennings
(1884).
Memoirs of the Life & Services of John Theophilus Lee (1836).

12. TRAFALGAR

I *H.M.C.*, 15th Report Appendix p. ii.
Eliot Hodgkin MS., p. 661. Contains Nelson's message to
Emma concerning Weymouth.

II *United Services Magazine* (1847), Pt. III. Includes little-known Trafalgar details.

N. & Q., 4th Series, II (1868), p. 357.

III *M.M.* (1950), pp. 281-321. Rear-Admiral Taylor's account of Trafalgar comprises an excellent summary of research.

IV *Authentic Narrative of the Death of Lord Nelson*, William Beatty (1807).

The Friend, S. T. Coleridge, Essay VI.

B.M. Egerton MS. 1614, ff. 125-6. Nelson's last letter to Emma Hamilton, and her sad postscript.

The Gibraltar Chronicle, issue of Thursday, 24th October 1805, had one of the biggest scoops in newspaper history, with the first news of Trafalgar. According to this account, published in English and French, Nelson's final words were: *"Thank God I have outlived this day, and now I die content."* It is a more journalistic conclusion than Doctor Scott's.

Chapter 1

LEGACY

Si monumentum requiris, circumspice

THE biographer of Nelson, like the classical trage-
dian, works upon material long and widely known.
The subject of his attention is buried in St Paul's,
beneath the centre of the most splendid dome in Northern
Europe. In Trafalgar Square rises a memorial column, a
copy of one belonging to the temple of Mars Ultor in Rome.
Above it, a limestone statue faces towards the sea. Impressive
as is the monument, it would not out-top the *Victory*, as her
builders designed her. This, Nelson's flagship, preserved in
her Trafalgar condition, though without her graceful spread
of sail, is a principal feature of Portsmouth, where the
admiral embarked for his final weeks at sea. Near that sea-
port, high on Portsdown Hill, stands the pillar erected by
his companions-in-arms, subscribed for out of their prize-
money.

Nelson memorials abound. The church at Burnham
Thorpe in which he worshipped as a boy has been restored
in his memory. Much of the National Maritime Museum is
illustrative of his exploits. There is an effigy of almost startling realism within the precincts of Westminster Abbey.
Edinburgh and Dublin have their statues, as has many
another city. His literature is greater than that of any other
fighting seaman, and one of his noblest interpreters, Alfred
Mahan, belonged to the American Navy.

Nelson has in fact suffered from much idolatry and some
attack; and perhaps the greatest danger in any new venture
in portraiture lies in distorting the trivial merely because it
includes details hitherto unpublished. Proportion is the first
essential, together with the need to recognise the fact that it
is possible to re-create a vivid image entirely from Nelson's
own surviving letters and despatches, so affectionately edited
by Sir Harris Nicolas more than a century ago. Most per-

sonal judgments on any question affecting Nelson's career may be tested against what he himself said on the subject, and Nelson had an immense range of experience, a broad mind, and, for all his occasional extravagances, a realist's view of himself and of the world in general. The duty is to rediscover not perfection, but the extent of the man's genius.

Nelson himself remarked that all his portraits differed; but posterity has never complained of their variety, or indeed of their number. In his own time he had his special place in folk art: that of the jug, the mug and the coloured glass-picture, as well as in that of the gallery, drawing-room and portfolio. His appeal continues on more than one level. As Mahan wrote: "so much being known, biographies of Nelson will contrast with one another, not in point of abundance of material, but as portraits do, according to the ability of the workman to reproduce, from the original before him, an impression of the man which shall be at once full, true and living."

Wealth of information carries obligations with it. It is almost as unpardonable to be dull about Nelson as to be untruthful. He packed into his forty-seven years enough incident, conflict and passionate feeling to suffice for a score of lesser and longer lives, but there is a sharp division of interest. While the seaman is impatient of the devotion to Lady Hamilton which coloured the last phase, the landsman may well become restive at the thought of long stretches of watch and ward on the sea blockade which occupied so much of his energies. It is the final years which have greatest momentum. Nelson's life, the service thread of which broke in his thirties, rises to a climax with the Battle of St Vincent in 1797, and holds its high strain thereafter. Yet for five full years, between the ages of thirty and thirty-five, he lived in obscurity. This period belongs rather to family than to national history. After his years on half pay, there followed the violently contrasting activity in command of the *Agamemnon*, sudden glory, the loss of his right arm at the repulse of Teneriffe, and, from 1798 onwards, general fame.

With the Battle of the Nile, such a light fell upon Nelson as might have distressed a man of another stamp. He welcomed it. He loved being a hero. If there had been nothing for his conscience to stifle, his life henceforward could have held boundless pleasure, marred only by the frailties of his body and slowly failing sight.

Nelson, the child of a pious household, needed to justify to himself his passion for a friend's wife. The task was difficult, and perhaps no great man has suffered more from the fact that so many private papers belonging to his later life were preserved and published. At least one Trafalgar captain recorded that he would gladly have opened his purse to buy and destroy letters which might, if printed, show his chief in a derogatory light. Although the honourable wish was not fulfilled, there is compensation. Nelson may be known as well as one human being may know another.

The preserved material is strangely consistent. "Good and evil lie close together," Lord Acton once said: "Seek no artistic unity in character." Acton no doubt would have admitted exceptions, for although good and less good lay side by side in Nelson, yet of few men in history may it be said with greater truth that they had "artistic unity in character". Twin ardours burnt in him. One was for fame: the other for Emma Hamilton: but whereas the first lasted his life long, the second belonged only to his years of renown.

Through his admiration for Lady Hamilton, Nelson made himself, at times, ridiculous. The evidence is overwhelming, some of it forced from reluctant friends. But, although that is true, it is only one of the many ingredients which make him of such unceasing interest. He hurt, deeply and permanently, two people in his life: himself and his wife. To set against that, he gave pleasure to all the rest of his immediate family, and to the thousands of officers and men who served with him by land and sea. He won for the sea profession laurels which still adorn it. "Not the least glory of the Navy is that it understood Nelson," wrote Joseph Conrad. "In a few short years he revolutionised not the strategy or tactics of sea warfare, but the very conception of victory itself. He brought heroism into the line of duty. Verily he is a terrible ancestor."

Where Nelson brought heroism, there it has stayed. No single man was more responsible for a tradition which, during the century and a half after Trafalgar, armed those who followed after him with a confidence in "combat supremacy" (to use Mahan's phrase) which no inequality in numbers could disturb. One of his favourite pupils, Sir William Hoste, flew the signal *"Remember Nelson"* at his victory of Lissa, six years after Nelson's death. Codrington, Captain of the *Orion* in 1805, commanded in chief at Navarino in 1827, the last fleet action wholly under sail. The change to steam was revolutionary, but accounts of Nelson's life were among the favourite reading of Lord Beatty, who led the battle-cruisers so unfalteringly at Jutland. The conscious or inherited memory of Nelson has been a factor on every occasion when his country has been at odds. He will always be the prototype of resolution, activity and thought within the province of the admiral, and the unwarranted, but touching, legend still persists that the three lines of piping which adorn the bluejacket's collar stand for his great victories, the Nile, Copenhagen and Trafalgar.

Chapter 2

PRELUDE

I

WHEN he was forty-one years old and a peer of the
realm, Nelson sent John M'Arthur, editor of the
Naval Chronicle, a sketch of his life. This, Nelson's
longest attempt at formal autobiography, contains a number
of omissions and one or two incidents which would not otherwise have been recorded. It is in a style of self-satisfaction
which, though justified, was perhaps superfluous in the
victor of the Nile. "I am sensible," said Nelson, "it wants
your pruning knife before it is fit to meet the public eye. I
trust you and your friend will do that, and turn it into much
better language." The "friend" was James Clarke, joint
editor with M'Arthur. They printed his sketch *verbatim* in
the official biography they compiled some years later. Short
as it is, the sketch is an essential document for the earlier
years.

Nelson was a parson's son. The father he so rightly respected was rector of Burnham Thorpe, which, together
with a cluster of other Burnhams ("homesteads by the
stream"), Burnham Westgate, Burnham Market, Burnham
Overy, Burnham Ulph, Burnham Norton, Burnham Sutton,
Burnham Deepdene, Burnham St Andrew and Burnham
Harbour, lies close to or upon the northernmost sea-coast of
Norfolk, the nearest town being Wells and the nearest port
of any size King's Lynn.

By most standards, Burnham Thorpe is still remote; it is
even quiet, on the rare days when machines from a nearby
airfield do not whirr and thunder overhead, portents of the
new air-sea power which Nelson, with his questing mind,
would well have understood. What is hard to apprehend, in
an age when it is difficult to reach any spot to which the
sound of speeding traffic does not penetrate, is the quiet of
such a hamlet in the eighteenth and early nineteenth century,

before even the railway had ramified into the district. When northerly and easterly winds did not roar inland from the North Sea, such stillness would descend as is today almost unattainable. The only sounds would have been those of nature, of the farm-yard, of the rare horse-drawn vehicle, of the tools of those working in the fields, of the windmill and the hand-pump. Countrymen knew places, and knew one another with a depth which time and settled propinquity alone could bring. Everything had individuality; everything, large and small, had its proportion and value. Nelson's attachment to his home has often been remarked, but it would have been stranger, in a man whose family had long roots in Norfolk, had it been absent.

From the earliest Ordnance Survey map, which was planned within Nelson's own lifetime and published not many years after his death, it is possible to realise a little of the nature of this undulating district. The Burnhams were within easy distance of the splendid estate of Holkham, planted and fostered by Coke of Norfolk. Houghton, the domain of the Walpoles, was within a tolerable walk; so was Sandringham, not then a royal property. There was a maze of lanes, with brick kilns and gravel and clay pits here and there at the roadside. A straight lane led from the parsonage to a signal staff on the sand-dunes. From these dunes, at almost any time of the year except mid-winter, the Nelsons would have seen a great variety of coasting vessels—galliots, busses, hoys, brigantines, sloops, wherries, billanders, luggers, cutters, snows—carrying a flow of goods now carried by rail and road. Inland, too, Norfolk was a maze of waterways. Ships and boats, mills, small neat farms, the beasts and implements of the land—these would have been the local commonplaces.

"We stand and look right across the North Sea to the North Pole," says the local guide. "There is nothing to break the sweep of tumbling waters, save the fields and cliffs of ice which ring it round. And well do we know all this when the Nor' Easters whistle in off our steel-gray sea every day from January to June; stiffening our backs and shutting tight our mouths. It may be a welcome thing for the wind to reach some land at last; but it can hardly expect a welcome from

the inhabitants." Nevertheless, they have proved a hardy
breed, and although, when opportunity afforded, the Nelson
family migrated to the softer climate of Bath, they never
settled there, and returned to renew their bonds with their
own village, and with the people they came to know so well.

Nelson's mother was the daughter of Doctor Maurice
Suckling, Prebendary of Westminster. His maternal great-
grandmother was sister to Sir Robert Walpole, statesman
and First Minister to the early Georges. The Nelsons and
Walpoles were friends as well as connections. The second
Lord Walpole of Wolterton, whom Nelson was later to
describe with perfect truth as a political cypher, was his god-
father, and it was from him that "Horatio" derived. One of
the more famous members of the Walpole family, stricken
with the same Christian name, wrote from Strawberry Hill
that he preferred to sign himself "Horace, an English name
for an Englishman". There is evidence that the youthful
Nelson felt the burden, for an entry in the registry at Burnham which he signed "Horace"—he then being aged eleven
—as witness to a marriage, was changed by his grave father
into the more pompous alternative. But "Horace" he remained to most members of the family.

Through both his parents, Nelson had many ties in East
Anglia. The Sucklings were high in the social scale, and
possessed landed property. The Nelsons, who had a small
patrimony at Hilborough, together with a gift of the living,
themselves inclined to learning, though an education at
Cambridge did not make the Reverend Edmund good at
spelling. Before Horatio became famous, his father contributed some notes on the family to an East Anglian newspaper. From this he made it clear that, although his own
father had been rector of Hilborough, an Etonian and a
member of Emmanuel College, Cambridge, his mother had
been the daughter of John Bland, a baker in Petty Cury in
the university town. Very remarkable she must have been:
she lived to be ninety-three, and a surviving portrait shows
whence her favourite grandson, Horatio, derived his eyebrows, nose and shape of face.

"I was born September 29th, 1758, in the Parsonage
House [Burnham Thorpe], was sent to the high school at

Norwich, and afterwards removed to North Walsham; from whence, on the disturbance with Spain relative to Falkland's Islands, I went to Sea with my uncle, Captain Maurice Suckling, in the *Raisonable* of 64 guns." The words are Nelson's. In point of fact, he went to three Norfolk schools. A weather-worn statue in the cathedral close at Norwich commemorates his connection with the Grammar School foundation, north-east of the Erpingham Gate. His next school was south-west of Burnham, at Downham Market, a fact which might have escaped record but for a note contributed anonymously to a service magazine, possibly by Captain George Manby. The Captain must have been a very small person at the time that he and Nelson were school-fellows, for he was seven years the Admiral's junior. He remarked three details which are not otherwise preserved: that their master was called Noakes; that Nelson wore a green coat; and that it was his pleasure to set smaller boys working the pump in the village street, so that he could sail paper boats in the resulting flood.

After Downham Market Nelson went to the eastern part of the county, to the Paston School, North Walsham. There his class-room education ceased. Such additions as would accrue would be made at sea, and they would not be inconsiderable. Nelson always read widely. Shakespeare and the eighteenth-century classics became his familiars, and in his later years he kept himself well supplied with new books.

"The disturbance with Spain relative to Falkland's Islands", which was the immediate cause of Nelson's leaving home at the tender age of twelve, was one of those international storms which soon subside. The wind-swept Falklands, far in the South Atlantic, had already been the subject of much official correspondence, and at least one touch of comedy. In 1764 de Bougainville, the French explorer, had established a settlement at Port St Louis, now Port Stanley. In the following year Captain Jack Byron arrived in H.M.S. *Dolphin*, made a claim for Great Britain, and formed a settlement at Fort Egmont, on the small island of Saunders.

French and English remained for some time in actual ignorance of each other's presence. By the time the true situation was apparent, Spain had asserted a formal claim to sovereignty. This was admitted by France; but finding that

there was no eagerness at Versailles to join forces and expel
the British, Spain withdrew as gracefully as she could.
Alarm died down, though the settlement at Port St Louis
remained for a short time longer.

II

Horatio was always small and seemed frail, though his
constitution proved to have tough qualities, and his moral
ascendancy over his older brother, William, seems ever to
have been plain. He was the sixth child and the fifth son
of his parents, who had a family of eleven, the first, second
and tenth of whom died in infancy. Of the rest, Maurice,
who became a clerk in the Navy Office, was five years older
than Horatio; Susannah, the eldest girl, was three years
older; William, who like his father took Holy Orders, was
a year older; Anne, who died in her twenties, was two years
younger; Edmund, who was four years younger, only lived
to be twenty-eight, while Suckling died in his thirties. The
baby of the family, Catherine or Kate, a general favourite,
the girl whom Nelson sometimes called Katty, was born in
1767.

To provide for such a brood out of the resources of a
country living was hard. It was not lightened for the rector
by the loss of his wife, she and her mother dying within a
week of one another in the bitter Christmas weather of 1767,
when Horatio was only nine. Catherine Nelson is shadowy.
Many years later her famous son said with the unabashed
sentiment which came so naturally to him: "The thought of
former days brings all my mother to my heart, which shows
itself in my eyes."[1] Whether he remembered her connectedly
is uncertain: but he cherished the idea of her, recalled that
she "hated the French", and must often have heard Susannah
say that "she was quite a heroine for the sailors".

To an only child, the death of a mother is always calami-

[1] This is one of Nelson's various half-remembered quotations from Shakespeare's *Henry V* (IV, vi) which seems to have been, not unnaturally perhaps.
his favourite play.

tous and sometimes irreparable. In the case of a large and vigorous family, headed by a father determined to spare nothing in devotion, and by a girl who, though only twelve, was of a cheerful and capable disposition, what was lost in guidance was to some extent at least made up for by independence of spirit and strong mutual affection. Nor was this all. Catherine Nelson left behind her an infant in arms, her namesake, and three other children of still tender years, and it is certain that the family owed much—how much will never now be known—to the nurse, Blackett, who afterwards married Mr High, landlord of the Old Ship Inn at Brancaster Bay, and to a succession of Burnham girls who would have been glad enough to take service in the rectory for the derisory wages which were then the rule.

"Nelson's nurse"—she would in fact have had little to do with him, Horatio being one of the older children—duly achieved immortality in local lore. Nearly two centuries after she first assumed her responsibilities, villagers of Burnham Thorpe remembered her married name, as well as the fact that one of her relations, Valiant High, was called after a Burnham man who fought at Trafalgar.

For all the care given them under the eye of their father, it was apparent that the Nelson children would need to fend for themselves as soon as they could be found openings away from home. Susannah, the first to leave, was apprenticed to a "reputable Milliner" in Bath, according to her father's careful notes. After three industrious years, she "went assistant into a shop". Then she had two legacies, one of £500 from a family friend, John Norris, and another from her uncle, Captain Maurice Suckling. Thus endowered, at the age of twenty-six she married Thomas Bolton of Wells, who was "in a prosperous way of trade in corn, malt, coals etc.". Later on, due partly to the wars, Bolton had his difficulties in a varied career which at one time included farming, and he was glad of anything his naval brother-in-law could do for him.

Maurice and William, the first through influence and the second after graduating at Cambridge, followed family habit in becoming professional men. Edmund, it was hoped, would become assistant in Bolton's business, that is, if his precarious health allowed. Suckling, who for some time was a worry to his father, since he could not settle down to anything, at last decided to take Orders, though he did not live long to help with the scattered parish and died, after what his father privately recorded as a *"very* convivial evening" in a farmer's parlour.

Lifelong habit, a feeling for the conservation of his health, the easy customs of incumbents of his time, and a longing for warmth made Bath a second home to the Reverend Edmund Nelson, and it was to the West Country spa that William, at Horatio's request, wrote in 1770 to say that his young brother wished to join the navy. The rector could see no objection. Maurice Suckling, his late wife's brother, was a post-captain of seniority and influence, and would surely help. It was so. "What has poor Horatio done, who is so weak, that he, above all the rest, should be sent to rough it out at sea?" asked Suckling. "But let him come," he added, "and the first time we go into action a cannon ball may knock off his head, and provide for him at once."

III

In the eighteenth century, as at other times, the success of a man's career hinged largely upon the influence he could summon. Merit might help, but it could go unrecognised for a lifetime. The powerful patron, on the other hand, could ensure position, and, in certain circumstances, the means of fortune.

It is unlikely that, in choosing the navy, Nelson was possessed of any but the broadest idea of what life in King's ships entailed. On the other hand, he did know his uncle, who kept the 21st of October with ceremony each year in honour of a fight he had had against odds in the West Indies in 1757, during the Seven Years War, when three ships, of which his was one, had attacked more than twice their number and worsted the enemy. As a small child Nelson would have heard the famous song "Heart of Oak", composed in celebration of the Year of Victories, 1759, when

Wolfe and Saunders had taken Quebec, Boscawen had defeated De la Clue off Lagos, and Hawke had won a triumph of Handelian grandeur on a lee shore at Quiberon Bay. He had, in fact, been born into an heroic age of naval achievement, though not long after he first went to sea, the War of American Independence placed the navy in adversity, from which it took time to recover.

The aim of an officer of the Georgian navy was to become a post-captain as soon as possible—to be "made" or "made post" in the phrase of the time. In war, promotion could result from distinguished conduct under fire, as well as through influence. In peace, influence was paramount. Two consequences followed from the attainment of post rank: the first was the lion's share in any prize-money which might accrue to the ship; the second, given time, was elevation to admiral's rank, which came strictly by seniority. How soon a flag was obtained depended much upon the circumstances of the nation. War speeded promotion, though there was always a long wait: sometimes it was interminable.

The hope of prize-money resulting from the capture of enemy merchantmen, of bounty for capture or destruction of enemy men-of-war, and freightage on bullion, was not illusory. Scattered about the countryside were estates acquired by admirals at the expense of their country's enemies. The most famous example was Lord Anson. Successors, though rarely on his scale of splendour, appeared throughout the century. If the navy was a lottery, and a career therein unlikely to be continuous in peace-time, when most of the ships were laid up "in ordinary" to use the phrase of the period, it offered at least the chance of wealth in periods of disturbance; and it was rare, throughout the century, for England not to be at war with France, or Spain, or both together.

Although, in Nelson's case, the attainment of even lieutenant's rank was looking well ahead, there was always a demand for places for youngsters as pupils of distinguished post-captains such as Suckling, since such patronage led to the quarter-deck. Meanwhile, the small boy who arrived at Chatham on 1st January 1771 was lonely and unhappy. The captain was ashore when he arrived, and it was some time before he could find anyone to look after him. The ordeal of a child facing the unknown world is repeated in every generation in a country in which, for the middle classes, the boarding-school system is traditional. In Nelson's case, separation from home arose from choice, though the motive was largely unselfish. He had already been away at school with his brother, and had survived the first sharp pangs of homesickness; but he was heard to murmur "too young" when, many years later, an awed youngster at his table told him at what age he had first gone to sea. The guest, who was then still a midshipman, had joined a first-rate on active service in the Mediterranean at the age of eleven, and he had not been exceptional.

After about a year's employment in the *Raisonable*, Suckling suggested that his nephew should go on a voyage in a West India ship, belonging to the firm of Hibbert, Purrier and Horton. The master, John Rathbone, had formerly been in the navy, and had served under Suckling in H.M.S. *Dreadnought*. The Caribbean adventure lasted about a year. "If I did not improve my education," wrote Nelson, "I returned a practical seaman, with a horror of the Royal Navy, and with a saying then constant with the seamen, 'Aft the most honour, forward the better man.' It was many weeks," he added, "before I got in the least reconciled to a Man-of-War, so deep was the prejudice rooted; and what pains were taken to instil this erroneous principle in a young mind!" The prejudice endured long after the coming of steam, and has not yet died.

The effect on Nelson of this foreign voyage was important. It confirmed him in his choice of a seafaring life. Moreover, throughout his career his understanding of the merchantmen's outlook, by no means general in the navy of his day, made him considerate of their difficulties, particularly in time of war. Many sea careers have started in the navy and ended in the mercantile marine. It is pleasing that his country's foremost admiral admitted that it was in a trading vessel that he learnt the rudiments of his profession.

Nelson re-entered the royal service, first as captain's servant and later as midshipman in H.M.S. *Triumph*. In

1773, when he was a month or so short of fifteen, he heard that two King's ships, the *Racehorse* and the *Carcass*, were being fitted out, at the instance of the Royal Society, to make scientific observations within the Arctic Circle. The commander was Constantine Phipps, later Lord Mulgrave. The captain of the *Carcass* was Skeffington Lutwidge, whom Nelson had met. Although no boys were to go, "as being of no use", "yet," said Nelson, "nothing could prevent my using every interest to go with Captain Lutwidge . . . and, as I fancied I was to fill a man's place, I begged I might be cockswain: which, finding my ardent desire for going with him, Captain L. complied with, and has continued the strictest friendship to this moment. Lord Mulgrave, who I then first knew, continued his kindest friendship and regard to the last moment of his life." Nelson could have added, with perfect truth, that to serve with him, either as superior or subordinate, was to become his partisan.

The expedition, which got to within ten degrees of the Pole before being stopped by ice, produced no valuable results. A dignified account was published by Phipps, and as the expedition happened to contain among its members John Cleveley the younger, the son of an admirable though neglected follower of Canaletto, and himself one of the better marine painters of his time, it is possible to know exactly what the vessels looked like as they lay immobile in the ice. It was thought at first that they would have to be abandoned. When boats were fitting out to leave the blocked-up ships, Nelson exerted himself to have the command of a four-oared cutter, "which was given me, with twelve men; and I prided myself in fancying I could navigate her better than any other boat in the ship".

Captain Lutwidge, who outlived Nelson by nearly ten years and rose to the top of the Navy List, used to tell a story about his youthful coxswain. It appeared that one night, in the middle watch, Nelson stole away from the ship with a seaman, taking advantage of a fog. The pair set off across the ice in chase of a polar bear. They were soon missed. The fog thickened, and Lutwidge became alarmed for their safety.

Between three and four o'clock in the morning the

H.M. SHIPS
RACEHORSE
AND *CARCASS*
IN THE POLAR
ICE

by John Cleveley

Nelson served
in 1773 as a
midshipman
in the *Carcass*,
which is to the
right of the picture

Victoria and Albert Museum

weather cleared, and the two adventurers were seen at a
considerable distance in the act of attacking the bear. The
signal of recall was made at once. Nelson's companion urged
him to obey it, but in vain. Though his musket had misfired,
his ammunition was spent, and a gap in the ice divided him
from the bear, he was determined to bring it back. "Do but
let me get a blow at this devil with the butt-end of my
musket, and we shall have him!" said Nelson. Lutwidge, no
doubt knowing more than Nelson about the capabilities of
the polar bear, fired one of the ship's guns. This frightened
the animal, which made off. The pair then returned, apprehensive of their reception. Lutwidge reprimanded Nelson
sternly, as being the leader in the affair, and asked what
motive he could have had for hunting under such conditions. "Sir," said the midshipman, "I wished to kill the bear
that I might carry the skin to my father."

IV

Not content with home waters, the West Indies and the
Arctic, Nelson, hearing of a squadron fitting out for the
East, discovered that "nothing less than such a distant
voyage could in the least satisfy my desire of maritime knowledge: and I was placed in the *Seahorse* of 20 guns, with
Captain Farmer, and watched in the foretop; from whence in
time I was placed on the quarter-deck having, in the time I
was in this ship, visited almost every part of the East Indies,
from Bengal to Bussorah." By "Bussorah" Nelson meant
Basrah, but this may be one of the rare mis-statements in his
Sketch.

Nelson's admiral in the East Indies, Sir Edward Hughes,
always showed him "the greatest kindness". He could have
afforded to do so. Having the enjoyment of two separate
periods as commander-in-chief on the East Indian station,
Sir Edward was able to bequeath his step-son a fortune of no
less than £40,000 a year. Many dukes would have exchanged
their worldly goods with him, and it was Nelson's fate
throughout life to serve under, or close to, men who made

large fortunes, but never to be outstandingly lucky himself in the matter of prize. It is untrue to say that he never valued money. All men do, who have ever felt the lack of it. He did not, however, care for money-making. ("I never did, or could," he wrote to his sister, Mrs Bolton), but he did not forget that there was a reason for being in the navy, through which it was possible to help his family. "All my money I have full confidence you will lay out to best advantage," he wrote many years later to his banker, Mr William Marsh. "I care not for myself, but as it may be useful to my friends, and it is this alone which drains my pocket."

The *Seahorse* sailed from Spithead on 19th November 1773 in company with the *Salisbury*, which flew Hughes's broad pendant. Nelson was at first rated midshipman, then —after April 1774—as Able Seaman. His lifelong friend Thomas Troubridge served with him. Years later he told Admiral Cornwallis that the Master of the *Seahorse* had been a "very clever man, and we constantly took the lunar observations". He added that he thought the log would be found to be among the best of those lodged in the Navy Office, and there is no doubt that he and all the other youngsters were well taught on this commission.

The ship called at Funchal, and long before they reached the Cape of Good Hope, on their way to Madras Roads, Nelson would have realised what service was like under a disciplinarian. The first lieutenant was court-martialled and relieved of his duties, and, in the course of the commission, no less than two hundred times men were lashed at the gratings.

After leaving the Cape, the ships had experience of the Roaring Forties, for they made what was known as the "outward passage", proceeding eastwards as far as the lonely islands of St Paul and Amsterdam before hauling northward towards India. To modern ideas, it was many hundreds of miles out of their course. After visiting Madras they made for the Hoogly River, which they left on 14th January 1775 loaded with "89 chests, said to contain ten lakhs of rupees for Madras". Captain Farmer would have received handsome freightage.

From Madras the *Seahorse* went to Bombay, and from

thence, in March, she sailed for Surat, which was found "insufferably hot". At the end of the month the ship was ordered to Bushire, which was reached on 25th May. There the seamen found that the staff of the English Factory at Basrah had been obliged to leave. The Turks and Persians were at war, and Basrah was infested by 30,000 armed men. It seems unlikely that if Nelson did in fact penetrate to the beleaguered port, details should have escaped notice.

In July 1775 the *Seahorse* was back at Bombay with a convoy. Thence she returned to Madras. On her next run westbound she called at Trincomalee, which Nelson thought the finest harbour in the world. On arrival at Bombay in December 1775, he was down with fever. The surgeon of the *Salisbury* pronounced that a voyage to England offered the only chance of recovery for the young man. He was transferred to the *Dolphin*, Captain James Pigot, and on 23rd March 1776 sailed for home, more dead than alive.

The *Dolphin* frigate was the first of the many ships in which Nelson served which were either famous in themselves or which he made so. Built in 1751 at Woolwich, she was sheathed with copper, the second ship in the navy to be so treated. She had been fitted up to take John Byron on his voyage of circumnavigation in the 'sixties. She made a second voyage round the world immediately after Byron's return, taking Samuel Wallis and his men into the Pacific, the first Europeans to enjoy Tahiti. She was now on her last commission, and her roomy quarters would have added to the comfort of a young invalid.

On his way back to England—the *Dolphin* took over six months for the journey—Nelson suffered from severe depression, caused first by his fever and then by his seeming lack of prospects. But the captain was kindness itself, and presently, health slowly returning, Nelson thought he perceived a radiant orb, which beckoned him on. "A sudden glow of patriotism was kindled within me," he would tell his officers later, "and presented my King and Country as my patron. My mind exulted in the idea. 'Well then,' I exclaimed, 'I will be a hero, and confiding in Providence, I will brave every danger.'"

V

Nelson made such a firm recovery, under the care of
Captain Pigot, that he was off to sea again immediately after
his return home. He owed his new appointment to his uncle,
who was now, as Comptroller of the Navy, head of the Navy
Board, which was concerned with the material as opposed to
the operational side of the service. Suckling was, in fact, very
influential. His brother had already been the means of ensuring a clerkship in his Department for Maurice Nelson,
the most silent and endearing of Nelson's brothers.

The *Dolphin* was paid off at Woolwich on 24th September
1776. Two days later Nelson received an order from Sir
James Douglas, who commanded at Portsmouth, to act as
lieutenant in the *Worcester*, a ship of the line of 64 guns. Her
captain was Mark Robinson, who paid the young man every
attention.

The War of American Independence had broken out in
1775, and although France had not yet become formally
allied with the revolted colonists, the convoy system was in
operation on the main routes of commerce. Nelson's first
employment was in escort duty to Gibraltar. He recorded
that he "was at sea with convoys till April 2nd 1777, and in
very bad weather; but although my age might have been a
sufficient cause for not entrusting me with the charge of a
Watch, yet Captain Robinson used to say 'he felt as easy
when I was upon deck, as any Officer in the Ship' ".

Winter duty in the Channel and the Atlantic, immediately
following a spell in the tropics, might have proved a strain.
It was, in fact, a tonic. Nelson continued in health for another
three years, which were vital in his service life. They gave
him the experience and promotion necessary if he was to
attain the highest rank.

On 9th April 1777 Nelson stood his examination for
lieutenant. The three post-captains who examined him included Suckling among them. In their life of the admiral,
Clarke and M'Arthur said that Suckling "purposely concealed his relationship from the other examining Captains.
When his nephew had recovered from his first confusion, his

answers were prompt and satisfactory, and indicated the talents he so eminently possessed. The examination ended in a manner very honourable to him; upon which his uncle immediately threw off his reserve, and rising from his seat, introduced his nephew. The examining Captains expressed their surprise at his not having informed them of this before. 'No,' replied the independent Comptroller, 'I did not wish the younker to be favoured, I felt convinced that he would pass a good examination; and you see, gentlemen, I have not been disappointed.' "

Nelson sent the good news to his brother William, then at Christ's College, Cambridge, in the first letter printed by Sir Harris Nicolas. "I passed my Degree as Master of Arts on the 9th instant," he reported jocularly, "and received my Commission on the following day, for a fine Frigate of 32 guns. So now I am left in the world to shift for myself, which I hope I shall do, so as to bring credit to myself and friends." Strictly speaking, Nelson should have been twenty years of age before being confirmed in the rank, but like so many regulations of the time, the relevant one was disregarded.

The "fine Frigate" was the *Lowestoffe*. Her captain was William Locker, who remained one of Nelson's friends and confidants until his death, twenty-three years later, as Lieutenant-Governor of Greenwich Hospital. Locker was a robust example of eighteenth-century clarity and assurance. Shrewd, sophisticated, capable, affectionate, he seems to have deserved the good fortune which attended him from the time when, as a young man, he followed Hawke's star and fought at Quiberon Bay, to his serene age when Nelson, having justified all his hopes, wrote: "I have been your scholar; it is you who taught me to board a Frenchman . . . and my sole merit in my profession is being a good scholar."

The *Lowestoffe* was ordered to the Jamaica station, to latitudes familiar to Nelson from his first voyage abroad, but he had a spell of shore leave before sailing. Part of this was spent in London. There, at the desire of Locker, he visited the studio of John Francis Rigaud. Locker, who had a marked sense of history, who kept all Nelson's letters, and whose pleasure was to encourage merit, put posterity in his debt by not only arranging the most famous of all portraits of Nelson from the life, that of Lemuel Francis Abbott, but suggesting the first.

The choice of artist was happy. Rigaud had already attempted one or two naval portraits. With Nelson he excelled himself. Although the picture—through a technical device—conveyed the impression that Nelson, though slender, was reasonably tall, instead of being short of five foot six, it has vitality and charm, enhanced by the tricorne hat, a shape which is so often becoming. Moreover, it was prophetic. Nelson, at eighteen, is seen with the assurance of command. It would not have been an unlikely prophecy on the part of one ignorant of what the subject afterwards became were he to have said, "That young man will either go far, or he will die an early and glorious death." No other certain likeness, except this, and a miniature painted at Leghorn by an unknown artist many years later, shows Nelson before wounds and suffering transformed him. Rigaud did not complete his canvas for some four years, when Nelson returned home. He was then instructed by Nelson to "add beauty", but it is probable that he merely inserted the insignia of rank, the figure of a coxswain waiting for his captain to embark, indications of tropical scenery, and, in the right background, Fort San Juan in Nicaragua, with the British flag above the Spanish. These touches add interest to what would in any event be one of the most precious memorials, and one which bears evidence of Nelson's recognition, from the start of his career, of the value of a clear record of personal achievement.

From England, the *Lowestoffe* proceeded to her station, but life even in a frigate soon proved to be insufficiently active for Nelson's zeal. Locker put him in charge of the schooner *Little Lucy*, which was the *Lowestoffe*'s tender. "In this vessel," said Nelson, "I made myself a complete pilot for all the passages through the Islands situated on the north side of Hispaniola." What Nelson called Hispaniola is the modern Haiti. It was then a French possession.

The *Lowestoffe*'s station was one of active service, and it was Nelson's first experience of war conditions. He proved himself an apt pupil of his captain, who in turn had learnt his business from one of the great admirals of the Seven

Years War, and Nelson's own prototype in tactical daring. Hawke's bold aphorisms would have been heard constantly on Locker's lips. As the old warrior himself survived until after Nelson had achieved post rank, it is just possible that his speculative eye, ranging the published lists of sea officers, may have marked the name which was to inspire as much fear in his country's enemies as he who, Hawke-like, had chosen "Strike" for his motto.

VI

In the summer of 1778 Sir Peter Parker arrived at Jamaica as commander-in-chief. Things then began to stir for Nelson. He was taken into the flagship *Bristol* as Third Lieutenant, rising quickly to become First. The French had now begun to appear in force in American and West Indian waters, adding to the embarrassments of the navy. The general feeling on the station was pessimistic. At home, political feuds embittered the higher ranks, and in the outposts admirals did not always find themselves well supported.

Within a very short time Nelson won Sir Peter's confidence. What was equally important, he was liked by Lady Parker. Before the end of the year, being then just over twenty, he was promoted commander, and appointed to the *Badger* brig. On the same date, 8th December 1778, Cuthbert Collingwood was made second lieutenant of the *Lowestoffe*. It was the first though not the last occasion on which the careers of these two men, who though so different in temperament remained lifelong friends, ran along similar channels, Collingwood, though older, always a step behind. Collingwood, who came from an equally modest background, was a Northumbrian who in appearance and character was in strong contrast to Nelson. His features were regular; Nelson's were otherwise. He was solidly built; Nelson was slim. His mind lacked gaiety; and where Nelson was active and resolute, ever ready to make up his mind and to take and even to enjoy responsibility, Collingwood was apt to slide into a sea of gloom and indecision, throwing himself into battle, where he always carried himself nobly, as if in relief from more perplexing circumstances.

In the *Badger* Nelson was "sent to protect the Mosquito shore, and the bay of Honduras, from the depredations of the American privateers". It was a strange situation, for these settlers, though living within the Spanish Captain-Generalship of Guatemala, had originally come from Jamaica, equipped with negro labour for the banana plantations. An informal protectorate, improvised against buccaneers, Caribs and every other kind of interloper, had been exercised by the island government for over thirty years.

Nelson's area of operations extended along the eastern littoral of what is now part of southern Mexico, Guatemala, Honduras, Nicaragua and Costa Rica. The settlers expressed approval of his services, and urged him to describe how difficult their situation would become in the event of Spain joining forces with France to aid the Americans. This in fact occurred during the course of the following year.

"Whilst I commanded the Brig," recorded Nelson, "H.M.S. *Glasgow*, Captain Thomas Lloyd, came into Montego Bay, Jamaica, where the *Badger* was lying: in two hours she took fire by a cask of rum:"—the steward had tried to steal spirit out of the after hold. "Captain Lloyd will tell you," said Nelson, "that it was owing to my exertions joined to his that her whole crew were rescued from the flames." He also secured a prize, *La Prudente* of eighty tons and nine men, about which he hastened to write to Locker, saying, "We have had a good deal of plague with her," and adding that it took two whole days to find her papers. "They had been concealed in an old shoe."

The rank of commander, which for some years to come was officially "master and commander", signified that the officer was qualified for the charge of a ship not big enough to carry a sailing-master of her own. It brought with it the courtesy title of captain, and it was not uncommon, particularly in war, for officers to hold it for a very short time. This was so in Nelson's case. Admiral Parker had noted him for the first vacancy of the status of post-captain—that is, charge of a ship of upwards of twenty guns.

On 11th June 1779 Nelson was appointed to the frigate

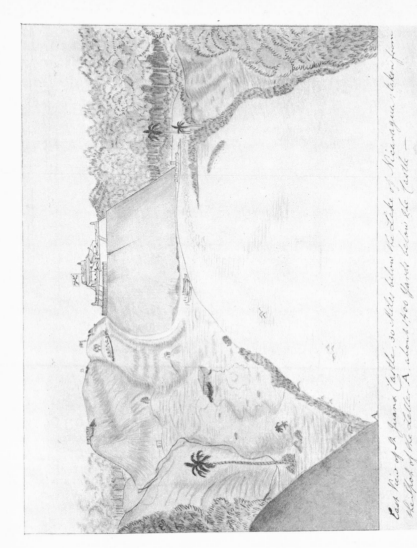

FORT SAN JUAN,
NICARAGUA

A sketch, probably
by Nelson, of the
principal fort captured
during the Expedition
to Nicaragua, 1780

Hinchingbrooke, 32 guns, named in honour of the estate of
the First Lord, the Earl of Sandwich. Her captain had been
killed by a random shot. Nelson was now "made". No one
could be jumped over his head. He had only to live long
enough, and one day he would achieve his flag.

Collingwood succeeded him in the *Badger*, and in time
also commanded the *Hinchingbrooke* as a post-captain. These
appointments, vital to the future of the two men, were confirmed in due course by the Admiralty. No commander-in-
chief could expect automatic approval of his local arrangements, even on active service, but this time no questions
arose. The patronage of Sir Peter was doubly welcome to
Nelson, since in the previous summer Maurice Suckling,
who had commended his nephew to the commander-in-
chief, himself passed beyond the reach of helping the young
man again, except through a legacy. No father could have
done more for him.

As the French admiral Count d'Estaing had by now
arrived at Hispaniola from Martinique, an attack on
Jamaica was expected. In August 1779 Nelson wrote to
Locker, who had by then gone home: "Jamaica is turned
upside down since you left it." The young man had been
entrusted with the command of the batteries at Port
Royal.

Nelson's letters at this time were full of foreboding, shared
by the station. He half expected to be taken prisoner. "I
think," he wrote to Locker, "you must not be surprised to
hear of my learning to speak French." His apprehensions
were in time removed, and French remained one of the
accomplishments he long pursued without notable success.

What Nelson learnt instead was even more useful: it was
the rudiments of amphibious warfare. "In January 1780,"
he wrote, "an Expedition being resolved on against St
Juan's, I was chosen to command the Sea part of it. Major
Polson, who commanded the soldiers will tell you of my
exertions: how I quitted my Ship, carried troops in boats
one hundred miles up a river, which none but the Spaniards
since the time of the buccaneers had ever ascended. . . . It
will then be told how I boarded (if I may be allowed the
expression) an outpost of the Enemy, situated on an Island

in the river; that I made batteries, and afterwards fought them, and was a principal cause of our success."

The success was relative; but Nelson did not exaggerate the merit of his own services, which were voluntary. Polson described them in warm terms. "He was the first on every service whether by night or day," ran the official despatch. "I want words to express what I owe to that gentleman." But the expedition itself, sound in intention, in that it was aimed at a Spanish outpost and offered possibilities of inflicting damage upon the enemy out of proportion to the cost, was, like so many operations of its time, conducted without regard to climate, the season of the year, the experience of the troops or the health of those concerned in its execution.

The plan was to ascend the river San Juan from Greytown, the modern San Juan del Norte, the full hundred miles or so to Lake Nicaragua. This lake, more than a hundred miles in length and more than a hundred feet above sea-level, with three volcanic cones protruding from its depths, lies towards the Pacific side of the isthmus. The modest force detailed for the adventure, drawn from the 60th and 79th Regiments, with some Loyal Irish and Jamaican volunteers, a little more than five hundred in all, was to obtain command of the lake, capture the reputedly rich cities of Granada and Leon, the second of which was beyond the head of Lake Managua, force a passage to the Pacific, and sever communications between north and south. It was a conception in which enthusiasm far outran sense.

As Nelson observed, no members of the force had ever been up the San Juan river, nor had they any idea where Spanish forts were sited. In April, when the campaign began, the river was low, and the men got soaked several times a day dragging boats through the shallows. Fever, snakes, insects, sun, all took their toll, and when Fort San Juan, which appeared to be the key to Granada and much territory beyond it, was at least reached, some thirty miles below the lake, the military insisted on a formal siege. Not for the last time in his life, the elaborate procedure which this entailed exasperated Nelson. He was for instant assault.

Bowing to superior knowledge, he helped to make batteries. Polson said that "there was scarce a gun but what was pointed by him or Lieutenant Despard". The officer referred to was Edward Marcus Despard, one of two Irish brothers attached to the 79th Regiment, skilled as an engineer. Twenty-three years later, when, as a colonel, Despard was on trial for high treason, having grown bitter from neglect, Nelson testified to his character in earlier life. "We served together on the Spanish main," he said. "We were together in the enemies' trenches, and slept in the same tent. Colonel Despard was then a loyal man and a brave officer." Together the pair had led an attack on a small fortified island called San Bartholomew. They had taken the Spanish garrison by surprise, and carried the place without loss.

Nelson was not present at the final operations against Fort San Juan, for he was recalled to Jamaica to command the *Janus*, of 44 guns. The order may well have saved his life, for he was by that time ill with fever. In some remarks which he wrote for an account of the expedition prepared later by his friend Dr Benjamin Moseley, he said, "In the *Hinching-brooke*, with a complement of two hundred men, eighty-seven took to their beds in one night; and of the two hundred, one hundred and forty-five were buried in mine and Captain Collingwood's time; and I believe very few, not more than ten survived of that Ship's crew." The disease which so afflicted the sailors on that steaming coast was known as Yellow Jack.

Nelson commanded the *Janus* until the end of August 1780, but in name only. He was forced to resign through persisting ill health, and was ashore most of the months following his return from Nicaragua. On 12th June he wrote from the Parker's house to Hercules Ross, a friend at Kingston: "Oh, Mr Ross, what would I give to be at Port Royal. Lady Parker not here, and the servants letting me lay as if a log, and take no notice." The next letter, recording his resignation, is the last preserved from his second spell of service in the West Indies. "My state of health was now so bad," said Nelson, "that I was obliged to go to England in the *Lion*, Honourable William Cornwallis, Captain: whose care and attention saved my life."

Cornwallis, with whom he had already lived ashore, was a notable figure in the navy of his time. A younger son of the first Earl Cornwallis, he was some fourteen years older than Nelson. He was stout, rubicund and known as "Billy Blue" or "Billy-go-Tight", though by nature the most abstemious of men. He proved a good friend to Nelson, but although he rose to the highest commands in the service, he was never fortunate in his opportunities. His name appears in the official battle-honours of the navy only by virtue of a masterly retreat, successfully carried out in 1795 in face of daunting odds.

VII

Nelson arrived in England in the autumn of 1780. After a brief visit to Locker and other friends in or near London, he went to Bath, which was his home for the winter. "This is like Jamaica to any other part of England," he wrote to Locker with all the feeling of one who, after three spells in the tropics, keenly disliked the cold.

It is hard to picture Captain Nelson, aged twenty-two, among the Rowlandsonesque figures, bloated and crotchety, who haunted the spa in search of easement for their complaints, many of which were the result of gross feeding. "I have been so ill since I have been here," he wrote to Locker in January from Pierrepont Street, "that I was obliged to be carried to and from bed, with the most excruciating tortures, but, thank God, I am now upon the mending hand. I am physicked three times a day, drink the waters three times, and bathe every other night, besides not drinking wine, which I think the worst of all." His doctor, Woodward, said he never had a better patient, and his fees were so modest that Nelson wished to increase them.

"Pray, Captain Nelson," said the generous man, who was well equipped to deal with gouty old peers with plenty of money, "allow me to follow what I consider to be my professional duty. Your illness, Sir, has been brought on by serving your King and Country, and believe me, I love both too well to be able to receive any more."

By the middle of February Nelson was able to report: "My health is very near perfectly restored; and I have the perfect use of all my limbs, except my left arm, which I can hardly tell what is the matter with it. From the shoulder to my fingers' ends are as half dead; but the Surgeon and Doctors give me hopes it will all go off. I most sincerely wish to be employed, and hope it will not be long." Six days later he was able to say that he felt "perfectly restored", though he intended to stay a few weeks longer, as he believed a cold spell was about to set in.

By 7th May he was in Kentish Town, staying with his uncle, William Suckling of the Customs and Navy Office. "I was with Lord Sandwich yesterday," he reported to his brother William, "and he could fix no time when I should be employed . . . and now you will say, Why does not he come into Norfolk? I will tell you: I have entirely lost the use of my left arm, and very near of my left leg and thigh, and am at present under the care of a Mr Adair, an eminent Surgeon in London; but he gives me hopes a few weeks will remove my disorder, when I will certainly come into Norfolk, and spend my time there till I am employed. When you write to my father do not mention my complaints, for I know it will make him very uneasy, and can do no good."

A few weeks later he was able to join the family for the first Burnham holiday since his boyhood. Maurice he had seen in London: as for his other brothers and his sisters, Susannah, now Mrs Bolton, was settled with her husband at Wells; William was a curate, much attracted to the idea of a chaplaincy in the navy; Anne was at home; Edmund was training to help his brother-in-law, Bolton, as his accountant at Ostend; and Suckling was apprentice to a linen draper at Beccles, where the Nelson parents had married.

It was Kate, the youngest sister, then aged fifteen, who seems most to have appealed to Nelson, though his affection for the rest of his family was boundless. They were all benefiting from the will of Maurice Suckling, and Nelson hoped that as Kate would by reason of the legacy be spared apprenticeship to a "respectable trade", she would marry a man of standing; for, he said later, "Although I am very

D

fond of Mrs Bolton, yet I own I should not like to see my little Kate fixed in a Wells society." When the time came, she did not disappoint him.

In August Nelson had the good news of his appointment to the *Albemarle*, a frigate of 28 guns, converted from a French prize taken the year before. This time he owed nothing to influence. The war was not going well, and any captain with an active record, willing to be considered for such a ship as this, need not fear unemployment.

While the *Albemarle* was having her bottom sheathed with copper at Woolwich yard, Nelson stayed with William Suckling at Kentish Town, whence he wrote to his brother William: "the Admiralty have been very civil, having given me the choice of all my Officers, which I am much pleased with". He asked William to arrange for any seamen who could be procured to come round to him in a Wells ship, adding, "I have talked with Mr Suckling about your going Chaplain in the Navy, and he thinks, as I do, that fifty pounds where you are, is much more than equal to what you can get at Sea; but in that I know you will please yourself." He knew his brother and his persistence, and added a few weeks later, "as to my real opinion whether you will like it, I say, as I always did, that it is five to one you will not. If you get with a good man, and with gentlemen, it will be tolerable; if not you will soon detest it." His last words at this time on the subject were written from Yarmouth Roads in December. "I hope you have lost all ideas of going to Sea," he said, "for the more I see of Chaplains of Men-of-War, the more I dread seeing my brother in such a disagreeable station in life."

Looking back on his services during the first part of the *Albemarle*'s commission, Nelson said, "it would almost be supposed, to try my constitution, I was kept the whole winter in the North Sea". Certainly the season was a hard one. The ship was first ordered into the Baltic, with the *Argo* and *Enterprise* in company, to escort a large convoy homewards, "laden with cargoes of the utmost national importance", including naval stores, many kinds of which came from the Northern countries. The King's ships chased a privateer, who got among the merchantmen, but she was too

speedy to be captured. The convoy itself, he told Locker
"behaved, as all convoys that I ever saw did, shamefully ill;
parting company every day".

After Nelson's return to home waters, gale followed gale
until the coasts were full of wrecks. The *Albemarle* herself
narrowly escaped. On 26th January 1782, while at anchor
in the Downs, "a large East India Store Ship drove from her
anchors, and came on board us", he wrote to William. "We
have lost our foremast and bowsprit, mainyard, larboard
cathead, and quarter gallery, and are stove in two places on
the larboard side—all done in five minutes. What a change!
But yet we ought to be thankful we did not founder."

Clarke and M'Arthur have a story that Nelson was ashore
at Deal at the time of the accident, and could not persuade
any boatman to get him out to the *Albemarle*, until an offer
of fifteen guineas at last proved too much to be resisted, and
he made his way through fierce surf at great risk to his life.
Nothing in Nelson's own correspondence records what
would have been one of the dramatic incidents of his sea
career.

In April Nelson was ordered to Cork, and thence
with a convoy to Quebec. He sailed for the New World full
of apprehension about his health. Locker had even tried to
effect an exchange of ships for him, though without success.
In the end he went in company with Thomas Pringle, a man
with whom he soon made friends. Moreover, he found that
the voyage agreed with him better than he had expected.
Pringle himself had not wished to go on this particular
service, but Nelson explained to Locker that his outlook had
been transformed by the fact that "a hundred thousand
pounds were going out to Quebec and he's got it all. See
what it is to be a Scotchman." Pringle was taking the bullion
in his own ship, and he would receive a liberal fee for
freightage.

Nelson took some prizes off the Canadian coast, but none
reached port. On 14th July he captured an American fishing
schooner belonging to Cape Cod, and, not having any officer
on board who knew Boston Bay and its shoals, he ordered
Nathaniel Carver, the master, to come aboard the *Albemarle*
and act as her pilot. Carver behaved so well that Nelson,

when his work was done, addressed him as follows: "You have rendered us, Sir, a very useful service, and it is not the custom of English seamen to be ungrateful. In the name, therefore, and with the approbation of the Officers of this Ship, I return your Schooner, and with it this Certificate of your good conduct. Farewell! and may God bless you."

This understanding treatment brought a double reward. The certificate long graced the walls of a Boston home, a cherished treasure; and when, a few months later, Nelson and his ship's company were "knocked up with the scurvy", the only occasion of the kind in Nelson's service, the intrepid Carver brought off to him, at considerable risk, a present of four sheep, several crates of fowls, and a quantity of fresh greens. It was with difficulty that Nelson persuaded him to accept any payment. The ship's company had not had a fresh meal for eight weeks, and the relief was proportionate.

Another adventure in the *Albemarle* is related in Nelson's Sketch of his Life. "During a cruise off Boston," he recorded, "I was chased by three French ships of the Line, and the *Iris* frigate: as they all beat me in sailing very much, I had no chance left, but running them amongst the shoals of St George's bank. This alarmed the Line-of-Battle Ships, and they quitted the pursuit; But the Frigate continued, and at sunset was little more than gun shot distance: when, the Line-of-Battle Ships being out of sight, I ordered the main top-sail to be laid to the mast; when the Frigate tacked, and stood to rejoin her consorts." Nelson's manœuvre was a challenge, presented at the right time, which ended an awkward encounter creditably.

In the fall of the year he was at Quebec, recovering his men, and finding the climate suited him so well that he wrote to his father: "Health, that greatest of blessings, is what I never truly enjoyed till I saw fair Canada. The change it has wrought, I am convinced is truly wonderful." He made many friends in the city, and formed a sudden attachment to a beauty of sixteen. It took all the tact of Alexander Davison, shipowner, merchant and firm friend, to persuade Nelson against proposing.

On 11th November the *Albemarle* anchored near Sandy Hook lighthouse. There are two letters extant from New

York; in one of which he said, not of the city but of the captains on the station: "Money is the great object here; nothing else is attended to." The other, hitherto unnoticed, to a fellow-officer about a boatswain, has one very Nelsonian sentence: "My interest at home you know is next to nothing," he wrote, "the name of Nelson being little known; it may be different one of these days; a good chance only is wanting to make it so. . . . ."

Nelson thought such a chance most likely under Lord Hood's flag, and Hood's squadron, battle-scarred from a great encounter under Rodney against de Grasse in the spring of the year, lay at anchor near the frigate. Nelson soon made it his business to get to know the man who, when England was ringing with Rodney's praises, was still furious that the victory off Dominica had not been annihilating as he believed he himself could have made it. There was not an admiral better worth knowing. The most illustrious of a family of sea officers, and sprung like Nelson from a country parsonage, Hood, at the time when Nelson first met him, was nearly sixty but still at the height of his powers, for he had great vitality and lived into his nineties. He was a man of imperious will: shrewd, outspoken, there was not a cleverer tactician alive, or a man with keener insight into his fellows. A valuable and generous friend, a powerful enemy, Hood was to hold Nelson's respect to the end of his life, and Nelson later came to know him as only a trusted subordinate can know his chief.

It was in Hood's ship, the *Barfleur*, that Prince William Henry, son of the reigning monarch and himself to figure in history as an eccentric sailor King, first beheld Nelson. His appearance made William stare. The prince was midshipman of the watch on deck, so he told Nelson's biographers many years later, "when Captain Nelson, of the *Albemarle*, came in his barge alongside, who appeared to be the merest boy of a Captain I ever beheld: and his dress was worthy of attention. He had on a full laced uniform: his lank unpowdered hair was tied in a stiff Hessian tail, of an extraordinary length; the old fashioned flaps of his waistcoat added to the general quaintness of his figure, and produced an appearance which particularly attracted my notice; for I had never seen anything like it before, nor could I imagine who he was, nor what he came about. My doubts were, however, removed when Lord Hood introduced me to him. There was something irresistibly pleasing in his address and conversation; and an enthusiasm, when speaking on professional subjects, that showed he was no common being. I found him warmly attached to my Father, and singularly humane: he had the honour of the King's service, and the independence of the British Navy, particularly at heart; and his mind glowed with this idea as much when he was simply captain of the *Albemarle*, as when he was afterwards decorated with so much well-earned distinction."

Hood assured the Prince that there was not a captain in the service who had made a closer study of tactics. This was either a polite guess, or it indicated that Hood, who had not previously met Nelson, had spoken to someone who had recognised his qualities. In point of fact, the Prince had himself been present at a bigger engagement than had yet come Nelson's way, for he was in Rodney's fleet at the moonlight battle off Cape St Vincent, won against the Spaniards two years before.

Prince William Henry believed it was Nelson's ambition at that time to command a line of battleship in Hood's fleet. Although he did not attain this wish, he was allowed, to his great satisfaction, to serve on what he thought of as the station of honour, the West Indies, and under the man he admired. Moreover, further acquaintance with the Prince enabled him to return the close scrutiny to which he himself had been subjected by protuberant royal eyes. "He will be," he told Locker, "I am certain, an ornament to our Service. He is a *seaman*, which you could hardly suppose. Every other qualification you may expect from him. But he will be a *disciplinarian*, and a strong one: he says he is determined every person shall serve his time before they shall be provided for, as he is obliged to serve his. With the best temper, and great good sense, he cannot fail to be pleasing to everyone."

In Jamaican waters Nelson had a piece of characteristic ill fortune in the matter of prize. The squadron wanted topmasts. None were to be had in the island. "The Fleet," wrote Nelson to Locker, "must have been sent to Sea short of masts, had not providentially a French mast ship, belonging to Monsieur Vaudreuil's Fleet come alongside the *Albemarle*, and was captured by her. She has nearly a hundred topmasts for large Ships, with a number of lower masts and yards. She will clear upward of £20,000. What a good prize if the Fleet had not been in sight. They do not deserve to share for her; we had chased to leeward, and she had passed every Ship in the Fleet without being noticed." In the circumstances of the capture, Nelson's share would have been small.

Nelson's last chance of action, in a war which was slowly dragging to a close, occurred one morning in March, when, a few leagues to the westward of Monte Cristi, the *Albemarle* fell in with the *Resistance*, Captain King, who reported that the French had taken Turks Island, in the Bahamas. Nelson collected a few other ships, made for the island, anchored close inshore, and sent off a flag of truce, calling on the enemy to surrender. The French Commander replied that he would certainly defend himself. He did so to such purpose next day that the attack of a landing party, supported from seaward, was driven off. The place was held in greater strength than Nelson thought, and the batteries were well sited.

The repulse left no mark on his determination, and it was soon forgotten in the flutter of a pretty piece of war-time courtesy. Off Curaçao the frigate fell in with a Spanish launch. Hailed in French by a French-built ship, she came alongside unsuspectingly, and was made prize. But on finding that she was full of illustrious savants, engaged on a scientific tour round Caracca de Leon, Nelson offered the party the best meal he could contrive, and then allowed his guests to resume their occupation.

His last service with Hood's squadron was to attend Prince William Henry on an official visit to Havana. On his return to England he had rewards which pleased him in their differing ways. His entire ship's company offered, if he could get another ship, to serve a further commission. This was a touching event at a time when there was a rising spirit of discontent among the sailors, due, as Nelson thought, "to the infernal plan of turning them over from Ship to Ship, so that Men cannot be attached to their Officers, or the Officers care two-pence about them".

On 11th July Lord Hood took Nelson to a levee at St James's, where he was graciously received by George III, and was commanded to Windsor to take leave of Prince William Henry, for whom a Continental tour had been arranged. "I have closed the war without a fortune," wrote Nelson to his Jamaican friend Hercules Ross, "but I trust, and from the attention that has been paid to me, believe that there is not a speck on my character."

VIII

Nelson was now in a condition common both in the eighteenth century and in our own time. He was war-weary. He had been eight years on active service, broken by one protracted period of sick-leave. Although his profession had taken him to the furthest quarters of the globe he was ever to reach, he had seen little fighting, and that of a desultory kind. If he had missed the prizes, he had also missed the major battles, and it was natural that he should seek a complete change from the ardours, loneliness and responsibilities of command of a ship.

Conversation with the Prince may have turned his mind to the pleasures of the Continent; for this reason or another, he determined to join the many Englishmen who, now that the statesmen had made peace, could make or renew acquaintance with France and Italy.

In late October, with Sterne's *Sentimental Journey* in his baggage, he set out. From an address which he gave his brother William, "chez Madame la Mourie, St Omer, en Artois, France", he wrote as follows on 10th November 1783: "On Tuesday morning, the 21st ult. I set off from Salisbury street, in company with Captain Macnamara of the Navy, an old messmate of mine. I dined with Captain Locker, my old Captain, at Malling in Kent, and spent the night at his house. The next day we slept at Dover, and on

Thursday morning we left England with a fine wind. In
three hours and twenty minutes we were at breakfast in
Monsieur Grandsire's at Calais. The quick transition struck
me much. The manners, houses, and eating, so very different
to what we have in England. I had thoughts of fixing at
Montreuil, about sixty miles from Calais, in the road to
Paris. We set off *en poste*, they called it: we did not get on
more than four miles an hour. Such *carriages*, with *horses*,
such *drivers*, and such *boots*, you would have been ready to
burst with laughing at the ridiculous figure they made together. The roads were paved with stones; therefore by the
time we had travelled fifteen miles we were pretty well shook
up, and heartily tired. We stopped at an inn—a clean pigsty
is far preferable. They showed us into a dirty room with two
straw beds: they were clean, that was all they could brag on.
However, after a good laugh we went to bed and slept very
soundly till morning."

Although the letter conveys the impression of the superior
Englishman abroad, odd in a much-travelled man, yet
shrewdness was mixed with denigration. Nelson observed
fine country, so much so that "sometimes for two miles
together you would suppose you were in a gentleman's park;
there was good cultivation, stately woods, abundant game,
partridges twopence-halfpenny a brace; a noble turkey
fifteen pence. But," he said, putting his finger on the cause
of revolution and the next European war, "amidst such
plenty they are poor indeed."

At St Omer, their destination, Nelson and Macnamara
came upon two naval officers whom they considered to be
"great coxcombs" because they affected the French style in
wearing epaulettes with their uniform. One of them, Alexander Ball, afterwards became Governor of Malta, patron of
Samuel Taylor Coleridge, and Nelson's devoted friend.
Epaulettes, a French fashion, did not officially become part
of the British naval uniform until 1795, and Nelson was
always conservative in matters of dress. Even when they
were adopted, only captains of over three years' seniority
wore them on both shoulders.

In France, early in his stay, Nelson had the sad news of
the death of his sister Anne, at Bath, "occasioned", so

William Suckling had heard, "by coming out of the ball room immediately after dancing". Meanwhile, he had received an unexpected letter from one of the savants the *Albemarle* had met with off Curaçao. This correspondent, it seemed was a very great man. On the Spanish Main he had gone under the name of the Count de Deux Ponts. Now it transpired that he was a Prince of the Empire (later to become Maximilian of Bavaria), a general of the French army, and a Knight of the Grand Order of St Louis. He had actually been second in command at the capture of Yorktown in the American war. He had been so charmed with Nelson's behaviour as host in the frigate that he begged him to visit Paris, promising pleasures of an esoteric kind. "You shall see here," he promised, "very pretty little midshipmans which I dare say will teach you French with a method which will please you and improve you."

Such things were not for Nelson, and on 4th December he wrote solemnly to William: "My heart is quite secured against the French beauties: I almost wish I could say as much for an English young lady, the daughter of a clergyman, with whom I am just going to dine and spend the day. She has such accomplishments, that had I a million of money, I am sure I should at this moment make her an offer of them: my income at present is by far too small to think of marriage, and she has no fortune." Her name was Miss Andrews, and she had the added attraction of a brother in the navy.

It was his desire for Miss Andrews which moved him to write to his uncle, William Suckling, on 14th January 1784 in rather ponderous terms. "There arrives in general a time in a man's life (who has friends), that either they place him in life in a situation that makes his application for anything further totally unnecessary, or give him help in a pecuniary way, if they can afford, and he deserves it." Nelson then continued: "The critical moment of my life is now arrived, that either I am to be happy or miserable:—it depends solely on you.

"You may possibly think I am going to ask too much. I have led myself up with hopes you will not—till this trying moment. There is a lady I have seen, of good family and connexions, but with a small fortune—£1000, I understand.

The whole of my income does not exceed £130 per annum.
Now I must come to the point:—will you, if I should marry,
allow me yearly £100 until my income is increased to that
sum, either by employment, or any other way? A very few
years I hope will turn something up, if my friends will but
exert themselves. If you will not give me the above sum, will
you exert yourself . . . to get me a Guard-ship, or some
employment in a Public Office where the attendance of the
principal is not necessary, and of which they must have such
numbers to dispose of. In the India Service I understand (if
it remains under the Directors) their Marine Force is to be
under the command of a Captain in the Royal Navy: that is
a station I should like."

The letter concluded that Nelson thought that life was
"not worth preserving without happiness; and I care not
where I may linger out a miserable existence. I am prepared
to hear your refusal, and have fixed my resolution if that
should happen."

The plea is expressive of that confidence which Nelson
felt in the liberality of his own family. He owed his position
to the characteristic, and when his own turn came, nobly
repaid it. As for the immediate cause of his request, although
Miss Andrews refused him, his uncle seems to have made
him a promise of help, and the generosity may have done
something to soften the disappointment.

Nelson had written to Suckling from London the instant
he returned home. A week later, from his pleasant lodgings,
he was explaining to William that "London has so many
charms that a man's time is wholly taken up", and he reported to Locker that he had called upon Lord Howe. At
the end of the month, when he was at Bath, he proudly
addressed a letter to William with the title "Rector", the
news having come of William's preferment to the Norfolk
living of Brandon Parva.

Howe, who was then First Lord of the Admiralty, had
asked Nelson if he wished to be employed, and had been told
that he did. The meeting was important both in its immediate results and in forming another link between Nelson
and the maritime succession. For Howe, one of the paramount figures in naval history, was a pupil of Anson, with

whom he had sailed in the early stages of the famous voyage of circumnavigation, begun in 1740. He had taken a notable part in the Seven Years War both as a commodore in amphibious operations and as one of Hawke's leading captains at Quiberon. Since that time he had been in politics; he had fought a superb defensive campaign against d'Estaing, and had relieved Gibraltar from the sea in the height of siege in the face of enormous superiority, his flag flying in the *Victory*. He was known to the fleet as "Black Dick" from his dark complexion, and his taciturnity was famous. "His rigid brow seemed to give to every lineament of his countenance the harshness of an Article of War," said one who knew him well; "yet under that unfavourable physiognomy a more humane mind never did honour to nature."

IX

Howe was one of those men who perform better than they promise. On 18th March 1784 he appointed Nelson to a ship named after the north wind. Nelson was pleased, but there was a perversity about his commission in the *Boreas*, a Hull-built frigate of twenty-eight guns, which, in every respect but climate, made his period of command one of the starker episodes of his career. "My wish," he told his brother, "is to get to the East Indies." In fact, he was ordered to the West. That was not all. After the relief of Gibraltar Howe had been glad to get rid of Sir Richard Hughes, whose squadron had taken part, but whose skill in fleet manœuvring was below acceptable standards. Hughes was now commander-in-chief on the Leeward Islands station, Nelson's destination. The captain, moreover, was required to take out Lady Hughes and a daughter to join Sir Richard.

William, to whom he complained, "I shall be pretty well filled with *lumber*", was not to be diverted from his aim of going to sea as a chaplain, and there was no reasonable excuse for not offering him quarters in the frigate. Horatio told him to bring his "canonicals and sermons". As William, throughout his life, showed the characteristics of a hard-headed, rough-mannered business-man, with but slight infusion of the predominantly Christian virtues, perhaps he contented himself with reading the sermons of better men than himself. Never noted for his tact, he had allowed himself to express surprise at Horatio's appointment. "You ask by what interest did I get a ship," said Nelson, a shade tartly. "I answer, having served with credit was my recommendation to Lord Howe."

There was certainly an imp somewhere about the *Boreas*. To begin with, the Chatham pilot ran her aground. "It makes me swear to think of it," wrote Nelson to Locker. "She lay with so little water that the people could walk round till next high water." When he reached the Downs he became involved in a dispute with the captain of a Dutch East Indiaman who had detained some Englishmen by force. Nelson had his way in the matter, and the Admiralty approved his conduct.

On 21st April he reported a John Gilpin episode. "I was riding a *blackguard* horse that ran away with me," he said, "carried me round all the Works at Portsmouth, by the London gates, through the Town out at the gate that leads to Common, where there was a waggon in the road—which is so very narrow, that a horse could barely pass. To save my legs, and perhaps my life, I was obliged to throw myself from the horse, which I did with great agility: but unluckily upon hard stones, which has hurt my back and leg, but done no other mischief. It was a thousand to one that I had not been killed. To crown all, a young girl was riding with me; her horse ran way with mine; but most *fortunately* a *gallant* young man seized her horse's bridle a moment before I dismounted, and saved her from the destruction which she could not have avoided."

Lady Hughes and her daughter joined the ship at Portsmouth. Nelson described his future admiral's wife as an "eternal clack", and her daughter lacked beauty. The *Boreas* sailed towards the end of May, and on the 30th, in the broad Atlantic, Nelson, exasperated by the numbers which congested his quarter-deck, made a list of those present, which included the two ladies, himself, two lieutenants, the master, the surgeon, the purser and his wife, Mr Lane of the Marines, and no less than twenty young gentlemen, two of whom, Talbot and Boyle, were in due time to achieve their flags. Still more were below.

The *Boreas* was at Madeira early in June, and the first surviving letter from the West Indies was written to Locker. It was dated from English Harbour, Antigua, on 24th September 1784. English Harbour, land-locked, and almost like the crater of an immense volcano, the hills all round forming the crater lip, then crowned with forts, has attracted attention in our own time as an almost perfectly preserved Georgian dockyard, equipped for the service and repair of the sailing navy. Having mouldered for nearly a century, it has now become a quarry for the historian and a paradise for yachtsmen. Nelson described it as an "infernal hole", whose *longueurs* were relieved only by the fact that his ship was well officered and manned, and by the pleasing society of Mrs Moutray, wife of the Commissioner of the Navy in the island. She, so Nelson confided to Locker, "is *very very* good to me". She was, he thought, the most accomplished creature it was possible to meet. "Her equal I never saw in any country or in any situation." He hoped, when she returned home, she would make herself known to his sister Kate. "What an acquisition to any female to be acquainted with; what an example to take pattern from."

It was example that Nelson needed. He did not find it in his admiral: indeed, he shared Lord Howe's feeling for Sir Richard Hughes, though for different reasons. "He bows and scrapes too much," said Nelson, adding, a few weeks later, "the admiral and all about him are great ninnies." Sir Richard's charms were not enhanced by the fact that in youth he has lost one of his eyes—not in action, but through an accident with a table-fork when chasing a cockroach.

If the admiral was uncongenial, there were few others to whom to turn, for even brother William soon departed, taking his canonicals and sermons with him. He found the climate bad for his health. In fact, until Nelson's attached friend Collingwood sailed into the harbour in November, in command of the *Mediator*, he was without a close confidant in his profession.

Whatever his opinion of the family, there is reason to
be grateful to Lady Hughes for a glimpse of Nelson in the
Boreas which she gave to his brother-in-law Matcham soon
after Trafalgar. What had struck her particularly was his
attention to those he called his children, the midshipmen, of
whom there was apparently a total of thirty attached to the
frigate. "Among the number," recalled her ladyship, "it may
reasonably be supposed that there must be timid as well as
bold: the timid he never rebuked, but always wished to show
them he desired nothing of them that he would not instantly
do himself: and I have known him say—'Well, Sir, I am
going a race to the mast-head, and beg I may meet you
there.'

"No denial could be given to such a wish, and the poor
fellow instantly began his march. His Lordship never took
the least notice with what alacrity it was done, but when he
met at the top, began instantly speaking in the most cheerful
manner, and saying how much a person was to be pitied who
could fancy there was any danger, or even anything disagreeable, in the attempt.

"After this excellent example, I have seen the timid youth
lead another, and rehearse his Captain's words. How wise
and kind was such a proceeding! In like manner, he went
every day into the School Room, and saw them do their
nautical business, and at twelve o'clock he was first upon
deck with his quadrant. No one there could be behind-hand
in their business when their Captain set them so good an
example.

"One other circumstance I must mention which was the
day we landed at Barbados. We were to dine at the Governor's. Our dear Captain said, 'You must permit me, Lady
Hughes, to carry one of my Aide-de-Camps with me'; and
when he presented him to the Governor he said, 'Your
Excellency must excuse me for bringing one of my midshipmen, as I make it a rule to introduce them to all the good
company I can, as they have few to look up to besides myself
during the time they are at sea.' This kindness and attention
made the young people adore him; and even his wishes,
could they have been known, would have been instantly
complied with . . . I hope my simple narration may, in a

faint degree, describe his Lordship's excellent manner of making his young men fancy the attaining nautical perfection was much more of a play than a task."

X

Things being as they were on the station, Nelson was ripe for trouble. This took the form of what was thought at first by all but Cuthbert Collingwood, Wilfred Collingwood, his brother, and one or two other sea officers, as excess of zeal. Some have seen officiousness and a desire to shine as motives behind the events in the months which followed, others a hope of money from prize. Nelson was not often officious; on the other hand, fame and duty were his watchwords, and to fulfil what he conceived his duty, he never lacked that moral courage which sometimes begins by disobeying orders and generally entails unpopularity.

Nelson put the matter pithily in the Sketch of his Life. One of the results of the War of American Independence had been to make foreigners of men and women who had formerly been British subjects. It was against the incursion of all foreigners into the Colonial trade that the current Navigation Act was designed, and it was strict upholding of this Act which was the subject of Nelson's crusade. The law enjoined that goods to and from Colonial territories should be carried either in ships of those territories or in those of the Mother Country.

"The Station," said Nelson, "opened a new scene to the Officers of the British Navy. The Americans, when colonists, possessed almost all the trade from America to our West India Islands; and on the return of Peace, they forgot, on this occasion, they became foreigners, and of course had no right to trade in the British Colonies. Our Governors and Custom-house Officers pretended, that by the Navigation Act they had a right to trade; and all the West Indians wished what was so much for their interest.

"Having given Governors, Custom-house Officers, and

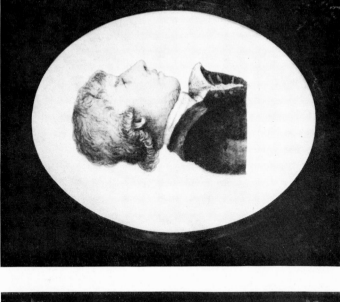

COLLINGWOOD by NELSON   NELSON by COLLINGWOOD

Portraits made of one another in the West Indies. Nelson wore a wig, his hair
being then shaved off owing to fever

Americans, notice of what I would do, I seized many of
their Vessels, which brought all parties upon me; and I was
persecuted from one Island to another, that I could not leave
my Ship. But conscious rectitude bore me through it; and I
was supported, when the business came to be understood,
from home: and I proved . . . that a Captain of a man of War
is in duty bound to support all the Maritime Laws, by his
Admiralty commission alone, without becoming a Custom-
house Officer."

These statements were amplified in a letter which he
wrote to Locker on 15th January 1785 when off Guadeloupe.
"The longer I am upon this Station the worse I like it. Our
Commander has not that opinion of his own sense that he
ought to have. He is led by the advice of the Islanders to
admit the Yankees to a Trade; at least to wink at it. He does
not give himself that weight that I think an English Admiral
ought to do. I, for one, am determined not to suffer the
Yankees to come where my Ship is; for I am sure, if once the
Americans are admitted to any kind of intercourse with
these Islands, the views of the Loyalists are entirely done
away. They will become first the Carriers, and next have
possession of our Islands, are we ever again embroiled in a
French war. The residents of these Islands are Americans by
connexion and by interest, and are inimical to Great Britain.
They are as great rebels as ever were in America, had they
the power to show it.

"After what I have said, you will believe I am not very
popular with the people. They have never visited me, and I
have not set a foot in any private house since I have been on
the Station, and all for doing my duty by being *true to the
interests of Great Britain*. A petition from the President and
Council has gone to the Governor-General and Admiral, to
request the admission of Americans. I have given my
answer to the Admiral upon the subject; how he will like it
I know not: but I am determined to suppress the admission
of Foreigners all in my power. I have told the Customs that
I will complain if they admit any Foreigner to an Entry:—
an American arrives; sprung a leak, a mast and what not,
makes a protest, gets admittance, sells his cargo for ready
money; goes to Martinico, buys molasses, and so round and

E

round. But I hate them all. The Loyalist cannot do it, consequently must sell a little dearer. . . ."

Nelson was no sooner committed to enforcement of the Navigation Act, single-handed if necessary, than he disturbed his admiral in quite another matter. The Commissioner of the Navy at English Harbour, Moutray, husband of the lady he so much admired, had been authorised by Sir Richard Hughes to order the hoisting of the broad pendant of a commodore, and to exercise the functions of command in the absence of the admiral.

Moutray had been a post-captain since 1758, and was therefore Nelson's senior officer by many years. But by taking employment under the Navy Board in a civil capacity, he had reverted to half pay, and was no longer on the active list. In effect, he was a civil servant with a nautical title. To object to taking orders from Moutray may appear to have been a quibble, but in fact it was not so. The personal history of the higher ranks in the eighteenth-century navy is full of disagreements of this sort: more often than not they relate to the objection of officers holding civil posts to forgo their chance of promotion to flag rank. In certain well-known cases, notably that of Lord Barham, they sustained their rights, though rarely without a struggle. Nelson would have maintained that, whether admiral or captain, such people were not actively re-employed as sea officers until they were appointed by the Admiralty to the command of a ship or squadron. They then at once resumed their seniority in the Navy List.

Nelson's account of the incident, given in a circumstantial letter to the Admiralty from Barbados, was as follows. "On the 5th of February, 1785, upon my arrival in English Harbour, I found the *Latona* with a Broad Pendant flying. As her Captain was junior to me, I sent to know the reason for her wearing it. Her Captain came on board, who I asked the following questions:

"Have you any order from Sir Richard Hughes to wear a broad pendant? *Answer:* No.

"*Question:* For what reason do you then wear it in the presence of a Senior Officer? *Answer:* I hoisted it by order of Commissioner Moutray.

"*Question:* Have you seen by what authority Commissioner Moutray was empowered to give you orders? *Answer:* No.

"*Question:* Sir, you have acted wrong, to obey any man who you do not know is authorised to command you. *Answer:* I feel I have acted wrong; but being a young captain, did not think proper to interfere in this matter, as there were you and other older Officers upon this Station."

Nelson added: "I did not choose to order the Commissioner's Pendant to be struck, as Mr Moutray is an old Officer of high military character; and it might hurt his feelings to be supposed wrong by so young an officer."

In their reply, Their Lordships informed Nelson that he should have submitted his doubts to the commander-in-chief. The immediate difficulty was resolved through the fact that Moutray sailed for England shortly afterwards. On longer consideration the Admiralty, recognising the difficulty of the matter, placed all Commissioners of the Navy on full pay, and appointed them to the nominal command of a ship.

Nelson did not take a biassed or exaggerated view of the general situation in the Leeward Islands. This was shown by two incidents. In March, when he was at St Kitts, he was constrained to refuse an invitation from the President since "the Irish colours, with thirteen stripes in them, was hoisted all over the town" on St Patrick's Day. "I mention it," he told Locker, "only to show the principle of these *vagabonds*." As for his fear that in a future war an American-French alliance might be as great a danger as it had been in the past, it was barely a year later that, when the *Boreas* was at anchor in Nevis Road, a French frigate passed to leeward, close along shore. Lieutenant Wallis of the *Boreas* described the episode as follows.

"Captain Nelson had information that this Frigate was destined on a survey of our Islands, and had on board two General Officers and some Engineers for that purpose, which information proved correct. Captain Nelson immediately determined to attend her, and prevent their intentions: therefore he immediately got under weigh and pursued her.

"On the next day we found her at anchor in the Road of St Eustatia, and the *Boreas* was anchored at about two cables length on the French frigate's quarter. After a reciprocity of civilities, salutes etc. had passed on all sides, Captain Nelson with his Officers was invited to meet the French officers at dinner next day at the Dutch Governor's, which was accepted; and it was at this dinner that Captain Nelson made known his intentions to the Captain of the French frigate.

"He said that understanding he intended visiting the English Islands, he thought it his duty to accompany him in an English Frigate, that attention might be paid to the Officers of his Most Christian Majesty, which he was sure every Englishman in the Islands would be proud of an opportunity of doing. This declaration did not appear palatable to the French generals, and was politely refused by them as well as by the Captain of the French Frigate, saying that their intention was only to take a cruise round the Islands, without stopping at any. However, Captain Nelson was determined not to be outdone in *civility*, and strictly adhered to his purpose. The Frenchman, perceiving the English Commander's drift, in a few days abandoned his project, got under weigh, and beat up to Martinique. Captain Nelson availed himself of the same opportunity, and beat up to Barbados, by which he never lost sight of the French Frigate until she got into Martinique, where she came from."

Meanwhile, the Navigation Act dispute dragged on. Nelson was soon involved with General Shirley, Governor of the Leeward Islands, who was prepared to wink his eye at the American traffic. In stating his position, he wrote with asperity to Nelson that "old respectable officers of high rank, long service and of a certain life are very jealous of being dictated to in their duty by young gentlemen whose service and experience do not entitle them to it". Wallis says that at this stage Nelson made the reply that he had the honour of being as old as the Prime Minister of England, and thought himself as capable of commanding one of H.M. ships as he (Pitt) was of governing the State. The remark does not appear in his correspondence, and Nelson may well have made it to Wallis in a private way.

With Governor and admiral forming a passive coalition
against him, Nelson's position was unpleasant. Sir Richard
was in fact about to supersede Nelson, but found that an
increasing number of officers agreed with his subordinate.
Although, in Southey's graceful words, the admiral "wanted
vigour of mind to decide upon what was right, he was not
obstinate in wrong, and had even generosity enough in his
nature to thank Nelson afterwards for having shown him his
error". Poor Hughes: to have escaped from Howe to
encounter Nelson was hard indeed.

But it was Nelson whose difficulties soon became urgent.
The island of Nevis was so roused at his action in seizing
four American vessels that he was forced to confine himself
to his ship. To have gone ashore would have meant arrest
for damages, laid by the traders and islanders at the enormous sum of £40,000. Fortunately he was able to amuse his
officers by encouraging "music, dancing, cudgelling etc.,
and the Officers and Young Gentlemen acted plays which
kept up their spirits, and kept their minds employed". Moreover, the local judge was worthy of his calling, and upheld
the seizures. What was even more remarkable, the President,
Mr Herbert, showed great generosity in offering to stand
bail for Nelson in the sum of £10,000 should he choose to
suffer arrest, though he had himself been a principal loser
by the case.

"I hate pity," said Nelson to Wallis, at this time of distress: "I shall live to be envied, and to that point I shall
always direct my course." What he was scarcely prepared
for was to hear that the Governor and admiral had been
commended from home for their zeal and activity in the
protection of English commerce. He was not of a temperament to savour such irony.

XI

Although troubles surrounded Nelson, life on the West
Indies station was not without relief. "*Entre nous*" a letter to
his brother William concluded, sent from St Kitts on 28th

June 1785, "do not be surprised to hear I am a Benedict, for if at all, it will be before a month. Do not tell."

Nelson had mentioned in a letter to his father, written a few weeks earlier, that he had "been visiting Miss Parry Herbert and a young widow" at Nevis. This same young widow had already received the following account of Nelson from one of her own sex: "We have at last seen the Captain of the *Boreas*, of whom so much has been said. He came up just before dinner, much heated, and was very silent; yet seemed, according to the old adage, to think the more. He declined drinking any wine; but after dinner, when the President, as usual, gave the following toasts, 'the King', 'the Queen and Royal Family', and 'Lord Hood', this strange man regularly filled his glass, and observed, that those were always bumper toasts with him; which having drank, he uniformly passed the bottle, and relapsed into his former taciturnity. It was impossible, during this visit, for any of us to make out his real character; there was such a reserve and sternness in his behaviour, with occasional sallies, though very transient, of a superior mind. Being placed by him, I endeavoured to rouse his attention by showing him all the civilities in my power; but I drew out little more than 'Yes' or 'No'. If you, Fanny, had been there, we think you would have made something of him; for you have been in the habit of attending to these odd sort of people."

The recipient of this well-observed glimpse was a little older than Nelson. Her name was Frances Herbert Nisbet, and she was the daughter of William Woolward, Senior Judge of Nevis. Her mother, who had died when she was a child, had been sister of the President, John Richardson Herbert, descendant of the fourth Earl of Pembroke. Her father lived just long enough to see her grow up, and shortly after his death she had married the doctor who attended him, Josiah Nisbet.

After eleven months, a son, Josiah, had been born, but the doctor, who had been in ill health even before departing for England for his honeymoon, had never fully recovered, and had died in a house near Salisbury Cathedral, a year and a half later. Having neither home, husband nor means,

Frances had appealed for help to her uncle in Nevis. He had invited her to return with her child, to help oversee his household. She had been a widow some four years when Nelson first met her.

The President was himself a widower, not at the moment on the best of terms with his only child, Martha, who intended to marry a man not of his choice. Miss Parry Herbert, another niece, had been brought to Nevis on a visit from Barbados (where she had another uncle) in Nelson's frigate.

Fanny, experienced in society, usually dispensed the hospitality of the President, but it so happened that it was her child, Josiah, then aged five, who first received Nelson. The President was astonished one early morning before the family were up to find "that great little man of whom everyone is so afraid, playing in the next room, under the dining table, with Mrs Nisbet's child". Nelson had a way with children, who enjoyed his company as much as he did theirs.

Portraits show Fanny slender and fine-featured; an anxious woman who had known misfortune. Her manners were elegant. She spoke French fluently, and surviving examples of her work show her to have been an exquisite needlewoman. Her eyes were dark, her colour charming. Recalling her over the years, a midshipman who had once known her well said that she "had at that time some beauty, and a freshness of complexion not common in that climate, but there was so remarkable an absence of intellectual endowment as to make it evident that Nelson's sagacious eye was content to dwell upon the blooming cheeks, without going in search of better graces which give permanence to conjugal felicity". This may well have been a judgment coloured by later events, for Nelson himself wrote to his uncle William Suckling that he thought "her mental accomplishments are superior to most people's of either sex", and he repeated the compliment to more than one other correspondent. Fanny's surviving letters show her to have been a good judge of people and a shrewd observer; they give little indication of questing interest in affairs beyond her immediate circle. She and Nelson both enjoyed gossip, and his first surviving letter to her, dated 19th August 1785 from English Harbour, Antigua, not only contains some hints of the indiscretions of

Sir Richard Hughes but a scratch or two in cypher. In his earlier years, at any rate, Nelson was a discreet correspondent.

Undoubtedly Fanny filled the gap in Nelson's life left by Mrs Moutray. "I wish you knew her," he enthused to Fanny. "Your Minds and Manners are so congenial that you must have pleasure in the Acquaintance." Within a few weeks of meeting his charming widow, Nelson had proposed, and by 11th September he was writing to her: "My greatest wish is to be united to you; and the foundation of all conjugal happiness, real love and esteem is, I trust, what you believe I possess in the strongest degree towards you."

Nothing was easily settled; no firm arrangements could be arrived at with the President, and even Fanny herself did not at first seem likely to be an energetic correspondent. But by November Nelson was writing to William Suckling in a familiar strain: "Herbert is very rich and proud—he has an only daughter, and this niece, who he looks upon in the same light, if not higher. I have lived at his house, when at Nevis, since June last, and am a great favourite of his. I have told him I am as poor as Job; but he tells me he likes me, and I am descended from a good family, which his pride likes; but he also says, 'Nelson, I am proud, and I must live like myself, therefore I can't do much in my lifetime; when I die she shall have twenty thousand pounds; and if my daughter dies before me, she shall possess the major part of my property. I intend going to England in 1787 and remaining there my life; therefore, if you two can live happily together till that event takes place, you have my consent.' This is exactly my situation with him; and I know the way to get him to give me most, is not to appear to want it: thus circumstanced, who can I apply to but you? Don't disappoint me, or my heart will break."

By the following March William Suckling had written, offering help if it should be necessary, though one sentence in his letter, which read, "your application has in a great degree deprived me of my free agency", caused Nelson considerable hurt. Actually, William Suckling was himself contemplating a regular instead of an irregular union, and his own burdens were likely to increase.

Nelson, who was by now fairly launched upon his wooing,

wrote to his beloved on 3rd March: "Separated from you, what pleasure can I feel? None, be assured: all my happiness is centred with thee; and where thou art not, there I am not happy. Every day, every hour and act, convince me of it. With my heart filled with the purest and most tender affection, do I write this. . . . Fortune, that is, money, is the only thing I regret the want of, and that only for the sake of my affectionate Fanny. But the Almighty, who brings us together, will, I doubt not, take ample care of us, and prosper all our undertakings. No dangers shall deter me from pursuing every honourable means of providing handsomely for you and yours; and again let me repeat, that my dear Josiah shall ever be considered by me as one of my own."

A few months later he was writing, "As you begin to know something about sailors, have you not often heard, that salt water and absence always wash away love? Now, I am such a heretic as not to believe that Faith; for behold, every morning since my arrival, I have had six pails of salt water at daylight poured upon my head, and instead of finding what the Seamen say to be true, I perceive the contrary effect. . . . I am alone in the Commanding Officer's house, while my Ship is fitting, and from sunset until bedtime I have not a human creature to speak to: you will feel a little for me, I think. I did not use to be over-fond of sitting alone. The moment old *Boreas* is habitable in my cabin, I shall fly to it, to avoid mosquitoes and melancholies. Hundreds of the former are now devouring me through my clothes."

By the beginning of November 1786, while he was still tangled in correspondence with officialdom of all sorts, arising from his enforcement of the Navigation Act upon reluctant colonies, he not only found himself temporarily in command of the station, Sir Richard Hughes having sailed for home, and Sir Richard Bickerton, his successor designate not yet having arrived, but he had under his care H.M.S. *Pegasus*, Captain H.R.H. Prince William Henry.

The Prince, on promotion to post rank, had quickly begun to fulfil Nelson's prophecy that he would prove a disciplinarian. He was now a martinet. Some of his officers, who were not a happy band, thought his sternness might have been partly Nelson's influence, but the truth was otherwise. It was, in fact, in the man's nature, and in that of his family, and it was Nelson who wrote to his brother soon after the Prince's arrival, "I begin to be very strict in my ship, and as I get older, probably shall be more so."

On 12th December Nelson wrote to Fanny from Antigua: "Our young prince is a gallant man: he is indeed volatile, but always with great good nature. There were two balls during his stay, and some of the old ladies were mortified that H.R.H. would not dance with them; but he says, he is determined to enjoy the privilege of all other men, that of asking any lady he pleased. I can tell you a piece of news, which is, that the Prince is fully determined, and has made me promise him, that he shall be at our wedding; and he says he will give you to me. His Royal Highness has not yet been in a private house to visit, and is determined never to do it, except in this instance."

But before that event, there was much trouble to be endured on the young man's account. He had reprimanded his first lieutenant, Isaac Schomberg, an experienced and zealous officer, specially appointed for those qualities so that he could remove irksome responsibility from his royal captain. Schomberg, rightly aggrieved, requested a court-martial, and Nelson soon discovered that he was not likely to be the last in the *Pegasus* to do so. His immediate solution of the matter, since there were not enough senior officers available to form a court, was to place Schomberg under arrest, which pleased nobody. The matter was only settled after many awkward weeks by Nelson ordering the *Pegasus* to proceed to another station, where the wretched lieutenant was transferred and affairs smoothed over. The incident, happily, did Schomberg no lasting harm; his next appointment was as first lieutenant in Lord Hood's ship, the *Barfleur*; and he died one of the Commissioners of the Navy Board.

Quite as awkward in its own way was the Prince's "volatile" though scarcely good-natured action in having a German artist who had been allowed to visit the *Pegasus*, and had caused some unwitting offence, cat-o'-nine-tailed on "that part of the body called the seat of honour". Reporting the incident later, midshipman Byam Martin said that "the fleshly wounds were healed with a plaster", but that William Henry was "put to the inconvenience of raising some hundreds of pounds" as compensation for less tangible injuries received.

Nor was the Prince's round of island visits without its drawbacks. Nelson wrote to Fanny on Christmas Eve 1786, to report: "We returned last Night from St John's and I fancy many people were as happy to see His Royal Highness quit as they were to see him enter St John's, for another day or two's racquet would have knocked some of the fair sex up. Three night's dancing was too much and never Broke up till Day. Miss Athell is the Belle of this island and of course attracted H.R.H.'s attention. I will tell you much when we meet, for you know the danger of putting too much upon paper." Activity and the Prince were inseparable, however the energies of lesser folk might tire.

"How vain are human expectations," wrote Nelson to his betrothed on 13th January 1787. "I was in hopes to have remained quiet all this week: but today we dine with Sir Thomas (Shirley); tomorrow the Prince has a party; on Wednesday he gives a dinner at Saint John's to the Regiment; in the evening is a Mulatto ball; on Thursday a cockfight, and we dine at Colonel Crosbie's brother's and a ball: on Friday somewhere, but I forget; on Saturday at Mr Byam's, the President. If we get well through all this, I shall be fit for anything. What is it to attend on Princes? Let me attend on you and I am satisfied. His Royal Highness often tells me, he believes I am married; for he never saw a lover so easy, or say so little of the object he has a regard for. When I tell him I certainly am not, he says, 'Then he is sure I must have a great esteem for you, and that is not what is (vulgarly) . . . called "love".' He is right: my love is founded on esteem, the only foundation that can make the passion last."

On Sunday, 11th March 1787, a date which the bride herself recollected as one day later, Prince William Henry was able to fulfil his wish, and Horatio Nelson and Fanny Nesbit were married at Nevis, in the principal reception-room at Montpelier. The service was performed by the

Reverend William Jones, Rector of the parishes of St John and St Thomas, and when, in the speechifying, the Prince spoke of Fanny as "the principal favourite of the island", he was loudly applauded. The couple were not long alone together, for a few days later, in a hastily written letter to Locker from his ship, the bridegroom spoke of wishing to refit the *Boreas* for the voyage to England. "Happy shall I be when that time arrives," he added, "no man has had more illness or trouble on a Station than I have experienced; but let me lay a balance on the other side—I am married to an amiable woman, that far makes amends for everything: indeed till I married her I never knew happiness. And I am morally certain she will continue to make me a happy man for the rest of my days."

Before the end of Nelson's one and only peace-time commission there were two more incidents which helped to make it memorable. The first concerned allegations by two merchants, Messrs Wilkinson and Higgins, who traded at St John's, Antigua. They testified to enormous peculations by Crown officials in the Leeward Islands. These were disclosed, to an officer known to be zealous, not merely from a sense of concern for the expenditure of public funds, but in the hope of a reward of 15 per cent. on any money recovered. Nelson had come up against much the same sort of thing himself. When, in 1889, the old dockyard at English Harbour was formally closed by Admiral Sir Herbert King Hall, he found two letters from Nelson in the archives, dated 1787. Both of them chided officials for negligence in furnishing accounts to justify their drawing money from the Government.

The matter of Wilkinson and Higgins led to tedious correspondence extending over many months, and although Nelson was assured, after his return home, that the whole matter would be laid before Mr Pitt by the Secretary of the Treasury, Mr George Rose, with whom he then had the first of many interviews, yet before matters were sorted out, at least one of the informants, Wilkinson, had been lodged in gaol in his home island. Nelson must have quickly realised that he had helped to further another business which was likely to be as troublesome as the Navigation Act. Seven

years later, in the earliest statement of his services which
Nelson set down, he recorded that he had had "the opportunity of discouraging great frauds in the expenditure of
Public Money, and as the Naval Storekeeper is punished by
fine and imprisonment it is to be hoped a stop will by this
means be put to further embezzlement". Mr Rose had been
as good as his word.

Finally, there was the matter of Able Seaman William
Clark, of H.M.S. *Rattler*, Commander Wilfred Collingwood. Clark had deserted his ship on 20th June 1786 at
English Harbour, had been at liberty a fortnight, and had
been retaken without resistance, "not perfectly sober". The
poor man was then confined for the greater part of a year,
with no tobacco or grog, until a court-martial could be
assembled. This met on 6th April 1787, under Nelson's
presidency.

The penalty for desertion was death, and this fact was not
formally altered in times of peace. The charge was proved,
and Clark was duly sentenced. All the dreadful formalities
were carried out, except the actual execution, for Prince
William Henry asked for a reprieve, and this was willingly
granted. "The Law might not have supposed me guilty of
murder," said Nelson in his report to the Admiralty, "but
my feelings would nearly have been the same." Nelson
added generosity to mercy. Clark, not unnaturally, wished
to be discharged from the Service, a wish which was supported by his captain. Nelson, considering that as he had
been pardoned, he became "new", and as there was "no
want of a good man to supply his place", granted him his
wish. Clark must have been deeply thankful to return to the
pleasures of Antigua, but Nelson, on his return home, was
severely rapped over the knuckles, for it was pointed out to
him that he had power only to suspend sentence, not to
pardon and certainly not to discharge.

The matter of Able Seaman Clark was, in its small way,
a distraction typical of a spell of service upon which Nelson
never could look back with pleasure. One of his last duties,
as acting Commander-in-Chief, was to inform Cuthbert
Collingwood of the release of another belonging to the
Rattler: her commander had died at sea on his way to

Grenada, "without a groan or struggle", said Nelson. "I have cried for him," wrote Prince William Henry, and Nelson hoped that this fact might afford his brother some consolation.

Nelson was only once again in the West Indies, in the last year of his life, and even that visit was not one of his more rewarding experiences.

XII

The *Boreas* sailed from the Leeward Islands station in May 1787, and arrived at Spithead on 4th July. Fanny and her son made the voyage independently in the West Indiaman *Roehampton*. The next five years belonged exclusively to Nelson's immediate family.

When the frigate anchored at Spithead there were, this time, no united offers from the ship's company to serve another commission. It was not that Nelson had lost the art of making himself beloved, but whereas he had himself been able to escape the tedium of shipboard in the tropics by spells ashore, the chances of subordinate officers and men for relaxation had been altogether more limited. They longed, one and all, for the pleasures of old England. As the ship was not paid off without protracted delay, there were desertions, as well as varied complaints addressed to the captain by the Admiralty. Nelson even had the mortification of hearing that as, in Their Lordships' view he had not been properly authorised to fill up appointments, those which he had made locally abroad would not be confirmed.

From Portsmouth, the *Boreas* was ordered to the Nore, whence Nelson was able to arrange for London lodgings for his wife. From the Nore he wrote to congratulate his brother on the birth of a daughter; William had married a Miss Sarah Yonge, daughter of the Vicar of Great Torrington in Devon, while Nelson was still away. After dull weeks, during which the frigate served as a sloop and receiving ship, at last, on 30th November, Nelson was free to discover the delights of married life without professional responsibilities.

His means were slender. William Suckling allowed him
£100 a year, and a similar supply came to Fanny through the
President of Nevis, who had fulfilled his intention of making
a home in England. Nelson's half pay as a post-captain
amounted to £53, 12s. 6d. paid every half-year, a sum
reduced to £51, 0s. 8d. by office commissions. Out of these
sources of income there were appearances to be kept up, and
Josiah's schooling to be paid for. There is no better illustra-
tion of the value of money in the eighteenth century than
the events of the next five years, for although it is true that
at one point (at the end of 1791) Nelson's credit balance
stood at only £1, 2s. 0d., the years on half pay were, though
retired, not altogether without diversion.

The Nelsons visited; in the earlier months they kept a
sailor servant, Frank Lepée, who had been with Nelson as
long ago as the expedition into Nicaragua, and they sent
Josiah to board at a school recommended by William.
Lepée, who was sent to Hilborough in charge of the lad, was
"desired to stay two or three days till the child becomes
reconciled. I am assured of your and Mrs Nelson's goodness
to him—that is, you will not allow him to do as he pleases;
it's mistaken kindness where it happens. I wish him at school
to have the same weekly allowance as the other boys, and
whatever else may be proper for him."

The first Christmas the Horatio Nelsons spent together
they were guests of the President of Nevis in Cavendish
Square. They then went on an excursion which included
Exmouth and Bath, and from there Nelson was able to make
his way to Plymouth, to which port he had been invited by
Prince William Henry. There were to be festivities celebrating the royal return.

It was midsummer 1788, more than a year after leaving
the West Indies, before Nelson was home again in Norfolk,
conducting Fanny on a round which included the William
Nelsons, the cheerful Boltons, and Katty, who had married a
man of substance, George Matcham, and taken the lease of
Barton Hall, near Neatishead. The Matchams lived in restless affluence, with a rapidly increasing family.

It was in Norfolk that the pair eventually settled. "I lived
at Burnham Thorpe, county of Norfolk, in the Parsonage-

house," said Nelson in that single sentence in the Sketch of his Life, which spans a long period. When winter approached, Fanny, who was always inclined to ill health, suffered greatly from the cold. When the village was snowbound, and when, in the Rector's words, all was "Hush, at High Noon as at Midnight", she suffered still more, and sometimes retired to bed for whole days together. But she soon won the Rector's heart by her kind attentions —they were semi-invalids together—and Horatio, even if confined, was able to enjoy fireside travel, discovering in Dampier's *Voyages* the most interesting book he had ever read.

With the coming of spring, Nelson renewed pleasures he had known as a boy, learning to farm the glebe, gardening and sometimes digging so hard "as it were for the purpose of being wearied", in the phrase of Clarke and M'Arthur. "At others, he would renew the early pastime of his childhood, and with a simplicity that was peculiar to him, would spend some part of the day amidst the woods, in taking the eggs of different birds, which, as he obtained, he gave to Mrs Nelson, who always accompanied him. The uniformity of a village life," these biographers add, "was occasionally diversified by professional calls to the Metropolis; by an annual visit, with Mrs Nelson, to Lord Walpole, at Wolterton; and by occasional visits to Mr Coke, at Holkham." A surviving business letter shows Nelson to have been at Bath in January 1790, and intending to be in London the following month on his way back to Burnham. The pair were soon in sole possession of the Parsonage-house, Edmund Nelson taking the lease of a cottage in Burnham Ulph, pleased to have his sailor son at home, but wishing to allow him all the privacy he could.

James Harrison, one of Nelson's earliest memorialists, recorded that he was particularly fond of coursing, but "though one of the best gunners in the world, he was a bad shot at a hare, a woodcock or a partridge. In pointing a great gun, however, on grand and suitable occasions, at a ship, a castle, or a fort, he was scarcely to be equalled: so well, indeed, was this talent known, and so universally recognised, by his frequently volunteering his services on shore, that he

LADY HAMILTON
AS A BACCHANTE

An enamel of 1803, by
Henry Bone, after a
painting by Vigée Lebrun
made at Naples in 1790

was familiarly called the Brigadier, ever after the affair of San Juan."

At least once, rude reminders of the stir Nelson had made in the West Indies broke in upon him. One day, when he had gone to a fair to buy a pony, two men served notification of an action on behalf of two American captains, who laid their damages at £20,000. Fanny was alarmed, but Mr Rose of the Treasury assured Nelson's friend Pringle that "Captain Nelson is a very good officer, that he need be under no apprehension, for that he will assuredly be supported by the Treasury."

Though active, Nelson was never reconciled to shore life. Time and again, whoever reigned at the Admiralty, he begged for employment, and he would have gone with Cornwallis to the East Indies had not that officer, wrongly concluding that Nelson's marriage would make him prefer home life, already filled his vacancies. "I made use of every interest to get a Ship," Nelson recorded in his Sketch, "even a boat, to serve my Country, but in vain; there was a prejudice at the Admiralty evidently against me, which I can neither guess at, or in the least account for."

One of Nelson's "interests" might have been Prince William Henry, now Duke of Clarence, but although the prince did in fact mention Nelson to Lord Chatham, nothing came of the matter. So far from allowing his acquaintance with royalty to drop, Nelson continued, for the rest of his life, to send regular, well-informed and courtly letters to the Duke; these were always answered, and the Duke had the good sense to preserve the correspondence. In December 1792, when actually nearing the end of his unemployment, the Duke asked Nelson how he stood with Lord Hood. Nelson replied: "I can readily and truly answer. We have not for a long time had any communication with each other. Our familiar correspondence ceased on a difference of opinion. However, in consideration of our former intimacy, whenever I have gone to London, I have hitherto thought it right to leave my name at his Lordship's door. I certainly cannot look on Lord Hood as my friend; but I have the satisfaction of knowing, that I never gave his Lordship just cause to be my enemy."

Nelson's past and future admiration for Hood make this letter of special interest. It is not less so from a sentence struck out, to the effect that Hood had told Nelson "that the King was impressed with an unfavourable opinion of me", a matter "never to be effaced from my memory". Nelson probably considered such a passage improper in a letter to the King's son. Reflection might have led him to ask himself whether the seeming prejudice which both the Admiralty and the King then had was not in fact connected with the Duke of Clarence. The King would no doubt have called for an account of the affair of Isaac Schomberg from the flag-officer under whom Schomberg next served, and Schomberg might well have given Hood a report unfavourable to Nelson. George III, who would have attended personally to Schomberg's appointment to the *Pegasus*, would not necessarily have taken his son's side in the matter.

In his same letter to the Duke, Nelson took pains to enlighten him with a carefully documented account of the plight of Norfolk labourers who tried to keep a family alive on total yearly earnings of £23, 1s. od. He concluded: "Not quite twopence a day for each person; and to drink nothing but water, for beer our poor labourers never taste, unless they are tempted, which is too often the case, to go to the Alehouse." Nelson blamed the landlords for "not making their farmers raise their wages, in some small proportion, as the prices of necessaries increased". He was right; but over half a century later, when the reign of the man he was addressing had come and gone, things were much the same. Another post-captain on half pay, writing in 1847 of a feast he had provided for his labourers at Langham, only a few miles from Burnham, said, "these poor men work hard all the year round, and never get anything to eat but bread for themselves and their wives and children: and they are thankful if, by hard labour, they can find bread to live upon". Frederick Marryat, novelist of Nelson's navy, had the same compassionate interest in the lives of those around him.

Chapter 3

PARTISAN

I

"*POST nubila Phoebus:*—After clouds comes sunshine." Nelson began the first important letter of the year 1793 with a burst of jubilation. He wrote thus to his wife from London, adding, "The Admiralty so smile upon me, that really I am as much surprised as when they frowned. Lord Chatham yesterday made many apologies for not having given me a Ship before this time, and said, that if I chose to take a Sixty-four to begin with, I should be appointed to one as soon as she was ready; and whenever it was in his power, I should be removed into a Seventy-four. Everything indicates War. One of our Ships, looking into Brest, has been fired into: the shot is now at the Admiralty. You will send my Father this news, which I am sure will please him. Love to Josiah, and believe me, Your most affectionate Horatio Nelson."

The writer may have been elated: it is questionable whether news of the appointment of her husband to a ship of the line, and of the imminence of war, fell pleasantly upon the ear of a woman not known for her serene acceptance of vicissitude.

Much had happened in the world since the paying off of the *Boreas*, however small a stir affairs had made in Norfolk. There had been serious threat of war with Spain over the rights of Britons to settle on the American coast of the Pacific. Nelson and others referred to this as "the Affair with Spain, relative to Nootka Sound", at which remote spot some merchantmen had been seized. Additional men-of-war had been commissioned for active service, and only concessions from Madrid saved an outbreak. Then, in November, 1792, the French, in defiance of treaty obligations, occupied the Austrian Netherlands. Thereupon, through their command of the Scheldt, they threatened trade routes vital to this country, and the prospect opened that, if the Austrians should be decisively defeated, Antwerp might become a French port and a rival to London.

Finally, after the execution of Louis XVI in January 1793, revolution stalked in Europe, and such a wave of horror, execration and loyalism swept across the United Kingdom as to make war almost inevitable. Opinion had already been inflamed by a decree of the Paris Convention which offered "assistance to all people who wish to recover their liberty". Britons might be nearer to slavery than popular songs indicated, but they had no intention of being liberated by regicides from across the Channel.

War was formally declared by France on England and Holland on 1st February 1793, so that Nelson's appointment offered the likelihood of immediate action in European waters. Two large fleets were organised: the first, for home and Atlantic waters, was put under the command of Lord Howe; the second, for the Mediterranean, under Lord Hood. Both admirals were elderly, and Hood was close on seventy; but had Nelson been offered his choice, there is no question which station he would have preferred, and it was in fact for Hood's he was destined. It seemed that when fortune smiled, she was not half-hearted. "Lord Hood," he wrote to Locker, "has been very civil indeed. I think we may be good friends again." And in the Sketch of his Life he proudly recorded: "On the 30th of January 1793 I was commissioned in the very handsomest way for the *Agamemnon*, 64; and was put under the command of that great man and excellent officer, Lord Hood."

From this time onward, the jubilant note was sustained. Nelson was back in his chosen profession; he could now be the patron of friends who wished to send lads to sea under his care; his officers (who included a Suckling) pleased him; Josiah was with him; and his muster-book soon began to fill with Norfolk and Suffolk names, all volunteers. These men were embarking on a hard, strange life, but Nelson himself had collected enough evidence to show that, whatever else it was, the eighteenth century was not that of the common man in rural England.

Nelson himself had no doubt that the exchange from the

simple pleasures of rural life to the austerities of seafaring
was a pleasing one, and as captain of a ship of the line he lived
in comparative comfort. In the *Agamemnon* he had a cabin
whose dimensions were those of a sizeable though low-
ceilinged room, embellished with pictures and bookshelves,
furnished with the amenities of a dining-room ashore. He
had a sleeping-place in which his cot could swing. He had his
silver, his own galley, his cook and steward, his own food.
To light him he had windowed galleries, with a view of the
sea through the square panes. By night, candle-lanterns
enabled him to entertain guests in style. For warmth he had
a charcoal brazier. Even the Mediterranean could be so
persistently chilly that Nelson recorded the use of his "fire"
for almost the whole stretch of a summer.

The officers had their ward-room beneath his cabin. The
men lived and slept among the weapons and gear of the gun
decks, their mess-tables fixed between the barrels, hooked
up to the beams when not in use. Every sailor had a knife,
which he wore about him, a spoon, an earthenware bowl and
a platter. The ship's cook used huge coppers in his galley
forward for boiling the salt junk. The regulation victuals
included biscuit, beef, pork, peas, oatmeal, sugar, butter and
cheese, but the quality varied from bad to atrocious, and the
quantity was strictly limited. The meat was gristly, fibrous,
dark, glistening with salt crystals. It was so hard that boxes
could be carved from it which would take a fine polish. The
water was bad, the beer a little better, and the rum better
still. Admiral Vernon made a name for himself earlier in the
century by his introduction of "grog", the daily allowance of
half a pint of rum being mixed with a quart of water in the
presence of the officer of the watch. Nelson, in his later
service, found wine better than spirits for the fitness of his
ship's company, though it was not so popular.

He was never a captain who kept aloof from the detailed
running of his command. He insisted that the men's quarters
were properly ventilated, and that stoves were used whenever necessary for drying out the recesses in the ship which
were most exposed to damp. He encouraged music and
dancing, and any other activity which could help to sustain
morale. All good captains did the same. "We have lately

been making musical instruments, and have now a good band," wrote the much more puritanically minded Collingwood from the Channel fleet. "Every moonlit night the sailors dance, and there seems as much mirth and festivity as if we were in Wapping itself." Nelson's crews were always in good heart, and although they had no more amenities than those of other ships, yet as early as the days of the *Lowestoffe*, when he was a lieutenant, the seamen were fond enough of him to present him with an ivory model of their frigate, filled with dominoes. It was a familiar sight in his cabin, a valued token of the affection of his "brave fellows".

One of the friends whose sons Nelson had taken to sea was a staunch Whig; Nelson's politics were less progressive. James Harrison records that the captain, thinking the youth "might possibly require some little counteraction of the principles of modern whiggism, which he did not think very conducive to the loyalty and subordination of a young British sailor, called him into his cabin and gave him a private piece of advice that soon became public. 'There are three things, young gentleman,' said Nelson, 'you are constantly to bear in mind: first, you must always implicitly obey orders, without attempting to form any opinion of your own respecting their propriety; secondly, you must consider every man as your enemy who speaks ill of your King; and thirdly, you must hate a Frenchman as you do the devil!' "

A few years before, in time of peace, his advice had been equally sound but rather different. Writing to the Earl of Cork about a protégé proposed to be sent to sea, he said: "In the first place . . . it is necessary he should be made complete in his navigation; and if the Peace continues, French is absolutely necessary. Dancing is an accomplishment that probably a Sea Officer may require. You will see almost the necessity of it, when employed in Foreign Countries; indeed the honour of the Nation is so often entrusted to Sea Officers, that there is no accomplishment which will not shine with peculiar lustre."

Obedience, loyalty, accomplishments; those were the qualities Nelson would expect from his officers. In the *Agamemnon*'s ward-room he was not disappointed.

So far as manning the ship was concerned, Nelson had

every help from Locker, who was then Commodore com-
manding-in-chief at the Nore, though he was soon to take
up a new and final appointment as Lieutenant-Governor of
Greenwich Hospital. Locker was in a position to draft good
men to his friends. Everything, indeed, seemed to conspire
to please. "I never was in better health," he wrote to Fanny
from Chatham on 15th March, "and I hope you intend a
new lease of your life." A month later he added, "I have
reason to be satisfied at present with every officer of the
ship"; later still: "nobody can be ill with my Ship's company, they are so fine a set".

As at many turning-points in his life, Nelson ascribed the
situation to Providence, and as a clergyman's son he did not
forget the spiritual welfare of those under his care. He wrote
from Chatham to the Society for the Promotion of Christian
Knowledge "soliciting a donation of Bibles and Prayer
Books for the use of his ship's company". The Society sent
Psalters, copies of the *Christian Soldier* and *The Seaman's
Monitor*. The author of the latter book, Dr Josiah Woodward
had been famous and popular as a preacher, and the *Monitor*
had had a huge circulation since its first appearance in the
early years of the eighteenth century.

Above all else, the *Agamemnon* pleased her captain. She
was then twelve years old. She had been built at Buckler's
Hard on the Beaulieu River, a place which has still a flavour
of the era of sail. In her first year afloat she had fought under
Kempenfelt, helping to snap up a French convoy in the
Atlantic under the eyes of its escort. She had been present
at Rodney's victory of the Saint's Passage in 1782. The
Admiralty could scarcely have chosen a ship more fitted to
capture Nelson's imagination. "*Agamemnon* sails admirably,"
he told Fanny. "We think better than any Ship in the Fleet."
She could certainly leave the 74-gun *Robust*, commanded by
George Keith Elphinstone, well behind her, a ship with
which she was often in company. In May, Maurice Nelson
joined his brother at Spithead on a brief visit, "and it blew
so hard I could not land him," said Nelson: "he consequently went to sea with us". Maurice no doubt enjoyed an
encounter with the fleet otherwise than through the papers
on his desk at the Navy Office.

Hood made a rendezvous for his ships in the Channel, saw a West India convoy safely home, and by the beginning of June was well on his way to Gibraltar. Part of the fleet, including the *Agamemnon*, put into Cadiz on a friendly visit, for the Spanish were temporary though rather uncertain allies. The officers were allowed to go over the arsenals and dockyard, and Nelson reported to Fanny that he thought the vessels he saw in commission "very fine ships, but shockingly manned.... I am certain if our six Barge's crews, who are picked men, had got on board one of their First-rates, they would have taken her. The Dons may make fine Ships—they cannot, however, make men." This axiom seemed to be reinforced when the fleet had reached the Mediterranean and a Spanish frigate came with a message saying that as the vessels co-operating with Hood had many sick, they were putting into Cartagena, adding it was no wonder, for they had been sixty days at sea! Nelson's comment was: "This speech was to us ridiculous: for from the circumstance of having been longer than that time at sea, do we attribute our getting healthy. It has stamped with me the extent of their nautical abilities." Nor did the land relaxations of his allies impress him, for while at Cadiz he had been with a party to a bullfight. His reaction was that of many Englishmen before and since. "It turned us sick," he wrote to Fanny, "and we could hardly go through it: the dead mangled horses with the entrails torn out, and the bulls covered with blood, were too much. However we have seen our bull-feast, and agree that nothing shall tempt us to see another."

By August, when the fleet was off Toulon, preparing for that long-to-be-continued work of blockade which played such a great part in the war now fairly begun, Hood had implemented the First Lord's promise of offering Nelson a bigger ship. It was declined. "I cannot give up my officers," Nelson told Fanny. "Lord Hood approved of my reasons: so far well." And in the same letter he said: "How I long to have a letter from you: next to being with you, it is the greatest pleasure I can receive. The being united to such a good woman, I look back to as the happiest period of my life; and as I cannot here show my affection to you, I do it doubly to Josiah, who deserves it, as well on his own account as on yours, for he is a real good boy, and most affectionately loves me."

II

The recollection of domestic felicity was present, but it was doomed to fade, for Nelson, a captain of fourteen years' seniority, in command of a ship of which he had reason to be proud, and on a station where he was trusted, soon became involved in larger affairs.

Hood was in treaty with a party in Toulon who wished to open the town to the British fleet, so inimical was the feeling generally to the revolutionaries at Paris. After the outlawing of the town by the Parliamentary Convention, the allied forces, British, Spanish and Sardinian, were admitted to the port, and Hood's immediate need was for troops to hold it against the attack in force which he knew to be preparing. He despatched Nelson to Naples, to seek men and munitions. On 11th September Nelson wrote to Fanny to say that the *Agamemnon* was "now in sight of Mount Vesuvius, which shows a fine light to us in Naples Bay, where we are lying-to for the night, and hope [to anchor early to-morrow".

"Tomorrow" brought Nelson his first acquaintance with King Ferdinand of Naples, Sir William Hamilton the British Minister, his wife (formerly Emma Hart), Sir John Acton, baronet of a Shropshire family who was then the Neapolitan Prime Minister, and other notables. The meeting was auspicious. Ferdinand, who had married a sister of Marie Antoinette, was full of zeal against the French republic, and assured Nelson that troops would be sent to Toulon. As for the Hamiltons, Nelson found Sir William a man after his own heart: "You do business in my own way," he said with admiration. Of Emma, Nelson wrote to Fanny that she had been "wonderfully kind and good to Josiah" (a sure way to a mother's heart), and he added that she "does honour to the station to which she is raised". Sir William had been equally impressed with Nelson, so he told his wife, who was fond of recalling how he said he was "about to introduce her to a little man who could not boast of being handsome, but who would become the greatest man that England ever produced".

It is most unlikely that the sophisticated Sir William said anything of the kind. He was a good judge of character, but there is no evidence that he added prophecy to his other gifts; however, it was plain fact that Nelson's mission was fruitful; that he was a personal success at the ceremonies arranged for his visit; that Sir William corresponded with him afterwards with confidence and increasing affection, and that, although he told Emma that he had never before entertained officers in his own house, he requested that Nelson should be lodged in the room prepared for a visit from the Duke of Sussex.

Although Nelson did not, at the time of his visit, record his impressions of Emma Hamilton except in general terms, he must have made apparent his pleasure in her society. For Hamilton, wishing to impress a kinsman, Thomas Graham, then serving at Toulon, with the virtues of his lovely wife, wrote from Naples: "I refer you to Captain Nelson . . . to give you an account of Lady Hamilton, who will never disgrace the family in which her merit has placed her. She makes me happy and is loved and esteemed by all. Come and see, and my life for it, she will gain you. You may well imagine that I should not have taken the step without having seen my way clearly. It was not a sudden passion for a pretty face, for she had lived with me five years, and you know that all faces in that space of time become pretty near equal."

The pair had then been legally married some two years.

Nelson's private Journal covering the period which includes this first Naples visit is in existence, though it has not been used by biographers. It gives a running record of events which began with a formal call on the King. Ferdinand had already heard of the fall of Toulon, but had understood it to have been taken by the "Spanish and English fleets". Nelson was able to tell him that in fact Lord Hood had made all arrangements to enter the port before the Spanish hove in sight. The King expressed surprise at this, and added that he was "sensible that to his Lordship and his fleet was Italie

indebted for security—that we were the saviours of Italie
and of his Kingdom in particular."

Nelson's next call, made with Sir William Hamilton, was
upon Sir John Acton, to discuss the despatch of troops.
Acton assured his fellow-Englishman that the King would
do everything required, but suggested that, as Hood was
known to be short of provisions, it might perhaps be better
to wait a week or so before embarkation, so that extra provisions could be collected. Sir William took up this point at
once, saying that 2,000 men in three or four days would be
better than a larger force delayed some weeks. Acton agreed.
At dinner the Prime Minister was careful to lay it down that
the Neapolitans should serve only under Lord Hood, not
under Spanish or Sardinian command.

On 13th September Nelson saw the King again, who
promised to dine aboard the *Agamemnon*. "The Queen being
eight months with child," wrote Nelson, "I was not presented to her."

Next day Acton produced a handsome letter from Ferdinand to Lord Hood, and Lady Hamilton (who was then first
mentioned in the Journal) introduced Nelson to the Princess
of Bellemont, who wished to see over the British ship. Next
day Nelson dined—at 1 o'clock—at the right hand of the
King, the swell being too great for H.M. to have his meal
afloat, as he had wished. He asked Nelson to accompany him
next day to see the troops, who, he promised, were "good
cannoniers and handled the broad-sword well".

At 6 o'clock in the morning on the 16th, drill took place.
"H.M. as soon as he saw us made his troops halt and dressed
them as they march'd by us," wrote Nelson. Socialities continued with a breakfast on board the *Agamemnon* to which
Lady Hamilton and other ladies were invited. But before the
time of the King's own visit, news came from Acton that
"there was anchored off the south of Sardinia one French
corvette with a small English ship her prize, and two ships
under her convoy from Smyrna bound for Leghorn, that
they would have sent but were otherwise employed."

Nelson, his eyes ranging round the splendid harbour, saw
seven Neapolitan men-of-war and a Spanish 40-gun frigate
"otherwise employed". "So," he told his brother William,

"unfit as my ship was, I had nothing left for the honour of our country but to sail, which I did in two hours afterwards." It was necessary to show allies what a British ship of the line could do, and the ladies, with every courtesy, were put ashore.

Nelson ended his Naples entries with significant comments on the Hamiltons and the King, though (careful of *lèse-majesté*) he left Ferdinand's title out. "I believe we carry with us the good wishes of Naples and of Sir William and Lady Hamilton in particular, which I esteem more than all the rest. Farewell Naples, may those who were kind to me be repaid tenfold. If I am successful I return, if otherwise go to Toulon. I should be wanting did I not say how active Sir William Hamilton has been in getting these troops sent off, for left to themselves I am sure they would not have sailed these three weeks, the Vanity of the —— is such that he wish'd to cut a great figure by sending his stipulated force all at the same time, and to that vanity are we now indebted for the 4,000 instead of the 2,000 at first promised."

Nelson's pursuit of the corvette was not successful, and it was some years before he returned to Naples. Meanwhile, his ship had only been twenty days at anchor since April, and his men were so worn out that it was necessary to put into Leghorn, a friendly port, "absolutely to save my poor fellows", wrote their commander. There, in Tuscan waters, he lay close to a French 40-gun frigate, which he intended to chase should she try to slip away. It seemed that she might prove an easy prize, for her men had, so Nelson heard, "deposed their Captain, made the Lieutenant of Marines Captain of the Ship, the Sergeant of Marines Lieutenant of Marines, and their former Captain, Sergeant of Marines. What a state!"

In her disorganised condition, the frigate did nothing so rash as to try to leave Leghorn, and it was Nelson who sailed, first for Sardinia and then for Toulon. There, on 1st October he had news from home that Fanny was ailing and fretting. His way of comforting her was to ask briefly: "Why should you alarm yourself? I am well, your son is well, and we are as comfortable in every respect as the nature of our service will admit. Lord Hood is now quite as he used to be: he is so

good an officer, that every body must respect him. All the
foreigners at Toulon absolutely worship him; were any
accident to happen to him, I am sure no person in our Fleet
could supply his place." He ended by saying that it "made
no difference" to a court-martial on which he had sat that
shot and shell had whistled overhead. It was all part of the
day's work. "Such is the force of habit, we seem to feel no
danger." The shell came from batteries some of which had
been sited by a young officer of artillery called Bonaparte,
who was infusing new life into a siege by the Republicans
which had been mounted since the end of August.

Nelson would have liked to be landed, to join Elphinstone
of the *Robust* and others, who, he heard, were doing gallantly
ashore; but, although disappointed, he did not have long to
wait for his first taste of close action since the War of
American Independence.

On 22nd October, while off Sardinia with only 345 men
at quarters, the rest having been landed to serve at Toulon,
he sighted and pursued five French ships smaller than his
own, including three frigates. He engaged them for four
hours, and would have continued action with an enemy who
had been reinforced but for grave damage to his masts and
rigging. The *Agamemnon* had one man killed and six wounded.

The engagement, unimportant in itself, though indicative
of Nelson's pertinacity, is interesting as showing, from a
surviving memorandum, that he was careful to consult his
officers before breaking off action in the face of odds. Moreover, to ensure that the affair was not overlooked at home, he
sent a brief but precise report to his brother Maurice at the
Navy Office (in addition to his despatch to Lord Hood),
knowing that it would be read by men of consequence in the
sea profession.

Privately, he felt both elation and relief at the result of the
encounter. "My thanks and offerings to the Almighty have
been nearly in the same words and certainly with the same
meaning as those so inimitably wrote in the *Spectator*,"[1] ran
the entry in his Sea Journal, affording posterity another

---

[1] For 20th September 1712, including lines beginning:
How are Thy Servants blest, O Lord,
How sure is their defence.

glimpse of his reading. The Journal continued with a passage, hitherto unpublished, expressive of that simple trust in Providence which never forsook him.

"When I lay me down to sleep I recommend myself to the Care of Almighty God, when I awake I give myself up to His direction, amidst all the evils that threaten me, I will look up to Him for help, and question not but that He will either avert them or turn them to my advantage though I know neither the time nor the manner of my death, I am not at all solicitous about it because I am sure that He knows them both, and that He will not fail to support and comfort me."

No sooner had he returned to his anchorage than Commodore Linzee, under whose orders Hood told Nelson to place himself, asked him if he would be ready to sail at once on an operation. Shattered as the ship was, "I would not say *Agamemnon* was ever unable to go in search of the enemy," wrote Nelson. "We worked all night fishing our masts and yards and stopping shot holes, mending sails and splicing our rigging."

Linzee had orders to expostulate with the Bey of Tunis for his partiality to French interests. Clarke and M'Arthur say that in Nelson's sole interview with the potentate, he discovered "such quickness as to have disconcerted even the captain of the *Agamemnon*". On being reminded of the excesses which the French Government had committed— including the murder of their King and Queen, the Bey drily observed "that nothing could be more heinous than the murder of their Sovereign; and yet, Sir, if your historians tell the truth, your own countrymen once did the same." Nelson himself reported to his uncle William Suckling: "You will believe the English seldom get much from negotiation except the being laughed at, which we have been; and I don't like it."

His Journal merely refers to a "damn'd Palaver" spread over the first five days of November. By the 10th of the month he recorded, in phrases which anticipate those used on later occasions, "My spirits are low indeed, had I been Commodore most likely I should have been broke by this time, for certainly I should have taken every Frenchman here without negotiating, even had negotiations took place I would have had the French men of war. I believe that the people of England will never blame an officer for taking a French Line of Battle Ship." Linzee was not only of another opinion, but his methods were such as to cause Nelson to draw a moral from his behaviour. "Beware of dilatoriness; expedition ought to be the universal *word* and *deed*."

His spirits were not elevated by the next event which reverberated throughout the Mediterranean. It was the end of the affair at Toulon. By the first week in December the French Republican forces had gained such ascendency that the fall of the port was inevitable. On the 19th Bonaparte had the satisfaction of seeing the last allied resistance crumble, and the Royal Navy in retreat. Although, in his withdrawal, Hood was able to destroy some of the French ships, demolition was by no means complete, the Spanish Admiral de Langara and Captain Sir Sidney Smith failing to co-ordinate their efforts. Nelson, who did not much care for Smith, said later: "Lord Hood mistook the man: there is an old saying, *Great talkers do the least we see*." Nor was the embarkation of troops and refugees satisfactory. Some of the Neapolitans, in their flight, hurled themselves into the sea, a course which had something to be said for it, in view of the protracted blood-bath which followed the occupation of the town.

Civil wars are notoriously brutal: that in France, in which the recapture of Toulon was an important incident, was no exception. Although he was not himself present, the episode affected Nelson deeply. His hatred of a Frenchman was heightened, and he felt he had shame to avenge.

It is unlikely that Hood or for that matter any experienced general could have held Toulon as an enclave within a hostile country, but the episode gave parties on the Continent, otherwise well disposed, an opinion which has not since been seriously modified, that help from a sea-power is a mixed blessing, likely to be followed by withdrawal, and by consequences, locally, of an unpleasant kind. Foreign "worship" of Lord Hood certainly did not survive the withdrawal of his ships, if indeed it ever existed outside Nelson's partial mind. "It is the poor inhabitants at Toulon that I feel for," he wrote to the Duke of Clarence from Leghorn Roads. "All is horror," he told Fanny. "Each teller makes the scene more horrible." There is no more vivid reflection of the effect of the massacres at Toulon than appears in the half-demented character of the orphaned Arlette, in Conrad's novel *The Rover*. Conrad knew the place, its legends, and living descendants of loyalists and republicans with the nearness of one who began his seafaring in their company. The legends he imbibed were not of a kind out of which fairy-tales arise.

III

No less than three times, in official correspondence, the Earl of St Vincent, who in due course became Nelson's commander-in-chief, described him as an outstanding "partisan". The term would be puzzling applied to one who gained a peerless reputation as a fleet tactician were not Nelson's partiality for land service remembered, and in particular his zeal in operations in Nicaragua and Corsica. It was perhaps in Corsica that the "brigadier" most fully justified his nickname.

Expelled from Toulon, Hood sought another base, and believed he had found it close at hand. He had been in touch with Paoli, the veteran Corsican patriot, friend of Johnson and Boswell during a long sojourn in London, and had reason to hope that the British might find a welcome in an island recently ceded to France by the Genoese. The Corsicans, in whom the flame of independence burnt as brightly as in the Poles, were in a perpetual state of revolt, active or passive, against foreign oppressors. Once before, in the reign of George II, they had offered to place themselves under the protection of the crown of England.

Paoli promised that if Hood would make an attack on St Fiorenzo from the sea, he himself would move against the place by land. Unhappily, he was not able to keep his word, and Commodore Linzee, who was charged with seaward operations, was repulsed with loss. Hood suspected Paoli of deceiving him, but later sent a party, which included

Lieutenant-Colonel (afterwards Sir John) Moore and Lieutenant Andrews of the Navy, brother of Nelson's lady of
St Omer, to confer on a further plan of operations. Sir
Gilbert Elliot accompanied them, and in the upshot Elliot
was appointed Viceroy of the island, representative of
George III. It was not a happy decision, for although Nelson
himself had witnessed the islanders' "wonderful attachment"
to Paoli, adding that he saw a gentleman "taking a miniature
of him from his bosom: he kissed it, and hundreds on their
knees immediately begged to do the same", yet Paoli, in the
end, returned to England, and Elliot, in accordance with
instructions from home, tried to rule Corsica on the lines
of a constitutional monarchy of the British pattern, a good
intention which did not fit the circumstances.

On 21st January 1794 Nelson had his own first brush
with the French occupying troops. This he described to
Fanny as follows: "Having their storehouse of flour near a
water-mill close to St Fiorenzo, I seized a happy moment,
and landed sixty soldiers and sixty seamen, in spite of opposition. At landing, the sailors threw all the flour into the sea,
burned the mill—the only one they had—and returned on
board without the loss of a man. The French sent one
thousand men at least against them, and Gun-boats, etc. but
the shot went over them, and they were just within reach of
my guns." It was a typical example of the kind of operation
which, to use Southey's phrase, "depresses the spirits of an
enemy more than it injures them, because of the sense of
individual superiority which it indicates in the assailants".
This was the essence of partisan operations, together with
the hope of containing substantial enemy forces.

The French soon abandoned St Fiorenzo and retreated to
Bastia. Hood tried to persuade Dundas, the general in
command of the army ashore, to attack the stronghold, but
failed. Dundas was expecting a reinforcement from Gibraltar, without which he would not proceed: moreover, it
was his view that the garrison of Bastia could be starved
into surrender. It was an opinion which proved his good
sense, and one which was shared by his successor,
d'Aubant.

Nelson himself was soon ashore, incessantly active. "My

seamen," he told Fanny, "are now what British seamen ought to be . . . almost invincible: they really mind shot no more than peas." They dragged guns up precipitous slopes, and, with the few soldiers who were spared to serve in forward areas, showed "zeal almost unexampled. There is not a man but considers himself as personally interested in the event, and deserted by the general. It has, I am persuaded, made them equal to double their numbers."

When it was first decided to attack the place, the French were believed to be much fewer than in fact they were. Nelson later had private information of the true force, which was three times that of the assailants, and was behind a strong position, but he kept the matter secret, feeling that if the odds were realised, the operation would be called off. "My own honour, Lord Hood's honour, and the honour of our country, must have been sacrificed, had I mentioned what I knew," he wrote to Fanny many months later. In fact, an assault was not only unnecessary, but would have led to very severe casualties, for the garrison were ready to surrender on terms, and on 19th May a treaty of capitulation was discussed. Dundas was right. Hunger had succeeded where arms would almost certainly have been repulsed.

Nelson, in a letter to Fanny written between 1st and 4th May, told her "as a secret, Bastia will be ours between the 20th and 24th of this month, if succours do not get in. Our Ships are moored across the harbour's mouth, and three boats from each Ship row guard every night."

It is difficult to draw any other conclusion than that, although Nelson at heart agreed with the soldiers as to how and why Bastia must fall, he yet thirsted to see what men under his command could do in a land attack, even at much cost in human life. On this, as on almost every other occasion before action, he prepared Fanny for the worst, the effect of which was to cause her almost a paroxysm of anxiety. He himself seems to have been one of those people, rare even among professional fighters, with a constant hankering for danger, prepared to die at any moment. To him danger was more than the spice of life: it was the means of glory, an idea which meant so much to Nelson that he would gladly sacrifice himself to achieve it. He said so again and again, and proved his words by his behaviour. "Life with disgrace is dreadful," he once told Fanny. "A glorious death is to be envied; and if anything happens to me, recollect that death is a debt we all must pay, and whether now, or a few years hence, can be but of little consequence."

By mid-June Nelson was back in Corsica, preparing for the siege of Calvi. The new general, Charles Stuart, was nearer than Dundas to his ideal of a soldier, though Nelson feared the influence of Colonel Moore, and wished that distinguished officer "100 leagues off". In fact, to Hood's annoyance, Nelson received no credit in Stuart's reports, though his zeal continued unabated. "We will fag ourselves to death," he wrote to Hood, "before any blame shall lie at our doors." It was not fag, however, but sickness which laid men low. "The climate here, from July to October, is most unfavourable for Military operations," Nelson wrote to the Duke of Clarence. "It is now what we call the dog-days, here it is termed the Lion Sun; no person can endure it: we have upwards of one thousand sick out of two thousand, and others not much better than so many phantoms. We have lost many men from the season, very few from the enemy. I am here the reed among the oaks: all the prevailing disorders have attacked me, but I have not strength for them to fasten upon. I bow before the storm, whilst the sturdy oak is laid low." In fact, he was up every day at the batteries with some of his young gentlemen, or with officers of the army.

It was at the batteries that Nelson received a serious wound. He had had some narrow shaves before, as on an occasion before Bastia recorded in the diary of Captain Thomas Fremantle under the date 19th April 1794: "Dine with Nelson," runs the entry, "take a view of the new battery at Torga. Walking with Nelson from thence a shot knocked him down and covered me all over with dirt. Determine never to go the short way again." This time it was more than a trifle.

Nelson wrote to Lord Hood on 12th July from Camp, to make a report of the situation, ending his letter, "I got a little hurt this morning: not much, as you may judge from my writing." Next day, to the same correspondent, he added,

"my eye is better, and I hope not entirely to lose the sight".
He did not mention the matter to Fanny in a few lines sent
on 15th, referring to Lord Howe's victory of the First of
June. Fuller news (though even then it was not much) was
given in a letter to William Suckling on 16th, when he said:
"You will be surprised when I say I was wounded in the
head by stones from the merlon of our battery. My right
eye is cut entirely down; but the Surgeons flatter me I shall
not entirely lose the sight of that eye. At present I can
distinguish light from dark, but no object: it confined me one
day, when, thank God, I was enabled to attend to my duty.
I feel the want of it; but, such is the chance of War, it was
within a hair's breadth of taking off my head."

Apparently what had happened was that the enemy, opening concentrated fire, destroyed three guns, and in the
course of the bombardment Nelson was struck violently in
the face and breast by splinters, stones and sand flung up by
a shell. He bled profusely. Examination showed that he had
received several superficial cuts in the face, and a deep one
in the right brow which had penetrated the eyelid and eye-
ball. He suffered much pain, and was in fact never again
able to distinguish more than "light from dark" with his
right eye, though he did not actually lose it. John Harness
and Michael Jefferson, the physician and surgeon who on
9th August signed the first certificate respecting the wound,
spoke of "an unnatural dilatation of the pupil and a material
defect of sight". Three days later, Mr W. Chambers, surgeon to the Forces in the Mediterranean, gave his judgment,
which proved to be accurate, that the "eye is so materially
injured that, in my opinion, he will never recover the perfect
use of it again". In the course of the following January he
told Fanny: "My eye is grown worse, and is in almost total
darkness, and very painful at times; but never mind, I can
see very well with the other." It is probable that the retina
was detached.

The effects were profound, though they could not then
have been realised. All Nelson's greater exploits were before
him, and eleven years of incessant activity, mental and
physical. The strain on his good eye soon became appreci-
able, and he later found some relief by having a shade made,

which subdued the Mediterranean light. Nelson's fortitude
was never better shown than in his immediate reaction to
the wound, and in the wonderful patience with which he
afterwards bore his handicap.

Calvi surrendered on 10th August, but Nelson got so
little glory from the affair that his name did not even appear
among the list of the wounded. "One hundred and ten days
I have been actually engaged, at sea and on shore, against
the enemy," he wrote. "I do not know that any one has done
more. I have had the comfort to be always applauded by my
commander-in-chief, but never to be rewarded: and what is
more mortifying, for services in which I have been wounded,
others have been praised, who, at the same time, were
actually in bed, far from the scene of action. They have not
done me justice. But, never mind, I'll have a 'Gazette' of
my own."

One of the saddest pieces of news Nelson received, before
his spell ashore was over, was that of the death, from fever,
of Lieutenant James Moutray, the only son of Captain and
Mrs Moutray, his friends at Antigua. He had known the
young man as a child, had heard of his good services under
Hood in the *Victory*, and that he would shortly be promoted.
With typical kindness, he placed an inscription to the lad's
memory in the church at St Fiorenzo, the stone being
"Erected by an Affectionate Friend, who well knew his
worth as an Officer, and his Accomplished Manners as a
Gentleman."

IV

Nelson's next duty was diplomatic. He had been successful at Naples; now he was to go to Genoa to interview the
Doge, and to request facilities in that port for British men-
of-war. From Genoa he wrote to Fanny on 20th September
1794, "this City is, without exception, the most magnificent
I ever beheld, superior in many respects to Naples, although
it does not appear quite so fine from the sea, yet on shore it
is far beyond it. All the houses are palaces on the grandest
scale. However, I trust we shall soon quit these magnificent

scenes, and retire to England, where all that I admire is placed."

He told Lord Hood "I was received in some state, the Doge advancing to the middle of the room to receive me, and I had the honours of a Senator." He added, for the admiral's private ear, that "never man was so unpopular as Mr Drake in Genoa"—Drake being the British Minister at Turin, and also concerned with affairs in the Republic. "The Nobles, Middle class and Lowest, equally hate him, even the boat people speak of him as being unlike any other Englishman." Nelson felt it doubly incumbent on him to show that an Englishman could be both liked and respected, though he came in time to have a far greater respect for Mr Drake than had the Genoese. He parted from the Doge with mutual assurances of friendship.

It was his last important service under Hood, for in October the commander-in-chief was recalled, an occasion which provoked an acidulated entry in the diary of Colonel Moore. "It is singular," he wrote, "that Lord Hood . . . should take the *Victory* home, when he might be conveyed equally well in a frigate." Inter-service criticism was seldom stronger than during Hood's Mediterranean command, and Moore's comment may have had something to justify it, though no one knew better than Hood the potentiality of his opponents at sea.

Early in November the new commander-in-chief, Vice-Admiral Hotham, sent the *Agamemnon* on a reconnaissance. She was to discover the force of the French in the neighbourhood of their chief base. "Not finding them in Hieres Bay," Nelson told the Duke of Clarence in one of his regular letters, "I stood close into Toulon Harbour, where are twenty-two Sail of Ships in the inner Harbour: we could only look over a point of land, therefore cannot say how many were of the Line. . . . I see plainly they will keep us in hot water the whole winter, and I think it probable may detach small Squadrons to get, for a few days at intervals, in the track of our Trade. . . ."

By the end of the month the weary ship and her company were at Leghorn, refitting. In Nelson's words, they had had "such a series of hard service, as has never before, I believe, fallen to the lot of any one ship". It was perhaps not surprising that although, as he told Fanny, "I have been offered every Seventy-four which has fallen vacant in this Country," he could not bring himself to part with men with whom he had been through so much. "It is misery for me to be laid up dismantled," he told his uncle, William Suckling; but in Leghorn he found compensations.

Among them was a woman, though it is unlikely that her name and nature will now be discovered. Leghorn, as appeared through some tart remarks of St Vincent after he had succeeded to the Mediterranean command, was in Hotham's time a place where ships repaired, and where officers made such sport with local beauties, Tuscan and otherwise, that they all too often found themselves in hospital.

Nelson, according to James Harrison, who wrote on Lady Hamilton's information, had only two faults: venery and swearing. Harrison said of him that "it is not to be dissembled, though by no means ever an unprincipled seducer of the wives and daughters of his friends, he was always well known to maintain rather more partiality for the fair sex than is quite consistent with the highest degree of Christian purity. Such improper indulgences, with some slight addition to that other vicious habit of British seamen, the occasional use of a few thoughtlessly profane expletives in speech, form the only dark specks ever yet discovered in the bright blaze of his moral character."

No one could have known the history of Nelson's affairs of the heart better than Lady Hamilton, and as his is one of the most thoroughly documented lives, even the circumstances of his milder loves not escaping record, Harrison's sententious remarks were based upon some evidence. They rested, in all probability, on an affair at Leghorn, dutifully suppressed by contemporary biographers, if indeed any shred of record was committed by Nelson to paper. It is only indicated today by some terse lines in the diary of Captain Thomas Fremantle, which were unknown to earlier biographers, and by one oblique reference.

The entries are few. Their tantalising brevity is in keeping with Fremantle's whole method, his own marriage being dismissed in a single sentence, and his courtship in not much more.

> "December 1794. Wed. 3. Dined at Nelson's and his dolly. Called on old Udney, went to the opera with him. He introduced me to a very handsome Greek woman."

(John Udney was the British Consul at Leghorn. He sometimes acted as agent for prizes: and he seems to have had other uses.)

> "August 1795. A convoy arrived from Genoa. Dined with Nelson. Dolly aboard who has a sort of abscess in her side, he makes himself ridiculous with that woman."

(Nelson's ship was in Vado Bay on the date concerned. Apropos of women on board H.M. ships, which was not uncommon even in time of war, he wrote to a brother-officer, "they always will do as they please. Orders are not for them —at least I never knew one who obeyed your most faithful Horatio Nelson.")

> "August. Sat. 28. Dined with Nelson and his Dolly.
> "September. Sun. 27. Dined with Nelson and Dolly. Very bad dinner indeed."

On the note of a bad dinner, the entries cease as abruptly as they were begun. On each date mentioned but the second, Nelson was at or near Leghorn, and as Fremantle became intimate with the Hamiltons as well as with Nelson—Emma made all the arrangements for the captain's wedding to Betsy Wynne in January 1797—it is most unlikely that the affair was not known to Emma in all its intricacy. She would have dropped the necessary hint to Harrison, hence his critical sentence, which would certainly not have been intended to refer to Nelson's relationship with her.

That Nelson's "dolly" was what the word implies admits no reasonable doubt, and his obvious, even "ridiculous" attraction is characteristic of many of his friendships, with men and women alike. But there is a final reference which may explain a little more. In a letter to Sir Gilbert Elliot in Corsica, dated from Leghorn Roads on 3rd August 1796, Nelson let fall the sentence: "One *old* lady tells me all she hears, which is what we wish." The humorous italics were his, and the implication is that his dolly had her qualities, as others of her kind have had in history, as an intelligence agent. In 1796 Nelson was in the *Captain*, a commodore engaged in the blockade of the port. Any scrap of port gossip might have its value.

Although it is natural to emphasise any fresh Nelson discovery, there is no ground for supposing that the affair affected his deeper feelings for Fanny. His letters home during the period when he was in or about Leghorn continued affectionate, though he did not often rise quite to the sentiment of a letter to his wife from Corsica, written early in May 1794, in which he averred: "all my joy is placed in you, I have none separated from you; you are present to my imagination be I where I will".

Nelson had been away from home for two years, on war service of the most taxing kind; his heart abhorred a vacuum; he had been wounded, and needed comfort; and he took comfort, pleasure and information where he could find it, in company with brother officers. Moreover, if Leghorn provided a diversion from Fanny, it gave her one consolation from which, during the rest of her life, she was never parted. She persuaded her husband in 1795 to sit to a local miniaturist, whose name, like that of the dolly, has not survived. The result was a strange Nelson, the first of several Italianate versions, and the least known. It is notable that the artist, perhaps at the sitter's direction, gave no indication that the light in the right eye was dimmed for ever. Nelson was portrayed in the uniform of a post-captain, and this of a pattern which, by its up-to-dateness, showed more concern for appearance than he had possessed in the days when he was scrutinised by young Prince William Henry.

v

One of the several ways in which Nelson's career resembled that of his prototype, Lord Hawke, was in the fact that, having waited many years to take part in a fleet action,

when first such an occasion arose it was indifferently conducted by the admiral concerned. Hotham fought the French
in March 1795 in much the same area of sea as had Admiral
Mathews half a century before, and with similar lack of
decision. Of the captains present, Nelson, like Hawke in
Mathews's time, was the only one commanding a ship of the
line to enhance his reputation, and this in spite of the fact
that there was but one other 64-gun ship present besides the
Agamemnon, all the others, French and English, being larger.
Nelson's principal opponent mounted no fewer than 84
guns.

As early as mid-January the *Agamemnon* had been re-
fitted. Nelson cruised with the fleet off Corsica in weather so
bad that ships were twelve days under storm stay-sails, the
Agamemnon, true to her reputation, behaving splendidly,
causing her captain to say once again that she was "the finest
ship I ever sailed in".

In March, the Toulon fleet of seventeen of the line and
five smaller vessels made a sortie, with the hope of retaking
Corsica. Hotham, then being at Leghorn, put to sea with
fourteen of the line and a Neapolitan, all the British ships
undermanned. The fleets manœuvred for some time within
sight of one another, and the French at length allowed
themselves to be chased. One of their number, the *Ça Ira*,
carried away her main and fore top-masts, and was promptly
attacked by Fremantle's frigate, the *Inconstant*. Two French
consorts moved to the *Ça Ira*'s support, and she was taken
in tow.

The *Agamemnon*, always a fast sailer, stood towards the
crippled ship, and gained so much on the rest of the fleet
that she was soon far ahead. When she came up with the
Ça Ira she was subject to accurate fire from the Frenchman's
stern guns, but Nelson, by skilful seamanship, was soon able
to bring his broadsides to bear in turn, and for two and half
hours pounded away at his big opponent. The *Ça Ira* lost
over a hundred men on 13th March, as against seven
wounded in the *Agamemnon*.

Nelson had a considerable share in the conclusion of the
engagement next day, during the course of which the
Censeur and the *Ça Ira* were taken, Lieutenant Andrews of

the *Agamemnon* having the honour of hoisting British colours on the captured ships.

Despite his battering in the two days' encounter, Nelson thirsted for more activity. He proposed that the prizes should be left with British ships damaged in the action, and that the rest of the fleet should follow up their advantage. Hotham's reply was much the same as one of Rodney's that had so enraged Hood in a previous war. "We must be contented: we have done very well." "Now," wrote Nelson, "had we taken ten sail, and allowed the eleventh to escape, when it had been possible to have got at her, I could never have called it well done. We should have had such a day as, I believe, the annals of England never produced. Nothing can stop the courage of English seamen. . . ."

The action proved three things, two of which were important. It confirmed Nelson's opinion of Hotham, who, he told Locker, is "very well, but I believe heartily tires of his temporary command; nor do I think he is intended by nature for a Commander-in-Chief, which requires a man of more active turn of mind". It strengthened Nelson's view of how much a well-handled ship could achieve; and it sealed his own ambition. "I wish to be Admiral, and in command of the English fleet," he told Fanny soon after the battle was over: "I should very soon either do much, or be ruined. My disposition cannot bear tame or slow measures. Sure I am, had I commanded our Fleet on the 14th, that either the whole French fleet would have graced my triumph, or I should have been in a confounded scrape."

The action saved Corsica for the time being, but, as the French were soon reinforced, it did not affect their margin of superiority. Lacking a tactical victory as decisive as that of Howe in the Atlantic the year before, the British position in the Mediterranean remained precarious.

In June, Nelson was given what, a year before, he had rashly said would satisfy him. This was a Colonelcy of Marines, an honorary command carrying emoluments but no duties, the reward of distinguished service. Nelson, despite his remark, was not satisfied, but he was grateful, and was careful to say so to Earl Spencer, the First Lord of the Admiralty.

His next employment was appropriate, for he was ordered to co-operate with an Austrian general, de Vins, whose task was to drive the French from the Genoese Riviera. Nelson sailed from St Fiorenzo on this service with a small squadron, but fell in with the French fleet, who gave chase. The affair lasted a day and a night, and on Nelson's return to Corsica the British, in the midst of watering and refitting, had the mortification of beating about vainly for seven hours before the wind allowed them to move to Nelson's support. After four days abortive manœuvring, a partial action took place on 13th July, during which the *L'Alcide* of 74 guns struck her colours, but took fire before she could be secured. Hotham recalled the *Agamemnon* and *Cumberland* just as they were beginning to press the enemy, for the wind blew directly into the French anchorage.

As soon as the encounter was over, Nelson proceeded to Genoa with his small squadron. Consultation with Mr Drake made it clear to Nelson that the object of the British should be to put a stop to all trade between Genoa, France and the occupied countries. The decision involved him in political responsibility which, then as at other times, he did not shirk. As a captain in the navy he was open to prosecution for detention and damages if he held up shipping, a fact which he knew only too well from earlier experience. "Political courage in an Officer abroad is as highly necessary as military courage," he wrote to Fanny. His way of showing it was to require that the British representatives should appoint agents to pay the freight, release the vessels, sell the cargo, and hold the amount till decision was arrived at in the courts. "I am acting," he said, "not only without the orders of my commander-in-chief, but in some measure contrary to them. However, I have not only the support of his Majesty's Ministers, both at Turin and Genoa, but a consciousness that I am doing right and proper for the service of our King and Country."

It was appropriate at this stage that Collingwood should have joined the Mediterranean fleet. In a letter to his old friend addressed from Vado Bay on 31st August, Nelson said, "the Genoese are going, it is said, to carry a convoy with provisions to their Towns in the Riviera of Genoa in

possession of the French army. However cruel it may appear
to deprive poor innocent people of provisions, yet policy will
not allow it to be done, for if the inhabitants have plenty, so
will the Enemy, and therefore I have directed them to be
brought into Vado. So far have I gone; and trust I have
acted, and shall act, so as to merit approbation. Our Admiral,
entre nous, has no political courage whatever, and is alarmed
at the mention of any strong measure; but, in other respects,
he is as good a man as can possibly be."

The situation, and the quality of the admiral, would have
recalled a West Indian situation to Collingwood's memory.
Actually, Nelson did Hotham rather less than justice, for
the commander-in-chief gave him full moral support, though
as Nelson's responsibility grew, he would not or did not
give him the reinforcement in ships which the operations
appeared to warrant.

Typical of Nelson's activity at this time, and of his way of
describing it, is a letter he sent to Hotham a few days before
he wrote to Collingwood. It was an example of Nelson's
official style at its best; it was characteristic of the generous
way in which he spoke of subordinates, and was illustrative
of the incessant service which made the commission of the
Agamemnon more like that of a crack frigate than of a ship
of the line.

Agamemnon, Vado Bay
August 27th, 1795

Sir,

Having received information from General de Vins, that a
Convoy of provisions and ammunition was arrived at Alassio, a
place in the possession of the French Army, I yesterday proceeded
with the Ships named in the margin[1] to that place, where, within
an hour, we took the Vessels named in the enclosed list.[2] There
was but a very feeble opposition from some of the Enemy's cavalry,
who fired on our boats after Boarding the Vessels near the shore,
but I have the pleasure to say no man was killed or wounded. The
Enemy had two thousand horse and foot soldiers in the Town,

[1] H.M. ships *Inconstant*; *Meleager*; *Southampton*; *Tartar*; *Ariadne*;
Speedy.
[2] *La Resolve*, corvette; *La Republique*, gunboat; *La Constitution*, galley; *La
Vigilante*, galley; two brigs; three barks; one galley unnamed, and a tartare.

which prevented my landing and destroying their magazines of provisions and ammunition. I sent Captain Fremantle in the *Inconstant*, with the *Tartar*, to Languelia, a Town on the west side of the Bay of Alassio, where he executed my orders in the most officer-like manner; and I am indebted to every Captain and Officer of the Squadron for their activity, but most particularly so to Lieutenant George Andrews, first lieutenant of the *Agamemnon*, who by his spirited and officer-like conduct saved the French corvette from going on shore.

I have the honour to be, Sir
With the highest respect
Your most obedient Servant
Horatio Nelson

Sea activities contrasted strongly with those in collaboration with General de Vins; these did not prove rewarding to the colonel of marines. At first Nelson had been impressed by the man's apparent qualities. Further acquaintance decided him that both he and the Austrian army were "slow beyond all description; and I begin to think that the Emperor is anxious to touch another four millions of English money. As for the German generals, war is their trade, and peace is ruin to them; therefore we cannot expect that they should have any wish to finish the war." Mr Drake, who was appointed to the Austrian headquarters, was of the same opinion.

Every scheme of annoying the enemy proved abortive, until an Austrian Commissary was robbed of £10,000 by the French in collusion with Genoese. The money was brought to Genoa by a French privateer, and men were then publicly enlisted in the town for the French army. Nelson arrived at Genoa on 18th November, and the authorities, knowing that they had connived at a breach of neutrality, did not demand, what Nelson would have in any case refused, that he should treat the port as neutral.

Loss of cash stirred de Vins in a way which no other circumstance could have achieved. He took possession of some empty French magazines, and pushed outposts to the very gates of Genoa. This provoked a battle, which began in the neighbourhood of Vado. No sooner had it opened than

de Vins gave up his post on the grounds of health. From then
onwards it was every man for himself. "I had a Lieutenant,
two Midshipmen and sixteen men taken at Vado," wrote
Nelson to Fanny on 2nd December: "the Purser of the ship
. . . ran with the Austrians eighteen miles without stopping;
the men without arms, officers without soldiers, women
without assistance." Many thousands fled who had never
seen the enemy, some of them being thirty miles from the
advanced posts. From being slow beyond description, the
Austrians had become the fastest army in Europe.

The defeat of General de Vins gave the French firm
possession of the coast from Savona to Voltri, and deprived
the Austrians of direct communication with the British fleet.
As the *Agamemnon* could no longer be useful on her station,
Nelson sailed for Leghorn to refit, and to relieve his feelings
on the subject of military allies. When his ship returned to
dock after her year's activity, she was in a deplorable state,
her hull being secured with cables. Even the exertions of
Nelson and his veterans could not be expected to keep her
in service many months longer.

Nelson expected to hear reports from the Austrians that
their defeat was solely due to lack of naval support. He was
not disappointed: de Vins produced a circumstantial tale
which would have wrung tears from anyone who had not
known the facts.

VI

At Leghorn, Nelson had news that Admiral Hotham had
gone home, and that his temporary successor, Sir Hyde
Parker, had been replaced by Sir John Jervis. Nelson and
Sir John had met only once, when Jervis, who for long was a
member of the House of Commons, espied a man in the
Treasury Passage whom he knew, from his curious habit of
looking through an eye-glass fitted to the head of his cane,
to be Captain Locker. He was fond of Locker, hailed him,
and was promptly introduced to "my *élève*, Captain Nelson".

Jervis was a thick-set, round shouldered, good-looking
man who, when younger, had sat to Francis Cotes. He was

then sixty, and although he long outlived Nelson, had been in command of ships when Nelson was a baby. He had carried home Wolfe's last message to his betrothed after the taking of Quebec, and had already flown his flag nearly ten years. Nelson revered him. He once said that Jervis used a hatchet where he himself would have used a penknife, but Jervis was an efficient disciplinarian by whom it was a pleasure for a zealous man to be commanded.

The pair took to one another instantly. They had their first official meeting at Fiorenzo Bay on 19th January 1796. Nelson told Fanny that he had been received "not only with the greatest attention, but with much apparent friendship". He was once again offered a bigger ship, and asked if he would have any objection to continuing in the Mediterranean if he were promoted. Nelson was high on the captain's list, and although his flag did not come for more than a year, it could have been expected earlier. "My answer was," he told Fanny, "that if I were ordered to hoist my Flag, I should certainly be happy in serving under him."

Meanwhile, he had good opportunity to study the day-to-day methods of Jervis, and was impressed. It was only a week after their first interview that he wrote to Fanny, "One Captain told me 'You did just as you pleased in Lord Hood's time, the same in Admiral Hotham's and now again with Sir John Jervis; it makes no difference to you who is Commander-in-Chief.' " Nelson said he "returned a pretty strong answer to this speech", but it was true. No admiral was so foolish as to undervalue intelligent activity, least of all Jervis.

By the end of February Nelson reported to Fanny that Jervis "seems at present to consider me more as an associate than a subordinate Officer; for I am acting without any orders. This may have difficulties at a future day; but I make none, knowing the uprightness of my intentions. He asked me if I had heard any more of my promotion; I told him 'No': His answer was, 'You must have a larger ship, for we cannot spare you, either as Captain or Admiral.' "

During the months that followed, Nelson's duty continued to be the familiar one of harrassing the French on the Italian mainland, and the blockade of ports through which

the enemy could draw supplies: but in the struggle between
land and sea power in the Mediterranean, between the
elephant and the whale, the elephant, now controlled by
Bonaparte, was in the ascendant. General Beaulieu, successor to de Vins, was not much improvement on his predecessor, and although Nelson gave him help, this was never
decisive.

On 4th April Jervis ordered Nelson to fly a pendant as
commodore, second class, an appointment which, then as in
later times, denoted a post rather than a rank, and enabled a
captain to exercise the duties of an admiral before being
given his flag. In days of iron seniority, and in time of war,
it had advantages.

On 11th June Nelson at last left what he now called the
"poor old *Agamemnon*" for the *Captain* of 74 guns. Not only
was the *Agamemnon* worn out, but almost all her original
officers were gone, and she no longer sailed with tolerable
speed. Exactly two months later, on 11th August, Jervis
appointed a captain to serve in Nelson's ship, thus making
him an established commodore. He thought the Admiralty
had "done handsomely" when he heard in the autumn that
the promotion was confirmed.

Nelson's captain was Ralph Miller, who became one of
his more ardent admirers. Miller had been born in New
York, and had learnt his seamanship under Rodney. The
circumstances of his move to the *Captain* reflect credit both
on him and on Nelson. "You will perhaps wonder," wrote
Miller to a friend, "to see me Captain under a Broad Pendant—I'll tell you how I came so. When I was lying by the
walls of Ajaccio in a ship that could not move, I thought
myself forgotten by all the Naval world. Captain Nelson,
then expecting a Flag, asked for me for his Captain. I did
not have this offer till after Sir John Jervis had given me the
Unité. I did not hesitate a moment to accept, and rejoiced
that having something to give up enabled me to show the
Commodore my sense of his kindness in asking for me from
a situation that was intolerable."

Although it was one of personal satisfaction to Nelson,
1796 was a year of disappointment and retreat, culminating,
in the autumn, in the decision to abandon Corsica, of which

H

island Nelson had the melancholy satisfaction of seeing "the first and the last". There followed the order to retire altogether from the Mediterranean, a sign of major reverse in Europe, though not of inevitable defeat. In the immediate future the fleet would be based on Portugal.

Even with Spain now ranged against Great Britain, the captains serving in Jervis's fleet retained their confidence. "Under such a Commander-in-Chief," wrote Nelson to the Duke of Clarence, "nobody has any fears . . . there is nothing we are not able to accomplish under Sir John Jervis."

As if to prove his high spirits, Nelson ended his first long spell of service in the Middle Sea with a burst of pugnacity. Early in December, whilst at Gibraltar, he shifted his broad pendant from the *Captain* to *La Minerve*, frigate. In her he sailed, with the *Blanche*, to bring away stores from Elba. The ships fell in with two Spanish frigates, the *Sabina* and the *Ceres*, off Cartagena. Nelson had not lost the art of handling frigates after years as a big-ship man; he engaged the *Sabina*, the larger of the two, and hammered away at her for three hours till she struck her colours.

The action, he told William, opened with his "hailing the Don", adding that his was an English frigate, and requiring surrender. Back came the answer: "This is a Spanish frigate, and you may begin as soon as you please." Nelson said, "I have no idea of a closer or sharper battle: the force to a gun the same, and nearly the same number of men; we having two hundred and fifty. I asked him several times to surrender during the action, but his answer was—'No Sir: not whilst I have the means of fighting left.' When only he himself of all the Officers was left alive, he hailed, and said he could fight no more, and begged I would stop firing."

When the prisoner came aboard, Nelson found reason for his prowess. His name was Don Jacobo Stuart. As a descendant of the Duke of Berwick, he had the blood of James II and Arabella Churchill in his veins. But hardly were the compliments exchanged, and Don Jacobo permitted to keep his sword, than other Spanish ships were seen approaching. Next day, Nelson was forced to leave his prize, together with a boarding-party which included Lieutenants Culverhouse and Hardy, in order to resume action. He drove his new opponent off, but although *La Minerve* was able to save herself, she could not prevent Spanish colours being rehoist in the *Sabina*.

It was not long before an exchange of prisoners was arranged. Meanwhile a foe of royal descent, not for the first time, found entertainment in a Nelson frigate. Don Jacobo was sent to Spain with a flag of truce, Nelson recording in his New Year letter to his father, "I felt it consonant to the dignity of my Country, and I always act as I think right, without regard to custom: he was reputed the best officer in Spain, and his men were worthy of such a commander. . . ." It seemed that the Spaniards could at times make men as well as ships. A tincture of English blood made all the difference.

Chapter 4

THE YEAR OF FAME

I

WHEN *La Minerve* returned to Gibraltar after her foray, she carried Sir Gilbert Elliot and his staff from Corsica. Among the party was an army officer, Colonel John Drinkwater, who had served throughout the four years of the siege of the Rock and became its historian. He also published a narrative of events of the year 1797 which included glimpses of Nelson. These were so vivid that Nelson referred biographers to his friend's account when, in the Sketch of his Life, he reached the time of the first successful fleet action in which he took part.

The frigate only stayed one day at Gibraltar, during the course of which Culverhouse and Hardy rejoined. On 11th February Nelson was away to Sir John Jervis, whose fleet was disposed to prevent a junction of French and Spanish forces. No sooner was *La Minerve* clear of the harbour than she was pursued by two Spanish ships of the line. Drinkwater asked the Commodore if there was likely to be an engagement. Nelson said he thought it very possible, adding, "but before the Dons get hold of that bit of bunting"—looking up at his broad pendant—"I will have a struggle with them, and sooner than give up the Frigate I'll run her ashore".

Not long after this conversation Nelson and his guests sat down to dinner, and while Drinkwater was congratulating Hardy on no longer being a prisoner of war, the cry was heard, "Man overboard!" "The Officers of the ship ran on deck," said Drinkwater: "I, with others, ran to the stern-windows to see if anything could be observed of the unfortunate man; we had scarcely reached them before we noticed the lowering of the jolly-boat, in which was my late neighbour, Hardy, with a party of sailors; and before many seconds had elapsed, the current of the Straits (which runs strongly to the eastward) had carried the jolly-boat astern of the Frigate, towards the Spanish ships. Of course, the first object was to recover, if possible, the fallen man, but he was never seen again. Hardy soon made a signal to that effect, and the man was given up as lost. The attention of every person was now turned to the safety of Hardy and his boat's crew; their situation was extremely perilous, and their danger was every instant increasing, from the fast sailing of the headmost ship of the chase, which by this time had approached nearly to within gun-shot of the *Minerve*.

"The jolly-boat's crew pulled might and main to regain the Frigate, but apparently made little progress against the current of the Straits. At this crisis, Nelson, casting an anxious look at the hazardous situation of Hardy and his companions, exclaimed 'by G——, I'll not lose Hardy: back the mizzen topsail'. No sooner said than done; the *Minerve*'s progress was retarded, having the current to carry her down towards Hardy and his party, who, seeing this spirited manœuvre, naturally redoubled their exertions to rejoin the Frigate.

"To the landsman on board the *Minerve*, an action now appeared to be inevitable, and so, it would appear, thought the Enemy, who surprised and confounded by this daring manœuvre of the Commodore (being ignorant of the accident that led to it), must have construed it into a direct challenge. Not conceiving, however, a Spanish Ship of the Line to be an equal match for a British frigate, with Nelson on board of her, the captain . . . suddenly shortened sail, in order to allow his consort to join him, and thus afforded time for the *Minerve* to drop down to the jolly-boat to take out Hardy and the crew; and the moment they were on board the Frigate, orders were given again to make sail. Being now under studding sails, and the widening of the Straits allowing the wind to be brought more on the *Minerve*'s quarter, the Frigate soon regained the lost distance, and at sunset, by steering further to the southward, we lost sight of him and his consort altogether."

The adventures of the evening were not over. After dark, Nelson found himself sailing through a patch of fog. When this lifted, he saw that he was surrounded by an enemy squadron. He kept close to it, undetected, long enough to discover intelligence useful to Jervis, and then made for the rendezvous off Cape St Vincent, which he reached on 13th February. Jervis was expecting battle. He had had four days' warning of the approach of a force close upon double his own, under Admiral Cordoba, whose orders were to make for Cadiz after passing through the Straits of Gibraltar. From Cadiz, Cordoba intended to sail north for Brest, to be ready to take part in an invasion of the British Isles in which French, Dutch and Spanish would combine.

After paying his respects to the Commander-in-Chief, Nelson rejoined the *Captain*. Elliot and Drinkwater asked to be given quarters in the *Victory*, Jervis's flagship, but the party were ordered to proceed to England in the frigate *Lively*. As a concession, her captain, Lord Garlies, was allowed to stay with the fleet, so that he might carry home news of the impending action. So it came about that Sir Gilbert Elliot, soon to become Lord Minto, and Colonel Drinkwater were eye-witnesses of one of the more important sea battles of the century.

England, as Jervis well knew, needed a victory, for the country was facing one of her darkest hours. The Continent was leagued, even though uneasily, in the interest of France; Ireland was in a state of ferment; commerce was distressed; the Bank had suspended cash payments; and the Channel fleet was approaching mutiny. But, outnumbered as he was, Jervis remained unperturbed, and confident of his ability to beat the enemy.

According to Spanish accounts, of twenty-seven ships which left Cartagena on 1st February, three had been detached off Algeciras, two had been ordered to cover the rear, and five were escorting a convoy. The squadron of seventeen directly under Cordoba, which bore the brunt of the battle, included one 68-gun ship laden with mercury, this commodity also being the principal cargo in the convoy. The mercury came from Almaden, about a hundred miles north of Malaga, and was destined ultimately for the Spanish colonies, where it was used in the amalgamation of silver ore. Had Jervis known this, he might have dealt a blow at

Spain's economy and filled the pockets of himself, his officers and men with prize-money.

A levanter, the same easterly wind which had sped Nelson through the Straits of Gibraltar, had driven the Spaniards far into the Atlantic. When Jervis first sighted them, they were scattered. The convoy, which was not recognised as such, was to leeward, making the best of its way towards Cadiz, the wind having veered to a direction rather south of west.

Jervis, seeing a gap in the Spanish force, which appeared to be in no regular order, intended to keep the enemy separated. He cut through them without much difficulty and then, in order to prevent them from uniting, ordered his ships to tack in succession: that is to say, they were to remain in the line formation with which they had begun action, but were to head about in the opposite direction, due north. Jervis's plan was to keep the Spaniards scattered and to deal with them as opportunity occurred.

The exact moment for the crucial signal was hard to judge from the *Victory*, which was not leading the line, and it is probable that Jervis, if he erred at all, delayed too long. Fortunately, one of his principal subordinates had courage to act for himself. Nelson's was the last ship but two in the British fleet, and he was in a good position to see that the leading vessels, after executing Jervis's order, would arrive too late to keep the gap open. Without a moment's hesitation, he wore the *Captain* out of the line, turned her before the wind in a direction heading at first *away* from the enemy: then, his movement completed, sped into the fast-closing gap, engaging seven Spanish ships with his single 74. Three of the enemy had over 100 guns, and one, the *Santissima Trinidad*, was the largest ship in the world, the only four-decked man-of-war ever launched.

Of the many acts of courage in Nelson's career, this was perhaps the most sublime, extraordinary—and rewarding. For the order of battle, the "line", was sacred. To leave it, without an instruction from the commander-in-chief, was an appalling professional lapse: it was usually held to betray cowardice, and carried with it the certainty of a court-martial, and almost inevitably disgrace and ruin. Even if the manœuvre brought with it complete success, as Nelson's did, it entailed such risk, such assumption of responsibility as no other officer of his rank, then or since, has incurred in the heat of battle. There have been times when it might have been profitable to do so, but such occasions have been rare, and subordinates have not often been in a position to judge them well. Even the imperious Hood, though he felt like Nelson more than once when serving under Rodney, never showed anything bolder than irritation at the way his chief was conducting operations. He never dared as did Nelson in this supreme moment of tactical perception. Recalling that it was not Hotham or Parker or even Hood himself under whom Nelson was fighting, but none other than the formidable Jervis, posterity may be as astonished at his audacity as were Nelson's own contemporaries.

For a short time Nelson fought alone, but he was quickly supported by his old friend Troubridge in the *Culloden*, by Frederick in the *Blenheim*, and Collingwood in the *Excellent*. Collingwood's training was so good that he expected to deliver three broadsides in a minute and a half, the Spaniards thinking themselves lucky if they took no more than five minutes for a single one. Not for nothing is the name of Collingwood's ship remembered in that of the gunnery school at Portsmouth.

The *Captain*, *Culloden*, *Blenheim* and *Excellent* bore the brunt of the action, had the greatest number of casualties, and used the most powder and shot. As Jervis himself said, "the Ships' returns of killed and wounded, although not always the criterion of their being more or less in Action is, in this instance, correctly so". The *Captain* had twenty-four killed, the *Blenheim* twelve, the *Excellent* eleven and the *Culloden* ten, out of a total British list of seventy-three.

The *Captain* was responsible for the capture of two of the four enemy ships taken, the *San Nicolas* of 80 guns and the *San Josef* of 112. Two others, the *Salvador del Mundo* and the *San Ysidro* were made prize, and it was thought that the towering *Santissima Trinidad* at one time lowered her colours, reconsidered the matter, and managed to get away in the confusion of the afternoon. Cordoba, in his account of the battle, admitted that the ship had been completely dismasted, and that he found it necessary to shift his flag to a frigate. The *Santissima* had indeed borne much of the attack, and was saved only by the appearance of undamaged escorts, whose main anxiety was to get her away, not to renew the action. Most of the Spanish ships were under-manned, and the crews raw; the fact told heavily.

Valentine's Day was short, and, in the mêlée which followed upon Nelson's manœuvre, ships were so damaged that no organised pursuit was possible. Even so, the victory was decisive. Four prizes were no inconsiderable gain for a squadron inferior in numbers; moreover, they had been taken with a modest toll of human life. By the wish of his sovereign, Jervis became Earl of St Vincent. He well deserved his laurels, though how the day would have gone without the independent act of the only man flying a broad pendant in the British fleet it is hard to say. What is certain is that Jervis being the man he was, Nelson was in greater trepidation at the thought of how he would be received after the action than ever he had been during its course. He had done what he always said he would do—something decisive: whether it would lead to a "confounded scrape" remained to be seen.

The details of the battle had been highly dramatic. The *Captain* wore out of the line before one o'clock, passed between the *Diadem* and the *Excellent*, which were the ships astern of him, and within ten minutes was hotly engaged. Troubridge joined him almost at once—he had obeyed Jervis's signal to attack the Spanish quicker than the Com-mander-in-Chief would have believed possible—and the *Blenheim* came up later. When Collingwood arrived, his fire soon compelled the *Salvador del Mundo* and the *San Ysidro* to lower their colours; but, Nelson added in his memoran-dum of the battle, "disdaining the parade of taking pos-session of beaten Enemies, he most gallantly pushed up to save his old friend and mess-mate, who was to appearance in a critical situation: the *Blenheim* having fallen to leeward, and the *Culloden* crippled and astern, the *Captain* at this time being actually fired upon by three First-rates and the *San Nicolas* and a Seventy-four. . . ."

"At this time," continued Nelson, "the *Captain* having

A. The main body of the Spanish Fleet hauling their wind on the larboard tack, and making sail in consequence of the spirited attack of Commodore Nelson, in the Captain, of 74 guns, supported by the Culloden, of 74 guns, commanded by Captain Troubridge.

B. The Captain engaged with the Santissima Trinidad, of 136 guns, and two other three-decked ships, which were seconds to the Spanish Admiral.

C. The Culloden, engaged with the rear ships of the Enemy's main body.

D. The Blenheim, a three-decker, of 90 guns, commanded by T. L. Frederick, advancing to the assistance of the Captain and Culloden.

E. Rear-Admiral W. Parker, in the Prince George, of 98 guns; with the Orion, of 74 guns; Irresistible, of 74 guns; and Diadem, of 64 guns; approaching to support the attack on the centre and rear of the Enemy's Fleet.

F. The Colossus of 74 guns, Captain G. Murray, disabled by the loss of her fore yard and fore-topsail-yard.

G. Spanish ships that attempted to join their main body, but were obliged to sheer off, and afterwards made all sail to the southward.

H. A Portuguese frigate, casually in company with the British squadron.

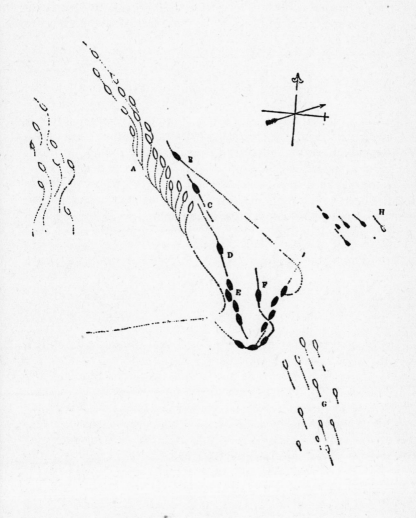

lost her fore-topmast, not a sail, shroud or rope standing, the wheel shot away, and incapable of further service in the Line or in chase, I directed Captain Miller to put the helm a-starboard, and calling for the Boarders, ordered them to Board.

"The Soldiers of the 69th Regiment, with an alacrity which will ever do them credit, with Lieutenant Pierson, of the same Regiment, were amongst the foremost on this service. The first man who jumped into the Enemy's mizzen-chains was Captain Berry, late my First-Lieutenant. He was supported from our spritsail-yard; and a soldier of the 69th Regiment having broke the upper quarter-gallery window, jumped in, followed by myself and others, as fast as possible. I found the cabin-doors fastened, and the Spanish Officers fired their pistols at us through the windows, but having broke open the doors, the soldiers fired, and the Spanish Brigadier (Commodore, with a distinguishing Pendant) fell as retreating to the quarter-deck.

"Having pushed on to the quarter-deck, I found Captain Berry in possession of the poop, and the Spanish Ensign hauling down. The *San Josef* at this moment fired muskets and pistols from the Admiral's stern-gallery on us. Our seamen by this time were in full possession of every part: about seven of my men were killed, and some few wounded, and about twenty Spaniards.

"Having placed sentinels at the different ladders, and ordered Captain Miller to push more men into the *San Nicolas*, I directed my brave fellows to board the First-rate, which was done in a moment. When I got into her main-chains, a Spanish Officer came upon the quarter-deck rail, without arms, and said the Ship had surrendered. From this welcome information, it was not long before I was on the quarter-deck, when the Spanish Captain, with bended knee, presented me his Sword, and told me the Admiral was dying with his wounds below. I gave him my hand, and desired him to tell his Officers and Ship's Company that the Ship had surrendered, which he did; and on the quarter-deck of a Spanish First-rate, extravagant as the story may seem, did I receive the Swords of the vanquished Spaniards, which as I received I gave to William Fearney, one of my bargemen, who placed them, with the greatest sang-froid, under his arm. I was surrounded by Captain Berry, Lieutenant Pierson, 69th Regiment, John Sykes, John Thompson, Francis Cook, and William Fearney, all old Agamemnons, and several other brave men, Seamen and Soldiers. Thus fell these ships."

Berry was at the time a passenger in the *Captain*, having been promoted master and commander for distinguished service in the Mediterranean. Miller had begged Nelson to allow him to be of the boarding-party, but Nelson said, "No, Miller, *I* must have that honour." On returning to the *Captain* after the action he exclaimed to Miller, "I am under the greatest obligations to you", and presented him with a Spanish captain's sword, and with a large topaz ring, set with diamonds, which he placed on his finger.

Lieutenant Pierson was a favourite with Nelson. He had served with the Neapolitans earlier in the war, and spoke Italian fluently. A detachment from his unit, now the Welsh Regiment, was serving with the fleet as marines. The 69th that day gained the second naval battle-honour in their history, a double distinction unique in the British army. A similar detachment had served with Rodney at the Battle of the Saints early in the previous decade.

Nelson ended his account: "There is a saying in the Fleet too flattering for me to omit telling—viz., 'Nelson's Patent Bridge for boarding First-rates,' alluding to my passing over an Enemy's 80-gun ship; and another of a Sailor's taking me by the hand on board the *San Josef*, saying he might not soon have such another place to do it in, and assuring me he was heartily glad to see me."

II

Before dark on Valentine's Day, Nelson's mind had been relieved of anxiety. "I went on board the *Victory*," he wrote in jubilation, "when the Admiral received me on the quarter-deck, and having embraced me, said he could not sufficiently thank me, and used every kind expression which could not

fail to make me happy." He then shifted his Pendant to the
Irresistible, and had a slight wound attended to. He had been
bruised in the stomach, though it proved to be nothing
grave.

Early next morning Nelson was rowed to the *Lively*. He
had hoped to see Elliot before he visited the Commander-in-
Chief. Elliot had already left, but Drinkwater was aboard,
and was given a private and detailed account of the battle as
seen from the decks of the *Captain* and her two prizes.

"Towards the conclusion of this interesting interview,"
wrote Drinkwater, "I adverted to the honours that must
attend such distinguished services. 'The Admiral,' I observed, 'will of course be made a Peer, and his seconds-in-
command noticed accordingly. As for you, Commodore,' I
continued, 'they will make you a Baronet.' The word was
scarcely uttered, when, placing his hand on my arm, and
looking me most expressively in the face, he said, 'No, no:
if they want to mark my services, it must not be in that
manner.' 'Oh,' said I, interrupting him, 'you wish to be
made a Knight of the Bath': for I could not imagine that his
ambition, at that time, led him to expect a Peerage. My
supposition proved to be correct, for he instantly answered
me, 'Yes, if my services have been of any value, let them be
noticed in a way that the public may know me, or them.' I
cannot distinctly remember which of these terms was used,
but, from his manner, I could have no doubt of his meaning,
that he wished to bear about his person some honorary
distinction, to attract the public eye, and mark his professional services." Drinkwater had long observed that "the
attainment of public honours, and the ambition to be distinguished above his fellows, were his master passions".

Nelson reinforced his view in a letter to Elliot; "You will
now, I am sure, think me an odd man, but still I hope you
will agree with me in opinion, and if you can be instrumental
in keeping back what I expect will happen, it will be an
additional obligation, for very far is it from my disposition
to hold light the Honours of the Crown; but I conceive to
take hereditary Honours without a fortune to support the
Dignity, is to lower that Honour it would be my pride to
support in proper splendour."

Iresistible off Lisbon feb:ry 26th
1797 —

Sir,

Having the good fortune on the
most glorious 14th febry & become possified
of the Sword of the Spanish Rear Admiral
Don Xavier Francisco Winthey sen in
the way sett forth in the paper transmitted
herewith. And being Born in the County
of Norfolk, I beg leave & present the
Sword & the City of Norwich in order &
it being preserved as a monento of this
event, and of my affection for my native
County. I have the honor & be Sir

Your most Obedient Servant
Horatio Nelson

To
The Mayor of
Norwich

One of Nelson's first thoughts, when the action was over, was to thank Collingwood for his support. "My dearest Friend," he wrote from the *Irresistible*, " 'A friend in need is a friend indeed' was never more truly verified than by your most noble and gallant conduct yesterday in sparing the *Captain* from further loss." Collingwood, in an equally affectionate reply, congratulated his "dear Commodore on the distinguished part which he ever takes when the honour and interests of his Country are at stake. It added very much to the satisfaction which I felt in thumping the Spaniards, that I released you a little."

Nelson sent the sword which he took from the Spanish Rear-Admiral, Don Xavier Francisco Winthuysen, who had been killed in action, to the Corporation of Norwich, where it has an honoured place in a trophy of arms in the mediaeval Guildhall. "I know no place where it would give me or my family more pleasure to have it kept, than in the Capital City of the County in which I had the Honour to be born," he wrote. Norwich voted Nelson its Freedom, and continued to follow his exploits with attention for the rest of his life.

Although he congratulated Nelson publicly on the quarter-deck of the *Victory*, Jervis has been blamed for according no praise in his public despatch to any officer except Robert Calder, his first captain, who carried home the official account of the battle and was knighted for his services.

Jervis was a wise man; never more so than in this reticence. It was less than three years since the battle of the First of June, and the discontent caused throughout the fleet at the way in which Lord Howe and his first captain, Sir Roger Curtis, had handled the matter of recognition was still active in the navy. A case in point was that of Collingwood, who had fought the *Barfleur* with distinction after his admiral, Bowyer, had had his leg blown off. Collingwood, through mischance, was omitted from the distribution of gold medals given to mark Howe's victory, as were one or two other captains who may also have deserved them.

Jervis played safe by making his commendations in general terms, although privately, in a letter to Earl Spencer, the First Lord, he gave credit where this was due. In the upshot, awards were appropriate. Jervis himself, in addition

to his earldom, got a pension of £3,000 a year. The grant of
so high a rank in the peerage was justified by the fact that
the King had been on the point of making him a baron when
news of the battle arrived. A baronetcy was given to the
second-in-command, and every flag-officer and captain in
the line received a gold medal. Collingwood, when told of
his award, said to St Vincent that he could not consent to
receive it while that for the First of June was withheld. "I
feel," he said, "that I was then improperly passed over; and
to receive such a distinction now would be to acknowledge
the propriety of that injustice." He was mollified by a
gracious letter from Lord Spencer, and the gift of medals
for both actions.

"Chains and medals are what no fortune or connection in
England can obtain," wrote Nelson to his brother William,
with entire truth, "and I shall feel prouder of these than all
the Titles in the King's power to bestow." The awards for
St Vincent were forwarded with commendable despatch, the
First Lord sending directions for "the Blue and White
Riband to be passed through the oval ring attached to the
Medal, and to be worn round the neck under the coat and
over the waistcoat, so that the Medal may hang about an
Inch above the pit of the stomach." Nelson usually wore his
higher, and was justly pleased with an emblem which showed
Victory, standing on the prow of an antique galley, placing
a wreath of laurel on Britannia. It figures in most of his
portraits. A riband similar in colours was later used for the
Naval General Service medal, and its tradition continues in
that rare distinction, the Conspicuous Gallantry Medal.

It was long held that Calder's jealousy prevented St
Vincent being more generous in his public despatch. This is
unlikely, for Tucker, St Vincent's secretary and biographer
recorded the following anecdote after the action: "In the
evening, while talking over the events of the day, Captain
Calder hinted that the spontaneous manœuvre which carried
Nelson and Collingwood into the brunt of battle was an
unauthorised departure by the Commodore from the pre-
scribed mode of attack. 'It certainly was so,' said Jervis, 'and
if ever you commit such a breach of your orders, I will
forgive you also.'" The remark has the Jervis touch, and it

is indeed improbable that he omitted names for any other reason than that he himself thought it proper so to do.

Experience over the centuries has proved that while honours and awards, if promptly and appropriately given, are a source of pleasure in quarters where they have been earned, they are also liable to cause ill feeling and jealousy. As Howe remarked in his own excuse, a commander-in-chief cannot see everything. He is dependent on reports from subordinates, whose standards will vary. After St Vincent, Nelson was the recipient of an acrimonious letter from Rear-Admiral Sir William Parker, who conceived that his own services had not had justice done to them. Nelson refused to argue the matter, for the excellent reason that he could only see and judge of what concerned his immediate command. But, as was his way, he was determined to make sure that his own exploits were recorded and made known to the world, as well as those which fell under his direct notice. This he did by forwarding his circumstantial memorandum of the action to Locker at Greenwich. It was signed by himself, Miller and Berry, Nelson writing to Locker that, if approved, Locker was at perfect liberty to send it to the newspapers, "inserting the name of Commodore instead of 'I' ". It was the publication of this account which annoyed Sir William.

Meanwhile, Nelson was the recipient of many congratulations, including those of Fanny, who, while she begged him for the future to "leave boarding to captains", said, with touching humility: "I can bear all my extreme good fortune." It was crowned by her husband's promotion, a week after the battle, to the rank of Rear-Admiral of the Blue, the flag-list then being divided into Red, White and Blue] Squadrons, the promotions, if the officer concerned was to remain on the active list, being according to this dispensation.

"I never saw anything elevate our Father equal to this," reported Fanny. Nelson himself did not get the news for some weeks. When he did so, it was accompanied by a touching letter from Edmund Nelson, who recalled Maurice Suckling's prophecy that he would live to see Horatio an admiral. Edmund said, "the height of glory to which your professional judgment, united with a proper degree of bravery, guarded by Providence, few sons, my dear child, attain to, and fewer fathers live to see. . . . The name and services of Nelson have sounded throughout the City of Bath, from the common ballad-singer to the public theatre. Joy sparkles in every eye, and desponding Britain draws back her sable veil, and smiles."

The rector's poetic allusion to desponding Britain was no exaggeration. When Drinkwater and Sir Gilbert Elliot arrived at Plymouth, they found the whole place sunk in gloom: every thought was of invasion: "nothing but England's disgrace and downfall foretold and talked of throughout the kingdom", said the surprised colonel. It took great powers of persuasion to induce the people of Devon to believe that a victory against odds had just been won off the coast of Spain, while to extract a mere fifteen guineas out of local resources, to defray some of the expenses of the journey to London, involved even harder talking. By the time Elliot's party reached the capital, Calder had shown the Government that there was indeed some cause for modest jubilation, and Elliot himself was able to make sure that Nelson, at least, had the Order of Chivalry which pleased him.

III

During April, Nelson made a brief excursion into the Mediterranean to cover the withdrawal of the remaining troops left in Elba. By the end of May he had rejoined Jervis off Cadiz, hoisting his flag in the *Theseus*, in command of the inshore squadron blockading the port, and keeping Miller as his captain. The *Theseus* was one of the ships which had been affected by the mutinies in home waters. Jervis hoped that Nelson would restore her discipline.

The effect of the appointment is best inferred through a letter which Nelson sent to Fanny on 15th June. "A few nights ago a Paper was dropped on the quarter-deck, of which this is a copy:—'Success attend Admiral Nelson! God bless Captain Miller! We thank them for the Officers they have placed over us. We are happy and comfortable, and will shed every drop of blood in our veins to support them, and the name of the *Theseus* shall be immortalised as high as the *Captain*'s. SHIPS COMPANY.'"

The sympathy for the lower deck which this paper reflects was not softness. Nelson wrote to a Norfolk friend: "We are a neglected set, and, when peace comes, are shamefully treated; but, for the Nore scoundrels, I should be happy to command a ship against them." Nelson referred to the more serious of the two mutinies of 1797, during which the seamen's Delegates for a time gained almost complete control; but he felt as much for those on active service as for their brethren of the fields. He wrote to Fanny, also from Cadiz: "I intend my next winter's gift at Burnham should be fifty good large blankets of the very best quality, with the letter 'N' in the centre that they may not be sold; I believe they may be made for about 15 shillings of the very best quality, and they will last some person or other for seven years at least. . . . I wish enquiry to be made, and the blankets ordered of some worthy man; they are to be at my father's disposal in November." Contented seamen abroad, and warmer labourers in Norfolk, were both near to his heart.

Meanwhile, the blockade of Cadiz was active enough even for his zeal. "We are looking at the Ladies walking the walls and Mall," he wrote, "and know of the ridicule they make of their Sea Officers. Thirty sail are now perfectly ready, and, the first east wind, I expect the Ships from the Mediterranean, which will make them forty Sail of the Line. We are now twenty; some of our Ships being always obliged to be absent for water, provisions etc. . . . I am of opinion that some morning, when least expected, I shall see them tumbling out. . . . We in the advance are, night and day, prepared for battle: our friends in England need not fear the event." All the same, he thought that Jervis should be reinforced.

On 3rd July Nelson conducted a bombardment of the town, and as a result was desperately engaged in his barge with a Spanish gunboat. Strictly speaking, he should have stayed aboard his ship, superintending operations. He had no need, and probably no business, to put his own life so

closely to the hazard: the service was of a sort which would
commonly fall to a lieutenant under the orders of a captain
or commander—typical boat-work. It was one more instance
of Nelson's sheer zeal for fighting that he was present at all,
and it was an affair which he singled out in the Sketch of his
Life as one when "my personal courage was more conspicuous than at any other period of my life. . . . I was boarded in
my barge with its common crew of ten men, Cockswain,
Captain Fremantle, and myself, by the Commander of the
Gunboats. The Spanish barge rowed twenty-six oars, besides
Officers, thirty in the whole; this was a service hand to hand
with swords, in which my Cockswain, John Sykes (now no
more), saved twice my life. Eighteen of the Spaniards being
killed and several wounded, we succeeded in taking their
Commander." Sykes, a Lincolnshire man, had been one of
the original muster in the *Agamemnon*. He had soon been
promoted to be ship's corporal, and was of sterling character. One of his finest moments had been at Nelson's side
in the triumphs at Cape St Vincent.

An account of the affair of the gunboat written from first-
hand experience provides further details: "The commandant
of the Spanish," says this narrative, which is, alas, anonymous,
"a gallant fellow, Don Miguel Tyrason, singled out the
Admiral's barge; in which was John Sykes, as gallant a
sailor as ever took up slops from a purser, or shared his grog
with his mess-mates. Don Miguel ordered his boat to be
placed alongside of ours; and, as you may suppose, we did
not object to the meeting, although she was a powerful
craft. . . . Don Miguel led his men bravely, and to give them
the credit they deserve, they were worthy of such a gallant
commander, and of the honour of being killed by us.

"Nelson parried a blow which would have saved him from
being at the Nile, and Fremantle (then commanding the
Seahorse) fought like himself, fore and aft, both boats. It was
a desperate struggle, and once we were nearly carried. John
Sykes was close to Nelson on his left hand, and he seemed
more concerned for the Admiral's life than his own: he
hardly ever struck a blow but to save his gallant officer.

"Twice he parried blows that must have been fatal to
Nelson; for Sykes was a man whose coolness gave him full

scope for the Science at Single Stick, and who never knew what fear was, any more than his Admiral. It was cut, thrust, fire, and no load again—we had no time for that. The Spaniards fought like devils, and seemed resolved to win from the Admiral the laurels of his former Victory; they appeared to know him, and directed their particular attack towards the officers.

"Twice had Sykes saved him; and now he saw a blow descending which would have severed the head of Nelson. In that second of thought which a cool man possesses, Sykes saw that he could not ward the blow with his cutlass; the situation of the Spaniard rendered it impossible. He saw the danger; that moment expired, and Nelson would have been a corpse: but Sykes saved him—he interposed his own hand!

"We all saw it—we were witnesses to the gallant deed, and we gave in revenge one cheer and one tremendous rally. Eighteen of the Spaniards were killed, and we boarded and carried her: there not being one man left on board who was not either dead or wounded.

" 'Sykes,' said Nelson as he caught the gallant fellow in his arms, 'I cannot forget this.' But my wounded shipmate only looked him in the face, and smiled, as he said, 'Thank God, Sir, you are safe.' "

It is scarcely surprising that Sykes was never the same man again. St Vincent, who seldom let merit go unrecognised, gave him a gunner's warrant, but he was killed a year later through the bursting of a cannon. Devotion to their officers was not uncommon in the men of Nelson's time, but there were few more splendid instances.

A second bombardment of Cadiz was mounted on the night of 5th July. The excitement was barely over when Nelson had a glimpse of how St Vincent dealt with mutiny— and criticism. Four men of the *St George* were to be tried by court-martial. If found guilty, they were to be hanged the same evening. The trial did not end until after sunset, but although the next day happened to be Sunday, Jervis ordered the sentence to be carried out.

The incident raised a protest from Vice-Admiral Thompson, who, in St Vincent's words, "presumed to censure the execution on the Sabbath, in a public letter; and I have

insisted on his being removed from this Fleet immediately,
or that I shall be called home; and I have stipulated for no
more Admirals!" The mutineers asked five days to prepare
for death, he told the First Lord, "in which they would have
hatched five hundred treasons; besides that, we are provok-
ing the Spanish Fleet to come out by every means in our
power". The Admiralty expressed "very high approbation"
of St Vincent's conduct "on that unpleasant and urgent
occasion". As for Nelson, he placed it on record, in a letter
to his Commander-in-Chief, "had it been Christmas Day
instead of Sunday, I would have executed them." Admiral
Thompson, needless to say, went home.

IV

Nelson had poor luck with islands. He had failed in his
attack on Turks Island in 1783; eleven years later he had
lost the use of his right eye in Corsica; nor was the next
adventure on which he embarked, an assault on Teneriffe in
the Canaries, to rank among his triumphs.

He and St Vincent had conceived a plan for seizing some
treasure ships with which the Viceroy of Mexico was believed to have reached Santa Cruz. It was a place memorable
in naval annals as the scene of the final exploit of Blake's sea
career, and although Nelson said with becoming modesty,
"I do not reckon myself equal to Blake," he believed his
predecessor's success and unimpeded withdrawal had been
due to the wind coming off the land at the right time:
"fortune favoured the gallant attempt," he added, "and may do
so again". In fact, Blake's ships were warped out after action.

The idea was discussed in April 1797, ordered in June,
and executed in July. Nelson had suggested the use of troops
from Elba who, he thought, would make sure of the business. They were not forthcoming: moreover, it was found
that the report about the Viceroy was untrue; but there was
indeed a homeward-bound Manila ship of size at Teneriffe,
and the expedition proceeded. England still badly needed
successes, and no officer was averse to prize-money.

St Vincent gave Nelson four ships of the line, three frigates and a cutter. He was allowed to choose his own officers, conspicuous among whom were Troubridge of the *Culloden*, Bowen of the *Terpsichore* and Fremantle of the *Seahorse*. Fremantle, amazingly to later ideas of war, was accompanied by his newly married wife, who was a great favourite with the Commander-in-Chief, and indeed with all who knew her. Seamen and marines were to form the shore parties, but Nelson was not expected to land in person unless his presence was absolutely necessary.

The original plan was that the frigates were to put boats ashore in the night, between the fort on the north-east side of Santa Cruz Bay and the town. It was hoped that the landing-parties would make themselves masters of the batteries, and then send a summons to the Governor. "I have had flattery enough to make me vain and success enough to make me confident," wrote Nelson to Fanny in high expectation.

From the first, conditions were against the attempt. Owing to a gale, and an inshore current, the ships were unable to get within a mile of the landing-place before day-break. By that time all element of surprise had been lost, and a more cautious man than Nelson might have called off the whole affair. But Nelson, on this occasion, was his own general. Backed by Troubridge and Captain Oldfield of the Marines, he favoured pressing on. The parties were put ashore with the hope of gaining possession of the heights above the fort. Nelson meanwhile stood inshore with his big ships, intending a bombardment to distract the garrison, but his movement was frustrated by the current.

The Spaniards were by this time thoroughly alerted, and the heights manned in force, so on the night of 22nd July Nelson withdrew his parties and prepared to try again later. This time, he would himself command. "Tomorrow," he wrote to St Vincent on 24th July, "my head will probably be covered with laurel or cypress."

Nelson realised the very hazardous nature of any further assault, and was anxious that Josiah at least should stay aboard the *Theseus*. "Should we both fall," he said, "what would become of your poor mother!" Josiah's place, said the admiral, was in charge of the ship. The young man's reply was that the ship must take care of herself. "I will go with you tonight," he said, "if I never go again." Nelson, who always responded to courage, let him have his way.

Mrs Fremantle presided at supper aboard the *Seahorse*, at which admiral and captains attended, everyone much cheered by the appearance of the *Leander* as a reinforcement. Nelson then went off with Fremantle on their perilous journey. Many wills had been made that night,[1] but the guests were so gaily mannered towards their hostess that she recorded in her diary: "As the taking of this place seemed an easy and almost sure thing, I went to bed after they had gone apprehending no danger for Fremantle." Though the battle of St Vincent may have led to over-confidence on the part of a few of those present, others concealed the fact that they had learnt, from experience, not to undervalue the opposition.

The boats drew away into the Atlantic darkness. The orders were to land at the mole, then to proceed to the main square of the town. The operation remained undetected until about half-past one, when the Spanish fire opened, and Nelson ordered everyone to make for the shore. The Spaniards were well prepared. Cannon and muskets commanded every approach. Many boats were holed when pounding through the heavy surf; some never reached land at all. Nelson himself, with Fremantle, Bowen and others, found the mole. It was stormed, and its guns spiked; but the port was so well defended that the seamen could get no further, almost every man being killed or wounded.

Nelson was shot just as he was in the act of drawing his sword and stepping out of the boat. This same sword, much treasured since it had once belonged to Galfridus Walpole, was transferred from Nelson's shattered right arm to his left, but Nisbet, who was near, saw that he could not stand, and heard him exclaim, "I am a dead man!" He placed him in the bottom of the boat, saw that a rush of blood was increasing his faintness, and concealed the flow with his hat. He then took a silk handkerchief from his neck and, helped by

---

[1] Including Nelson's own. He left £200 to his brother Maurice and £500 to Josiah, the rest of his property to go to Fanny or to Josiah if she predeceased him. It was the last will in which Emma Hamilton did not figure.

one of the bargemen, Loval, bound the silk tightly round and above the lacerated arm. Loval then made a sling from his shirt, helped to get the boat away, with Nisbet himself at one of the oars, and steered close under the guns of the batteries so as to be safe from their fire.

The next serious casualty was the cutter *Fox*, which was holed below the water-line and sank quickly, the commander and over half the ship's company being drowned. Nelson, despite his pain, insisted on rescuing all he could from the water. He was then rowed back through the fire and confusion to the ships in the offing.

It was the *Seahorse* they first sighted, but nothing would induce Nelson to go aboard, though he was assured that it would be at the risk of his life if they attempted to find another vessel. "Then I will die," he said, "for I would rather suffer death than alarm Mrs Fremantle by her seeing me in this state, and when I can give her no tidings of her husband."

The boat then made its way to the *Theseus*, where Nelson refused all help in getting on board. "Let me alone," he said. "I have yet my legs left, and one arm. Tell the surgeon to make haste and get his instruments. I know I must lose my right arm, so the sooner it is off the better." Young Hoste— a favourite Norfolk midshipman from the *Agamemnon*—was aboard, and watched Nelson in consternation, "his right arm dangling by his side, whilst with the other he helped himself to jump up the ship's side." Hoste thought of him as "a second father" and envied Nisbet his chance to save his life. Shattered and blood-soaked as he was, Nelson was received on the quarter-deck with all the usual ceremony, and he returned the salutes as punctiliously as ever

It was fortunate for Nelson that he had not been attended to in the *Seahorse*, for when Fremantle returned, with a flesh wound in the arm, he suffered great and continuous pain which lasted many months, perhaps due to unskilful treatment. The surgeon in the *Theseus* was Thomas Eshelby, and it was he who performed the operation which Hoste said Nelson bore with such "firmness and courage". What pained him most was the shock of the cold knife. No sick bay, in any future ship under his command, but had water warming before action! Eshelby was probably helped by Louis Remonier, a royalist refugee from Toulon who had been allowed to join the navy in his professional capacity, and who, like his chief, had followed Nelson from the *Captain*.

The operation took place in the early hours of the morning, and the medical journal of the *Theseus* duly recorded: "1797. July 25. Admiral Nelson. Compound fracture of the right arm by a musket ball passing through a little above the elbow, an artery divided: the arm was immediately amputated and opium afterwards given." Nelson was tough as well as brave and considerate. Next day the surgeon wrote that he "rested pretty well and quite easy. Tea, soup and sago. Lemonade and Tamarind drink." He had a "middling night" with no fever. By the 29th, the "stump looked well. No bad symptom whatever occurred. The sore reduced to the size of a shilling. In perfect health. One of the ligatures not come away."

There was everything to distract the admiral's attention from his own mutilated condition. The expedition was in ruins. Troubridge, presenting his official account, said that he had waited about an hour in the Square, "during which time I sent a Sergeant with two Gentlemen of the Town, to summons the citadel. I fear the Sergeant was shot on his way, as I heard nothing of him afterwards."

As the ladders had been lost in the surf, no attempt could then be made against the out-works. Daylight showed Troubridge the extent of his resources, "about eighty Marines, eighty Pike-men, and one hundred and eighty small-arm Seamen," the latter with wet ammunition. The Spaniards were by this time beginning to surround them, the boats were all stove in, so Troubridge sent a flag of truce to the Governor saying he had no wish to burn the town, but was prepared for the attempt. The Governor, who was perfectly ready to treat, behaved in "the handsomest manner, sending a large proportion of wine, bread, etc. to refresh the people, and showed every mark of attention in his power", even including the loan of local boats!

Nelson, not to be outdone in the courtesies of war, on 26th July addressed his Excellency Don Antonio Gutierrez, Commandant General of the Canary Islands, in the following

Theseus. Augt 16th 1797,

My Dear Sir,

I rejoice at being once more
in sight of your flag, and with your permission will come on board the Ville de Paris & pay
you my respects. If the Emerald has joined, you
know my wishes, a left handed Admiral will
never again be considered as useful therefore
the sooner I get to a very humble cottage the better
and make room for a better Man to serve the State
but whatever be my lot Believe me with the most
sincere affection &c Your most faithful

Horatio Nelson

ONE OF NELSON'S EARLIEST LEFT-HANDED
LETTERS: TO LORD ST. VINCENT

terms, from *His Majesty's Ship* Theseus, *opposite Santa Cruz de Teneriffe:*

"Sir, I cannot take my departure from this Island, without returning your Excellency my sincerest thanks for your attention towards me, by your humanity in favour of our wounded men in your power, or under your care, and for your generosity towards all our people who were disembarked, which I shall not fail to represent to my Sovereign, hoping also, at a proper time, to assure your Excellency in person how truly I am, Sir, your most obedient, humble servant, *Horatio Nelson.*" He added in a postscript that he trusted the Governor would "accept of a cask of English beer and a cheese". His letter breathed the same friendly spirit which was shown in the note of personal reassurance he wrote to Mrs Fremantle with his left hand. The expedition might have been a picnic, not a defeat with the gallant Bowen and many others among the slain.

On 16th August the squadron rejoined the main fleet, and Nelson wrote to his Commander-in-Chief: "I rejoice at being once more in sight of your Flag, and with your permission will come on board the *Ville de Paris*, and pay you my respects . . . a left-handed Admiral will never again be considered as useful therefore the sooner I get to a very humble cottage the better, and make room for a better man to serve the State. . . ." St Vincent was all sympathy. "Mortals cannot command success," he replied. "You and your companions have certainly deserved it, by the greatest degree of heroism and perseverance that ever was exhibited. Give my love to Mrs Fremantle. I will salute her and bow to your stump tomorrow morning, if you will give me leave."

St Vincent decided that Nelson should go home with the Fremantles, for he perceived that only a change of climate could give assurance of a proper cure for the two wounded officers. "I hope both of them will live to render important services to their King and Country," he wrote in his official despatch.

The news that Nelson was to travel in the frigate made Betsy Fremantle and her husband "exceedingly happy"; Nelson came aboard at twelve o'clock on Sunday, 20th August. "He is quite stout," recorded Mrs Fremantle, using

an adjective never before applied to her guest: "but I find it
looks shocking to be without one arm. He is in great spirits."
Dr Eshelby came too, which was a comfort to the suffering
Fremantle, and gave relief to Betsy, for she was carrying her
first child, and feeling the effects. "It is easy to guess what is
the matter with me," she wrote.

Nelson proved a bad patient, particularly when winds
were contrary: but the party were cheered with a glimpse of
Scilly light—the round white tower on the island of Agnes
—before the end of August, and the *Seahorse* anchored at
Spithead on Friday, 1st September. After dinner, though the
weather was blustery, Nelson was rowed ashore, setting foot
on English soil for the first time in more than four years.
Formal leave of absence was quickly given him, through the
channel of his old friend Sir Peter Parker, then in charge at
Portsmouth. On receiving it, Nelson made straight for Bath.
He was eager to cheer Fanny with the news of Josiah's
promotion to be commander of the *Dolphin* hospital ship.
Once again, regulations had been flouted. Josiah was short
of the necessary sea-time, but, earlier in the year, Nelson
had written to Maurice at the Navy Office, so he told Fanny,
"to see if he cannot get a little cheating for him: it might
be done and would be invaluable". It proved so.

v

Nelson's companion on the journey to Bath was his
eccentric and devoted servant Tom Allen, a seaman of the
Agamemnon who had looked after him since the autumn of
1795. He had replaced Frank Lepée, who had been dismissed "for Drunkenness, and when so, Mad", as Nelson
duly reported to his father from the Mediterranean.

The excited pair arrived in the evening on 3rd September,
to find Fanny and her father-in-law in a furnished house,
with Mrs Bolton on a visit. "The first you hear of me will
be at the door," Nelson had written from sea, and he was
with them almost as soon as his letter.

Overjoyed as she was, Fanny's anxieties were not quite

over. Nelson was home, but she had to accustom herself to a change which had worried others than Betsy Fremantle. A greater trial, for an ailing and timid woman, came with learning to dress a still grim wound. Nelson's stump proved painful; there was persisting trouble with a ligature; it was probably septic, and opium was needed to ensure, to one who always refused to regard himself as an invalid, a reasonably quiet night. But suspense at last was over; Nelson brought welcome accounts of Josiah; and as he now needed Fanny in a way he had never done before—she wrote some of his letters, and finished others which he had begun—her cup of happiness was brimming.

Despite his injuries, Nelson seemed the same man as ever; eager, affectionate, direct, and with a circle of relations and friends who were all the more warmly attached by reason of his fame, which they had prophesied, and his misfortunes, which were honourable. As he longed to be, he was recognisable as a hero: "my reception from John Bull has been just what I wished," he wrote to St Vincent. He had assumed the look and the bodily state by which posterity remembers him. His hair, once sandy grey, was nearer white: premature age and youthful eagerness were strangely mingled in face and character. He was still so active that there could never be a dull moment in his company.

The newspapers, in a dark year, made the most of the repulse at Teneriffe, but no blame was attached to the tactical commander. Instead, the purveyors of prints began the work of complicating his iconography, an industry pursued tirelessly for the next half-century. Locker's oil by Rigaud, Fanny's miniature from Leghorn were pressed into service as the basis of representations designed for popular sale. The results were indifferent, the remedy obvious. Nelson, unlike the Duke of Wellington, was a patient sitter, and at least three portraits from the life, including the most famous, derive from his spell of convalescence.

William Nelson, now possessed of the Hilborough rectorship, hastened westward to join his brother, and, at the advice of a local doctor, the family decided to obtain more expert opinion than was available at Bath. Maurice, serviceable and unobtrusive as ever, found lodgings in Bond

Street, and Nelson was examined by a series of medical experts, including his friend of Nicaragua days, Dr Moseley. The last of these doctors, Keate by name, had the sense to suggest that healing be left to "time and nature".

One night, the exhilarating news of Duncan's victory over the Dutch fleet at Camperdown threw the town into an uproar. The Bond Street lodging was not lit up, since Nelson had retired early, hoping for a little rest after a day of pain. The mob knocked repeatedly and violently, asking the reason for such lack of enthusiasm. When a servant came to the door and said that the badly wounded Nelson lodged there and was asleep, the leader of the party, all sympathy, at once assured the household, "You will hear no more from us to-night."

Keate's advice was obeyed, the pain was surmounted, and one December day the ligature came away almost at a touch. Nelson thereupon sent a note to Mr Greville, of St George's, Hanover Square, saying: "An Officer desires to return Thanks to Almighty God for his perfect recovery from a severe Wound, and also for the many mercies bestowed upon him." One effect of his injury (not uncommon in cases of amputation) was that Nelson sometimes had the sensation of a "phantom" right arm. It helped to confirm his belief in the immortality of the soul!

In the meantime he had visited two old friends at Greenwich, the senior of whom, Lord Hood, had written him, in Fanny's words, "*such* a letter". Hood was Governor of the Hospital, living in an opposite wing to Locker in that palace which is still one of the glories of London river. Locker insisted on a new portrait. This time, the favoured artist was Lemuel Abbott, an impoverished, hard-working man, who, rising to an occasion, created the best-known image of his illustrious subject.

Fanny and Edmund Nelson were enchanted when, in due time, the canvas was completed. Abbott, in the six years of life which remained to him, was besought again and again for replicas of a picture which found general favour: some of these were in hats, some without; some half length, some longer. Nearly all had that quality of fire and aspiration which is more pronounced than in any other rendering.

SIR HORATIO AND LADY NELSON
by Henry Edridge, A.R.A.

Drawings made in 1797. That of Lady Nelson is reproduced from a water-colour copy, now lost.

It is not altogether easy to credit the fact that Abbott's subject was the same man who was drawn by Edridge the miniaturist that autumn. Edridge's precise style was more suited to Fanny, and indeed, though he made another drawing of Nelson five years later, he again failed to indicate where his strength and attraction lay. Lawrence Gahagan, who showed a sculpture at the next Academy based on seven sittings which Nelson gave him in Bond Street, and who continued to produce versions after the turn of the nineteenth century (one other of which was made direct from life), also lacked magic.

The great event during Nelson's stay in London was his investiture as a Knight of the Bath. It had been arranged that Lord St Vincent should deputise for his sovereign in this matter, but Nelson had meanwhile returned home, and it was fitting that the King whose name was so often on Nelson's lips should bestow the star in person. The wife of his future flag-captain, Edward Berry, is the authority for a fragment of conversation at the ceremony. "You have lost your right arm," said the King solicitously. "But not my right hand," replied Sir Horatio, "as I have the honour of presenting Captain Berry to your Majesty." Lord Eldon used to relate that George III, after acknowledging Nelson's outstanding services, added, "but your Country has a claim for a bit more of you".

Among the more renowned figures at St James's was Earl Howe, now Admiral of the Fleet. He wore the insignia of the Garter, the only Knight of that exalted Order ever to have been granted the dignity for services wholly naval in character. Nelson revered Howe, and as it was the last time he ever saw him alive, it was well that he made the most of the occasion. The senior flag-officer asked warmly after St Vincent, and sent him many messages. As Howe never had a firmer admirer than St Vincent, the compliments were welcome.

Nelson was now entitled to a coat of arms, described as "or, a Cross flory sable, a Bend gules surmounted by another engrailed of the field charged with three Bombs fired proper". His crest was, "on a wreath of the Colours, the stern of a Spanish Man of War proper, thereon inscribed *San Josef*".

K

He attended at least two other public ceremonies, one before and the other after Christmas. The first was a thanksgiving service at St Paul's at which the King and the Royal Family were present, to signalise victories gained in the war. The second was in the City, where Nelson received an address from the Chamberlain, an office then held by that celebrated champion of liberty, John Wilkes. He was made a Freeman, the honour being accompanied by a gold box of the value of a hundred guineas.

He was soon haunting the Admiralty—through whom he had received a pension of £923, in consideration of wounds and services—pressing for a new appointment. To console Fanny, and also to secure his retreat, he laid out the sum of £2,000 on the purchase of Roundwood, a property near Ipswich which was intended as the "cottage" he had referred to so often in letters from the Mediterranean. For the first time, he and his wife might look forward to a home of their own. But not yet could they keep house together, for Nelson's thoughts were seaward.

The ship appointed for his flag was the *Vanguard* of 74 guns, and her captain, Edward Berry, was newly married to a Norfolk woman. His was particularly quick promotion, for he had been a lieutenant less than two years before. It would have been some compensation for an abrupt break with conjugal felicity. The two men prepared at Spithead and St Helen's for the voyage to Lisbon, where Nelson had been ordered to rejoin St Vincent's fleet. Without the least suspicion of so doing, he was breaking with his old life for ever.

Chapter 5

THE NILE

I

"READ a Letter from Adm: Sir Horatio Nelson Bart." recorded the Secretary of the Society for the Promotion of Christian Knowledge, on 6th February 1798 (bestowing on the sender a dignity he never held), "in which he observes that when he went out in the *Agamemnon* in the year 1793, he had been supplied by the Society with a quantity of Common Prayer, and religious tracts, which he flatters himself answer'd the good purposes they were intended for; and requests that he may be favor'd with as many Bibles and Prayer Books, as may be consistent with the regulations of the Society, for the use of such of H.M. Ships, as he may hoist his flag in." Nelson intended that his men should not lack proper guidance. For their part, the Society promised to fulfil any application with which they were favoured by Sir Horatio. Such zeal was to be encouraged.

It had been a struggle to get equipped. The *Foudroyant* had originally been intended for Nelson's flag, but she was not far enough forward, and he had to be content with a Deptford-built ship, just ten years old, with a name whose battle-honours stretched back to the Armada. The *Vanguard* was ready for commissioning in December 1797, but before she had been worked up in preparation for foreign service, Nelson had time for another stay in Bath. From there, on 4th January 1798, he wrote a letter to his friend Bertie of the *Ardent*, who had given him an account of the trial of Captain John Williamson for misconduct at the battle of Camperdown, which included some views on war. Williamson had a sad record: he had witnessed Cook's death at Hawaii, and indeed might have saved him had he acted with more vigour; he showed up equally badly under Duncan. The Court on which Bertie had sat was patient and, in

Nelson's view, lenient. It sentenced Williamson to be placed at the bottom of the Captain's list, and rendered him ineligible for further naval service.

"As to myself," said Nelson, "upon the general question, that if a man does not do his utmost in time of Action, I think but one punishment ought to be inflicted. Not that I take a man's merit from his list of killed and wounded, for but little may be in his power; and if he does his utmost in the station he is placed, he has equal merit to the man who may have his Ship beat to pieces, but not his good fortune. I dare say there were some favourable circumstances in W's trial, but it is a virtue to lean on the side of mercy; and I have only to hope it will have its effect upon Officers going into Action. I would have every man believe, I shall only take my chance of being shot by the Enemy, but if I do not take that chance, I am certain of being shot by my friends."

Nelson's thoughts were not wholly of war. He had a box lent him by Lord Lansdowne at the Bath theatre; this he enjoyed, since, he told a friend, "generally some of the handsomest ladies . . . are partakers . . . and as I am possessed of everything which is valuable in a wife, I have no occasion to think beyond a pretty face".

From Bath, early in March, the Nelsons returned to Bond Street. While in their lodgings, a friend from far-off days in Nicaragua, Richard Bulkeley, brought his boys on a visit. Nelson, with his usual instinct where children were concerned, showed the eldest his sword. From that hour, the lad was a dedicated sailor. For some months he cherished his ambition secretly, but out it all came in the end, and through Nelson's help, he lived to serve as a midshipman at Trafalgar.

Official leave of the King was taken on 14th March, and on the 29th of the month Nelson hoisted his blue flag in the *Vanguard* at Spithead. On 10th April the ship left St Helens with a convoy. "I am very happy to send you Sir Horatio Nelson again," wrote Lord Spencer to St Vincent from the Admiralty, "not only because I believe I cannot send you a more zealous, active and approved officer, but because I have reason to believe that his being under your command will be agreeable to your wishes." Spencer was right. "The arrival of Admiral Nelson has given me new life," replied St Vincent thankfully: "you could not have gratified me more than in sending him."

Lord Spencer and his Countess had had the opportunity of getting to know Nelson during his convalescence, and, after the first shock, Lady Spencer had been impressed. "The first time I saw him," she recalled in later years, with uncommon frankness, "was in the drawing-room of the Admiralty, and a most uncouth creature I thought him. He was just returned from Teneriffe, after having lost his arm. He looked so sickly, it was painful to see him, and his general appearance was that of an idiot; so much so, that when he spoke, and his wonderful mind broke forth, it was a sort of surprise that riveted my whole attention." She even forgave him for upsetting her table arrangements with his plea that he might sit next his wife at dinner. His reason was that he had too little of her society; but Fanny was also invaluable to a one-armed man who never became dexterous at cutting up what was on his plate.

Nelson, when once again on active service, found St Vincent facing serious problems. The fleet was splendidly ordered, but chafed under the ruthless discipline imposed upon it. Even the flag-officers were restive: they grew vocal when it was rumoured that a junior admiral would be picked as the man to re-enter the Mediterranean on a special mission. The need was to discover the destination of a great French armament preparing at Toulon and Genoa, rumours of which had put every Power of the Middle Sea into a state of tension.

St Vincent, as so often, was concerned that no junction should be made by the French with the Spaniards in Cadiz Bay. If, however, the enemy design was eastward, towards the Levant, a squadron must be formed to intercept it in passage. There was one person pre-eminently fitted to command such a force: Nelson. Many people in high places later claimed to have chosen him—the Duke of Clarence even wrote to his old friend that it was the King in person —but Nelson was the proper candidate, in St Vincent's judgment, which was the one that mattered. He was quite prepared to endure the protests of aggrieved subordinates.

One of them, Sir John Orde, later challenged St Vincent to a duel, which was forbidden from the Palace.

On 4th May Nelson was at Gibraltar, writing home to Fanny that although the company there was merry, "we had better be alongside a Spaniard". On the 6th, with the *Orion*, *Alexander* and attendant frigates in company, he prepared to watch Toulon, giving strict orders to his ships not to become separated. A French corvette, captured on 17th May, confirmed that Bonaparte was himself soon about to embark, but no one yet knew for what quarter the expedition was bound. It was thought that Admiral Brueys, who had his flag in *L'Orient*, would lead the covering force of thirteen ships of the line and attendant frigates. Brueys would have to protect some three hundred transports of various sizes, conveying 35,000 troops. He would be subject to the orders of Bonaparte, who commanded both land and sea forces, and this was why Nelson later told Fanny "it would have been my delight to have tried Bonaparte on a wind". Nelson recognised in the Corsican a tactician who would demand his best, one who had already humiliated the navy at Toulon, and a man with whom Nelson was destined to strive continuously, though never in direct combat.

Bonaparte's new and secret project, ambitious and wonderful, with scientists and savants on the staff, was in fact an enforced alternative to an assault on the United Kingdom. In February, while Nelson was still at Bath, Bonaparte had made a visit to Dunkirk and the Flemish coast and had concluded, regretfully, that, bearing in mind the state of the French navy, invasion was impracticable except as a desperate measure, though he urged on his government the importance of keeping up a pretence of it. England, he said, must be attacked in her trade and possessions.

For the time, Nelson was in no strength to do more than keep watch on his opponent, but he was confident in his small squadron, and had redoubtable captains in his two ships of the line, Sir James Saumarez and Alexander Ball. Saumarez had been knighted for his brilliant capture of a frigate early in the war, and he had fought at St Vincent. Ball and his admiral had regarded one another coldly at St Omer many years before, when Nelson had conceived a prejudice against Ball's sartorial niceties. "What," said Nelson when Ball came to pay his respects, "are you come to have your bones broken?" Within a very short time Ball had rendered Nelson such service as bound the two in lasting friendship. Ball was indeed a friend worth making. He had regular and most handsome features, bold, clear eyes, and a forehead almost Shakespearian in appearance. He was, in fact, a man of intellect as well as of action. Proof of his quality lies in the devotion he inspired wherever he went, by sea or land, and in the fact that his character and conversation enthralled even Coleridge, who was certainly the most brilliant talker and one of the profoundest thinkers of all time.

The incident which brought Nelson and Ball together is best described in a letter which Nelson wrote to Fanny from Sardinia on 24th May. "I ought not to call what has happened to the *Vanguard* by the cold name of accident," he related: "I believe firmly that it was the Almighty's goodness, to check my consummate vanity. I hope it has made me a better Officer, as I feel confident it has made me a better Man. I kiss with all humility the rod.

"Figure to yourself a vain man, on Sunday evening at sunset, walking in his cabin with a Squadron about him, who looked up to their Chief to lead them to glory. Figure to yourself this proud, conceited man, when the sun rose on Monday morning, his Ship dismasted, his Fleet dispersed, and himself in such distress, that the meanest Frigate out of France would have been a very unwelcome guest. But it has pleased Almighty God to bring us to a safe Port, where, although we are refused the rights of humanity, yet the *Vanguard* will in two days get to sea again, as an English Man of War."

The ship had been taken unawares by a sudden storm, dismasted, nearly wrecked, and saved only by the exertions of Ball and Saumarez, the former of whom took the flagship in tow. At one time the danger was so great that Nelson urged Ball to cast off and to leave him to his fate, but met a stubborn refusal. When the ships were at last safely anchored, Nelson went aboard the *Orion* to thank his deliverer in the same words which he had used to Collingwood after the

battle of St Vincent, "A friend in need is a friend indeed!"
Ball had proved himself unforgettably.

Berry wrote home that at the time of greatest danger he
could himself "easily distinguish the surf breaking on the
rocky shore", and recorded that a young gentleman called
Meek, recommended by Coke of Norfolk, had been lost
overboard, and others hurt. It had been one of the closest
things in Nelson's sea life. Yet in a mere four days, thanks
largely to the skill of the carpenter of Ball's ship, the *Vanguard* was re-equipped and actually at sea, cruising after the
enemy on their own coast, in her captain's words, "with a
main top-mast for a fore-mast, and a top-gallant-mast for a
top-mast, consequently everything else reduced in proportion. With such perseverance you will say we deserve
success."

If, by prodigious exertions, Nelson was operational once
more, he was without frigates. Having suffered some
damage, they had separated from the big ships in the stress
of weather, and—not allowing for the energy which would
stir in any vessel wearing Nelson's flag—their captains concluded that the *Vanguard* would return to Gibraltar for
repairs, and did not keep on station. The miscalculation had
results which Nelson never forgot; indeed, the first of a
string of mischances had begun. Bonaparte, favoured with
a north-west wind, sailed from Toulon on 20th May, and
passed near Nelson in the storm. Even had he been in a fit
state to do so, Nelson could not have challenged a fleet with
any hope of useful result, but the enemy would have lost
the advantage of surprise, and might have been watched and
harried.

St Vincent had promised to reinforce him the moment
Sir Roger Curtis joined with fresh ships from England. He
was a man so much of his word that as soon as the top-masts
of the expected squadron were made out, the captains of ten
of the best 74-gun ships were signalled away. St Vincent
called them "some choice fellows of the in-shore squadron",
and the names are a roll of honour. There was Troubridge
in the *Culloden*, a favourite of the Commander-in-Chief,
Nelson's friend of old, and in his opinion "the very best
Sea-officer in His Majesty's Service". There was Foley in

the *Goliath*; Louis in the *Minotaur*; Peyton in the *Defence*; Darby in the *Bellerophon*; Westcott in the *Majestic*; Samuel Hood in the *Zealous*; Hallowell in the *Swiftsure*; Miller in the *Theseus* and Gould in the *Audacious*. The smaller *Leander*, under Captain Thomas Thompson, also joined Nelson.

Troubridge, characteristically, was out of sight of St Vincent before Curtis anchored, and by 7th June Nelson was in command of what was perhaps the finest squadron of its size ever assembled in the era of sail. The brig *Mutine* (her Captain was Thomas Hardy), which had come up on the 5th, was the only lighter vessel at his disposal, but he told Berry he now conceived he would be a match for any hostile force in the Mediterranean. His orders were, on falling in with the French armament "to use your utmost endeavours to take, burn, sink or destroy it", a sentence which coincided precisely with his own wishes.

The correspondence which Nelson had conducted with Sir William Hamilton at Naples, ever since his visit in 1793, now quickened. The Admiralty told him he might look for "favourable neutrality" from Tuscany and the ' Two Sicilies ' —i.e. the Kingdom of Naples and Sicily. He requested Hamilton's good offices over water, supplies, pilots and even frigates. He was asking too much, though by the pressure of Sir William on King Ferdinand through the Prime Minister, Acton, and of Lady Hamilton directly upon the Queen, he was later able to get necessities. The arrangements were "under the rose", for Ferdinand's neutrality was conditioned by fear of the French, whose agents were ubiquitous, and he was not then prepared to come out as an open friend of a country which was only strong at sea, and which had but a single squadron to protect his territories.

Meanwhile, nearly two months of tension, frustration and disappointment had begun. They were among the most trying in Nelson's career, for he knew that, having been given a finely tempered instrument, command of the first effective squadron to enter the Mediterranean since the ignominious withdrawal nearly two years before, much would be expected of him. But where were the French? If Nelson now had strength enough to fight their covering force, lack of frigates seriously reduced his chance of intercepting them on passage, and their destination could still only be guess-work.

On 14th June he wrote to Sir William Hamilton that he had been told the enemy had been seen off the north-west end of Sicily, steering east. Troubridge was sent in to Naples with the letter. He was ordered to get any later news he could, to press for such help as Naples could be induced to give, and to state his admiral's view of the strategic situation. Nelson summed up his opinion in a note to Lord Spencer at the Admiralty. "If they pass Sicily," he said, "I shall believe they are going on their scheme of possessing Alexandria and getting troops to India." He added that he would lose not a moment in bringing them to action, and that his squadron was "remarkably healthy, and perfectly equal to meet the French fleet".

He himself hove-to in Naples Bay, and it was not long before Troubridge hurried back with a report that Bonaparte had gone towards Malta. "My distress for frigates is extreme," wrote Nelson to Hamilton in a sentence he was to repeat again and again during the weeks which followed. "I cannot help myself, and no one will help me. But, thank God, I am not apt to feel difficulties."

The squadron then weighed, and headed for Messina, with Malta their destination. But before they reached the island, news came that it had fallen, and Nelson realised that he must look for his opponent either at Corfu, which was then in Venetian hands and at the disposal of the French, or, more probably as he thought, in Egypt.

Bonaparte's attack on Malta had scarcely been opposed. The island, in which both Naples and Russia had interests or designs, was then held by the Knights of St John, the last of those companies of Christian warriors who had once waged war on the infidel in Palestine. They had a German Grand Master, and were in the last stages of disunity and decay, surrounded by rebellious Maltese. The French Knights refused to fight their countrymen, and the Grand Master surrendered to Bonaparte after nothing more than a token defence. In a few days Bonaparte had abolished the Order, drafted new regulations for the island, rearranged the curriculum of the University, loaded the holds of *L'Orient* with the Knights' treasure, installed a garrison, and sailed for Egypt.

During the night of 22nd June, in thick weather, Nelson actually drew so close to the French that Brueys, hearing in the distance the signal-guns of the British ships, knew serious alarm; not so Bonaparte. Trusting his star, untroubled by nautical minutiae, he devoted most of the passage to browsing in an extensive library of historical and geographical works, which included the *Voyages of Captain Cook*.

Sailing faster and straighter, Nelson reached Alexandria first, on 28th June, and it was only his lack of frigates which, preventing an extended search, deprived him of the pleasure of intercepting his opponent shortly before he disembarked. Alexandria was indeed the scene of activity, but this was Turkish. It was empty of the French, though Nelson's sails had scarcely disappeared over the north-eastern horizon when watchers on the Pharos saw the Republican flotillas come into view in the north-west.

Three years later, Nelson had a letter from a Mr George Baldwin, who had been Consul at Alexandria at the time. He had been away from the city some weeks when the British fleet appeared, and his deputy proved unintelligent. Baldwin wrote to ask Nelson what effect it might have had if he, Baldwin, had been there in person. Nelson was in no doubt as to the answer. "I should have been off Alexandria when the French fleet arrived," he wrote, "and most assuredly the Army could not have landed in the complete order it did, had an action taken place on the first of July, which . . . it would have done had the Turks received me as a friend instead of an enemy, for the answer I received was that neither English nor French should enter the port of Alexandria. And I believe if you had been there to explain between me and the Turkish Government that I should have remained a few days to get some water and refreshments."

As it was, Bonaparte had won the first round, and landed unopposed at Marabout. Three weeks later a dejected admiral wrote to Hamilton to bemoan the fact that the Devil's children had the Devil's luck, and that he himself was still without news. He also despatched long and ably reasoned letters to St Vincent and the Admiralty, stating the grounds for his various courses and decisions. He was disregarding Ball's sage advice that "I should recommend a friend never to begin a defence of his conduct before he is accused of error". Nelson held that the commander of what he described as the finest ships in the service must justify his view that "under all circumstances I was right in steering for Alexandria, and by that opinion I must stand or fall".

Meanwhile, having reached Sicily on what was in effect a journey of baffled retreat, Nelson had need to water and provision. Two hundred and fifty tons of water were wanted per ship, each drop entered by manual labour; and he insisted on stores of the first quality. "As no Fleet has had more fag than this," he wrote to Hamilton, "nothing but the best food and the greatest attention can keep them healthy. At this moment, we have not one sick man."

On 22nd July he found refreshment in a classical scene, the island of Ortygia, in Syracuse harbour, where there was a famous fountain associated with a nymph propitious to sailors. Blending fact with allusion, he made a graceful bow to the Hamiltons before renewing his search: "Thanks to your exertions," he wrote, "we have victualled and watered: and surely, watering at the Fountain of Arethusa, we must have victory. We shall sail with the first breeze, and be assured I will return either crowned with laurel, or covered with cypress."

II

There had been one compensation in Nelson's weeks of quest. They had enabled him to transform a splendid squadron into an invincible one. On every occasion when the wind dropped, the captains were rowed across to the *Vanguard*. Consultations were detailed and friendly. Everyone had the chance to know Nelson's intentions under any circumstance in which the enemy might be found. More than that, the ships' companies had time to learn to know one another, to act as a team. Gun crews were under regular exercise. Fire drill was efficient: nothing was left to chance.

If the spirit he felt growing around him only heightened Nelson's disappointment in not being able to bring it to the test, it assured him that anything he ordered would be carried out with a resolution equalling his own.

From Syracuse the squadron proceeded to Greek waters, and on 28th July Troubridge, sent into the Gulf of Koroni for intelligence, returned with a prize, a French brig laden with wine, and with news that Bonaparte's fleet had been seen about four weeks earlier, steering south-eastwards from Crete. As Ball in the *Alexander* had similar news from another vessel, Nelson, who was then off Cape Matapan, immediately bore up, under all sail, for Alexandria. He had indeed been right before, but too quick!

At noon on 1st August the squadron saw the Pharos at Alexandria for the second time. At two-thirty that day Captain Hood of the *Zealous* made the hoped-for signal. He could see the French, and they were anchored in Aboukir Bay, which extends from Aboukir Point to the Rosetta mouth of the Nile. They had been unable to use the harbour at Alexandria, which had become silted.

"The utmost joy seemed to animate every breast on board the squadron at sight of the Enemy," recorded Captain Berry, "and the pleasure which the Admiral himself felt was perhaps more heightened than that of any other man, as he had now a certainty by which he could regulate his future operations." Nelson had been intolerably restless during the later stages of the passage, scarcely slept at all, and made the life of the officers of the watch anything but tranquil. Now at last he could calm down, and, as was his way before action, he ordered dinner to be served. He could cease from fretting, and could savour in anticipation the fulfilment of that wish for annihilation of the foe which was one of his major contributions to the naval doctrine of his country. By temperament an artist, he now had before him the raw material for a masterpiece, which could be executed at a speed which matched his inclination. "Before this time tomorrow," he said at table, "I shall have gained a Peerage, or Westminster Abbey."

When he first sighted Nelson's ships, Admiral Brueys could not have felt unduly apprehensive. His own force—

thirteen of the line, including his flagship of 120 guns, three ships of 80 guns, and four frigates—was stronger in weight of metal, and although parties were ashore watering, he was anchored in a position which, to most adversaries, would have seemed impregnable. On two sides he was protected by shoals and breakers. Frigates and gunboats were on his flank, and there was a battery on Bequier Island, towards which his van was headed. Even the time of day was in his favour, for sunset was not many hours away.

It would not have escaped the memory of the older officers in both fleets that there was an admiral still living, Samuel Barrington, who, twenty years before, during the War of the American Revolution, had repulsed a vastly superior force under Count D'Estaing, relying on the strength of similar dispositions at anchor. St Lucia, in the West Indies, had been the scene of the action, and it could have been a valuable reassurance to the French. Lord Hood had also distinguished himself in that area, in operations not dissimilar. French admirals were not always confident by nature, but on the afternoon of 1st August 1798, Brueys, who had been taking counsel as to the most picturesque way of celebrating in the fleet Bonaparte's victory at the Pyramids, was known to have felt it unlikely that Nelson would attack before the next day.

Years later Bonaparte, while on the way to St Helena, told Admiral Cockburn that Brueys and he, while on passage to Alexandria, had discussed just such a situation as Brueys was now in, and that Brueys had actually proved, to Bonaparte's satisfaction, how disastrous it could be if an admiral were caught embayed and at anchor! Bonaparte added that Nelson's appearance, and its consequences, "exemplified the correctness of Brueys's ideas, and the impropriety of his conduct".

The hour had now come. Nelson, like Hawke at Quiberon had waited too long for his opportunity to postpone the decisive moment. He would strike at once. He had achieved surprise; the wind, a little west of north, was favourable; he was concentrated. He had already summoned the *Alexander* and the *Swiftsure*, which were reconnoitering in the direction of Alexandria; he now made the signal to prepare for battle, adding that it was his intention to attack van and centre, according to a plan developed in the weeks of preparation. "His idea," said Berry, "was first to secure the victory, and then to make the most of it according to future circumstances." An overwhelming force was to be opposed to part of the enemy line; ships were to anchor by the stern, with springs upon the cable, in order to help manœuvrability; they were to make ready four horizontal lights at the mizzen peak, so that there should be no confusion when daylight was over, and to keep sounding as they stood in. Hawke had had no pilots at Quiberon, remarking that his flying foe would serve for guidance; Nelson, on this memorable day, reasoned that where there was room for an enemy to swing at moorings there was room for him to anchor, and showed the same boldness as his predecessor. There were in fact great risks: Troubridge's *Culloden* actually grounded on a northern shoal, but the rest of the line, led by Foley in the *Goliath* and the *Zealous* under Hood, approached the French before a slight breeze. By sunset, which was at half-past six, action began. It did not cease for most of that summer night.

Signals had been few, a sure sign of understanding. Nelson twice gave the order to prepare for action, once after Hood's report, and again at 4.22. Just over an hour later, the squadron was instructed to form line as best they could, ahead and astern of the *Vanguard*. Only then did Brueys inform his fleet that he intended to engage the enemy at anchor! He seemed, indeed, half stunned at Nelson's impetuosity in coming into action so close upon nightfall, and with none of those meticulous preliminaries which went to the formation of a proper line of battle.

At 5.40 Nelson signalled for close action, and at 6.28, just before sunset, when the French were hoisting their colours, Foley in the *Goliath* steered for the anchor-cable of the French van ship, *Le Guerrier*, passed between her and the battery on Bequier Island, and was followed to an inshore position by the *Zealous* and the *Theseus*. The *Orion* and *Audacious* also penetrated the enemy line, achieving a massive concentration, and making certain of the destruction of the leading enemy vessels. The *Majestic* and *Alexander* broke through at a later stage of the battle.

Foley indeed, without explicit orders from Nelson, who could scarcely have anticipated Brueys exact defensive arrangements, equalled his admiral in tactical boldness by taking his ship inshore of the French. A big man in every sense of the adjective, with more battle experience than any officer in the squadron, he had fought under Keppel, Rodney, Hood and Jervis, had been a flag-captain at St Vincent, and knew just when to exercise his own judgment. Although it was a stroke of initiative after Nelson's own pattern, it was a great risk for the leading ship to take the *Goliath*'s course. Foley, with experienced shrewdness, surmised that the French would not have ventured to anchor too close to the shoals, that they would have left a generous margin of safety, and that, as they would certainly never anticipate that they would be attacked on their most protected side, they might not even have run out their shoreward-pointing guns. Events justified him. *Le Guerrier* was dismasted in less than twelve minutes, and the incident enabled Nelson, who was the first to anchor on Brueys's seaward side, to direct the following ships to take up their stations ahead, ensuring immediate pressure on the French centre. He himself gave the *Vanguard*'s opening broadside to *Le Spartiate*. Her surrender was acknowledged within two hours of the opening of the battle, after Nelson himself had been wounded.

In modern naval warfare the first minutes of action between capital units are always critical and often decisive. In the era of sail the agony was more prolonged. Ships came into battle slowly, and the effect of gunfire upon strong wooden sides was so gradual that battle-damage rarely sank a major vessel, though it often battered one into helpless surrender. At the Nile, it was the first two hours that were most crucial. By the time *Le Spartiate* was ready to submit, *Le Guerrier*, *Le Conquerant*, *L'Aquilon* and *Le Peuple Souverain* had also ceased resistance, while *L'Heureux*, *Le Tonnant* and even the flagship were closely beset, the great *L'Orient* being seventh in the line of thirteen. She was by far the largest vessel in Aboukir Bay.

Legends have clustered round *L'Orient*'s last hours. Brueys, the Commander-in-Chief, met a gallant end. After receiving three wounds, one in the head and two in the body,

LADY HAMILTON AND LORD NELSON AT VIENNA

pastels by Johann Schmidt, 1800

Lady Hamilton wears the insignia of the Order of the Knights of Malta

he persisted in remaining on deck, propped upon an arms-chest, until a fourth shot cut him in two. Among other stalwarts, Commodore Casabianca and his son, a boy of ten, became the subject of heroic verse, while the fact that *L'Orient* carried in her holds more than half a million in gold, besides much of the treasure of the Knights of Malta, three tons of plate, the gates of Valetta Cathedral, and life-sized statues of the twelve Apostles made of solid silver, added further melancholy to her end.

In *Le Tonnant* resistance was equally stubborn. Dupetit Thouars, the captain of the ship, had his right and left arms hit and a leg shattered. He would not move or go below; ordering a tub of bran to be brought, he had himself placed in it, and his last order, before he bled to death, was to direct the colours to be nailed to the mast.

Soon after nine o'clock the soft Egyptian night, already lit by the continuous flash of guns, was still brighter illuminated by a fire which was seen to be devouring *L'Orient*. It was later found to be partly due to some inextinguishable chemicals with which the French had been experimenting. Nelson, who was below having his wound dressed, was told the news by Berry, and gave orders that as many lives as possible should be saved. The *Vanguard*'s only serviceable boat was sent across, and the errand of mercy was followed by other ships. About seventy Frenchmen were saved from a ship, obviously doomed, from which they had jumped. Everyone on both sides knew just when a fire had grown beyond control.

The blaze served to show up the position of both fleets, the British slowly advancing towards the rear of the French line, blasting it as they progressed. Only the last few ships in Brueys's squadron were not yet fully in action. At about ten o'clock *L'Orient* exploded. In a night of noise and violence, this was by far the most sensational incident. It startled troops at Alexandria, fifteen miles away. Many men below decks in ships on both sides thought that their own magazines had been penetrated. The shock was such that, in Berry's words: "there was an awful pause and death-like silence for about three minutes". This was enlivened by a huge shower of debris, masts, yards, parts of guns, tackle of

L

every kind, which fell into the mêlée. A fragment even caused a small fire in one of the loftiest sails of the *Alexander*.

Once this awe-inspiring spectacle was over, the battle continued until after ten o'clock. Then there was another brief pause, due to exhaustion. Ball told Coleridge that both his own men in the *Alexander* and their French opponents slept for twenty minutes, and then "started up . . . more like men out of an ambush than from sleep, so co-instantaneously did they all obey the summons!" The pause was followed by partial resumption of activity until three o'clock in the morning. By dawn only the two rear French ships, *Le Guillaume Tell* and *Le Généreux* were still intact, and of the four French frigates one, *L'Artemise*, had been set on fire by her own captain, and another, *Le Serieuse*, had been sunk by the *Orion*, though her poop remained above water. At about eleven o'clock the two undamaged French ships of the line, in one of which, *Le Guillaume Tell*, was Villeneuve, Nelson's future opponent at Trafalgar, cut their cables and stood out to sea, together with the two surviving frigates, *La Justice* and *La Diane*. By that time the crews of the British ships were in no condition to chase, though Hood of the *Zealous* did his best to do so. As there were none to support him, Nelson regretfully ordered him back.

The fates of certain individual British vessels deserve remark. Darby in the *Bellerophon* had been so roughly handled in a first attempt on the massive *L'Orient* that his ship drifted out of the line, helpless, without masts or cables. As she had nowhere to place her four distinguishing lanterns, she narrowly escaped still harder treatment from the last approaching ships of her own side. She and the *Majestic*, whose captain, Westcott, was killed, had the heaviest casualties among the victors. Of a complement of just under six hundred, the *Bellerophon* and *Majestic* had 49 and 50 killed respectively; three times that number were wounded.

The *Culloden*, on which Nelson had greatly depended, never recovered from her grounding on the shoal running off Bequier Island. The situation nearly drove Troubridge crazy, for it was the second great fleet action which he had been compelled to witness as a spectator, the earlier occasion being the First of June 1794, when he had been a prisoner aboard one of the French ships captured by Howe. The limit of his satisfaction was that, after prodigies of exertion, he was able to get his ship free and later to save her, while his lights and signals enabled him to prevent the three ships following him from suffering his own fate.

The small *Leander*, unfitted by her size to lie in the line, was ordered to support the bigger ships as and where she could. Disdaining to attack the frigates, which were nearer her own weight, Captain Thompson at first placed his ship between *Le Peuple Souverain* and *Le Franklin*. As she later managed to rake *L'Orient*, she took a full part in a battle where each gun counted. It was fitting indeed that every captain of a ship of the line—even including Troubridge, by Nelson's pressing request—received a gold medal for the action from the King, while Hardy was promoted from the *Mutine* to become Nelson's flag-captain, after Berry was ordered home with despatches. Through this appointment, Hardy became the only officer of post rank to take part in every one of Nelson's greater battles.

III

At about half-past eight in the evening, when he was looking over a rough sketch of Aboukir Bay which had been given him a day or two before by Hallowell of the *Swiftsure*, Nelson was wounded. He was hit in the forehead by a piece of iron shot. The skin hung down over his face, and this, together with the blood which flowed from his head, rendered him temporarily blind.

Berry, who was standing near him, caught him in his arms, and heard him exclaim: "I am killed: remember me to my wife." He was carried below to the cockpit, where Jefferson the surgeon was already busy. The pain was intense, but in spite of this, when Jefferson broke away from a patient he was attending, Nelson said: "No, I will take my turn with my brave fellows." He waited some moments in the darkness, sure in his own mind that his end was near.

Jefferson was soon free to give his whole mind to the

admiral. A few seconds' inspection were enough: there was no great danger. After the battle, he entered in his journal: "Sir Horatio Nelson K.B., Rear Admiral of the Blue . . . wound on the forehead; over the right eye; the Cranium bare for more than an inch; the wound three inches long." It was messy and painful, and the cut was immediately over the bad eye, but Jefferson was soon able to assure Nelson that it was nothing much to worry over. The doctor "brought the edges of the wound together, and applied strips of adhesive". Yet Nelson's anxieties still continued. He gave the chaplain his last remembrances to Fanny, and ordered the *Minotaur* to be hailed, so that he could thank Louis for his noble support.

Jefferson begged him to remain quiet for a time in the bread-room, but, once reassured that he was in no danger of sinking, Nelson ordered his Secretary to be called, so that he could at least begin the draft of a despatch. Campbell, the man in question, had himself been wounded, and was so affected by his own misfortunes and that of his master that he could not write. The Chaplain was then summoned, but he, too, was inexpert, so Nelson, with his own hand, "contrived to trace some words which marked at that awful moment his devout sense of the success he had then obtained": the phrase is that of his official biographers. The victory was by no means complete, but Nelson wished to achieve some immediate record of his intentions and their fulfilment, in this as in other ways showing the nature of an artist.

When he received the message from Berry that *L'Orient* was on fire, he managed to make his way to the quarter-deck, to everyone's astonishment. Later, after much trouble, he was persuaded to go to bed. Still restless, he got up, signed Hardy's commission for the *Vanguard*, and arranged that Capel, his signal lieutenant, should take command of the *Mutine*, which would be sent home with duplicate despatches. It was not until 3rd August that the brief despatch, by which Georgiana Duchess of Devonshire thought that "Nelson had turned all our heads", was composed for the information of the Earl of St Vincent and the Lords Commissioners of the Admiralty.

"My Lord," wrote Nelson to his Commander-in-Chief,

"Almighty God has blessed his Majesty's Arms in the late Battle, by a great Victory over the Fleet of the Enemy, whom I attacked at sunset on the 1st of August, off the mouth of the Nile. The Enemy were moored in a strong Line of Battle for defending the entrance of the Bay . . . flank'd by numerous Gun-Boats, four Frigates and a Battery of Guns and Mortars on an Island in their Van; but nothing could withstand the Squadron your Lordship did me the honour to place under my command. Their high state of discipline is well known to you, and with the judgment of the Captains, together with their valour, and that of the Officers and Men of every description, it was absolutely irresistible. Could anything from my pen add to the character of the Captains I would write it with pleasure, but that is impossible. . . ."

Many months later, a letter came to Nelson from Lord Howe. It was brief, and one of the most beautifully written in all the ninety volumes of Nelson Papers. Adding his congratulations to the stream, Howe pointed out how notable he thought it was that *every* captain had done his duty, for such had not, alas, always been the case in his own long experience. It was a courtesy which moved Nelson to venture into his best-known account of the battle.

"My Lord," he wrote to Howe from Palermo, "it was only this moment (8 January, 1799) that I had the invaluable approbation of the great, the immortal Earl Howe—an honour the most flattering a Sea-officer could receive, as it comes from the first and greatest Sea-officer the world has ever produced. I had the happiness to command a Band of Brothers; therefore, night was to my advantage. Each knew his duty, and I was sure each would feel for a French ship. By attacking the Enemy's van and centre, the wind blowing directly along their line, I was enabled to throw what force I pleased on a few ships. This plan my friends readily conceived by the signals, (for which we are principally, if not entirely, indebted to your Lordship), and we always kept a superior force to the Enemy. At twenty-eight minutes past six, the sun in the horizon, the firing commenced. At five minutes past ten, when *L'Orient* blew up, having burnt seventy minutes, the six Van ships had surrendered. I then pressed further towards the Rear; and had it pleased God that I had not been wounded and stone blind, there cannot be a doubt but that every Ship would have been in our possession. But here let it not be supposed, that any officer is to blame. No; on my honour, I am satisfied each did his very best. I have never before, my Lord, detailed the Action to any one; but I have thought it wrong to have kept it from one who is our great Master in Naval tactics and bravery."

Such was Nelson's semi-official account. Two years later, while at Vienna, he had one or two more details to impart to Lady Minto and Lord Fitzharris concerning those moments of charged silence when the squadron, in the evening light, was bearing down upon the anchored French.

"Without knowing the men he had to trust to," Nelson said, "he would not have hazarded the attack: there was very little room, but he was sure each would find a hole to creep in at." Lord Fitzharris noted the admiral's actual words at one point in the conversation. "When I saw them," said Nelson, "I could not help popping my head every now and then out of the window (although I had a damned tooth-ache), and once, as I was observing their position, I heard two seamen quartered at a gun near me, talking, and one said to the other, 'Damn them, look at them. There they are, Jack, if we don't beat them, they will beat us.' I knew what stuff I had under me, so I went into the attack with a few ships only, perfectly sure the others would follow me, although it was nearly dark and they might have had every excuse for not doing it, yet they all in the course of two hours found a hole to poke in at." He added that "if I had taken a fleet of the same force from Spithead, I would sooner have thought of flying than attacking the French in their position, but I knew my captains, nor could I say which distinguished himself most."

IV

The state of Aboukir Bay on the morning of 2nd August 1798 was one of the most extraordinary in history. "Victory is not a name strong enough for such a scene," said Nelson. He had set a new standard of conquest. Of the seventeen

French ships which had opposed him the previous evening, all but the four, which were beating out of the bay, were either smoking hulks or flew the British flag. No British victory at sea had ever been so complete, and obtained without the loss of a single ship. Losses of the enemy "taken, drowned, burnt and missing", some 5,225 men in all, were nearly six times greater than those of the attackers. The masterpiece had been achieved, and it was almost flawless. With a mixture of humanity and a wish to embarrass French resources, the great majority of prisoners were sent ashore under cartel, and one of Troubridge's principal contributions to the amenities of a day of tired festivity was a supply of fresh provisions for the wounded. The night following, the battle was illuminated from the shore by Arabs and Mamelukes, fuel being readily obtainable from the masses of wreckage.

One of Nelson's first commands on 2nd August was a Service of Thanksgiving. "This solemn act of gratitude to Heaven," said Berry, "seemed to make a very deep impression upon several of the prisoners, both officers and men, some of the former of whom remarked 'that it was no wonder we could preserve such order and discipline, when we could impress the minds of our men with such sentiments after a victory so great, and at a moment of such seeming confusion.'"

Having rendered acknowledgment in the highest quarters, compliments could then be exchanged between Nelson and the incomparable men he led. Nelson's message to those he had commanded breathed his affection and pride. His squadron, in its turn, expressed its deep appreciation, and at a meeting on 3rd August, under the presidency of Sir James Saumarez in the *Orion*, a resolution was passed, in the following terms: "The Captains of the Squadron under the Orders of Rear Admiral Sir Horatio Nelson K.B., desirous of testifying the high sense they entertain of his prompt decision and intrepid conduct in the Attack on the French Fleet, in Bequier Road, off the Nile, the 1st August 1798, request his acceptance of a Sword; and as a further proof of their esteem and regard, hope that he will permit his Portrait to be taken, and hung up in the room belonging to the Egyptian Club, now established in commemoration of that glorious day." The Club, established so fittingly, had, alas, no permanent quarters, and the captains in the end contented themselves with replicas of a formal portrait by a Neapolitan, Leonardo Guzzardi, or by copies of the later and better picture by Sir William Beechey.[1] The Sword was ordered at once and became a favourite possession of the admiral.

Nelson, remembering his East Indian experiences as a youth, and having world strategy in mind, sent off a lieutenant, Duval, with news of Bonaparte's movements in Egypt, and of his own victory, to the British settlements east of Suez. Duval, a nephew of Drake of Genoa, was a linguist, and performed his mission so ably that the East India Company voted Nelson a present of ten thousand pounds. It was a liberal offering from an organisation which had itself been saved much expense in defensive dispositions owing to the exertions of the navy.

Two sets of despatches were prepared, one to go in the *Leander* to St Vincent, the other to Naples in the *Mutine*. Berry accompanied Thompson in the larger vessel, Hoste being with Capel in the brig. Alas, the *Leander* was captured off Crete on 18th August by *Le Généreux* of 74 guns, after a fierce resistance, during the course of which Berry and Thompson were both wounded. They were badly treated in the aftermath of this single French success, were stripped of all their personal possessions, and eventually reached home overland. The two captains were honourably acquitted at a court-martial on the loss of the ship, and both were knighted.

It was the little *Mutine* which was the means of spreading the news of triumph through Europe. The Queen of Naples and Lady Hamilton both fainted with excitement, so Capel told Nelson. It was a foretaste of Nelson's own reception. When Capel reached London, on 2nd October, there were scenes of wild jubilation, and much private relief. The First Lord fell flat on the floor outside his room in the Admiralty, so great had been his suppressed anxiety, and when the good

---

[1] Ball related that an artist was actually commissioned, but was reluctant to begin. When pressed, he said he would never do it. "There is such a mixture of humanity and ambition in Lord Nelson's countenance that I dare not risk the attempt."

news reached Windsor, King George III was said to have remained silent for a few moments, which was perhaps one of the most astonishing effects of the battle.

Of the countless effusions directed at Nelson, perhaps only one—that written by Lady Hamilton—was as fully charged as that which he received from Lady Spencer. "Joy, joy, joy to you, brave, gallant immortalised Nelson!" wrote this distracted patrician. "May that great God, whose cause you so valiantly support, protect and bless you to the end of your brilliant career! Such a race surely never was run. My heart is absolutely bursting with different sensations of joy, of gratitude, of pride, of every emotion that ever warmed the bosom of a British woman, on hearing of her Country's glory —and all produced by you, my dear, my good friend. . . . All, all I *can* say must fall short of my wishes, of my sentiments about you. This moment the guns are firing, illuminations are preparing, your gallant name is echoed from street to street, and every Briton feels his obligations to you weighing him down. But if these strangers feel in this manner about you, who can express what *We* of this House feel about you! What incalculable service have you been to my dear Lord Spencer! How gratefully, as First Lord of the Admiralty, does he place on *your* brow these laurels so gloriously won. . . . I am half Mad, and I fear I have written a strange letter, but you'll excuse it. Almighty God protect you. Adieu! How anxious we shall be to hear of your health! Lady Nelson has had an express sent to her."

It is only by such impetuous messages as this, by the glowing newspaper accounts, and by the flowering of popular art, mugs and prints, patriotic handkerchiefs and swinging inn-signs, that the temperature of that faraway autumn can still be felt. If news took long to reach its destination, yet when at last it did so, how richly was it realised.

"*Honor est a Nilo*"—so ran a contemporary anagram on Nelson's two names. It was true. Had he himself chosen to go to Gibraltar with the prizes, instead of sending them under the charge of Sir James Saumarez, the lustre of that honour might have remained undimmed. But the *Vanguard* called for immediate repair, and Nelson saw his duty at Naples.

Chapter 6

NAPLES AND SICILY

I

"NAPLES is a paradise," wrote Goethe of a visit made more than a decade before the Battle of the Nile. "Everyone lives, after his manner, intoxicated in self-forgetfulness." In the years that had passed since that time, much had changed, though intoxication of one kind or another was still in the air, and an illustrious newcomer was likely to be offered heady draughts. It was so with Nelson. "All here are drunk with joy," said the Neapolitan Queen, speaking of the immediate effect of the victory. It was not anticipated that the principal hero would be one of the more sober persons after the event.

Nothing is further from the truth than the belief that, after his defeat of Brueys, the wounded Nelson sank rapidly into fuddled indolence, listening to siren voices. So much remained to be done. The battle was of world consequence, but, strategically, it only settled one immediate matter—that the mass of Bonaparte's army could not return to France, and that even the General in person could only do so by slipping through a close blockade. Bonaparte's sources of supply were too uncertain to enable him to advance far into Asia Minor, so, with wisdom and application, he set himself to learn what he could from his enforced sojourn in Egypt. It was much. Moreover, the French left an impression on the country which has never been effaced. Although Bonaparte was soon to meet defeat on land, as well as by sea, from the hands of the British, at the siege of Acre, his nuisance value remained considerable, and required the attentions of a naval squadron continually on the watch. Three years later, a large expedition under Keith and Abercrombie extinguished the French forces in Egypt. By that time Bonaparte, long returned home, was again contemplating the invasion of England.

When, after the Nile, Nelson wrote to Lord Spencer that

if he died, want of frigates would still be written on his
heart, he then meant that if his strength in lighter vessels
had been greater, he might have exploited his success by
destroying Bonaparte's transports in Alexandria and elsewhere. It is possible that he was too sanguine. The French
had had time to attend to the seaward defences of Egypt,
and any such attempt, even supported by landing-parties,
might have been costly and ineffectual. Nelson was in fact
always luckier as an admiral than as a brigadier.

In deciding that the scarred *Vanguard* should go to Naples
for repair, off which city she arrived in tow on 22nd September, after a stormy passage, Nelson was guided by various
considerations, all of them sound. At home, Pitt, as so often
during his career as a war minister, was in process of building up new combinations of Powers against France, in place
of those which had dissolved before French muskets. The
strength of any coalition would greatly depend upon Britain's
use of her newly won sea power in the Mediterranean. The
central position of Naples and Sicily offered a good base for
activity, and in fact, by the time Nelson had returned to the
Bay from which he had begun his chase of Brueys, Ferdinand
IV was preparing to resume an active part against the French
Republic.

Nelson's interest in Naples was not sudden. No less than
four times, in the summer of the previous year, he had expressed the opinion that Ferdinand had been by far the most
faithful and cherishable ally of Great Britain; and although
it was true that he had not been markedly impressed by the
monarch's personal qualities during the visit he had paid on
Hood's behalf soon after the opening of the war, and had
been disappointed at the lack of active help in the campaign
of the Nile, he knew from experience that he had a business-
like friend in Sir William Hamilton, and that Acton, the
Neapolitan Prime Minister, was English in blood and
sympathy. In no other quarter could a naval force have been
more useful and acceptable, if renewal of war on the Continent were to take place. Nelson's view was shared by his
superiors; though he was inclined to wonder whether his
own health would stand further active service.

If, from the nature of eighteenth-century communications, the admiral could expect a long silence, both from Lord St Vincent and from home, he was soon left in no manner of doubt as to how Naples felt about his success. The enthusiasm was frantic. It was led from the throne. Ferdinand, who prided himself on being a seaman, had himself rowed three leagues in his state barge to greet Nelson, the moment he heard that the *Vanguard* was in sight, calling him his "Deliverer and Preserver". Acton and Hamilton had already written glowing letters, Hamilton remarking on the hawk-like way in which the vital chance was seized. "That is the way to do business," he wrote. "How proud I am of feeling myself an Englishman at this moment. Great Britain alone has truly faced the enemy in support of the good cause, and Nelson is the greatest hero of Great Britain." He promised "a pleasant apartment ready for you in my house, and Emma is looking out for the softest pillows, to repose the few wearied limbs you have left."

Emma's own boudoir had a curving balcony, one end of which looked upon Vesuvius and the other on the lovely slopes of Posillipo, with Capri within sight. Hamilton was promising much.

The most significant letter of all was in a fast-flowing feminine hand which conveyed the sentiments not only of the writer but of her close friend the Queen of Naples. "I am delirious with joy," wrote Emma Hamilton on 8th September, "and assure you I have a fever caused by agitation and pleasure. Good God what a victory! Never, never has there been anything half so glorious, so complete!" Capel had not exaggerated in his account of the scenes after his arrival. "I fainted when I heard the joyful news, and fell on my side, and am hurt, but what of that . . ." she continued. "I should feel it a glory to die in such a cause. No, I would not like to die till I see and embrace the *Victor of the Nile*. . . . Sir William is ten years younger since the happy news. . . . My dress from head to foot is *alla Nelson*. Even my shawl is in Blue with gold anchors all over. My ear-rings are Nelson's anchors; in short, we are all be-Nelsoned. . . ." If Lady Hamilton's punctuation, like Nelson's own, needed to be added by the reader, neither characters left their correspondents wondering at their meaning.

The scene in the boat when Emma and Nelson met was described to Fanny as "terribly affecting; up flew her Ladyship, and exclaiming: 'O God, is it possible?' she fell into my arm more dead than alive. Tears, however, soon set matters to rights."

Constant as had been their correspondence, neither Emma Hamilton nor her husband had seen Nelson in person for some five years. Physically, he had been transformed in that time. His right eye was sightless, his right arm a mere stump, and although the surgeon of the *Vanguard* officially discharged his patient a month after the Nile, the head wound being then healed, he added in his Journal that "as the integuments were much enlarged I applied every night a compress, wet, with a discutient embrocation, which was of great service". For some months the place was red and visible. Later, on Emma's suggestion, Nelson wore his hair in a way which helped to cover it. He still suffered much pain. "My head is ready to split, and I am always so sick," he wrote to St Vincent; "in short, if there be no fracture, my head is severely shaken." He had need of every comfort. He had had fever on the way to Naples, and may well have felt a return of the complaint which he described while in the *Agamemnon* as being "as if a girth were buckled taut over my heart". At one point he even wrote to his Commander-in-Chief: "I never expect, my dear Lord, to see your face again," so low were his spirits. Reaction from the strain of the months since Teneriffe would in any case have been considerable, but it is likely that a modern doctor might have suspected some degree of concussion accompanying the new wound, even though the outward damage was superficial. This probability, apparent to Nelson, and added to the state of his frame in general, makes it more than ever necessary to recall the months of pain and anxiety he had already endured.

The palliation of suffering which Nelson obtained through living with the Hamiltons was great, and their tender care of him was the result of quickly growing pleasure in his society. The Minister and his wife, through their long residence at the Court, could spare him decisions which would have taxed his resources even further, but the complexity of the business he had necessarily to manage, his incessant public and private social obligations, and the size of his correspondence, the greater part written or at least drafted in his own left hand, would in later times have been eased by a trained staff. It was small wonder, in the circumstances, that Sir William Hamilton thought him the most energetic man he had ever known.

Where the Hamiltons could not help him directly was in the regulation of his squadron; the administration of blockades at Alexandria and at Malta, in which he had the rather ineffectual assistance of some Portuguese ships under the Marquis de Niza; and in the difficult dovetailing of movement and supply. Almost at once upon his arrival he added to the duties of an admiral those of strategic adviser to the King of Naples. From being a junior flag-officer in command of a detached squadron, he found himself in the centre of political activities whose effects must be felt far beyond that Italian kingdom whose guest and prop he was. If his private hope had been to return home after a short stay, matters were soon taken out of his own hands, for he became increasingly involved in the affairs of those who looked to him as their Protector.

The chief characters in the drama soon to be played out were the King and Queen, the two Hamiltons, and Sir John Acton. Ferdinand IV, who had been on the throne since boyhood, was a Spanish Bourbon known to his subjects as "Il Re Lazzarone", from his fondness for the proletariat and beggars with whom it was his pleasure to mingle, or "Il Vecchio Nasone"—old Nosey, from his most prominent feature. He fried and sold the fish he had caught at Fusaro and Posillipo in his own cook-shop; excelled in knowledge of the vernacular in all its luridness; and found his main outlet for activity in the chase. The bigger the slaughter, the more delighted he became. His idea of government, the routine exercise of which bored him, was summed up in the words "*Festa, forca, farina*"—feasts, force, and flour. By these means he kept the *lazzaroni* attached to him, the State being a partnership of crown, church and mob. As a result, the professional and trading classes, neglected or exploited, became greedy listeners to those who, for whatever reason, promised a different kind of tyranny.

Ferdinand's Queen, Maria Carolina, was a sister of Marie Antoinette, and a person so formidable that even Bonaparte, much as he hated her, said that she was the only man in Naples. It was she who exercised most power, and with her advantages of beauty, strength of character and exalted position she had always to be reckoned with, though she was without the wisdom and prudence of her mother, the Empress Maria Theresa of Austria. She was reactionary, firm and opportunist, and for nearly a quarter of a century, after the death of her sister by the guillotine, she did her utmost to frustrate the expansion of France. Her success was limited. Twice she and her husband were turned out of Naples by force of arms, but in the end, after Bonaparte's downfall, the Bourbon power was restored, and her aim fulfilled.

Sir John Acton, the Prime Minister, was one of those expatriate Englishmen who have so often played a part in Continental affairs, generally in the armed forces. Some twenty years older than Nelson, he had been born in France and brought up as a sailor, serving in the French, Tuscan and Neapolitan navies. Settling down in the employment of Ferdinand and his Queen, he soon discovered that his true gifts were bureaucratic. His position was strengthened and secured by his integrity and industry in a country where those virtues were uncommon. He had inherited a baronetcy fairly late in life, and although there is no evidence of his ever having visited England, he wrote and spoke English, in addition to French and Italian, with a fluency which was perhaps more surprising than the oddities of phrase of which he was self-conscious. He had the interests of Great Britain as well as those of Naples at heart; but, although his ambition was to be regarded as the Pitt of Southern Europe, he was in fact lacking in those qualities of prescience and single-mindedness which could have given him the status of a European statesman.

Sir William Hamilton, descendant from a ducal line, was, at the time of the admiral's return to Naples, approaching seventy, and had already served some thirty-five years as plenipotentiary to the Bourbon Court. Earlier in life he had been a soldier. He had married an heiress, with property in

Wales, who had been entirely devoted to him. Her money, together with the opportunities offered by his official duties, which in time of peace had not been arduous, enabled him to follow his real interests. These were classical archaeology, the study of earthquakes, and the collection of works of art. He had made twenty-two ascents of Vesuvius, and had been a man of exceptional physique. In mind, he represented the flower of eighteenth-century aristocratic civilisation, with easy charm, a great range of curiosity, discernment and natural ability.

"My study of antiquities," wrote Hamilton to his second wife, "has kept me in constant thought of the perpetual fluctuation of everything. The whole art is, really, to live all the *days* of our life; and not, with anxious care, disturb the sweetest hour that life affords—which is, the present. Admire the Creator, and all His works, to us incomprehensible; do all the good you can upon earth; and take the chance of Eternity without dismay." In thus summing up his Horatian view of life, he drew a self-portrait whose attraction is lasting.

Emma, Lady Hamilton, has become the centre of an extensive romantic literature. It is one which may be illustrated with scores of interpretations of her loveliness put upon canvas by the infatuated Romney, who never tired of her variety. But in her Romney days she was a young girl whose beauty, then still plastic, appeared to be of the passive kind. By the time Nelson came into her life she was in her middle thirties and an active, even a dynamic force in Naples.

An accurate physical description, written by a woman who, though hostile, saw clearly, was given by a Mrs Trench, in recollections published many years later. The lady had dined with the Hamiltons and Nelson only two years after the Nile, and noted in her diary that her hostess was "bold, forward, coarse, assuming and vain". She continued: "her figure is colossal, but, excepting her feet, which are hideous, well shaped. Her bones are large, and she is exceedingly *embonpoint*. She resembles the bust of Ariadne; the shape of all her features is fine, as is the form of her head, and particularly her ears; her teeth are a little irregular, but tolerably white; her eyes light blue, with a brown spot in one which, though a defect, takes nothing away from her beauty of expression. Her eyebrows and hair are dark, and her complexion coarse. Her expression is strongly marked, variable and interesting; her movements in common life ungraceful, her voice loud yet not disagreeable."

In supplement to this account, the pastel drawn by Johann Schmidt of Dresden in 1800, which Nelson liked so much that he was never parted from it, is in point. Schmidt's is the representation of an active woman, and the insignia of the Order of the Knights of Malta which she wore on her breast, conferred—at Nelson's request—by the Czar of Russia in his capacity as Grand Master for her services in the relief of that island, emphasises that her abilities were not merely those of the courtesan. Southey, on the whole not a sympathetic witness, went so far as to say of her that she was "a woman whose personal accomplishments have seldom been equalled".

It was Samuel Johnson who, in Emma's own day, remarked how uncommon was personal beauty among those in the humbler spheres of life. Wind and weather, incessant work, rough housing and coarse food may have made for toughness, but not for bloom. Beauty indeed was not often lasting even among those who had no anxieties, servants to wait upon them, and the best of food and drink, since indifferent medical skill, uncontrolled child-bearing and the ravages of the small-pox were all liable to take their toll. Emma Hardy, daughter of a smith of Neston, Cheshire, was one of those exceptions which make a mockery of rules. By the time she became hostess to Nelson she had already had a career of exceptional vicissitude and adventure. It had been a fairy-story which seemed to have ended happily, for she had been married to Hamilton seven years, and although the pair had had no children, these years had been, in other directions, a time of fulfilment.

Emma's only child hitherto had been the result of an affair which occurred when she had been living under the protection of Sir Harry Fetherstonehaugh at Up Park, a great estate on the Sussex Downs which still contains the lovely furnishings which she knew in her brief stay there.

M

Today's visitor may even see the polished dining-table on which she was said to have danced, in a state of nature, for the pleasure of Sir Harry and his friends.

Emma had first yielded her virtue to the persuasion of a sea officer. She had then gone from one occupation or owner to another until Sir Harry, for some reason which had never been satisfactorily explained, sent her home to Cheshire. While there, she sent such piteous letters to her friends in a higher walk of society that one of them gave her the means by which to return south to London. There she lived under the protection of Charles Greville, Sir William Hamilton's nephew. Greville had her educated, and even made some small provision for the babe she had left behind her in the north. Her mother, who went by the name of Mrs Cadogan, was henceforward her companion and adviser.

While on a visit to England, Hamilton, then a widower, met and admired her, and it was arranged that she and Mrs Cadogan should visit him at Naples. Greville, who was hoping to make a rich marriage, planned to sell his mistress to his uncle. Very difficult he found it, for Emma had become deeply attached to him, and would certainly have remained faithful had the young man wished it. The letters which unfold Emma's agony of mind may still be read. They present an instructive though not an edifying picture of the ways of eighteenth-century male society, and they do credit to at least one human heart. One of Emma's most notable characteristics was her abiding interest in her former lovers, however indifferently they had treated her.

Having at length made her his mistress, Hamilton proceeded to marry her in the course of his next visit home. It was ironic that it should have been Emma, not Greville, who made the rich marriage, and in fact, had the Hamiltons had children, Greville would have stood to lose much, for he was his uncle's heir. The pair soon returned to Naples, whose admiration Emma had already won both by her beauty and her talent for singing and posing in decorous classical attitudes. "*Damn* Mrs Siddons!" exclaimed Nelson after seeing one of her performances: and even Goethe, a less biassed judge, wrote that "in her, Hamilton finds the charm of all antiques, the fair profiles on Sicilian coins, the Apollo

Belvedere himself. . . ." The collector had gathered his
choicest piece. "A masterpiece of the arch-artist," was
Goethe's enthusiastic summing up.

For many years Emma had made Hamilton an admirable,
affectionate wife, and although he himself wrote that he
expected to be "superannuated", so great was the difference
in their ages, yet on both sides the marriage was satisfactory.
Sir William had given his wife position; for her part, she
graced his bed and board. Naples, from the Queen down-
ward, increasingly became her conquest. "Sir William,"
wrote a friend, "has lately got a piece of modernity which
will fatigue and exhaust him more than all the volcanoes and
antiquities in the Kingdom of Naples."

In such circumstances, it was not long before Emma
yielded to a wish to take part in politics. She had ample
opportunity to indulge her inclination, from her husband's
position, the Queen's partiality and her own skill with people
and languages. Emma was, indeed, a compound of what her
century knew as "Nature and Sensibility". Her best biographer, the late Walter Sichel, quoted a passage from
Byron's *Don Juan* which, as well as anything else, seems to
sum up her characteristics:

> *So well she acted all and every part*
> *By turns—with that vivacious versatility*
> *Which many people take for want of heart.*
> *They err—'tis merely what is called mobility.*

Emma was colourful, restless, and far more alive than those
poses, delineated by the many artists who persuaded her to
sit to them, would serve to indicate. Their renderings may
have been good as paintings, but in day-to-day life Emma's
was the poetry of motion. Indeed, Gillray's brutal cartoon,
showing her as a billowing creature bemoaning the departure
of Nelson on a mission at sea, leaving her to the "old
antique" and displaying a drawing of a nude in an attitude
suggestive of anything but classical restraint, is a whole-
some antidote to the sentimental confections by which she
was so often "immortalised", as her contemporaries would
have put it. Whatever Emma was, she was neither fool nor
victim. Like Nelson himself, she was sometimes over-

generous, and if she lacked his customary (though not invariable) cool judgment of fellow-creatures, yet the only woman she consistently and irreparably wronged was the one she might well have had most reason to fear, her rival, Fanny.

It was in fact an ironic situation which she expressed to Nelson very soon after they had met again, and before their intimacy developed. "I would not be a lukewarm friend for the world," she wrote to him in October 1799. "I cannot make friends with all, but the few friends I have, I would die for. . . . I told her Majesty we only wanted Lady Nelson to be the female *Tria juncta in Uno*, for we all love you, and yet all three differently and yet all equally, if you can make that out." Her Latin reference was to the motto of the Order of the Bath, worn both by Nelson and Hamilton. But neither such allusions, nor such emotional leaps into the sublime as were suggested by this letter, could have been understood by such a limited, virtuous and passive figure as the wife who was to be swept aside by the whirlwind.

"I hope one day to have the pleasure of introducing you to Lady Hamilton," wrote Nelson to Fanny on his arrival at Naples. "She is one of the *very* best women in this world. How few could have made the turn she has; she is an honour to her sex & a proof that even reputation may be regained, but I own it requires a great soul." Nor did he stop there: in a passage hitherto unpublished he added, "her Ladyship, if Josiah was to stay, would make something of him & with all his bluntness I am sure he likes Lady Hamilton more than any female. She would fashion him in six months in spite of himself.

"I believe Lady Hamilton intends writing you. May God Almighty bless you my dearest Fanny, and give us in due time a happy meeting. Should the King give me a peerage, I believe I need scarcely state the propriety of your going to Court. Don't mind the expense, money is trash, again God Almighty bless you, Ever your most affectionate Horatio Nelson."

Nelson, in his time, wrote more tactful letters than this.

II

The admiral's fortieth birthday was by far the most festive of his life. "The preparations of Lady Hamilton for celebrating . . . are enough to fill me with vanity," he wrote to Fanny. "Every ribbon, every button has '*Nelson*' etc. The whole service is marked '*H. N. Glorious 1st of August!*' Songs and Sonnetti are numerous beyond what I ever could deserve. I send the additional verse to 'God Save the King,' as I know you will sing it with pleasure. I cannot move on foot, or in a carriage, for the kindness of the populace; but good Lady H. preserves all the papers as the highest treat for you. . . . The more I think, the more I hear, the greater is my astonishment at the extent and good consequences of our Victory."

The additional verse referred to, attributed to a Mr Davenport, ran as follows:

> *Join we great Nelson's name*
> *First on the rolls of fame*
> *Him let us sing.*
> *Spread we his fame around,*
> *Honour of British ground,*
> *Who made Nile's shores resound,*
> *God Save the King!*

Whether Fanny sung this verse, or indeed any of the various songs composed in Nelson's honour by the Hamilton's prolific friend Cornelia Knight, is not recorded, but one immediate satisfaction she did enjoy. Abbott had put the finishing touches on his portrait, and it had been delivered to Roundwood. "The likeness is great," she wrote. "I am well satisfied with Abbott. It is my company, my sincere friend in your absence."

Nelson's successes moved his father—not usually an eloquent man—to the composition of an affecting letter to an old friend and neighbour. "My great and good son," he wrote to the Reverend Brian Allott, "went into the world without fortune, but with a heart replete with every moral and religious virtue: these have been his compass to steer by, and it has pleased God to be his shield in the day of battle, and to give success to his wishes to be of service to his country. His country seems sensible of his services, but should he ever meet with ingratitude, his scars will plead his cause: for at the siege of Bastia he lost an eye; at Teneriffe an arm; on the memorable 14th of February he received a severe blow on his body, which he still feels; and now a wound in his head. After all this you must allow his bloom of countenance must be faded, but the spirit beareth up yet as vigorous as ever. On the 29th of September he completed his fortieth year, cheerful, generous and good; fearing no evil, because he has done none; an honour to my grey hairs."

In addition to the immediate festivities—eighteen hundred guests were invited by the Hamiltons, and the occasion was marred only by the fact that Josiah, whose ship was in Naples, got offensively drunk—Nelson was in process of receiving those honours which, when they once began to flow, resembled a cascade. They included the peerage he had mentioned to Fanny, which was gazetted in November, and another gold medal from the King. Nelson became Baron of the Nile and of Burnham Thorpe. Some thought it an elevation too modest. Among them was Hood, who, on the strength of a conversation with Pitt, committed the indiscretion of mentioning to Fanny that he had an idea she would find herself a Viscountess. Even the quiet Maurice, who at the Minister's invitation found himself at a public dinner, felt that a mere barony was inadequate, though he was assured that the Admiralty could not do more, for the time at any rate. But in addition to the barony there was a pension of £2,000 a year from Parliament, for the admiral and the next two successors to the title; and the munificent gift from the East India Company, much of which Nelson promptly gave away among his immediate relations. There was another medal from his friend and prize agent, Alexander Davison, who made a general distribution throughout the fleet at a cost to himself of about two thousand pounds; there was a sword from the City of London; a diamond chelengk, or Plume of Triumph, and a rich pelisse from the Sultan of Turkey, the battle having been fought in waters where Turkey held at least nominal sovereignty; and diamond boxes from more than one monarch, including the Czar.

The chelengk long excited interest. Together with the scarlet pelisse, lined and enriched with sable, it is a principal feature of a portrait commissioned for the Sultan a few months later from the Neapolitan artist, Leonardo Guzzardi, replicas and variations of which soon proliferated. The decoration represented a hand with thirteen fingers covered with (indifferent) diamonds, allusive to the ships taken or attacked in the battle. The letter accompanying it stated that it was "a blaze of brilliants, crowned with a vibrating plumage, and a radiant star in the middle, turning on its centre by means of watch-work which winds up behind". It was a theatrical decoration which Nelson seems to have enjoyed, though a simple offering pleased him even more. This was a gold-headed sword and cane from the Island of Zante, whose inhabitants assured him that "had it not been for the Battle of the Nile, they could not have been liberated from French cruelty".

By contrast with these scintillating gifts, Hallowell of the *Swiftsure*, wishing to remind Nelson of his mortality, sent him a coffin made of part of *L'Orient's* main-mast, "that, when you are tired of Life, you may be buried in one of your own Trophies". Far from resenting this grim offering, Nelson had it placed upright against the bulkhead of his cabin, behind the chair on which he sat at dinner. It was only after repeated entreaties from Tom Allen that he allowed it to be removed below. He swore that no one else should use it, and as in due time he was buried inside it, he kept his word.

Official excuse for the bestowal of a barony only lay in the fact that Nelson was not a commander-in-chief, and that there was no precedent for bestowing a peerage of any kind upon so comparatively junior an officer. But, as Nelson's friends soon retorted, there was no precedent for such a victory, and Duncan had been made a Viscount for Camperdown, a less distinguished battle than the Nile.

Actually, whatever he himself may have been persuaded into thinking, Nelson was in fact splendidly rewarded. The Admiralty paid at least something for the French ships he had been forced to destroy; saw to it that Troubridge had his medal; attended to most of Nelson's recommendations, and even confirmed Josiah as a post-captain! Although

Nelson could run his eye down the Navy List and see other peers therein of but moderate professional abilities, his were days when the award of titles to serving officers was far more frequent than it ever has been since. There were fewer alternative distinctions. Indeed, he probably spoke from his heart when he wrote to Cornwallis, "my honours, my riches, the gifts of a gracious sovereign are beyond my deserts", and it was not until later that grumbles penetrated beyond the circle of his friends. They were not always those of a reasonable man, and there were none to remind him that Hawke had waited seventeen years for the peerage which should have been his after his great victory at Quiberon.

III

Though Naples was jubilant, affairs in Italy were favourable chiefly to the French. After the signing of the Treaty of Campo Formio in the previous year, the only sovereigns in the peninsula who had retained any degree of independence had been the Pope and Ferdinand. Their status was precarious.

Pius IV was the first victim of renewed French aggression. The death of the ambassador Duphot at the hands of pontifical troops, the result of a brawl, furnished excuse for intervention. In February 1798, Berthier had entered Rome without serious opposition and established a Republic, the aged Pope being deposed and taken to France. Henceforward, a French army was within a few days' march of the Neapolitan border. Menacing claims were soon made by the Republic to suzerainty over the two Sicilies, and to control of Ferdinand's ministers and policy. Ferdinand defied the threat, moved troops towards the frontier, and renewed his persecution of those in Naples who professed liberal views.

Nelson's arrival gave the King the stimulus he needed to attack the French; the Queen needed none. Negotiations were in train for a new Coalition against France, which would include Britain, Russia and Austria as formal allies. It was Nelson's opinion that there was no time like the present; Ferdinand should either "advance, trusting to God for his blessings in a just cause . . . or remain quiet and be kicked out of his dominions". Ferdinand, at first pacifically inclined, at length decided to become a hero after the Nelson pattern. His army would be led by an experienced Austrian general, Mack, who arrived early in October. The Hooligan King would become Ferdinand Victorious.

Nelson's advice did not conflict with his orders from home, for the Admiralty sent directions to St Vincent that the duties of the squadron employed in the Mediterranean were to protect the coasts of Italy, and in the event of war becoming active, to co-operate with the Austrian and Neapolitan armies. Communications between France and Egypt were to be severed; Malta was to be blockaded, and liaison was to be established with the Turkish and Russian squadrons whose help, it was anticipated, would soon be added to that of the Portuguese. Every one of these aims was now to be implemented, though Nelson, with long and bitter experience of Continental generals, was alarmed to perceive that Mack could not move without an inordinate amount of personal baggage. He soon doubted whether the man knew his business. Moreover, he had no illusions as to the quality of Neapolitan leadership. The Ministry would order whatever he suggested; execution was dilatory or not attempted. "The miserable conduct of this Court is not likely to cool my irritable temper," he wrote to St Vincent. "It is a country of fiddlers and poets, whores and scoundrels." Less than a week later he added; "This Country with its system of procrastination will ruin itself: the Queen sees it, and thinks as we do. The Ministry, except Acton, are for putting off the evil day, when it will come with destruction. War at this moment can alone save these Kingdoms." His letter, dated 4th October, ended with the significant comment, "I am writing opposite Lady Hamilton, therefore you will not be surprised at the glorious jumble of this letter. Were your Lordship in my place, I much doubt if you could write so well; our hearts and our heads must be all in a flutter: Naples is a dangerous place, and we must keep clear of it." Events were about to speed him away.

On 14th October he sailed for Malta with four ships of

the line, saw to his satisfaction that the Maltese, who were fighting under joint Neapolitan and British colours, were in good heart, received the surrender of the nearby island of Gozo, and encouraged Ball in his long and protracted campaign against the French commandant, Vaubois, who was to hold out at Valetta for many more months on very little food.

By 23rd November Mack and the Neapolitan army, urged on by Ferdinand, had crossed the frontier in five columns, while Nelson embarked four thousand men aboard the British fleet and sailed north-west to seize Leghorn and cut the French communications, Tuscan neutrality being blandly disregarded.

Success was immediate, though brief. The French withdrew from Rome to Civita Castellana, leaving a small garrison in the Castle of St Angelo. On 29th November Ferdinand entered the Eternal City with appropriate pomp. But his troops showed no eagerness in fighting, allowing themselves to be separated, and then defeated in detail. On 7th December the King left the city; the retreat of the Neapolitans soon became a rout, and Ferdinand had not long been back in his capital before the enemy turned the tables on him by crossing his frontiers. "If Mack is defeated," said Nelson, "in fourteen days this country is lost, for the Emperor has not yet moved his army, and Naples has not the power of resisting the enemy."

In the event, Mack made a poor show of leadership; as for the Neapolitans, "the officers did not lose much honour," said Nelson bitterly, "for God knows they had not much to lose—but they lost all they had." The general who commanded their right wing, 19,000 men strong, fell in with about 3,000 of the enemy. As soon as he was near enough to establish contact, he deserted. One of his sergeants had virtue enough to shoot him in the arm, but even this did not deter him from joining in the chase of his own side. By 18th December Mack appeared at Court with the news that nothing could stop a general French advance, and that the best hope of safety for the royal family lay in flight to Sicily, under Nelson's protection. The white bird of good omen which had fluttered about the *Vanguard* after the Nile had now flown away, and however passionately Nelson might exclaim *Down, down with the French!* and urge that every opportunity be seized to attack them, yet, on land at any rate, the day of their ascendancy would long remain.

Nelson's advice had been a blunder. Ferdinand's fate was to be similar to that of his brother monarch, the King of Sardinia, who was to be driven from his territories in Piedmont to his island refuge, also under British escort. As Nelson had been the instrument of misfortune, he felt himself in honour bound to secure the royal escape, and to devote himself henceforward to the protection of the Court. It was his expiation.

Escape was not easy. As the French began to advance, the *lazzaroni* prepared to give them their first taste of real fighting. Simultaneously, the Francophile element at the Court, headed by the Marquis de Gallo, whom Nelson detested, were so active that they even formed a plan of seizing Nelson and the Hamiltons as hostages.

Meanwhile, with secrecy and speed, Lady Hamilton and Nelson made every necessary arrangement for the removal of the royal family, and of a treasure estimated at two and a half millions sterling. British merchants and their stocks were also embarked on men-of-war and in transports. There was a subterranean passage from the palace to the shore, which was guarded by seamen armed with cutlasses, under Nelson's personal direction. By the night of 21st December, the *Vanguard* was fully laden. Two days later, she sailed for Sicily.

Secrecy had been most necessary, for the *lazzaroni* believed that they could save Naples, and were insistent that the monarch to whom they were so attached should not desert them. The Queen had vivid memories of the arrest of the flight of her sister to Varennes, and of the fatal consequences. "Once aboard the British flagship," said Nelson, "not a word of uneasiness escaped the lips of any of the Royal Family."

Within a day of the fleet leaving Naples bay, such a storm arose as even the admiral, in his long experience, had never before encountered. The *Vanguard*, weakened by her hard service, was in some danger of foundering, and the congestion on board, including many land-lubbers, taxed the seamen's endurance to the full. Many were soon laid low with sea-sickness, and at one stage Sir William Hamilton was found in his cabin with a pistol in each hand, determined to blow his brains out rather than experience the "guggle, guggle, guggle of salt water in his throat". His wife, active and stout-hearted, attended night and day upon the royal children. Throughout the voyage to Palermo she was tireless in attendance, "nor did her Ladyship enter a bed the whole time they were aboard", reported Nelson. Yet even her incessant care could not prevent the youngest royal child from dying in her arms on the second day out.

A nightmare voyage ended early in the morning of 26th December. "At 9 a.m. His Majesty went on shore," wrote Nelson to St Vincent, "and was received with the loudest acclamations and apparent joy." Not a soul on board seems to have cared that Christmas Day had come and gone without observance. Certainly there had been no appetite for feasting.

No sooner had Nelson arrived at Palermo than he had a fresh annoyance. Captain Sir Sidney Smith had been charged with naval command in the Levant, besides exercising diplomatic powers in that area, jointly with his civilian brother Spencer. He announced his advent to Nelson in the highfaluting terms which were his natural mode of expression. It was exactly the kind of situation to wound Nelson's feelings, and he sent a spate of letters of complaint to St Vincent, one of them on 31st December beginning: "*I do feel, for I am a man*, that it is impossible for me to serve in these Seas, with a Squadron under a junior Officer." St Vincent, as so often, was wholly sympathetic at the difficulties in which Nelson found himself. He understood his indignation, and promised that so far as he, St Vincent, was concerned, Smith should in no way interfere with existing dispositions.

It was an odd trick of fate that caused the man whom Nelson called "the Swedish knight" to cross his path at this particular moment. For Sir Sidney—he held the Order of the Sword of Sweden—was a histrionic creature a little after Nelson's own style, and, like Nelson, he could perform as

well as talk. Even Lord Spencer, in despatching him eastwards, had realised that "there might be some prejudices"
against him in the fleet, but he was the sort of man who could
always argue his way into important missions, and this was
exactly what he had now done. After some acid letters from
Nelson, and effusive assurances from Smith, the latter sailed
to the Levant, there to gain a stirring success against Bonaparte at the defence of Acre. Smith, in fact, became the first
Englishman to defeat Bonaparte ashore, which was something to boast about.

"Knowing your magnanimity," wrote St Vincent to
Nelson, "I am sure you will mortify him as little as possible,
consistently with what is due to the great characters senior
to him on the List, and his superiors in every sense of the
word." Nelson did his best to obey the injunction, and in
the end the Swedish Knight even persuaded himself that
Nelson had forgiven him for being sent to operate in an area
in which he might have occasion to give orders to Samuel
Hood and others among the veteran Nilers. "I should not
(if I am not greatly mistaken in my ideas of the gallant Hero
of the Nile) be surprised to see my brother his flag-captain,
if they ever served three months together": such was the
view of Spencer Smith, expressed to Sir William Hamilton.

Hamilton escaped the "guggle, guggle" in his throat
which he so dreaded, but flight to Palermo brought him loss
and misfortune. He had caused the pick of his classical vases
to be sent to England in a transport. While sheltering in
Scilly Roads, the ship dragged her anchor, and sunk in deep
water near the shore. Charles Greville was enjoined to save
what he could, and some months later a few cases were
salvaged from the wreck.

IV

If the matters of state in which he was now involved
brought Nelson little but disappointment, his personal
affairs were also in curious case, and were beginning to cause
anxiety to his friends. He made no secret to Fanny of what

he felt he owed to the Hamiltons, without whose support he would have pressed to go home, leaving the direction of affairs to his trusted friend Troubridge. "Lady Hamilton's goodness forces me out at noon for an hour," he wrote to his wife, shortly before the passage to Sicily. "What can I say of hers and Sir William's attention to me? They are, in fact, with the exception of you and my good father, the dearest friends I have in this world. I live as Sir William's son in the house, and my glory is as dear to them as their own; in short, I am under such obligations, as I can never repay but with my eternal gratitude. The improvement made in Josiah by Lady Hamilton is wonderful; your obligations and mine are infinite on that score." Feeling that he had perhaps again advanced a shade beyond the frontiers of tact in writing thus to a mother, he added, "not but Josiah's heart is as good and humane as ever was covered by a human breast."

Josiah's conduct had so improved that Nelson felt able to arrange for him to take the Turkish ambassador to Constantinople in his sloop; but, in the upshot, the trust was not justified. Apart from his liking for the bottle, the young man was unfitted for the ardours and loneliness of naval command, and in a letter to Fanny of January 1799, Nelson said: "I wish I could say much to your and my satisfaction about Josiah, but I am sorry to say and with real grief that he has nothing good about him, and must sooner or later be broke, but I am sure neither you or I can help it. I have done with the subject, it is an ungrateful one."

Nelson's second thoughts were right. So far as Josiah's service career was concerned, he did little good after his promotion. Although he conducted his mission to Turkey without trouble, and in March 1799 was posted to the frigate *Thalia*, his activities ceased soon after the turn of the century. In later life he discovered some talent for making money, and became affluent. Nelson put immediate troubles down to the fact that he had spoilt him, and this may well have been the truth.

Sir Harris Nicolas dates the beginning of Nelson's increasing irritability, even towards his best friends, from the ending of the year which had seen his universal fame. His temper was not eased by the fact that he heard so little from home. He wrote to his parson brother William on 2nd January 1799, to say that he had only had one letter from Fanny, besides the note from William which he was answering, since the arrival of Captain Capel in London with the Nile despatches, though if one thing is more certain than another it is that Fanny was an attentive correspondent. The regularity of the postal service was in fact far in the future, and war did nothing to ease communications.

In the uncomfortable winter months at Palermo, Nelson had more time than usual to reflect, and his thoughts were not pleasant. He wrote to Admiral Goodall that he did not feel he had long to live, and to Lady Parker: "You who remember me always laughing and gay, would hardly believe the change, but who can see what I have and be in health?" And if the first Italianate picture by Guzzardi dates from this time, so, too, does a far more illuminating pencil portrait by Charles Grignion, an English artist resident in Italy. Grignion depicted a weary man who, so far from displaying the star of the Bath of which he was usually so proud, seemed indifferent as to whether it was seen or not.

v

In Naples, the struggle was continued by the stout-hearted *lazzaroni* until the end of January 1799, when the French, aided by the liberal aristocracy and the middle classes, established what was called the Vesuvian or Parthenopian Republic. It was in no sense a popular revolution, less so in the provinces even than in Naples. It rested mainly upon the strength of French arms, a fact which was soon clear to the Court at Palermo.

The first form of attack on the new dispensation was the despatch of an agent to Calabria, to excite a peasant rising. The man commissioned to lead this enterprise was Cardinal Fabrizio Ruffo. His family owned big estates in Calabria, and his personal following, once it could be assembled, was equal to a small army.

Ruffo was one of the few capable men upon whose loyalty

Ferdinand could rely, though in other respects he had the complexity of mind which seems to have belonged to many who have adorned his holy office, and his interests ranged from the habits of pigeons to infantry drill. His authority was in wide terms: it included powers of life and death, and a great measure of political discretion. In February he landed on the beach of La Catona near Bagnara, without money and without arms, on what must have seemed, to anyone less familiar than he was himself with the nature of those to whom he was about to appeal, a forlorn venture.

His success was startling. Three hundred recruits from among his family's vassals quickly rallied to him. Within a few months he had spread the flame far and wide. He allied himself with other partisans, drawn from more doubtful sources, including the jails, and soon a White Terror was established throughout Southern Italy which presented the waverer with a grim alternative to such persuasion as was offered by the Jacobins, and which showed no mercy whatever to the collaborator.

The final development which cheered the Court was that war had at last broken out between France and Austria, that 120,000 Austrian and Russian troops were on their way to Italy under Suvarov, and that General Sir Charles Stuart, with commendable initiative, had landed a small force of British troops to help in the fortification of Sicily. Stuart was Nelson's old acquaintance of Corsica. He had just been made a Knight of the Bath for the capture of Minorca from 3,700 Spaniards without the loss of a man. Nelson wrote to St Vincent: "he has probably, by his quick decision, not only saved this Kingdom, but may be the instrument of driving the French out of Naples. It will be an electric shock both to good and bad subjects." Stuart's own opinion was that Sicily could best be helped by ousting an administration in which the islanders themselves were scarcely represented.

Troubridge, like Ruffo, had early success, and the islands of Procida and Ischia, which command the western entrance to the Gulf of Naples, were soon in his hands. He found that the character of the inhabitants took some getting used to. "I have a villain by name Francesco on board," he wrote to

Nelson, "who commanded the castle at Ischia, formerly a Neapolitan officer, and of property in that Island. The moment we took possession of the castle, the mob tore this vagabond's coat with the tricoloured cape and cap of liberty button to pieces, and he then had the impudence to put on his Sicilian Majesty's regimentals again; upon which I tore his epaulette off, took his cockade out, and obliged him to throw them overboard; I then honoured him with double irons."

Nelson, delighted at such vigour, replied that he was sending Troubridge some soldiers and a Judge. "Send me word some proper heads are taken off," he wrote: "this alone will comfort me. . . ." It was not said in jest. "I ever preach," he wrote to the Duke of Clarence, "that rewards and punishments are the foundation of all good Government." Troubridge agreed. Indeed, he told a Neapolitan general who would not fight for his King that Ferdinand would never do well until he had hanged half his officers, though when he managed to infuse zeal for service into what was so often indifferent material the results were sometimes embarrassing. "Sir," wrote a Neapolitan to him from Salerno, "as a faithful subject of my King, Ferdinand IV (whom God preserve) I have the glory of presenting to Your Excellency the head of D. Charles Granozio di Giffoni, who was employed in the Administration. . . . The said Granozio was killed by me . . . as he was running away, I beg Your Excellency would accept the said head, and consider this operation as a proof of my attachment to the Royal Crown."

It was against such a bizarre background that Nelson's much criticised conduct in the Bay of Naples had to be considered. Political opinions of a liberal kind, such as moved his biographer Southey to rebuke his illustrious subject, seldom touched Nelson. His humanity was personal, not general. He believed passionately in the war he was fighting. "It is their infernal principles I dread, not their prowess," he said of the French. He was not merely exercising his professional skill, as were so many of his contemporaries. He believed, further, in the *status quo*, however gross might be its defects, and he saw affairs in terms of black and white. His own side, for all practical purposes, was garbed in

N

unsullied vesture, and it was soon apparent that he regarded revolted Neapolitans, whatever their circumstances or temptations, like so many mutinous seamen. They were to be treated accordingly, and his own verdict on that subject had long been given to St Vincent. He would have hanged such men even on Christmas Day. "I own myself, my dear Lord," he wrote to his Commander-in-Chief, "much fitter to be the actor, than the counsellor of proper measures to be pursued, in this very critical situation of public affairs."

While events were ripening for a reappearance of the Bourbons at Naples, the situation was complicated in May by the entry of a French squadron into the Mediterranean. The enemy had in fact made for Toulon, with St Vincent and George Elphinstone (now Lord Keith) in pursuit. Nelson was for some time unaware of this development, news reaching him merely that the Brest fleet had been sighted off Oporto, and that its destination was thought to be Malta and Alexandria. He decided that his most favourable course was to cruise to westward of Sicily.

"I do not forget for a moment that they [the Bourbon Family] are in my *charge*," he wrote to Sir William Hamilton from sea on 27th May, adding, "I have not been free from head-ache, sickness and with want of rest, for I know not what sleep is since I left Palermo. I have given notice to my squadron that if I am asked to blockade Toulon that my health will not allow it and I will give up."

The current rumours had put the Neapolitan Court into a flurry, for the belief was that the French, if they succeeded in withdrawing their troops from Egypt, would attack Sicily. Nelson ordered Troubridge to concentrate the greater part of his squadron, which it was his intention should be employed as St Vincent might direct. It was some time before the exact disposition of the enemy was known to him: the main force was actually at Toulon, and a subsidiary Spanish fleet, which had slipped out of Cadiz, at Cartagena. When Nelson knew for certain that the opposition was thus divided, he returned to Palermo, where he could cover both Sicily and the blockade of Naples. Meanwhile the Neapolitan Jacobins were looking westward, hopefully, in the expectation that a combined Franco-Spanish fleet would release

them from pressure by land and sea and ensure the continuance of the Parthenopean Republic.

On 5th June a small squadron of reinforcement reached
Palermo, under Rear-Admiral John Duckworth. Among the
four ships of the line was the new Plymouth-built 80-gun
Foudroyant, to which Nelson shifted his flag from the battered
Vanguard. The *Foudroyant* was in fact so stout that she was
afloat for a century. Nelson's flag was now that of a Rear-
Admiral of the Red, for in a large general promotion dating
from the previous February he had skipped the section of
the junior flag list devoted to the White Squadron.

It was probably the arrival of Duckworth's force, added
to the continual pressure put upon him by the Queen
through her friend Lady Hamilton, which determined him
to go to Naples. This was not an easy decision, for Nelson's
first duty was not to restore the Bourbons but to keep his
force in the best position to reach St Vincent quickly at his
rendezvous at Minorca, or to damage the enemy if they
made towards Malta and Egypt. This could best be done
from Sicily. He told St Vincent that he expected merely to
put in an appearance at Naples, and that he did not intend
to risk a mast of his squadron. He embarked the Hereditary
Prince as official cover for his operations.

The coast-line had hardly disappeared when two seventy-
fours were sighted. They proved to be the *Bellerophon* and
the *Powerful*. They had been sent by Lord Keith, who was
about to supersede St Vincent as Commander-in-Chief, and
who was already known to Nelson from his gallant service
at Toulon nearly six years before. The news was that it was
believed the French were bound for Naples, but that an east
wind had prevented Keith from following them to make
certain. Nelson's squadron was too weak to engage the
enemy with any chance of success, so he stood back for
Palermo, where he arrived, to the consternation of the
Court, on the morning of the 14th June. There he landed
the Prince, got under way again with only a short delay, and
proceeded to the island of Maritimo, westward of Sicily,
where he proposed to await such further reinforcements as
would enable him to go in search of the enemy. Then, so he
told Keith, "not one moment shall be lost in bringing them

to battle, for I consider the best defence for his Sicilian Majesty's dominions is to place myself alongside the French."

It was at this point that the Court heard that Ruffo, then investing Naples, was in negotiation with the rebels as well as with the French. Unconditional surrender on the part of his refractory subjects was a matter upon which the King felt strongly and the Queen tempestuously. A message was sent to Nelson, via Sir William Hamilton, urging him to fulfil his promise to appear with his squadron before Naples.

The receipt of this letter placed Nelson in a trying position. "To fight is nothing," he told Hamilton, "but to be continually on the stretch for news and events of the greatest importance is what I find my shattered carcase very unequal to." He had to decide whether he was justified in abandoning a strong position, in which he covered both Sicily and the way to Malta and Egypt, for the purpose of bringing matters to a conclusion at Naples. His mental anguish was considerable, but he decided at length to risk all on one throw, and to sail at once with his squadron on the King's errand. "I am full of grief and anxiety," he wrote to Hamilton. "I must go. It will finish the war. It will give a sprig of laurel to your affectionate friend Nelson." His own belief differed from that of Keith as to the French admiral's intentions.

He returned to Palermo, and was there authorised to summon the forts which commanded Naples to immediate surrender. If this was declined, he was given full liberty to take them by storm. He embarked Sir William and Lady Hamilton as intermediaries and interpreters, and proceeded northwards in a very bad temper, saying to a messenger from Naples who reached the flagship in a light vessel: "Tell the people on shore when you return that I will batter down their city."

Sir William, who had found being with the fleet "stealing on with light winds" a pleasant experience, told the messenger privately not to repeat Nelson's remark, adding: "I hope he will be calmer tomorrow, and think differently"; for her part, Lady Hamilton did her experienced best to soothe the admiral's agitation. He had made his first decision between love and duty—for there is no question that, without the

indirect pressure of the Queen through Emma Hamilton,
he would have kept his station off Maritimo—but his professional instincts warned him that his true direction might
not be that in which his ships were heading. This was, in
fact, one of the crises of his life; much of the future would
be affected by his choice. The dilemma, painfully resolved,
not only altered the course of events in Naples, but caused
Nelson's relations with Keith, never likely to be easy, to
deteriorate very seriously. Nelson had begun to put himself
in the wrong, and it was never his way to do things by halves.
His dependence upon Lady Hamilton was already beginning
to be general talk, and as early as May 1799 he made the
first of many codicils to his will in her favour, leaving her a
gold box set with diamonds "as a token of regard and respect
for her every eminent virtue (for she possesses them all to
such a degree that it would be doing her injustice was any
particular one to be mentioned)".

VI

The affairs in Naples consequent upon Nelson's arrival
were of such complication that they produced a barbed
library of controversy. The salient facts were that when
Nelson's squadron, seventeen strong, was within easy sail of
the town, news was received in the flagship, not very accurate
in its details, that an armistice had been granted by Ruffo to
the Jacobins for twenty-one days, at the end of which time
they were to evacuate the castles of Uovo and Nuovo, which
they held, and were to be taken to France if the Combined
Fleet had not, meanwhile, come to their relief.

Nelson at once committed his own views on the subject to
paper. He reasoned that an armistice was an agreement
determinable at the option of either party on due notice
being given, adding that in this instance it was clearly
intended that the arrangements should cease to be valid on
the arrival of reinforcements to either side. He therefore
proposed that a declaration in the joint names of Ruffo and
himself should be sent both to the French, who occupied the

castle of St Elmo, and to the Jacobins, annulling the agreement. The French should be given two hours in which to leave the fort, whereupon they would be sent to France, "without the stipulation of their being prisoners of war". As for the Jacobins, "rebels and traitors" as Nelson termed them, "no power on earth has a right to stand between their gracious king and them; they must instantly throw themselves on the clemency of their sovereign, for no other terms will be allowed them, nor will the French be allowed even to name them in any Capitulation".

On the morning of 24th June the British ships passed the straits which separate the island of Capri from the mainland, and stood into the Bay of Naples. Their appearance was quite unexpected, except by Ruffo. It was hailed with delight by the royalists, whilst the Jacobins in the castles, who had at first believed that it was the Combined Fleet coming to their succour, gave vent to their feelings by tearing up their handkerchiefs and showing other signs of mortification.

As the flagship drew nearer to the city, Nelson and the Hamiltons saw that the white flag was flying from the castles of Uovo and Nuovo, and also on board the familiar frigate *Seahorse*, whose captain, Edward Foote, had been left in charge of operations in the absence of Troubridge. The admiral at once signalled to Foote that the truce was at an end. Shortly afterwards he received copies of a French and rebel capitulation which had been agreed by the Cardinal and Foote, and by the representative of the Russian and Turkish forces then operating against the city.

A formal capitulation was a very different matter from an armistice, and when Nelson realised its terms, it did nothing to ease his state of mind. In consideration of the delivery of the Castles of Uovo and Nuovo to the allied forces, the Neapolitan Jacobins were to march out with all the honours of war, their property was to be respected, and they were to be given the choice of embarking under safeguard to Toulon, or of remaining at Naples "without being molested either in their persons or families". The terms were subject to the approval of the French commandant of the Fort of St Elmo, which had in fact been given. Such terms would have been generous to a distinguished enemy; to "rebels and traitors" they seemed to Nelson to go beyond all reasonable concession. He noted with approval that although Foote had signed the document, he had returned it with a protest against anything that might be contrary to British interests. Nelson described the whole affair as infamous.

Troubridge and Ball, the most trusted of his captains, were promptly sent to Ruffo by Nelson to explain his views. The discussion was so heated that nothing was agreed upon except that the French in St Elmo should be summoned to surrender within the space of two hours.

At a second interview, equally abortive, Ruffo flatly refused to send a document to the Jacobin castles in the following terms "Rear-Admiral Lord Nelson, K.B., Commander of his Britannic Majesty's fleet in the Bay of Naples, acquaints the rebellious subjects of his Sicilian Majesty's in the castles of Uovo and Nuovo that he will not permit them to embark or quit those places. They must surrender themselves to His Majesty's royal mercy." Ruffo said that he had concluded the capitulation "as best he could do in his weak state, to save the city of Naples from destruction" and that he could not repudiate what he had signed. He admitted that Nelson was under no obligation to respect the treaty, and could do "what he thought best for the king's service". Troubridge then put the plain question: "If Lord Nelson breaks the armistice, will your Eminence assist him in his attack with men or guns?" Ruffo gave the only possible answer: "I will neither assist him with men or with guns."

On the afternoon of 25th June, in accordance with an arrangement made by Ball and Troubridge, Ruffo visited Nelson on board the *Foudroyant*, the Hamilton's acting as interpreters. The result was another long and profitless discussion. "Nothing but my phlegm," wrote Hamilton afterwards to Greville, "could have prevented an open rupture on the first meeting between Cardinal Ruffo and Lord Nelson. Lord Nelson is so accustomed to dealings fair & open, that he has no patience when he meets with the contrary, which one must always expect when one has to deal with Italians &, perhaps, His Eminency is the very quintessence of Italian finesse." Nelson's own verdict was simpler. "An admiral is no match in talking with a Cardinal." He committed his view to writing, in a few lines. "Rear-Admiral Lord Nelson arrived with the British fleet the 24th of June in the Bay of Naples, and found a Treaty entered into with the rebels, which, in his opinion, cannot be carried into execution without the approbation of his Sicilian Majesty." The most satisfactory result of the meeting was that Ruffo promised that he would let the garrisons of all three castles know that he could not answer for Lord Nelson's allowing the armistice to continue.

Ruffo not only kept his word, but during the course of the next twenty-four hours Nelson's own mood softened. It is likely that, on reflection, he realised that Ruffo had as firm an idea of honour as he had himself. No doubt Sir William had meanwhile explained some of the intricacies of life in an occupied city. The upshot was that the Jacobins were allowed to withdraw from their castles and to embark in a number of polaccas which were lying in the harbour; Ruffo accepted the help of 1,500 marines to operate against St Elmo, about which he had previously made difficulties; finally, at an early hour on 26th June, Hamilton wrote to Ruffo, by Nelson's direction, saying that the admiral had decided to do nothing which might break the armistice. The same afternoon a force under Troubridge occupied Uovo and Nuovo. Next day, Ruffo attended at a celebration of the *Te Deum* in the church of the Carmine, and wrote letters of thanks to Nelson and Hamilton expressing his gratitude to them for rescuing him from an unpleasant predicament.

Such a reversal of affairs was too good to last.

VII

In treating with the Jacobins at all, Ruffo had in fact exceeded his authority, and on the morning of 28th June letters arrived from Palermo which left no doubt as to the Royal feelings. Nelson, who had been given what Hamilton described as "full powers", was advised by the Queen, through Emma, "to treat Naples as if it were a rebellious Irish town". She recommended that an example should be

made of some of the leaders, and stated it as her view that
"our future tranquillity and position" depended upon "the
greatest firmness, vigour and severity". Nelson was enjoined
to repeat what he had already told the Cardinal, that the
Jacobins were to have "no conditions." The first effect of these
instructions was that the polaccas were seized by armed boats,
and were moved under the guns of the British men-of-war.

Ruffo's answer was to refuse to take any further part in
the measures then being planned for the reduction of St
Elmo. He even threatened to withdraw his forces altogether,
and his attitude was such that Nelson and Hamilton contemplated his arrest, for which extreme measure they had
the King's warrant. Fortunately, both parties showed restraint in a situation of increasing tension.

Nelson urged the King to return speedily to Naples. His
letter on the subject to Acton (addressed by Emma, and
dated 29th June), stressed the value of the sovereign's
physical presence, but underlined the Queen's name three
times and Acton's once—effectively showing the relative
value Nelson placed upon their energies. The same day he
issued a printed notice in Italian, giving civil and military
officers in Naples who had served the Republic twenty-four
hours in which to give themselves up to the royal clemency.
Those living outside Naples had a further day's grace.

Before the King's arrival, Ruffo unbent sufficiently to
renew his promise of help in the defeat of St Elmo, and to
accept the hospitality of the flagship. On 10th July the
burden of responsibility was lifted from British shoulders,
for the King appeared in a frigate. An appalling series of
judicial executions then began, which horrified the conscience of Europe. They were a fitting continuation to that
of Caracciolo. This, a direct consequence of Nelson's intervention, was the most macabre incident by which his
appearance in Naples is remembered.

Admiral Prince Francesco Caracciolo was known to
Nelson from earlier service in the Mediterranean with the
British fleet. He was a man of forty-seven, esteemed by
many of his countrymen. On the day that the polaccas were
moved to their new position Caracciolo, who had taken an
active part in the maritime affairs of the Republic, and who

had fled from the city in disguise, was seized and brought on board the *Foudroyant*. He was bound, and was in an exhausted condition. Captain Hardy, who remembered him well, treated him with courtesy, and ordered him to be received as an officer. Nelson, with the Queen's letter before him pointing to the value of severe example, at once ordered Count Thurn to assemble a court-martial of Neapolitans. Caracciolo was then summarily tried, without benefit of witnesses or counsel. His plea that he hoped that a lifetime of service might weigh against a few days of aberration was disallowed. He was condemned—the result was a foregone conclusion—and was hanged the same day at the yard-arm of a Sicilian frigate, his request that he might have a death more becoming to a nobleman being disregarded. His body was later cut down.

Harsh, even brutal as was his fate, it was merciful compared with that of the many condemned to linger, before going to the scaffold, in the miseries of a Neapolitan prison. Ferdinand had a fright when, later, he saw Caracciolo's corpse rise from the water and appear to bobble towards him. He was not much comforted by the jest that the admiral had risen to ask his Majesty's forgiveness.

Nelson has been arraigned on two serious charges in connection with the restoration of the monarchy at Naples. The first was for his unwillingness to honour a capitulation which had been signed by one of his own subordinates; the second, that he showed excessive harshness to Caracciolo. Yet he himself never doubted that he had acted rightly; his conduct was approved in generous terms by the Admiralty; and he put on record, not in connection with rebellious subjects but of established enemies, that, had he been Commander-in-Chief at the time, he would have refused to ratify a solemn agreement made by Sir Sidney Smith in Egypt, by which the French were allowed to leave the country with the honours of war. Smith had disobeyed Nelson's express direction "never to give any French ship or man leave to quit Egypt", and even Lord Keith, a very different type of officer, found himself so much in agreement with Nelson over Smith's treaty that he refused to honour it until the matter had been referred to the home government. The case of Ruffo was even simpler. He had not disobeyed his instructions, he had exceeded them, and caused his allies to do the same. The action, in Nelson's view, was *ultra vires*.

Nelson needed no telling what the French would have done had the situation been reversed in their favour. He had had experience of Bonaparte, who in flagrant defiance of arrangements made with Nelson through subordinates after the Nile had used the prisoners Nelson had landed in Egypt as the nucleus of "maritime battalions".

As for harshness, there was an entry in the log of the *Foudroyant*, under the day preceding Ferdinand's return, which refers to a court-martial, as a result of which two seamen of the British squadron were condemned to 250 and 50 lashes respectively for breaking into and looting the quarters of an officer of one of Ruffo's Calabrian units. The first sentence was so frightful in its severity, having in mind the nature of the naval cat-o'-nine-tails, that no Neapolitan sadist could have exceeded it; while even the second was one to which a quick death might have seemed a happy alternative. Two days earlier a marine, John Jolly by name, had been sentenced to death for striking and threatening to shoot his superior officer.

In Jolly's case Nelson acted somewhat as he had done in the case of the desertion of Able Seaman Clark in the West Indies twelve years before. He instructed Troubridge to "prepare everything for the execution of the sentence of the Court Martial held on John Jolly; but when all the forms, except the last, are gone through, you will acquaint the prisoner, that, although there has been no circumstance to mitigate the severity of the law, yet that I have reason to hope that the sparing of his life will have as beneficial an effect for the discipline of the Service, as if he had suffered death, you will therefore respite the prisoner from the sentence of death, till his Majesty's pleasure is known". Unlike Clark, Jolly was not given the chance of discharge from his Majesty's service, for this time Nelson did not make the error of formally "pardoning" him. An official pardon came later.

Troubridge soon had more congenial occupation than unsatisfactory interviews with ecclesiasts and the punishment of marines. It was he who, with a land force which included Russians and Calabrians, obtained the surrender of St Elmo, close upon the King's return, after the French commandant had vainly tried to sell him the place in consideration of 150,000 ducats. He afterwards continued his able work in command of a still larger body which, operating inland, secured the reduction of Capua, the principal stronghold remaining in enemy hands. Nelson by sea and Troubridge ashore had succeeded in making the Bourbon restoration temporarily secure.

On 5th August Nelson terminated his visit to Naples, sailing to Palermo with the King as his guest. He had spent six extraordinary weeks in that bay, by nature so favoured, to which no persuasion could make Ferdinand return, at a time when his continued presence was necessary to the well-being of his own affairs. That they deteriorated was only to be expected. No city could be envied or secure which was subject to a White Terror, least of all when the Fountain of Clemency removed itself to enjoy the irresponsibilities of the chase.

VIII

Nelson's conduct at Naples in support of the reactionary government which he served but did not respect was, as an example, shockingly unfortunate. Ferdinand had succeeded in making a tool of the illustrious admiral for serving his own narrow vengeance. While the King could now hunt and idle the months away at Palermo, the gallows and jails of Naples would create martyrs, and much of the odium for their suffering would be remembered against the British fleet. Nelson had not merely been used successfully, he made no serious effort to urge a policy of conciliation, and treated the political affairs of Ferdinand's mainland capital, once kingly authority was restored, with the indifference he may by then have felt.

Whatever else he may have been, it is not as a liberal zealot that Nelson has gone down to history. He was born in the mid-eighteenth century, in the county of the Walpoles. Oligarchy was in his blood, and tyranny he understood: he would remain ignorant of the enlightenments of democracy, as unfolded during the course of the nineteenth century, and it would be his friend Prince William Henry who would be styled by his future subjects (quite against his desire or expectation) "the Reform Monarch of England".

"The common English traveller," wrote Ruskin many years later, "if he can gather a black bunch of grapes with his own fingers, and have his bottle of Falernian brought him by a girl with black eyes, asks no more of this world, nor the next, and declares Naples a paradise. But I knew, from the first moment when my foot furrowed volcanic ashes, that no mountain form or colour could exist in perfection where everything was made of scoria, and that blue sea was little to be boasted if it broke on black sand."

IX

Nelson's life over the next year may be summarised in the words—disobedience, rewards, frustration. He continued to be tied to the Court of Naples by way of the apron-strings of Lady Hamilton, and the whole station knew it. Rumours to this effect were reaching home, and it was an odd fact that, however broad the allusions made to the situation by familiar friends, Nelson himself took no trouble to counter them. He was lavishly rewarded for his attention; but he was frustrated in the wider field of his career, first by the decision of the Admiralty, right in the circumstances, not to entrust him with the formal dignity of the command-in-chief, and then by his inability to crown his subordinates' resolute work in the blockade of Malta with the capture of Valetta. Moreover, a Venetian frigate wearing the flag of Rear-Admiral Ganteaume evaded the forces blockading Egypt, and in October 1799 took Bonaparte to Toulon. Although, as Nelson wrote to Sir Sidney Smith, "no Crusader ever returned with more humility", Bonaparte in France was soon the most dynamic force in Europe, and Nelson's ships had lost the chance of gathering their greatest prize.

In July, Lord Keith, who had reason to fear a French

attack on Minorca, ordered Nelson to join him off Port Mahon with every ship he could spare. Nelson refused. He did not believe that the island was in any danger; moreover, he had landed so large a part of his ships' companies for service inland that, with the reduced complements with which they would have had to sail, they would not have been effective. "I am fully aware of the act I have committed," he wrote to Earl Spencer, "but, sensible of my loyal intentions, I am prepared for any fate which may await my disobedience. Capua and Gaeta will soon fall; and the moment the scoundrels of French are out of this Kingdom, I shall send eight or nine ships of the line to Minorca." A more peremptory order was needed before Nelson would reinforce Keith with any ships at all.

On the question of obedience, Nelson was not always consistent. Possessing boundless moral courage, he was himself prepared to disobey if he thought it to the advantage of his country (or of Naples), and he was often right, as in this case. Capua and Gaeta did in fact soon fall, and although the French and Spanish fleets eventually joined forces, they accomplished nothing. They were chased by Keith into the Atlantic, though neither there nor in the Mediterranean did he have the chance to bring them to battle.

"To serve my King, and to destroy the French, I consider as the great order of all, from which little ones spring; and if one of these little ones militate against it (for, who can tell exactly at a distance?), I go back and obey the great order and object, to *down, down* with the damned French villains." He ended his diatribe, addressed to the Duke of Clarence: "Excuse my warmth; but my blood boils at the name of a Frenchman." Nelson was in fact always urging others, even allies, superiors and officers of the army, to disregard their orders, if necessary, in what he thought to be the general interest of the cause. Where he was on dangerous ground was in the fact that he could not always discern what was a "little order" and what, coming with the authority of central direction of affairs, was a big one. Had Keith been right, as he might well have been, and had he been forced to abandon Minorca in the face of greatly superior force,

Nelson would have been disgraced. Further, although Nelson was willing to risk disobedience himself, he did not relish it in others when it conflicted with his own requirements. For instance, he would certainly have court-martialled the Portuguese captain who destroyed Neapolitan ships, in disregard of instructions, soon after the flight from Naples, had he been able to do so. So strongly did he feel on the subject that it took all the tact of the Court, who were the principal sufferers, to make him withdraw his displeasure from the officer in question.

While the *Foudroyant* remained at Naples, serving both as Nelson's flagship and as the seat of government of Ferdinand, there were celebrations other than those connected with the restoration of the monarchy. On the First of August, the anniversary of the Nile victory, there were notable festivities, about which Nelson took the trouble to tell Fanny. "The King dined with me," he wrote, "and when His Majesty drank my health, a Royal salute of twenty-one guns was fired from all his Sicilian Majesty's Ships of War, and from all the Castles. In the evening there was a general illumination. Amongst other representations, a large Vessel was fitted out with a Roman galley; on its oars were fixed lamps, and in the centre was erected a rostral column with my name: at the stern were elevated two angels supporting my picture. In short, my dear Fanny, the beauty of the whole is beyond my powers of description. . . . An orchestra was fitted up, and filled with the very best musicians and singers. The piece of music was in great measure to celebrate my praise, describing their previous distress, 'but Nelson came, the invincible Nelson, and they were preserved, and again made happy'. This must not make you think me vain; no, very far from it, I relate it more from gratitude than vanity. . . . Pray say what is true," he added, feeling that some apology was needed for the lack of more regular letters, which Fanny was in fact the first to condone, "that I really *steal* time to write this letter, and my hand is ready to drop, and out of my eye I cannot see half what I write. My dear father must forgive my not writing so often as I ought, and so must my brothers and friends."

There were not those wanting in the fleet who discerned

in the angelic figures supporting Nelson's picture the linea-
ments of Emma and the Queen of Naples, though the
Queen had not come in person to the capital for fear of
assassination, and even the King, for all the festivities, never
set foot ashore. Emma was in her element as organising
hostess both of Court and naval squadron, and Troubridge
was not the only officer who found the "buzz" in the
Foudroyant bewildering.

Nelson was relieved to return to Palermo with the
King. They reached Sicily on 8th August, and almost
at once Nelson was offered a dukedom. It was that of Brontë,
under the shadow of Mount Etna in the eastern part of the
island, and the accompanying estate was said to be worth
£3,000 a year, though it had never yet yielded that sum, and
was unlikely to do so in the immediate future. It was some
days before Nelson could be persuaded to accept this magnificent gift. The argument which finally prevailed, which
was put forward by the Queen, was that he considered his
own honour too much, if he persisted in refusing what those
he had benefited felt to be necessary for the preservation of
theirs. "Lord Nelson," said the King, "do you wish that your
name alone should pass with honour to posterity; and that
I, Ferdinand Bourbon, should appear ungrateful?" Nelson
had in fact fairly won his Dukedom, as well as the diamond-
hilted sword with which he was now presented, by restoring
Ferdinand to his mainland possessions. Nelson said that the
reward was worthy of a king, and he was determined that
the inhabitants on his estate "should be the happiest in all
his Sicilian Majesty's dominions". The name Brontë, appropriately enough, signified *Thunder*. Nelson liked it, and he
began signing himself "Brontë Nelson", or "Brontë Nelson
of the Nile". After he had received his own King's formal
permission to use the title, he settled upon the simpler
"Nelson and Brontë", which led a Greenwich pensioner to
remark that it was a pity he had taken a partner! A clergyman of Irish descent and eccentric notions, Prunty or
Brunty by name, also fancied the sound of Brontë, and
bestowed the surname upon children whose literary fame
sustained it with honour into the reign of Victoria.

One of Emma Hamilton's first acts in celebration of the

gift was to commission a young artist to draw a profile of the
new Duke. Perhaps the most appropriate comment on this
little-known version, which was copied in a miniature the
following year, signed "E. Nash", and which served (be-
hatted) as the basis for a print by Burke, was that Nelson
at this time deserved to be represented in so Italianate a
fashion. Keith wrote home to his sister saying that he was
"cutting the most absurd figure possible for folly and
vanity", and when Sir John Moore later had what he
thought was the misfortune to come into brief contact with
the Neapolitan Court, he said of his companion-in-arms of
days in Corsica: "He is covered with stars, ribbons and
medals, more like a Prince of an Opera than the Conqueror
of the Nile. It is really melancholy to see a brave and good
man, who has deserved well of his country, cutting so pitiful
a figure."

x

Keith's Atlantic foray in pursuit of a French fleet left
Nelson exercising the functions of chief command in the
Middle Sea, without the title of that office. It is significant
that in the instructions he received from the Secretary of the
Admiralty, dated 20th August, the affairs of Naples were
not specifically mentioned. Nelson's duty, it is true, was still
to co-operate with all His Majesty's allies, but his detailed
orders were to keep an important part of the fleet off the
coast of Genoa on blockade, to protect Minorca, and to seal
Cadiz, which was a westward extension over which he could
hope to exercise little direct control. Their Lordships expressed the view, which was in fact too sanguine, that the
French would soon be expelled from Egypt, and that Sir
Sidney Smith's squadron might be found new duties.

Whatever the distractions of Palermo—they included
gambling, for which Emma Hamilton had an appetite not
shared by Nelson—the ardours of command kept the
admiral at a stretch. In October he sailed for Minorca, where
he stayed five days. He then returned to Palermo, which he
did not leave until the following January, though his corre-

spondence grew in complication. His most pressing problem was the relief of starvation in the Maltese countryside. It was not a new one; he had been urging the matter upon Acton for a full year; but it was one which Troubridge and Ball found increasingly distressing. "I am not very tender-hearted," wrote Troubridge, "but really the distress here would move even a Neapolitan." In desperation, the captains effected their purpose by taking corn vessels from the eastern ports of Sicily, in defiance of the government; nor did they ever hear a word of reproach from a Court which appeared indifferent to anything which did not lie beneath its immediate notice.

Troubridge was by now sickened with everything Sicilian and Neapolitan, and was shocked at the apparent deterioration in Nelson. "Your lordship is a stranger to half that happens and the talk it occasions," he wrote with the frankness of long acquaintance. "If you knew what your friends feel for you, I am sure you would cut out all the nocturnal parties. The gambling of the people of Palermo is publicly talked of everywhere. I beseech your lordship leave off. I wish my pen could tell you my feelings, I am sure you would oblige me. Lady Hamilton's character will suffer; nothing can prevent people from talking. A gambling woman, in the eyes of an Englishman, is lost."

Bracing was at hand, but from a superior, not a subordinate, for with the New Year and century, Lord Keith returned to his command. One of his first actions was to summon Nelson to join him at Leghorn. The *Foudroyant* arrived in the Roads on the 20th January. Nelson wrote to the Hamiltons to say that his reception had been chilly. This was only to have been expected from a man to whom he had made no effort to be either obedient or conciliatory. Keith was a Scot, of a race towards whom Nelson seems to have had some antipathy, but he was an officer whom to know was to respect, and Nelson had known him many years. He was twelve years Nelson's senior in age, and three years senior as a flag-officer. Although his service had not been spectacular it had been gallant and distinguished, and his forbearance, over many months, towards his brilliant junior was a matter for admiration. Nelson, his vanity increased by

months of adulation in a country where he had no rival,
bitterly resented the position of second-in-command, and
Keith's frigid reception by the Neapolitan Court, when the
fleet sailed to Palermo from Leghorn, did not ease relation-
ships.

It was ironical that Keith's activity should have been the
means through which Nelson increased his fame. After nine
days in Sicily, the Commander-in-Chief, with Nelson in
company, set sail for Malta. Off Cape Passaro the *Foudroyant*,
Northumberland, *Audacious* and *Success* fell in with a French
squadron under Rear-Admiral Perrée in *Le Généreux*, and it
was typical of Nelson's luck that, on his sole incursion into
the Maltese area during many months, he should have met
with one of the two ships of the line which had escaped from
Aboukir Bay eighteen months before. While he wrote from
sea to Lady Hamilton: "to say how I miss your house and
company would be saying little; but in truth you and Sir
William have so spoiled me that I am not happy anywhere
else but with you, nor have I an idea that I ever can be".
Ball reported a few days later to the same correspondent:
"With what joy you must have received the news of his
Lordship's success in the capture of the French Admiral's
ship, *Le Généreux*, with a corvette, and the dispersion of the
rest of the enemy's squadron bound for Malta, not one of
which will ever attempt to make for the destined port. We
may truly call him a *heaven*-born Admiral, upon whom
fortune smiles wherever he goes. We have been carrying on
the blockade of Malta sixteen months, during which time
the enemy never attempted to throw in succours until this
month. His Lordship arrived here the day they were within
a few leagues of the island, captured the principal ships and
dispersed the rest, so that not one has reached the port." In
his loyalty to Nelson, it escaped Ball's remark that it was
Keith's energy which had brought about the result.

Sir Edward Berry had recently rejoined the Mediterranean fleet, and had replaced Hardy as Nelson's flag-
captain. Serving in the *Foudroyant* at the time of the action
was a young midshipman, G. S. Parsons, who later recorded
his impressions of the event. After four days of groping
about in a heavy sea, interspersed with fog, Nelson heard the

sound of firing, and steered towards it. When it was apparent
that it was *Le Généreux* which was being chased, he said:
"Make the *Foudroyant* fly! . . . This will not do, Sir Ed'ard,
it is certainly *Le Généreux*, and to my flagship she can alone
surrender. Sir Ed'ard, we must and shall beat the *North-*
umberland."

"I will do my utmost, my lord," said Berry. "Get the
engine to work on the sails[1]—hand butts of water to the
stays—pipe the hammocks down, and each man place shot
in them—slack the stays, knock up the wedges, and give the
masts play. Start off the water, Mr James, and pump the
ship." The *Foudroyant* drew ahead, and at last took the lead.
"The Admiral is working his fin" (the stump of his right
arm): "do not cross hawse, I advise you." Such was Parsons's
thought at the time: how right he was soon appeared in
Nelson's act of turning furiously on the petty officer who
was conning the ship.

"I'll knock you off your perch, you rascal," he said, "if
you are so inattentive! Sir Ed'ard, send your best quarter-
master to the weather wheel."

"A strange sail ahead of the chase," called the look-out
man.

"Youngster, to the mast-head! What—going without
your glass and be damned to you! Let me know what she is
immediately."

"A sloop of war or frigate, my lord."

"Demand her number."

"The *Success*, my lord."

"Signal her to cut off the flying enemy. Great odds,
though! Thirty-two small guns to eighty large ones."

"The *Success*, my lord, has hove to athwart-hawse of *Le
Généreux* and is firing her larboard broadside. The Frenchman has hoisted the tricolour with a Rear-Admiral's flag."

"Bravo, *Success*, at her again!"

"She has wore, my lord, and is firing her starboard broadside. It has winged the chase, my lord. Her flying kits are
flying away together."

1 The "engine" was the fire-engine, hand-pump and hoses. In light airs,
it was customary to wet the sails by hosing them, for the canvas was then
supposed to hold a better wind, the water closing the interstices.

"*Le Généreux* now opened fire on the frigate and every-one stood aghast, fearing the consequences. But when the smoke cleared there was the *Success*, crippled it is true, but bull-dog like, bearing up for the enemy.

"Signal the *Success* to discontinue the action and come under my stern", said Nelson. "She has done well for her size. Try a shot from the lower deck at her, Sir Ed'ard."

"It goes over her."

"Beat to quarters and fire coolly and deliberately at her masts and yards."

"*Le Généreux* at this moment opend her fire on us," continued Parsons, "and, as a shot passed through the mizzen stay-sail, Lord Nelson, patting one of the youngsters on the head, asked him jocularly how he relished the music; and observing something like alarm depicted on his coun-tenance, consoled him with the information that Charles XII ran away from the first shot he heard, though afterwards he was called 'The Great', and deservedly, from his bravery. 'I therefore,' said Nelson, 'hope much from you in the future.'

"Here the *Northumberland* opened her fire, and down came the tricoloured ensign, amidst the thunders of our united cannon."

Berry boarded the prize and received the sword of Rear-Admiral Perrée, who was dying of wounds. Keith was un-moved when, after recounting his triumph next day, Nelson added that he had made a vow that if he took *Le Généreux* he would strike his flag. Keith gave his subordinate every praise in his despatch to the Admiralty; but his mind soon turned to other matters; his immediate business lay east-wards, in Egyptian waters. In leaving Nelson in charge of the Malta blockade, he pointed out that Syracuse, Augusta or Messina were all better bases or *rendez-vous* than Palermo for the conduct of operations in hand.

Nelson, as usual where Keith was concerned, was of another mind. He was tired of being at sea, ailing, and home-sick for the Hamiltons. Not even an agonised letter from Troubridge, written on 24th February and referring to some wholly fancied slight to Nelson, the very thought of which had reduced the captain to tears, could move the admiral. It was a strange mood which necessitated entreaties to stay at his post, with promises from his friend and subordinate that "everything shall be done to make it comfortable and pleasing for you". The innate fire and devotion to duty had been temporarily dulled; even the spur of the late successful action was not enough to goad Nelson into further activity.

A very few days after Keith's sails were below the horizon, Berry was ordered to make for Palermo, where Nelson arrived on 16th March. There he hoisted his flag on a transport, sending the *Foudroyant* back to her station. Nelson was just in time to hear news of the marriage of Sir John Acton, then aged sixty-four, to his niece, aged not quite fourteen, by special dispensation. It was the sort of event to excite more interest at Palermo than a first-hand account of the taking of a ship of the line.

Before the month was out, Berry and his ship were present at the taking of the very last of Brueys's battle-fleet, *Le Guillaume Tell*, which failed in an attempt to evade the Malta blockade. Much of the credit for the action went to Captain Henry Blackwood, of the frigate *Penelope*. Nelson was not yet acquainted with him, though he played an important part in the last days of the admiral's sea career. "Is there a sympathy which ties men together in the bonds of friendship without having a personal knowledge of each other?" he wrote after the action. "If so, I was your friend and acquaintance before I saw you. Your conduct and character in the late glorious occasion stamps your fame beyond the reach of envy; it was like yourself, it was like the *Penelope*." This was just the sort of generous recognition of which Nelson was capable even in his most self-indulgent hour, and it ensured men's devotion. As for Berry, he wrote from the "*Foudroyant*, at Sea, Cape Passaro North by East Eight or Nine Leagues", on 30th March: "My very dear Lord, Had you been a partaker with me of the glory, every wish would have been gratified. How very often I went into your cabin, last night, to ask you if we were doing right; for, I had nothing to act upon! . . ." This action of going to Nelson's empty cabin in search of advice was in fact typical of Berry's dependence, for Nelson had confided to Fanny in a letter written a few months before, "I shall be worn to death by being obliged to fag and think of those things

which . . . excellent Captain Hardy takes entirely from me."
Berry was a good fighter, but Nelson had by now discovered
his ideal flag-captain, from whom, in the future, he would
rarely be separated. It was, of course, that massive figure,
Thomas Masterman Hardy. Dorset bred, largely self taught,
sure in his reactions though not in his spelling, Hardy had
attracted Nelson when still a lieutenant. It was he whom
Nelson had rescued so spectacularly from the Spaniards,
shortly before the Battle of St Vincent; it was he whom he
had promoted on the evening of the Nile. A firm disciplinarian, a man with all the intricacies of ship management at
his command, Hardy stood no nonsense from anyone whatever—even from Emma Hamilton when she tried to interfere in sea matters. Nelson came to rely upon him, whenever
they were together, to ease the detailed running of the
squadron. He won the big man's lasting devotion. Grave,
constant, modest, Hardy was completely dedicated to his
profession, and remained so to the end of his life.

In a jubilant letter reporting Berry's action to Lord Keith,
Nelson could not resist including the sentence: "I thank
God I was not present; for it would finish me, could I have
taken a sprig of these brave men's laurels. They are, and I
glory in them, my darling children; served in my school;
and all of us caught our professional zeal and fire from the
great and good Earl of St Vincent." It was not the most
tactful sentiment to convey to the officer under whom
Nelson was then serving.

Nelson spent most of April 1800 at Palermo, but on the
24th, after the *Foudroyant* had returned from her foray, he
took the Hamiltons with him in the flagship to Malta, where
Emma, who professed not to like being at sea, had a taste of
fire from a shore battery, and relished it. A year later, from
the remoteness of a Baltic shore, Nelson referred to the
"days of ease and nights of pleasure" which the voyage
unfolded. He was well and truly in love; and his passion was
by this time actively returned.

Malta itself provided cold comfort, for Valetta's resistance
was still stubborn, and when, in the following September,
Vaubois at last surrendered, telling the British that his men
had only consumed seven months' provisions in two years,

it was Keith who got much of the credit for the capitulation, for by then Nelson was far away. The very day after the *Foudroyant* sailed on Nelson's visit to Malta, Lord Spencer wrote to Nelson: "If the Enemy should come into the Mediterranean, and whenever they do, it will be suddenly, I should be much concerned to hear that you learnt of their arrival in that Sea, either on Shore or in a Transport at Palermo." By taking the Hamiltons with him, Nelson had managed, temporarily at least, to reconcile duty with pleasure. It was now his hope that Berry and the *Foudroyant* would carry him and his friends to England, for Sir William was about to be replaced at the Court of Naples by Arthur Paget, and without the Hamiltons the station seemed unthinkable.

On his return to Palermo, early in June, Nelson received a final gift from the sovereign he had served so well. The King had instituted a new Order, that of St Ferdinand and Merit of the Two Sicilies, and Nelson had another star with which to decorate his coat. He was one of the first three to be given the Grand Cross, the others being Marshal Suvarof and the Czar of Russia. Troubridge, Hallowell and Ball were also made members in the lesser degree of "Commandeurs".

If anything could have reinforced Nelson's decision to leave the Mediterranean it was the letter he received from Lord Spencer, whose polished and tactful phrases had their barb, and their truth to fact. "It is by no means my wish or intention to call you away from service," wrote the First Lord, "but having observed that you have been under the necessity of quitting your station off Malta, on account of the state of your health, which I am persuaded you could not have thought of doing without such necessity, it appeared to me much more advisable for you to come home at once, than to be obliged to remain inactive at Palermo . . . and I believe I am joined in opinion by all your friends here, that you will be more likely to recover your health and strength in England than in an inactive situation at a Foreign Court, however pleasing the respect and gratitude shown to you for your services may be. . . ."

Nelson sailed in the *Foudroyant* for Leghorn on 10th June,

where he proposed to join Lord Keith, whose ships were co-operating with the armies of Austria. He had on board the Queen of Naples, Prince Leopold, three Princesses, the Hamiltons, Miss Knight and an attendant retinue, and it was but natural that Keith should have expressed a fear of being "bored by Lord Nelson" with requests to take the Neapolitan royal family to all quarters of the globe. Entirely conciliatory and even considerate as he continued to be in his correspondence, Keith was firm: he could not spare the *Foudroyant*, even at the plea of Majesty, made in person. The very day Nelson arrived at Leghorn, 14th June, Bonaparte had won the resounding victory of Marengo against the Austrians, and Italy was once more at his feet. Every British ship of the line would be needed for active service. Under the circumstances, it was generous of Keith to offer Nelson the *Seahorse*, in which he had returned wounded with the Fremantles after Teneriffe, or any troop-ship, for the accommodation of himself and his friends.

One expression of farewell on the occasion of leaving his flagship was as touching as any message Nelson ever received. "My Lord," said a letter in an unpractised hand, "it is with extreme grief that we find you are about to leave us. We have been along with you (although not in the same ship) in every Engagement your Lordship has been in, both by Sea and Land; and most humbly beg of your Lordship to permit us to go to England, as your Boat's crew in any Ship or vessel, or in any way that may seem most pleasing to your Lordship. My Lord, pardon the rude style of Seamen, who are but little acquainted with writing, and believe us to be, my Lord, your ever humble and obedient servants—*Barge's Crew of the Foudroyant.*"

In the end, Nelson shifted his flag to the *Alexander*, as a temporary measure, and on 13th July 1800 ended his service under Keith. He had decided on the risky adventure of crossing a Continent which was in as grave a state of tension as it had been when he had sailed from home in the *Agamemnon*, seven long years before.

Chapter 7

HOMECOMING

I

NELSON'S journey home was an appropriate rounding-off to his two years' commission abroad. It started precipitately. While he was lying in his cot one morning in the *Alexander*, a message came from the Queen of Naples to say that the local people were restive, and that she feared danger. A French army was then less than thirty miles away, at Lucca, and the idea of the Tuscans was to seize the Queen in order to detain Nelson, who, they knew, would not leave Leghorn without her. He, they hoped, would command them in person against the invaders.

The leaders were treated to a balcony speech made on Nelson's behalf by Emma Hamilton. She begged them to return the arms which they had purloined from the arsenal, saying that Nelson could under no circumstances hold the smallest communication with them until they had done what he asked. When, at her bidding, they had dispersed, the Queen and her party retreated on board the *Alexander*. After dark they set out for Florence, Nelson, the Hamiltons, Miss Knight and Mrs Cadogan following next day. The parties were conveyed in no fewer than fourteen carriages. As there were three large baggage-waggons in attendance, royalty and flag-officers did not travel light.

Miss Knight wrote to Sir Edward Berry to say that Lady Hamilton still could not bear the thought of going anywhere by sea, and that although Nelson appeared to be in good spirits, Sir William was "broken, distressed and harassed". She and Mrs Cadogan were the most practical members of the joint party, whose object was Vienna. There the Queen proposed to visit her daughter, and to request continuance of support in the war with the French.

On their way to Florence, the cavalcade at one stage

passed within two miles of the advanced posts of the enemy.
From Florence they proceeded to Ancona, which was then
within the boundaries of the States of the Church. There
they were detained nearly a fortnight while arrangements
were completed for their transport across the Adriatic to
Trieste, which lay in the Emperor's dominions. Emma, who
wished to visit the various Courts of Germany, was by this
time more cheerful, despite the prospect of a sea trip. Sir
William, for his part, thought he was likely to die by the
way. "He looks so ill," reported Miss Knight, "that I should
not be surprised if he did."

At Ancona the Queen found an Austrian frigate, the
Bellona, fitted up for her reception with silk hangings,
carpets and eighty beds; but as most of her guns had been
removed, and as her men had recently mutinied, she did not
deem this vessel a safe conveyance. She was right, for the
French knew all about the *Bellona*, and she was captured on
her way back. An alternative was provided by a Russian
squadron of three frigates and a brig under Commodore
Count Voinovitsch. One of the frigate captains was an
Englishman, Messer, who had served under Lord Howe.
He and Nelson had many animated talks on naval subjects,
but it was Miss Knight and Mrs Cadogan who had the
pleasure of sailing with him. The grandees, Nelson included,
had a miserable voyage in the Commodore's ship, Nelson
audibly sighing for the *Foudroyant*.

At Trieste, which was reached on 2nd August, the day
after the second anniversary of the Nile, the admiral was
"followed by thousands", so Miss Knight related; "there
were many *Viva Nelsons* prepared". It was a foretaste of the
acclamation with which he would be greeted wherever he
travelled in Europe. In a Continent which had already
grown weary of French victories and would grow wearier
still, it was refreshing to greet a man who had won his
peerage by an unparalleled victory over the common
enemy.

A few days' journey from Trieste brought the party to
Vienna. There Nelson and his friends were presented to the
Emperor and Empress, and they found pleasure in the
attention of Nelson's old friend, Gilbert Elliot, Lord Minto,

who was Minister Plenipotentiary. "You can have no idea of the anxiety and curiosity to see him," recorded Lady Minto of Nelson. "The door of his house is always crowded with people, and when he went to the play he was applauded, a thing which rarely happens here."[1]

Knowing little German between them, Nelson and the Hamiltons engaged an Englishman, Francis Oliver, as courier, interpreter and confidential secretary. Oliver had long been known to Sir William, who took him back with them to England. He proved useful in many ways, for, like Mrs Cadogan, he was one of those people who were able to slide without fuss into the background, holding their tongue whenever necessary.

"I don't think him altered in the least," recorded Lady Minto of Nelson. "He has the same shock head and the same honest simple manners; but he is devoted to *Emma*, he thinks her quite an *angel*, and talks of her as such to her face and behind her back, and she leads him about like a keeper with a bear. She must sit by him at dinner to cut his meat, and he carries her pocket-handkerchief. He is a gig from ribands, orders and stars, but he is just the same with us as ever he was." Lady Hamilton shocked many observers by her appetite, and by her fondness for gambling. Moreover, for all her attention to Nelson, she was not always as successful as Tom Allen in keeping him from drinking too much champagne. Allen, who once at least was ordered from the *Foudroyant*'s cabin for over-familiarity to senior officers, had the excellent habit of regulating Nelson's glasses, reminding him aloud, on the very rare occasions when he needed it, that strict moderation was best for his health. "You will be ill if you take any more," Allen would say, and he knew to a drop when his master's modest needs were met.

Quizzical people thought the English made a curious party. Franz Collenbach, for instance, wrote to a niece to tell her that "our little queens of society have for some time been crazy about wigs—brown, blonde, ashen—and on diamonds, pearls, laces and gold chains. One would take

---

[1] Artists were also in attendance. Nelson was painted by Heinrich Füger, though he did not complete the canvas, and at least one sculptor modelled his head.

them, the whole bunch, for miraculous Virgins, decorated
with all the offerings of pilgrim sinners.

"Lady Hamilton brought us fashions of her own, and
others borrowed from the different places she has visited.
They say it is to her we owe the light diaphanous draperies
which leave nothing to be guessed at by lovers of the fair
sex. After a stay in Vienna, this lady has just left us, taking
with her Nelson, the most favoured lover in her empire of
hearts.

"I often found myself in the company of this odd pair,
and Lady Hamilton never stopped talking, singing, laughing, gesticulating and mimicking, while the favoured son of
Neptune appeared to leave her no more than did her shadow,
trying to meet with his own small eyes the great orbs of his
beloved, and, withal, as motionless and silent as a monument, embarrassed by his poor figure and by all the emblems,
cords and crosses with which he was be-decked. In a word,
the Lord of the Nile seemed as clumsy and dim on land as
he is adroit and notable at sea."

Before leaving Vienna the party attended an aquatic fête
given on the Danube by Count Bathiani. There Nelson was
invited to see some experiments made with a large vessel,
which had been equipped with machinery for working
against the current. Nelson's view was that the contrivance,
though "prodigiously ingenious", would be unlikely to
answer the inventor's purpose at sea. His opinion would
have been made with an open mind, for he was interested
in all forms of mechanical progress, and is said to have
been enthusiastic at the idea of Henry Bell's experimental
Clyde paddle steamer, which had been rejected by the
Admiralty.

On 26th September the Hamiltons and Nelson bade a
ceremonial and tearful farewell to the Queen of Naples, and
their party, which numbered seventeen including servants,
then proceeded to Prague. There Nelson found pleasure in
the society of the Archduke Charles, accounted the ablest of
the Austrian generals. He called him a man after his own
heart, as he had Hamilton, two years before. At Prague a
grand entertainment was given in honour of Nelson's birthday, Sir William remarking during the course of dinner that

he had the honour to be between the greatest naval and the greatest military character in Europe.

Dresden was the next city on the route. After a few stages by coach, the party quitted the direct road, turning off towards the Upper Elbe in order to embark at Leitmeritz, and to proceed to the Saxon capital by river. "His lordship," recorded James Harrison, who got his information direct from Lady Hamilton, "was much amused by this fresh-water voyage, and viewed with delight the stupendous rocks of basaltes through which the Elbe here securely wound its way, amidst scenes of impressive grandeur."

Lord Minto's brother, Hugh Elliot, was Minister at Dresden, and it was he who arranged for pastel portraits to be made both of Nelson and Lady Hamilton by Johann Heinrich Schmidt, the Court painter. The results were of exceptional interest. A boyish Nelson was recorded, his hair nearly white, with a patch of white powder covering the Nile scar. It was a picture as realistic as any photograph, and much more vivid. Lady Hamilton wore her Maltese decoration for her sittings, and as the picture afterwards hung in Nelson's cabin as what he called his "Guardian Angel", Schmidt's rather than Romney's Emma was the one with whom he was in love.

At Dresden an unprejudiced German onlooker, Kosegarten by name, noted Nelson as being as "one of the most insignificant looking figures I ever saw in my life. His weight cannot be more than seventy pounds, and a more miserable collection of bones and wizened frame I have never yet come across. His bold nose, the steady eye and the solid worth revealed in his whole face betray in some measure the great conqueror. He speaks little, and then only English, and he hardly ever smiles. I have no doubt of his high ability, but one cannot look without astonishment at his slender body, although this can of course have no immediate connection with a great soul. He was almost covered with orders and stars.

"Lady Hamilton behaved like a loving sister towards him; led him; often took hold of his hand, whispered something into his ear, and he twisted his mouth into the faintest resemblance of a smile. She did not seek to win hearts, for everyone's lay at her feet."

The Saxons liked their women stout, but one Dresden heart which was not prostrate was that of Hugh Elliot. He called the pair "Antony and Moll-Cleopatra", and found Emma so loud and exhausting that he said to his wife when the party had gone: "Now, don't let us laugh tonight. Let us all speak in whispers and be very, very quiet."

Mrs St George, a friend of the Elliots, wrote in her private journal: "It is plain that Lord Nelson thinks of nothing but Lady Hamilton, who is totally occupied by the same object. Sir William is old, infirm, all admiration of his wife, and never spoke but to applaud her. Miss Cornelia Knight seems the decided flatterer of the two, and never opens her mouth but to show forth their praise; and Mrs Cadogan, Lady Hamilton's mother is—what one might expect. After dinner we had several songs in honour of Lord Nelson, written by Miss Knight and sung by Lady Hamilton. She puffs the incense full in his face; but he receives it with pleasure, and snuffs it up very cordially."

The next call was Magdeburg, the journey being continued by water. There another German observer, Alexander von Dalwick, noted that excitement was intense, the King of Prussia ordering a guard of honour to attend his lordship. He was astonished at the way in which Lady Hamilton managed Nelson's food, added that there was nothing noticeable about his sightless eye, and he was struck by the way in which Emma showed the admiral off to the crowds like a curiosity, telling them of his hundred engagements.

Nelson was interested to meet some young Englishmen from the commercial school. Von Dalwick said that Nelson "assured them he was nothing less than a great man", and insisted that they must be loyal and industrious, when they would do equally well. He urged upon them, above all, an eternal hatred of the French.

On leaving Magdeburg Nelson stood alone with doffed hat on the deck of his gondola. "Die Hamilton," concluded von Dalwick, "must be well on in her thirties, but is a woman full of fire, in whom one can clearly see the beauty of youth. . . . It is a strange sensation that takes possession of us when we see so great a man as Nelson. But what a typical Englishman!"

At Hamburg Nelson had hoped to find a frigate waiting to take the party on its final stage home. He was disappointed, but he received two compliments which particularly gratified him. The elderly pastor of a village forty miles away requested that he would inscribe his name in the first leaf of the parochial Bible, Nelson being, to the pastor's mind "the Saviour of the Christian World", while an equally patriarchal wine-merchant begged his acceptance of some Rhenish of the vintage of 1625, which had been in his own cellars more than half a century. He would have offered six dozen of this incomparable wine, but Nelson, taking him kindly by the hand, consented to accept only six, on the strict condition that the merchant would dine with him next day. A less pleasing incident, not without its significance, concerned the poet Klopstock, who planned a composition in praise of Emma and Nelson which was to be called "The Innocents". Further investigation of the circumstances of the party led him to withdraw his homage. He concluded that things were not quite what they seemed.

The tour ended in November. Nelson hired a packet from Cuxhaven, which was sent up the river to a point about five miles outside Hamburg. After a stormy voyage of five days, England was sighted, clouded in mist and settled in autumnal chill. Even so, Nelson was anxious to land quickly, and he persuaded the local pilot, rather against his better judgment, to take the ship across the bar without delay. Yarmouth was made, said Harrison, "not without a considerable degree of that horrible grating of the ship's bottom, while forcing its way through the sands, which so often thrills those who navigate this perilous Road".

II

Landing once more in his own country, Nelson met with a reception whose warmth equalled anything which the Continent had provided. Crowds took the horses from his carriage and drew it to the Wrestlers Inn, where the landlady, Sarah Suckling, claimed relationship, and asked leave to rename her hostelry the Nelson Arms. "That would be absurd," said Nelson, "seeing that I have but one."

The Mayor and Corporation waited upon him with the Freedom of the town, "but," recorded Harrison, "with the blundering fatality that seldom fails to mark some member in almost every town-corporate on any extraordinary occasion, when the usual oath was tendered to his lordship, who placed his left and only hand on the Book, the officer who administered it incautiously exclaimed—'Your *right* hand, my lord!' His lordship, with a good-humoured smile, mildly reminded him that he had no right hand. The surrounding company, however, were less merciful; and not only indulged an immediate hearty laugh at his expense, but sarcastically fastened on the little clerk for ever after, the unfortunate phrase—'*Your right hand, my lord!*' "

Soon after the ceremony, Nelson went to an upper window at the inn and waved at the throng gathered in his honour in the pouring rain, saying, "I am myself a Norfolk man, and glory in being so." At his side stood Lady Hamilton, wearing a muslin gown decorated with flounces and embroidered with oak leaves and acorns, with coronets, anchors and oval garlands enclosing the words "Nelson" and "Brontë". This dress, with its delicate fresh greens and browns, and the gold of its sequins, was made for a Sicilian fête. It still exists, far more restrained in its beauty and careful in its workmanship than highly coloured contemporary descriptions indicate. Nelson and Emma had the art of pleasing the crowd, and Emma intended to show her proprietorship, even in Nelson's own county. "I believe you could *hip, hip, hip!* your Nelson when every other power was exhausted," wrote Alexander Ball, and it was true.

During a service in the parish church the congregation gave thanks for the Victory of the Nile and Nelson's safe return. As the admiral entered the nave, the organ played *See the Conquering Hero Comes* in the approved style. The rest of the day was taken up with celebrations. Troops from the barracks paraded, salutes were fired, bands played martial tunes. At night the town was illuminated, and Nelson dined with the Mayor at his house in King Street.

Before departing for London next day, the Hamiltons

P

gave one of the several versions of Nelson by Guzzardi to a local artist to copy. The man chosen, Matthew Keymer, did his best to fulfil the commission, but, being dissatisfied with his brother-craftsman's version, determined to attempt a likeness for himself. This he had the chance to do when Nelson visited the town in the following year, on his way to the Baltic. The Keymer rendering still hangs at Great Yarmouth, and it is almost as bizarre as anything by the Neapolitan.

Nelson was escorted southward by the local Volunteer Cavalry, who rode with him as far as the county boundary. At Ipswich, the people dragged his carriage a mile into the town, and accompanied him to his property at Roundwood, which he then visited for the first and last time in his life. The house was empty, for Fanny and Edmund Nelson were awaiting the admiral in London, to which the party at once pushed on. They arrived on Sunday, 9th November, in a thunderstorm, and proceeded to Nerot's Hotel, King Street, St James's. Fanny and her father-in-law were living there while the house taken by Davison in Dover Street was being made ready. Nelson had already written to request an appointment from the Admiralty. "I trust that my necessary journey by land from the Mediterranean will not be considered as a wish to be a moment out of active service," he said.

This wish for immediate employment, on the part of a man who had been so long from home, and who had left Lord Keith on the grounds of ill health, indicated three things; hunger for activity after idle weeks; recovery of health, and a realisation that, domestically, he was about to plunge into an intolerable situation. During the years he had been away, Fanny had waited for him in lonely virtue. During the time when Nelson's dependence upon another woman had been continuously growing and was now mounting to a climax, the image of his wife must necessarily have become dim. A man so without hypocrisy could not simulate an emotion he did not feel.

When Emma and Fanny at last met face to face, at three o'clock on that dark afternoon, Emma, in her own words to Mrs William Nelson, felt "an antipathy not to be described".

It was no wonder. Not only was she confronted with a rival of impeccable morals, breeding and good manners, standing well with Nelson's oldest friends, and entrenched in the affection of a father-in-law whom Nelson called "the very best man that ever I saw", but she was at grips with conventional English society. As she herself quickly understood, Emma was unlikely, whatever her future behaviour, to find welcome in those circles where Fanny moved by right, and within which she would always be appreciated. Emma was a woman without inhibitions, but wholly lacking that self-control through which Fanny had endured her years of anxious vigil. It was the quality which had given her the strength to tend her husband in the darker hours of his last visit home.

Although, on superficial consideration, it may seem to have been Emma who needed sympathy, in fact it was Fanny. Emma's feelings, once she had survived her early betrayals, ran wide rather than deep. Nothing could long withstand her overflowing passionate vitality, or withhold from her anything on which she had firmly set her mind. She guessed from the outset that it was she and not her rival who commanded Nelson's closest allegiance. She had been his mistress many months; she was then carrying his child; she had been present at some of the most glowing episodes of his life abroad. Fanny had known no Neapolitan sunlight, nor had she, in Edmund Nelson's graphic words, "soared in spheres unknown to private stations". Only a miracle could have made the two women find tolerance of one another.

Biographers of Nelson have found it almost impossible not to take sides with Fanny or with Emma. Fanny, so limited and colourless, has come off poorly, but it was she who deserved pity, for upon Emma was lavished henceforward Nelson's burning devotion; it was she with whom his name would be linked in the nation's story, and it was she who held the attention of most of Nelson's family until the closing years of her life.

The way in which the Nelson relations sided with Emma, natural enough in view of the fame and position of their brother, and of his generous care for them all, could only have added to the sharp and prolonged pain of losing a husband to whom, until her death, Fanny remained devoted, and whom she had never failed, except in a matter she could not help, that of providing him with an heir. "You must expect to find me a worn out old man," Nelson had written to her from Vienna. To Fanny, it was so, although to Emma he remained the fervent adorer which he had been ever since she had nursed him on his return from Aboukir Bay.

Fanny, it is true, had her son Josiah, who returned in the frigate *Thalia* before the end of the year. She also retained the affection of Edmund Nelson, which seemed proof even against the anonymous letters which Emma was capable of sending him, and which were echoed by quite unworthy insinuations from Nelson himself. Maurice Nelson also continued her friend for the few months of life which remained to him, and he (as Fanny wrote across one of his letters) was indeed an honourable man. But perhaps nothing in the family history is more revealing of character than the way in which the Reverend William Nelson and his wife, when they thought Fanny was in favour, told her that they would rather their beloved daughter was with her than with anyone else, and then, as soon as they realised it was Emma who mattered, made an obsequious turn-about. Not merely did they attach themselves henceforward to the Hamiltons, which bored Sir William, but they were among the first and most eager to refer to Fanny and Josiah as "Tom Tit and Cub", in the unfortunate phrase so often used by Emma, one of whose firmest beliefs was that the best form of defence was attack. When William Nelson looked at his clerical face in the glass of a morning, glowing with good living, it seems unlikely that Charity, so rightly emphasised in the religion which he expounded for a living, occurred to him as an attribute which he himself might cultivate with profit.

It was Troubridge, then in London and about to take up an appointment in the Channel fleet, who completed the dissolution of the travelling party by warning Miss Cornelia Knight, in the way of friendship, that she would be well advised to steer clear of the Hamilton *ménage* if she wished to further her own interests in London society. For all her apparent sycophancy, Miss Knight was a woman of character who in a very short time found a position at the Court

of George III. She took Troubridge's advice, and was given
hospitality by Mrs Nepean, wife of the Secretary of the
Admiralty, though she had the good feeling not to sever her
friendship too abruptly.

Miss Knight has more than a passing interest in the
Nelson story. She herself was a link between the age of Dr
Johnson and that of Southey and Coleridge. Johnson had
been a friend of her sailor father and had supervised her early
education; she recorded in her *Autobiography* that he "had a
great respect for men who served their country by sea or land
and was heard to say, let a man be ever so distinguished for
rank or abilities, he could not help thinking that he must,
when in company with an officer of long and splendid
services, feel himself his inferior".

Progressing through the austerities of Latin composition,
she later tried her hand at romantic verse, anticipating the
manner of Byron at his most facile:

> *Come cheer up fair Delia, forget all thy grief;*
> *For thy shipmates are brave, and a Hero's their chief.*
> *Look round on these trophies, the pride of the Main,*
> *They were snatched by their valour from Gallia and Spain.*

She was among the last to believe in the purity of the relations between Emma and Nelson, though she had herself
been in the *Foudroyant* at the time of their spring excursion
to Malta. She had in fact heard Nelson say to her mother,
before Lady Knight's death in 1799, that the happiest day of
his life was not that of the Nile, but that on which he married
Lady Nelson; and she was with Nelson in Hamburg when
he chose costly gifts not only for his wife but for a woman
who had been good to her. A final anecdote that puts the
biographer in her debt is that it is she alone who records
that, when he was a youth in the East Indies, Nelson once
rose from the gaming table £300 to the good. When he
pondered over the predicament he would have been in had
he lost, he never again gambled, until Emma, with her usual
masterful persuasion, changed his habits, temporarily at
least, by playing his cards for him.

Nelson made an attempt to live with Fanny for what
remained of that sad opening year of the nineteenth century,

but his position grew progressively more intolerable. Whatever the impression his wife had made upon his heart during their years in Norfolk together, and during the winter months of 1797 when she had tended him so carefully, it was now obliterated. He found her refusal to minister to his vanity, her lack of exuberance, even her elegance and dignity oppressive: nor, so rumour said, could she altogether forbear to recriminate. It was the gossip of the newspapers, and the insinuations of popular cartoons that she dwelt upon, not the glorification due to the victor of the Nile. So it was with Sir William Hamilton that Nelson attended the City banquet given in his honour; with the Hamiltons that he visited Beckford, to spend Christmas at the fantastic great house of Fonthill, surprising his host by his nervousness at being driven by four horses in a phaeton; and it was to the Hamilton's house that he returned one night after wandering distractedly through the streets of London. He had already upset yet another of Lady Spencer's formal dinner parties by his brusqueness to his wife, so different from the time when he had insisted on sitting next to her at table. Moreover, there had been an unfortunate scene at a theatre when Fanny had actually fainted, it was supposed at her husband's attentions to Emma, and it was noted that while she and old Edmund Nelson saw Fanny home, Nelson himself sat out the rest of the performance. Fanny's indisposition was perhaps not surprising in a woman so sensitive that a letter from Nelson abroad had been known to render her temporarily sightless. Emma's condition, for all her natural amplitude, must by now have been clear to eyes on the look-out for such things.

Public events continued to crowd upon Nelson, not all of them pleasant. Charles Greville had written to his uncle as long ago as the summer of 1799 to say that the Prince of Wales had told him that, after the Queen of Naples's account of Lady Hamilton's services to her, "she might be assured that all would be made pleasing to her when she arrived again in England", but Emma was not in fact received at Court, and Sir William had to make his bow alone. Nor was the King gracious even to Nelson. After a curt enquiry after his health, George III turned to engage in nearly half an

hour's conversation with an obscure military character. As
Collingwood remarked, it could scarcely have been about
his successes, for the army as yet had few to show in the war
with France. "I found St James's as cold as the atmosphere",
Nelson reported to Emma, and it was a fact that he never
again enjoyed the personal approbation of his sovereign.

Lady Elizabeth Foster, who overheard his remark about
the Court, recorded Nelson's appearance at this time as
"interesting and animated, his manner simple and unaffected". She added later that she noted melancholy in his
face, and that she found his voice very agreeable in tone. He
had, she considered, the mildest and most unassuming way
with him she had ever met with in Society. A few months
later, old Lord St Vincent told her and her friend the
Duchess of Devonshire that Nelson, "that foolish little
fellow, has sat to every artist in London". This, alas, was an
exaggeration, but it was quite true that Nelson, as well as
taking his seat in the House of Peers and putting in an
occasional appearance there when Parliament was sitting,
had in fact been sketched by a Dutchman, Simon de Koster,
whose work pleased him, and sat to the sculptress Mrs Anne
Damer, protégé of Horace Walpole, who in due time produced a bust for the City Guildhall. She presented a copy of
her insipid work to Bonaparte, during the Peace of Amiens,
and the First Consul of France kept it about him as the likeness of a foe he could respect. Nelson may also have visited
Hoppner's studio soon after the turn of the year 1801, and
he told Henry Aston Barker, son of the proprietor of a
nautical panorama shown in Leicester Fields which was so
realistic that it made Queen Charlotte feel sea-sick, that by
his ingenuity in presenting the battle, he had kept the fame
of the Nile bright for "a year longer that it would otherwise
have been, in public estimation".

Nelson's contacts with artists and writers not only helped
to keep his image fresh for posterity, it was part of that
appreciation of publicity which made him say in his eager
fashion to Colonel Drinkwater, who had done much for his
fame after the battle of St Vincent: "Why were you not with
us at Aboukir?" It was also that facet of his character which
had caused him to write from Palermo to Fanny, just a year

before his return: "I find it good to serve near home; there a man's fag and services are easily seen—next to that is writing a famous account of your own actions." This aside is one of the more notable glimpses of a nature which saw in action the material for glowing representation. There is evidence that Nelson was a subscriber to the work of Thomas Campbell, author of "Ye Mariners of England" and other rousing verse, and if he appreciated Campbell it is likely that he would have understood, more than many of his fellow-officers, the flamboyancies of Turner, who in so many canvasses glorified an era of achievement at sea.

Fanny's mind did not incline towards the heroic or romantic. Early in 1801, soon after her husband's promotion to the rank of Vice-Admiral of the Blue, the last reserves of her patience seem to have become exhausted. The most familiar story of the estrangement has it that the break occurred at the breakfast-table, with guests present. If this were true, the state of her emotions, which she seldom revealed in public, must indeed have been extraordinary. Mr William Haslewood, an attorney who was transacting some business for Nelson in connection with an action against Lord St Vincent's nominee over prize-money, when enjoined to recall the scene many years later, said: "A cheerful conversation was passing on indifferent subjects when Lord Nelson spoke of something which had been done or said by 'dear Lady Hamilton'. Lady Nelson rose from her chair and exclaimed with much vehemence, 'I am sick of hearing of dear Lady Hamilton, and am resolved that you shall give up either her or me.'

"Lord Nelson, with perfect calmness said: 'Take care, Fanny, what you say. I love you sincerely; but I cannot forget my obligations to Lady Hamilton, or speak of her otherwise than with affection and admiration.' Without saying one soothing word, but muttering something about her mind being made up, Lady Nelson left the room, and shortly after drove from the house. They never lived together again. I believe that Lord Nelson took a formal leave of her ladyship before joining the Fleet under Sir Hyde Parker."

Such was the version accepted, for want of a better, by Nelson biographers, after the story had been extracted from

Haslewood over forty years later. Fortunately another has
been preserved, though it has escaped general notice.

On 13th December 1805, very shortly after the news of
Trafalgar had reached England, when Nelson was still glowing in men's hearts, Joseph Farington, R.A., who was
extremely interested in all that concerned the admiral, and
who was one of the first and most observant pilgrims to
Burnham Thorpe, dined with Samuel Lysons the antiquary.
Sir Thomas Lawrence was a fellow-guest, and in the course
of conversation he gave the following account of the episode.
He said that Sir Andrew Hamond, Comptroller of the Navy,
"had told him that when a separation between the late Lord
Nelson and Lady Nelson his wife had been agreed upon, at
their last interview she was in bed. In that situation she put
out her hand to him, and taking his, she said, There was not
a man in the World who had more Honour than his Lordship, and that she conjured him to say upon his Honour,
whether he had ever suspected or heard from anyone anything that rendered her fidelity to him disputable. To which
he replied *Never*. They then parted, with natural respect of
each other, on all essential points, but their tempers not
calculated to suit each other." On this Farington shrewdly
observed "that before Lord Nelson's unfortunate acquaintance with Lady Hamilton, it does not appear that anything
had interrupted their domestic happiness".

Sir Andrew Hamond, a much older man than Nelson,
was well known to and much respected by both him and
Fanny. He represented Ipswich in the House of Commons
for ten years, and it is very possible that Fanny told him
herself, in one of her rare confidences. It is unlikely that
there was any such scene, before comparative strangers, as
Haslewood suggested, and it was all too probable that the
advent of Emma drove Fanny to take refuge, as so often, in
ill health. Although Farington's *Diary* was not published
until the present century, the entry itself was contemporary,
and his version has as much interest as Haslewood's,
and is altogether more in character with Fanny.

Later glimpses of the eclipsed wife are sad. Nelson rejected all attempts at reconciliation, once, at least, unkindly;
he sold Roundwood, and henceforward made his home,

whenever he was ashore, with the welcoming Hamiltons. Four years later, a niece of Nelson's old friend Admiral Cornwallis caught a glimpse of Fanny on Christmas Day, at Bath. "I went yesterday to call upon a good lady, a Litchfield clergyman's wife," she reported to her uncle at sea, "and who should be there upon her sofa but Lady Nelson, with a lameness like a sprain, by her manner of walking, which she immediately did out of the room. Poor creature! I felt ashamed of my red eyes for *tiny* sorrows in comparison with hers, and longed to support her down the stairs, had I not been a stranger to her."

Long afterwards, when she was living in Paris, Fanny's eldest Nisbet grandchild, who bore her Christian name, remarked her grandmother's invariable sweetness of temper, perhaps the result of age and resignation. She would often see her take her precious Leghorn miniature of Nelson from its casket—it was one of the few relics she possessed of her husband, apart from his letters. She would look at it affectionately, kiss it, and then turn and say: "When you are older, little Fan, you too may know what it is to have a broken heart."

Chapter 8

THE BALTIC

I

D URING the course of the year 1800, fate severed
more than one link with Nelson's earlier life. First he
found himself executor for the estate of William
Suckling; then old William Locker, his beloved "sea
daddy", died the day after Christmas. The funeral journey
to Addington in Kent would have revived memories of West
Indian waters and apprenticeship in the American war.

In mid-January, immediately after the break-up of his
home, Nelson went down to Plymouth on service. His offer
to the Admiralty had been seized upon at once, the state
of the nation not permitting the unemployment of so outstanding a flag-officer. He had been appointed to St Vincent's
fleet, with the prospect of detachment on special duty as soon
as the weather allowed. His ship was to be the great *San
Josef*, which he had himself boarded and captured four years
earlier, and which he thought an incomparable vessel. Hardy
was to be her captain, a fact which gave him satisfaction.

"Read a Letter from Lord Nelson," recorded the Secretary of the Society for the Promotion of Christian Knowledge on 13th January, "in which he states his trust that
'the conduct of the *Agamemnon* and *Vanguard* has been such
as to induce a belief that good to our King and Country may
have arisen from the Seamen and Marines having been
taught to respect the establish'd religion'." Nelson further
observed that "Kings have been shown that our Seamen are
religious", adding a request that the Crew of the *San Josef*,
his new flagship, "consisting of nearly 900 persons, may be
favor'd with a suitable supply of books". The original letter
to the Society has vanished, but great satisfaction at his
Lordship's request was officially expressed, and books were
duly sent.

On his way to join his command, Nelson called on the

widow of Captain Westcott, the only member of the "Band of Brothers" to have lost his life at the Nile. He found her in humble circumstances, and gave her one of Davison's gold medals commemorating the victory. His commander-in-chief was at Torre Abbey, and when the two men met, certain subjects were tacitly avoided in their conversation; the first was prize-money, upon which the Courts later showed St Vincent to have been in the wrong; another was Lady Hamilton, whose intimacy with Nelson was thought to be doing him increasing harm. St Vincent's idea was that Nelson's object was to get Emma received at St James's. He felt that Nelson would get himself badly embroiled in a forlorn undertaking; Troubridge agreed.

The Earl's impressions were set down in a letter to Nepean at the Admiralty. "Nelson was low when he first came here," he reported on 17th January. He "appeared and acted as if he had done me an injury, and felt apprehensive that I was acquainted with it. Poor man! He is devoured with vanity, weakness and folly; was stuck with ribbons, medals, etc. and yet pretended that he wished to avoid the honour and ceremony he everywhere met with upon the road."

Nelson had reason for feeling low. His eye was troubling him. The immediate treatment included rest, a dark room, and bathing every hour. Moreover he was enjoined to use a green shade, and not to touch wine. He hoped that Emma would make him shades, and, whatever the doctor's restrictions, he could not resist writing to her every day, often more than once. For the first time in many crowded months he was far from her, and the stream of passionate messages which continued henceforward, whenever they were separated, were soon to be concerned with the birth of their child. This was expected hourly, and would need to be concealed from all but Mrs Cadogan, who was her daughter's stay and confidant in everything, and possibly Francis Oliver, who had become "confidential steward". Nelson invented the fiction of a character aboard his ship who had got his sweetheart—Mrs Thomson or Thompson—into trouble, but would marry her when his "uncle" was out of the way. It was in terms of "Thompson" that the pair corresponded.

A few days of indisposition on Emma's part were natural enough not to arouse any stir of suspicion, particularly as her first chilly London winter for many years must in any case have been trying. Never was her ample figure—Lord Minto had once remarked it as being "monstrous for its enormity" —allied with a fashion which placed the waist-line high, of better service than in concealing what, on 29th or 30th January 1801, was delivered as a baby girl, the survivor of twins. Horatia, for such she became, was spirited away to a Marylebone wet-nurse concealed in a muff, though if ever the "shameful bundle" of popular melodrama was welcome to parents, it was Nelson's child.

It is most unlikely that Emma and Nelson deceived Sir William: indeed, it would have been hard for them to have done so: but appearances were successfully kept up: the world in general knew nothing of the event. Emma was equally skilful in causing Nelson to believe that Horatia was her first-born. In fact, a girl now grown to womanhood, Emma Carew, was living in the north of England, distressed that her parentage could not be acknowledged; while to her dying day Emma kept the facts of her own maternity from Horatia. It was then, and it continued to be, a situation fitted for the stage. So far as society was concerned, Sir William remained the unwearyingly doting husband, and indeed the truth need never have been known at all but for Emma's indiscretion, wanton or calculated, in keeping the entire sequence of Nelson's letters to her, some of which actually passed out of her possession before her last months of life. "I burn all your dear letters," wrote Nelson to her in March 1801, with a blend of chivalry and sense. "It is right for your sake," he added, "and I wish you would burn all mine— they can do no good, and will do us both harm, for any seizure of them, or the dropping even one of them, would fill the mouths of the world sooner than we intend." Emma's two last missives never reached their intended recipient, and if the general level of zest to which she attained on paper was as great as that shown in the surviving effusions of October 1805, her share of the correspondence must be accounted a sad loss in helter-skelter outpouring.

Various and distinct threads of interest appeared in

Nelson's letters at this time. One was his fear, which Emma played upon violently for many weeks to come, that Sir William would invite the Prince of Wales to dine, and that the Prince would scheme to seduce his hostess. "I own I wonder that Sir William should have a wish for the Prince of Wales to come under your roof," wrote Nelson on 26th January: "no good can come from it, but every harm. You are too beautiful not to have enemies, and even one visit will stamp you as his *chère amie*, and we know he is dotingly fond of such women as yourself, and is without one spark of honour in those respects, and would leave you to bewail your folly. But, my dear friend, I know you too well not to be convinced you cannot be seduced by any Prince in Europe. You are, in my opinion, the pattern of perfection."

On 1st February, when the *San Josef* was at Torbay, Nelson had news of the birth of Horatia. "I believe poor dear Mrs Thomson's friend will go mad with joy," he wrote. "He cries, prays, and performs all tricks, yet dare not show any of his feelings. . . . He swears he will drink your health this day in a bumper, and damn me if I don't join him in spite of all the doctors in Europe. . . . I cannot write, I am so agitated by this young man at my elbow. I believe he is foolish; he does nothing but rave about you and her." Two days later Mrs Thomson's friend "swears before Heaven that he will marry you as soon as is possible, which he fervently prays may be soon", and within a few weeks, eschewing fiction, Nelson confided: "If you was single and I found you under a hedge, I would *instantly* marry you."

Nor did Nelson neglect to pass on every pressing detail of his professional life. He informed Emma that he had just found "an order to hoist my flag in the *St George*, as Lord Spencer says I must go forth as the Champion of England in the north". A change of ships was necessary owing to a vessel of shallower draught being needed for the Baltic, for which sphere Nelson was now destined. He was pleased with the Admiralty: "in this instance," he said, "they have behaved handsomely—could not be better", and he hoped to snatch a brief leave, later, from Portsmouth. He was to sail as second-in-command of an expedition under Sir Hyde

Parker; but if Their Lordships in Whitehall had done well
in the matter of a ship for a brilliant subordinate, they were
not inspired in their choice of a leader. Parker was elderly,
rich, cautious, and recently married to a girl of nineteen,
known to some irreverent spirits as "batter pudding".
He was in no hurry to face chill and shot in a northern
latitude.

Meanwhile, Emma continued to provoke Nelson into a
frenzy of loverly jealousy about the Prince, poured out in a
succession of letters which became at times distracted. She
would tantalise, then relent; and if he was jealous, she was
possessive. She did not like Nelson to dine ashore, even with
staid old friends, if there were any other women present, and
he made her a promise not to do so without her consent,
"although", he added in a letter of 22nd February from
Spithead, "with my present feelings, I might be trusted with
50 virgins naked in a dark room".

The next day, the Admiralty granted a short leave of
absence, and Nelson raced to London, where he saw his
child, and arranged for the William Nelsons to stay near
Emma, at his expense, whenever she wished for his clerical
brother's society. With his sharp clarity he told Emma,
"Reverend Sir you will find a great bore at times, therefore
he ought to amuse himself all the mornings, and not always
dine with you, as Sir William may not like it. They can twice
or thrice a week have a beef-steak at home, for some people
may say bye and bye that Sir William maintains the family
of the Nelsons, which would vex me." Whether Nelson
saw any resemblance to himself in the infant who was
in the care of Mrs Gibson of Great Titchfield Street is
not recorded. Drawings dated from her childhood give little
indication: but by good fortune Horatia lived on into the
era of photography, and her appearance in age affords en-
thralling speculation as to how Nelson might have appeared
in his later years, had he survived Trafalgar.

No sooner had Nelson returned to the *St George* than
Oliver arrived hot-foot with letters. "When he was announced by Hardy," reported Nelson, "so much anxiety for
your safety rushed into my mind that a pain immediately
seized my heart, which kept increasing for half an hour, that,

turning cold, hot, cold, &c., I was obliged to send for the surgeon, who gave me something to warm me, for it was a deadly chill." Nelson was in that state where he could truly say: "I am all soul and sensibility; a fine thread will lead me, but with my life I would resist a cable from dragging me."

On 1st March Oliver was despatched with a long letter which began: "Now, my own dear wife, for such you are in my eyes and in the face of heaven, I can give full scope to my feelings. . . . You know, my dearest Emma, that there is nothing in this world that I would not do for us to live together, and have our dear little child with us. I firmly believe that this campaign will give us peace, and then we will set off for Brontë . . . for unless all matters accord it would bring 100 of tongues and slanderous reports if I separated from her (which I would do with pleasure the moment we can be united; I want to see her no more), therefore we must manage till we can quit this country or your 'uncle' dies. I love, I never did love anyone else. I never had a dear pledge of love till you gave me one, and you, thank God, never gave one to anyone else. I think before March is out you will either see us back, or so victorious we shall insure a glorious issue to our toils. Think what my Emma will feel at seeing return safe, perhaps with a little more fame, her own dear loving Nelson. You, my beloved Emma, and my Country, are the two dearest objects of my fond heart—*a heart susceptible and true.*"

His excitement mounting, he added: "My longing for you, both person and conversation, you may readily imagine. What must be my sensations at the idea of sleeping with you! it setts me on fire, even the thoughts, much more would the reality. I am sure my love & desires are all to you, and if any woman naked were to come to me, even as I am this moment from thinking of you, I hope it might rot off if I would touch her even with my hand. No, my heart, person and mind is in perfect union of love towards my own, dear beloved Emma."

Four days later, in cold contrast, Nelson wrote his last surviving letter to Fanny. It was from the *St George* at sea, and he seems, almost unbelievably, to have sent a copy to Emma. "Josiah is to have another ship," he reported (wrongly as it proved), "and to go abroad, if the *Thalia* cannot soon be got ready. I have done *all* for him, and he may again, as he has often done before, wish me to break my neck, and be abetted in it by his friends, who are likewise my enemies; but I have done my duty as an honest, generous man, and I neither want or wish for anybody to care what becomes of me, whether I return, or am left in the Baltic. Living, I have done all in my power for you, and if dead, you will find I have done the same; therefore my only wish is to be left to myself; and wishing you every happiness, believe that I am, your affectionate Nelson and Brontë."

Only the top half of the original of this missive survives. Upon this Fanny wrote: "This is my Lord Nelson's letter of dismissal, which so astonished me that I immediately sent it to Mr Maurice Nelson, who was sincerely attached to me, for his advice; he desired me not to take the least notice of it as his Brother seemed to have forgot himself."

Maurice Nelson was at the time a very sick man, but his advice was perhaps no better and no worse than anyone else's would have been who cared sincerely for Fanny. Not even he, with fraternal knowledge and insight, could have apprehended how intense was Horatio's new attachment, or that it would be constant for the rest of his life, growing rather than diminishing with every month that passed.

II

"I am brushing these fellows up," wrote Nelson of the officers and men he now commanded. "I do not find that activity which my mind carries with it." Lethargy indeed pervaded the direction of affairs in the northern expedition as he first found it. It had been conceived by Pitt's government with the bold imagination befitting a nation facing a hostile Continent, but dilatory execution could spoil the best-laid plan.

Paul of Russia had become soured in his relations with Great Britain, largely because he had been unable to share in the liberation of Malta, the surrender of which had actually been offered him by Bonaparte, who played upon his fancy for the rôle of Grand Master of the Knights. The Czar had not merely transferred his friendship to the French but, in conjunction with the government of the other Baltic powers, Denmark—which then included Norway—Sweden, and Prussia, he had revived the old political combination known as the Armed Neutrality of the North. An association of the same sort had been formed twenty years earlier, during the course of the American war, to try to enforce the principle that neutrals might trade with immunity even along belligerent coasts, freed of the fear of search.

As Great Britain was once again alone in her fight with France, it was essential to her interests, perhaps even to her existence, that Scandinavia, rich in the raw materials of shipbuilding, should be prevented from combining to supply the enemy with sinews of war; it was equally important that a large share of Baltic exports should continue to strengthen the resources of a nation then straining every nerve to maintain the status of a world power.

Incidents between Danish and British vessels had already occurred, but war was not formally declared by or against the Northern Powers either before the sailing of Parker's expedition or during its actual course. It was, however, intended that Paul's menacing combination should be met with stern counter-measures, in which fighting was by no means excluded. One of the axioms of the earlier Armed Neutrality had been that: "a blockade to be respected must be efficient". Britain meant to make hers so.

In order to reinforce the complements of Parker's ships and to provide a landing-force, the 49th Regiment and a company of riflemen were embarked at Portsmouth. Nelson had the good fortune to receive into the *St George* an officer after his own heart. Lieutenant-Colonel the Honourable William Stewart, the man concerned, was a Scot, a son of the Earl of Galloway; he was a rifleman, and was senior military officer afloat. Stewart was then twenty-seven; he had already been in many fights, and was to survive many more. Sir Charles Napier, who knew him well, wrote of him that he was "open-hearted and honourable in the highest degree, but with much passion, much zeal—and not the least judgment". That was an opinion based upon experience in later years. Nelson's reactions were less qualified. "I love, honour and respect you," he wrote to Stewart after they had parted. "I hope whenever we serve together that you will command the troops."

Just as it is to a military officer, Colonel Drinkwater, that posterity owes the most detailed portrait of Nelson at the time of the battle of St Vincent, so it was Stewart who, out of material from his Journal of the Baltic Expedition, provided the closest account of Nelson at Copenhagen. He had a vivid first impression: for immediately upon Nelson's return to Portsmouth from his London leave he sent for the Colonel and told him that the troops were to be embarked at once, as he would sail on the next tide. He intended to take the caulkers and painters who were then in the ship away with him to St Helens, so that not a moment should be lost. Nelson in a hurry allowed nothing, not even a dockyard worker, to stand in his way.

Hardly had the *St George* put to sea than Stewart had a glimpse of a side of Nelson's character familiar to Hardy, who used to say that the reason they never quarrelled was because when Nelson wished to be captain, he, Hardy, played first lieutenant, but when being an admiral took Nelson's fancy, Hardy assumed his proper rôle. "His Lordship," wrote Stewart, "was rather too apt to interfere in the working of the ship, and not always with the best success or judgment. The wind, when off Dungeness, was scanty, and the Ship was to be put about; Lord Nelson *would* give the orders, and caused her to miss stays," that is, she failed to tack. "Upon this he said rather peevishly to the Master or Officer of the Watch: 'Well, now, see what we have done. Well Sir, what do you mean to do?' The Officer saying with hesitation: 'I don't exactly know my lord; I fear she won't do', Lord Nelson turned sharply towards the cabin and replied: 'Well, I am sure if you don't know what to do with her, no more do I either.' He then went in, leaving the Officer to work the Ship as he liked."

Nelson joined Parker at Yarmouth Roads on 6th March, and found the Commander-in-Chief living on shore. The fact disturbed him. Nelson, said Stewart, duly "reported his arrival, and announced his intention of waiting on Sir Hyde the next morning. We breakfasted, as usual, soon after six o'clock, for we were always up before daylight. We went on shore, so as to be at Sir Hyde's door by eight o'clock, Lord Nelson choosing to be amusingly exact to that hour, which he considered a very late one for business."

Parker's attitude exasperated Nelson. Not only did he not open his mind, but his energies, such as they were, seemed directed to arranging a ball. This was altogether too much for Nelson. It happened that Troubridge had just been appointed to the Board of Admiralty, under the presidency of St Vincent, and to him he wrote post-haste: "if a Lord of the Admiralty—and such a Lord—had not told me that the Baltic fleet had orders to put to sea, I would not have believed it; and forgive me, I even think seriously that, by some accident, they have not arrived, for there is not the least appearance of going. . . . I know, my dear Troubridge, how angry the Earl would be if he knew I, as second-in-command, was to venture to give an opinion, because I know his opinion of officers writing to the Admiralty. But what I say is in the mouth of all the old market-women at Yarmouth. . . . Consider how nice it must be laying in bed with a young wife, compared to a damned cold raw wind. But, my dear Troubridge, pack us off. I am interested, as I want to return."

Imperative orders to sail soon arrived. Nelson's first act in a new campaign—typically independent of the orthodox chain of command—had its effect. Lady Parker's gaiety was postponed.

Nelson kept a rough Journal of notes on the Baltic campaign, loose sheets of foolscap which have been unused in earlier biographies, having been long in private hands. "The fleet in general," he wrote the first full day at sea, 13th March, "keep very badly their stations, for although the Commander-in-Chief made the signal for close order of sailing, yet scarcely one have kept their stations and in particular the good going ships."

He had seen Davison at Yarmouth; indeed, Nelson's old friend and prize agent was his channel of communication with London. To Davison he wrote, on 16th March from sea: "Our weather is very cold, we have received much snow and sharp frost. I have not yet seen my Commander-in-Chief, and have had no official communication whatever. All I have gathered of our first plans, I disapprove most exceedingly; honour may arise from them, good cannot. I hear we are likely to anchor outside Cronenburg Castle, instead of Copenhagen, which would give weight to our negotiation: a Danish Minister would think twice before he would put his name to war with England, when the next moment he would probably see his Master's Fleet in flames, and his Capital in ruins; but 'out of sight out of mind' is an old saying. The Dane should see our Flag waving every moment he lifted up his head."

What Nelson omitted to mention was that, although there had been no opportunity to consult Sir Hyde since the expedition sailed, he had at least won his approbation. Parker liked good living, and a certain Lieutenant Layman, serving in the *St George*, happened to mention, in Nelson's presence, that some years before he had caught a very fine turbot on the Dogger Bank, near which the fleet must pass. When the right moment came, Nelson asked Layman if he thought he could catch one this time. After a try or two, a fish was caught. Nelson at once said: "Send it to Sir Hyde." Somebody murmured about the risk of sending over a boat in a rising sea so near to nightfall, but Nelson was insistent that Parker should have his delicacy. Back came a note of compliment, and from that moment communication was less constrained. Layman said afterwards that a turbot gained Nelson a victory. Nelson's Journal omits the incident, but mentions that Parker sent him a private note on 14th March containing among other things "a little of his intentions".

If the fish did something to put Sir Hyde on easier terms with his subordinate, the instructions which were forwarded soon after the expedition sailed might well have upset his complacency: for he was enjoined to see that the Danes agreed to a settlement, of British demands, either by "amicable arrangement, or by actual hostilities". He was then to push on to Reval, where he was to "make an immediate and vigorous attack" on the Russians if the measure proved to be practicable, and then to proceed against Cronstadt, still further eastward. In the hands of a Nelson, such orders would have been all the excuse needed for the most pressing and diverse activity. They merely served to emphasise Parker's indecision. Good strategy dictated that the Powers should be defeated as soon as possible: above all, in detail, for the Danes were reported to have twenty-three ships of the line, the Swedes eighteen, and the Russians no fewer than eighty-two, though it was known that they were ill manned and worse equipped.

By 19th March the fleet had reached the Skaw, the northernmost tip of Denmark, whence the broad channel of the Kattegat extends southward, between Sweden and Denmark, until it reaches the isle of Zealand, on the eastern shore of which lies Copenhagen. The entrances to the Baltic are upon either side of Zealand, the westerly being the Great Belt, and the easterly the Sound. Although the wind was fair for Copenhagen, there was no sign that Sir Hyde would act with despatch. Meanwhile, Nicholas Vansittart from the Foreign Office was sent ahead of the fleet with official instructions to allow Denmark forty-eight hours to withdraw from the Northern Coalition, otherwise she would have to take the consequences.

On the evening of the 20th the fleet anchored in the Kattegat, about eighteen miles above Cronenburg Castle and Hamlet's town of Elsinore. Both Danish and Swedish shores were hostile, and Parker would not attempt to force a passage until he had heard the result of Vansittart's mission. On the 23rd the diplomatist returned, with the terms rejected, and with news of great preparations being made for the defence of Copenhagen. Sir Hyde then called a council. "Now we are sure of fighting," wrote Nelson to Emma, with reasonable asperity, "I am sent for. When it was a joke I was kept in the background."

Nelson disliked councils, except those over which he could himself preside, and thus, at a pinch, ensure his own way. "If a man consults whether he is to fight, when he has the power in his own hands," he wrote later, *it is certain that his opinion is against fighting.*" The italics were his. The dismal history of many eighteenth-century operations sup-

ported this view as realistic. His own bravery was exceptional, but he knew that, in battle, it represented the victory
of exaltation over self-preservation, and he knew, moreover,
that many of his fellows lacked his vital fire.

Nelson rarely wished to challenge unreasonable odds, but
he had a practical view of the opposition, and a clear recollection of what, within his own lifetime, enemies had and
had not achieved at sea. He was, therefore, at all times
prepared to work to a lower factor of safety than men of less
combat experience than himself—and few admirals had
more. He was generally, though not always, right, and the
Baltic provided as perfect an instance as could be conceived
of judgment so nice that the loss or absence of one ship
might have reversed the fortunes of encounter.

In Parker's council all was gloom. Nelson's first task was
to dissipate an atmosphere which he deplored. Having heard
from Vansittart that the great strength of the Danes was at
the head of their line, he at first proposed that the attempt
should be made from the tail—that is, that the fleet should
negotiate the difficult passage of the Belt, and take the
enemy from the south. But "go by the Sound, or the Belt,
or anyhow," was his repeated advice, "only lose not an
hour". What he feared was that Sir Hyde would wait inactive in the Kattegat until the combined fleets chose to
come out and fight. His hope was to get in a shrewd blow
first, what he called a "*home* stroke". He would himself have
favoured that the stroke should have been upon the Russians
at Reval, a small force being left to cover Denmark, but that
was an idea hopeless to implant in minds already beset with
irresolution.

After returning to his own ship, he composed an urgent
but considered appreciation. "The more I have reflected,"
he told Sir Hyde, "the more I am confirmed in opinion, that
not a moment should be lost in attacking the Enemy: they
will every day and hour be stronger; we never shall be so
good a match for them as at this moment. The only consideration in my mind is, how to get at them with the least
risk to our ships. Here you are, with almost the safety,
certainly with the honour, of England more entrusted to you
than ever yet fell to the lot of any British Officer. On your

decision depends, whether our Country shall be degraded in the eyes of Europe, or whether she shall rear her head higher than ever; again do I repeat, never did our Country depend so much on the success of any Fleet as this." Nelson then weighed the pros and cons of the Belt and the Sound passages, concluding with the maxim from Chatham which he so often liked to quote. "I am of opinion the boldest measures are the safest; and our Country demands a most vigorous exertion of her force, directed with judgment."

His Journal stated laconically that his conversation with Sir Hyde had been "too important to be quoted, but I trust it was for the honour of our country, and that I had the satisfaction of altering the very erroneous opinion given by . . ." The name omitted may have been that of Domett, Sir Hyde's captain of the fleet.

On 25th March Captain Otway of the *London*, came across to the *St George* with a message that Sir Hyde "was uneasy about going round by the Belt in case of accidents, and therefore he thought of going by Cronenburg, to which," said Nelson, "I cordially assented". Otway, who had some local knowledge, and whose record acquitted him of pusillanimous instincts, supported the Commander-in-Chief's opinion.

"I don't care a damn by which passage we go," Nelson said, "so that we fight them." But despite his vehemence, then and later, he showed more patience with the very senior Sir Hyde, who had been a post-captain when Nelson was a child, and had served as chief of staff to Lord Hood, than he ever extended to Lord Keith. "Sir Hyde Parker," he wrote complacently to Emma, "has by this time found out the worth of your Nelson, and that he is a useful sort of man on a pinch; therefore, if he has ever thought unkindly of me, I freely forgive him. Nelson must stand among the first, or he must fall." In this expedition it seemed he was unlikely to meet with competition.

By the evening of 26th March the fleet were anchored six miles above Cronenburg, and on that day Nelson noted that he "received directions to take under my direction 10 sail of the line, 4 frigates, 4 sloops, 7 bombs, 2 fire-ships and 12 gun-brigs which were to be engaged on a particular service;

our day employed in arranging and explaining to the
different officers the intended mode of attack. In the evening
shifted my flag from the *St George* to the *Elephant*. Very
unwell all day."

The detachment given to Nelson was to be employed in
the tactical assault on Copenhagen, the plan being a bombardment, possibly followed by a landing. For the second
time within a short time he found himself under the necessity
of flying his flag in a ship of shallower draught; in this
instance the *Elephant* had Foley as her captain, the man
who, when in command of the *Goliath*, had led inside the
French position at Aboukir Bay. It was a good omen. Nelson
was cheered next day, when the fleet were held up by head-
winds and calms, by some vessels coming through the
Sound, "who report the consternation and confusion at
Copenhagen."

On the 30th, the wind being from the north-west, the
fleet weighed, and passed the massive Danish fortress at
Cronenburg. It had been thought that the Swedes would
also open fire, but finding that the guns on their side of the
channel remained silent, the column inclined eastwards, thus
keeping out of range of the Danish batteries, which blazed
away in useless noise. "More powder and shot, I believe,
never was thrown away," wrote Nelson to Emma, "for not
one shot struck a single ship of the British fleet. Some of our
ships fired; but the *Elephant* did not return a single shot.
I hope to reserve them for a better occasion." He added
that he had "just been reconnoitring the Danish line of
defence. It looks formidable to those who are children at
war, but to my judgment, with ten sail of the line I think I
can annihilate them; at all events, I hope to be allowed to
try."

The reconnaissance was made towards nightfall in a
schooner, in which Sir Hyde and others accompanied Nelson.
"We soon perceived," wrote Colonel Stewart, "that our
delay had been of important advantage to the enemy, who
had lined the northern edge of the shoals near the Crown
batteries, and the front of the harbour and arsenal, with a
formidable flotilla. The Trekroner, or Three Crowns, battery
appeared in particular to have been strengthened, and all

the buoys of the Northern and of the King's Channel had been removed."

The night was employed, by those most skilled in surveying, in laying down fresh buoys. On the 31st Sir Hyde, together with Nelson, Stewart and others, proceeded in the *Amazon* frigate, Captain Riou, to a closer examination of the whole Danish position. "Captain Riou became on this occasion first known to Lord Nelson," recorded Stewart, "who was struck with admiration at the superior discipline and seamanship that were observable on board the *Amazon* during the proceedings of the day." Riou was in fact a superb frigate officer. He had already made a reputation in the navy by saving the *Guardian* of 44 guns by extraordinary exertions, after severe damage from an iceberg. Nelson himself noted "the ability and judgment of Captain Riou", whose sailing-master, appropriately called Mr Channel, did his work in a most satisfactory manner. In the Council of War that followed, Sir Hyde not only left all the tactical details to Nelson, but generously gave him two more line-of-battleships.

"During this Council of War," recorded Stewart, "the energy of Lord Nelson's character was remarked: certain difficulties had been started by some of the members, relative to each of the three Powers we should have to engage, in succession or united, in those seas. The number of the Russians was, in particular, represented as formidable. Lord Nelson kept pacing the cabin, mortified at everything which savoured either of alarm or irresolution. When the above remark was applied to the Swedes, he sharply observed 'The more numerous the better', and when to the Russians, he repeatedly said 'So much the better, I wish they were twice as many, the easier the victory, depend on it.' He alluded, as he afterwards explained in private, to the total want of *tactique* among the Northern Fleets. He used to say: 'Close with a Frenchman, but out-manœuvre a Russian.'" Sir Hyde's chaplain, Mr Alexander Scott, who afterwards became a devoted member of Nelson's retinue, wrote on the day of the Council, "I fear there is a great deal of Quixotism in this business; there is no getting any positive information of their strength."

III

The intention at Copenhagen was not to devastate a capital city, but to reduce a potentially dangerous fleet to the point at which it could serve no immediate purpose in the war. The attackers had the sole advantage of mobility; the Danes for their part were able to use shore fortifications to aid their ships; and they had at their backs the resources of a base and indeed of a countryside. Mr Scott had some reason for his use of the word "Quixotism". Windmills were a feature of the landscape spread before the fleet.

There were two ways by which Copenhagen could be approached. The inner or westernmost passage was known as the King's Channel, the easterly as the Outer Deep. Between the two was a shoal, called the Middle Ground. The Danish defence was concentrated along the King's Channel. It consisted of a line of nineteen hulks and floating batteries, mostly mastless, flanked at the northern end by the great Trekroner Fort. The Fort also guarded a narrower channel to the harbour, where a small mobile squadron was placed. This, in the upshot, was never seriously engaged.

The strength of the Danish position lay in the size and siting of the Trekroner. An advance upon it from the north needed a northerly wind, and if the movement were unsuccessful, the attacker had no hope of return. Attack from the south presupposed successful navigation of the Outer Deep on a southerly wind—no mean feat without local pilots—then anchorage, beyond the shoals of the Middle Ground until a change of wind enabled an approach to be made along the line of the moored hulks, which were more vulnerable than the Battery.

Once a southerly position was gained, the squadron would be interposed between the other Baltic fleets and Denmark, which could not be reinforced until the British were defeated. Nelson's plan was that, with his own detachment, he should pass along the Outer Deep, gain the southern flank and then, when the wind changed, carry out the main assault. Parker intended to support him as best he could with a demonstration against the northern end, but the wind would be against him, as would the fact that most of his ships were of deep draught.

Nelson accomplished the first part of his design on 1st April, the *Amazon* leading. "Not one accident occurred," noted Stewart approvingly. "12 ships of the line, frigates, bombs, gun-vessels all were safely anchored to the southward of the Middle Ground by 5 o'clock," noted Nelson in his Journal. "The Danes threw a few shells, but did no damage." The anchorage was satisfactory, and as the *Elephant* came to rest, Nelson exclaimed: "I will fight them the moment I have a fair wind."

Stewart thought that the enemy could have done much harm among more than thirty vessels grouped so close together within long range, but, he said, they were "too much occupied during this night in manning their Ships, and strengthening their Line; not from immediate expectation, as we afterwards learned, of our Attack—conceiving the Channel impracticable to so large a Fleet, but as a precaution against our nearer approach". Brueys, three years earlier, had reasoned very much the same at the Nile.

After dark Hardy actually rowed as far as the outermost Danish ship, "sounding round her, and using a pole when he was apprehensive of being heard". Meanwhile, on board the *Elephant* Stewart recorded that "the gallant Nelson sat down to table with a large party of his comrades in arms. He was in the highest spirits, and drank to a leading wind, and to the success of the ensuing day." Stewart felt privileged to be present with Foley, Fremantle, Riou, Rear-Admiral Thomas Graves (Nelson's second-in-command), and a few others to whom he was particularly attached. "Every man separated with feelings of admiration for their great leader," he said, "and with anxious impatience to follow him to the approaching Battle."

Riou and Foley were left with Nelson to arrange the Order of Battle, and to draft the plans to be issued to each ship on the following morning. "From the previous fatigue of this day," added Stewart, "and of the two preceding, Lord Nelson was so much exhausted while dictating his instructions, that it was recommended by us all, and, indeed, insisted upon by his old servant, Allen, who assumed much

command on these occasions, that he should go to his cot.
It was placed on the floor, but from it he still continued to
dictate. The orders were completed about one o'clock, when
half a dozen Clerks in the foremost cabin proceeded to
transcribe them. Lord Nelson's impatience again showed
itself; for instead of sleeping undisturbedly, as he might
have done, he was every half hour calling from his cot to
these Clerks to hasten their work, for that the wind was
becoming fair: he was constantly receiving a report of this
during the night. Their work being finished about six in the
morning, his Lordship, who was previously up and dressed,
breakfasted, at about seven made the signal for all captains.
The instructions were delivered to each by eight o'clock;
and a special command was given to Captain Riou to act as
circumstances might require." Riou had two frigates in
addition to the *Amazon*, two sloops, and two fire-ships.

Daylight showed that the wind had indeed changed. "It
was characteristic of the fortune of the 'heaven-born' admiral,
that the wind which had been fair the day before to take him
south, changed by the hour of battle to fair to take him
north," says Mahan in his tribute to Nelson, adding, "but
it is only just to notice also that he himself never trifled with
a fair wind, nor with time."

The directions were that the three leading ships, originally the *Edgar*, *Ardent* and *Glatton*, should pass along the
Danish line, engaging as they went, until the foremost
reached the fifth Dane, a blockship inferior to herself,
abreast of which she was to anchor by the stern. It was a
general order to anchor thus, as it had been at the Nile.
Numbers Two and Three were to pass number One, and
anchor successively ahead of her, while Four and Five were
to anchor astern of her, engaging the two flank blockships.
Nelson hoped that the two southernmost Danes would be
speedily silenced. Their immediate antagonists had orders,
when that was done, to cut the cables and go north, rein-
forcing the fight in that quarter. The dispositions for the
other ships allowed them to pass along the outer side of those
engaged, each one anchoring as it cleared the foremost
vessel already in action.

In the circumstances of the day, the plan became confused.

The pilots—merchant marine navigators, pressed into the service of the fleet owing to their local experience—showed much hesitation, and indeed they seemed to Nelson to "have no other thought than to keep the ship clear of danger, and their own silly heads clear of shot". At last the Master of the *Bellona*, Mr Briarly, offered to lead in, and he was transferred to Captain Murray's ship, the *Edgar*. She was followed by the *Agamemnon*, Nelson's old favourite. But the *Agamemnon* was so placed that she could not clear the Middle Ground, and never got into action at all. Two others, the *Bellona* and the *Russell*, stuck on the west side of the Middle Ground, but they could at least use their guns, and did so to some purpose against the southernmost enemy. Nelson quickly made new dispositions, and managed to complete a line of nine ships closely engaged. Riou found himself bombarding the Trekroner, and a blockship south of it, with his light squadron; long odds in weight of metal, but the best position in the circumstances, since his proper target, the Danish division in the harbour, did not come out. Henceforward it was sheer slogging.

"It is warm work," said Nelson cheerfully to Colonel Stewart, "and this day may be the last to us at any moment. But mark you! I would not be elsewhere for thousands!" His conversation, said Southey, "became joyous, animated, elevated and delightful". Truly was Lord Malmesbury right when, in a later eulogy, he said, "he added to genius, valour and energy the singular power of electrifying all within his atmosphere".

A lieutenant who had reported the grounding of the *Bellona* and *Russell* was reprimanded by Foley, not for the information but for the way in which he conveyed it. When he heard of the incident, Nelson supported his flag-captain. "I think," he said, "at such a moment, the delivery of anything like a desponding opinion, unasked, was highly reprehensible." No one knew better than Nelson the value of morale, and the swiftness with which, in a time of acute crisis, it could be shattered. He remembered the salutary example of Jervis before the battle of St Vincent, who, when more and more Spanish ships were reported to be in sight, cut the information short with: "Enough Sir, no more of that. The die is cast, and if there are fifty sail I will go through them!"

If the heavier units had been unlucky, Parker's two extra ships were justified, for those which contrived to take up position did their work, and this despite the fact that all but one of the gun-brigs were prevented by baffling currents from weathering the Middle Ground, and that few of the bomb-vessels reached a station where they could use their mortars against the arsenal, lobbing their shells over both fleets.

Meanwhile the Commander-in-Chief, who was near enough to know the unfavourable accidents which had weakened Nelson, yet too distant to follow the intricacies of the fighting, suffered painful anxiety. Wind and current prevented him from direct support, and at one o'clock, seeing the Danish fire still fierce, he began to despair of success. He had never been in action with Nelson.

Southey, whose brother Tom was present at the battle and gave him first-hand details, recorded Sir Hyde as saying to Domett, "I will make the signal of recall for Nelson's sake. If he is in a condition to continue the action successfully, he will disregard it; if he is not, it will be an excuse for his retreat, and no blame can be imputed to him." Domett urged his chief to delay, and to let Otway row to the scene and signal the true state of affairs, but before Otway could reach Nelson, Sir Hyde's opinion hardened. "The fire was too hot for Nelson to oppose," he said, "a retreat he thought must be made—he was aware of the consequences to his own personal reputation, but it would be cowardly in him to leave Nelson to bear the whole share of the failure, if failure it should be deemed." Under a mistaken though sympathetic impulse, the signal was flown.

Sir Hyde, as Southey said and Nelson would not have disputed, showed "disinterested and generous feeling", but his act might have been disastrous, and it had, in fact, some grievous consequences. His offence was that of the desponding lieutenant writ large.

The immediate effect has long passed into legend. Stewart recorded that when signal No. 39 was made—to discontinue action—the lieutenant reported it to Nelson.

"He continued his walk, and did not appear to take notice of it. The lieutenant, meeting his Lordship at the next turn, asked 'whether he should repeat it?' Lord Nelson answered, 'No, acknowledge it.' On the officer returning to the poop, his Lordship called after him, 'Is No. 16, for close action, still hoisted?' The lieutenant answering in the affirmative, Lord Nelson said, 'Mind you keep it so.' He now walked the deck considerably agitated, which was always known by his moving the stump of his right arm. After a turn or two he said to me, in a quick manner, 'Do you know what's shown on board of the Commander-in-Chief? No. 39!' On asking him what that meant, he answered, 'Why, to leave off action.' 'Leave off action!' he repeated, and then added, with a shrug, 'Now damn me if I do!' He also observed, I believe to Captain Foley, 'You know, Foley, I have only one eye—I have a right to be blind sometimes'; and then, with an archness peculiar to his character, putting the glass to his blind eye, he exclaimed, 'I really do not see the signal!' "

Rear-Admiral Graves, from his leading station in the *Defiance*, saw it immediately and duly repeated it, but either by accident or design he too kept No. 16 flying, and continued in action. Riou's division, who were under deadly fire from the Trekroner, obeyed No. 39 and hauled off. Riou, said Stewart, "was sitting on a gun, encouraging his men, and had been wounded in the head by a splinter. He had expressed himself grieved at being thus obliged to retreat, and nobly observed, 'What will Nelson think of us?' His Clerk was killed by his side; and by another shot, several of the Marines, while hauling on the mainbrace, shared the same fate. Riou then exclaimed, 'Come, then, my boys, let us all die together!' The words were scarcely uttered when the fatal shot severed him in two. Thus, and in an instant, was the British service deprived of one of its greatest ornaments, and society of a character of singular worth, resembling the heroes of romance."

The fighting continued without a break until about two in the afternoon, when the greater part of the Danish line was silent. Some of their smaller ships were on fire, and the carnage on board was dreadful, since reinforcements, including students from the university, were continually being

drafted from the shore to serve the guns. Taking possession
of such ships as had struck was a matter of difficulty, partly
because they were fired at by shore batteries, and also
because fire was kept up spasmodically from the ships themselves whenever British boats approached.

Even the *Dannebrog*, the flagship, presented a problem,
for although she was on fire and had struck, the commodore
having removed his pendant, she broke away from her
moorings and drifted in flames before the wind, spreading
terror throughout the enemy line. Boats rowed away to save
the crew, who threw themselves out of every port-hole, but
the rescuers were hampered in their work by shots from the
shore. In the end, the *Dannebrog* drifted to leeward and blew
up at about half-past three.

Before this climax, Nelson had become so exasperated at
the way in which humanity was impeded that he exclaimed:
"Either I must send on shore, and stop this irregular proceeding, or send in our fire ships and burn them." He
thereupon wrote as follows:

"TO THE BROTHERS OF ENGLISHMEN, THE DANES

Lord Nelson has directions to spare Denmark, when no longer
resisting; but if the firing is continued on the part of Denmark,
Lord Nelson will be obliged to set on fire all the Floating-batteries
he has taken, without having the power of saving the brave Danes
who have defended them. Dated on board his Britannic Majesty's
Ship *Elephant*, Copenhagen Roads, April 2nd 1801.

NELSON AND BRONTE, Vice-Admiral, under the
Command of Admiral Sir Hyde Parker."

This letter was sent ashore through the contending fleets by
the hand of Captain Sir Frederick Thesiger, who had extensive knowledge of Denmark, and who was serving on
Nelson's staff. Thesiger found the Prince Regent near the
Sally-port, cheering on his people. He delivered his letter
under a flag of truce.

The missive itself was written with care, the Purser of the
Elephant recalling that it was composed at the casing of the
rudder-head, and that as the Admiral wrote, he, Wallis, took
a copy, both of them standing. "The original," said Wallis,

R

"was put into an envelope and sealed with his Arms; at first I was going to seal it with a wafer, but he would not allow this to be done, observing that it must be sealed properly, or the Enemy would think it was written and sent in a hurry." The man first sent below for a candle was killed on his way, but another succeeded. "The wax told no tales," said Nelson. A wafer would still have been wet when it reached the Prince.

The Prince enquired more minutely into Nelson's intention in sending to him. "Lord Nelson's object in sending the flag of truce was humanity," he replied. "He therefore consents that hostilities shall cease, and that the wounded Danes may be taken on shore. And Lord Nelson will take his prisoners out of the vessels, and burn and carry off his prizes as he shall think fit. Lord Nelson, with humble duty to His Royal Highness the Prince of Denmark, will consider this the greatest victory he has ever gained if it may be the cause of a happy reconciliation and union between his own most gracious sovereign, and His Majesty the King of Denmark." Firing ceased.

It was a good thing that it did so, for although Nelson's ships had inflicted great damage on the enemy, they had suffered much themselves. Conference with Fremantle and Foley, which Nelson held while Thesiger was away, had shown both these officers to be strongly against an advance on that part of the Danish line which was still unsubdued, particularly as the Trekroner was capable of battering any ship which came within the range of her guns. The opinion of these officers, neither of whom could be accused of timidity, was that the squadron should extricate itself as best it could while the wind was favourable and while the armistice continued. How wise this advice was, was soon proved by the fact that no less than four ships, the *Monarch*, the *Defiance*, the *Elephant* herself and the frigate *Desiree*, all ran aground while within range of the guns of the battery. "Had there been no cessation of hostilities," said Stewart, "their situation would certainly have been perilous." After the *Elephant* had grounded, Nelson followed the Danish Adjutant General, Lindholm, to a conference aboard the *London*.

So ended the fiercest and saddest fight of Nelson's life, in which "there was nothing," in Southey's words, "of that indignation against the enemy, and that impression of retributive justice, which at the Nile had given a sterner temper to his mind, and a sense of austere delight, in beholding the vengeance of which he was the appointed minister". The casualties were awe-inspiring, some nine hundred British and some six thousand Danes killed, wounded and prisoners. Of them, a few at least were needless, particularly among soldiers of the 49th Regiment. Southey relates that "the commanding officer of the troops on board one of our ships, asked where his men should be stationed? He was told that they could be of no use; that they were not near enough for musquetry, and were not wanted at the guns; they had, therefore, better go below. This, he said, was impossible— it would be a disgrace that could never be wiped away. They were, therefore, drawn up upon the gangway, to satisfy this cruel point of honour; and there, without the possibility of annoying the enemy, they were mowed down." Nearly fifty years earlier, Lord Howe had ordered his men to lie down in action when not serving at rope or gun, but neither in the army nor navy was his sensible example widely followed.

For the second time in his life after a general action, Nelson went aboard the commander-in-chief's flagship half expecting a reprimand, even though his disobedience had brought about a victory. But, as at St Vincent, there was nothing but praise for his initiative and determination. Nelson's entry in his Journal concerning the longest day of his life was laconic, and by a curious slip he recorded the action as starting an hour earlier than in fact it did. "April 2. Moderate breezes southerly, at 9 made the signal to engage the Danish line; the action began at 5 min. and lasted about 4 hours, when 17 out of 18 of the Danish line were taken, burnt or sunk. Our ships suffered a good deal. At night went on board the *St George* very unwell."

If unwell, Nelson's night was free at least of the sound of gunfire, for Lindholm advised that the armistice be continued, and the unsecured prizes formally surrendered. He can rarely have snatched rest with the consciousness of duty more ably fulfilled, courage longer sustained, or tactical

experience put to better use. Over forty years old, battered
by arduous service, he had shown himself capable of exertions which would have prostrated many a younger officer.
Since he had shifted his flag to the *Elephant*, six days before,
he had conducted his squadron through exceptional hazards
of navigation, had surveyed the enemy position, planned and
issued written instructions to every individual captain and
then—on a change of wind—had fought an action of acute
severity, ending it with a piece of what might be called
martial diplomacy which not only saved his squadron from
further damage but won his way with his opponents.

Nelson can have slept little since 29th March, for he had
needed to make a succession of difficult and vital decisions,
often from moment to moment, and to watch them carried
out. He had exposed his person to every danger, as was his
custom and, perhaps, his relish. Tom Allen would have been
glad enough, on the night of 2nd April, to see the sheets
of his master's manuscript Journal fall from his hand and
his eyes close in slumber.

IV

It was typical of Nelson that his first duty next day, one
on which he noted "a very cold wind", was "to inspect the
ships which had been in action". Among the badly wounded
was Captain Thompson of the *Bellona*, who had fought the
Leander so bravely at the Nile. Thompson had lost a leg,
and his ship suffered much through the bursting of her own
guns. Thompson preserved an affectionate note from Nelson
in which he was told, "My Dear Fellow, Patience is a Virtue
(I know it but I never profest it in my life, yet I can admire
it in others)". It was one of a stream of small kindnesses.
The *Bellona*'s casualty list included Lieutenant Tom
Southey, who proved so helpful to his brother when he came
to write about the battle. Captain Mosse of the *Edgar* had
been killed, like poor Riou, as had Captain James Rawden
of the Cornish Miners, a volunteer rifleman serving in the
Elephant under Colonel Stewart.

His preliminary visits over, it was Nelson's turn for diplomacy. "At noon," he recorded, "Sir Hyde Parker sent me on shore to talk with the Prince of Denmark. Dined in the Palace and had two hours' conversation with him. At 8 returned on board the *London* to communicate the result of my business. Very tired." No action of Sir Hyde's was more extraordinary than the fact that he allowed an already weary man to conduct delicate negotiations which he could perfectly well have undertaken for himself.

Hardy was staggered at Nelson's versatility. "The more I see of his lordship," he wrote, "the more I admire his great character, for I think on this occasion his Political Management was *if possible* greater than his bravery."

Nelson's reception in the city where he had done so much to bring sorrow showed a mixture of admiration, curiosity and displeasure. He was given a strong guard, though there were no demonstrations. He told the Prince, who congratulated him on his humanity, that he had been in more than a hundred engagements, but that this had been the hardest of them all. "The French," he said, "fought bravely, but they could not have stood for one hour the fight which the Danes had supported for four."

Nelson reported the conference at some length to his friend Henry Addington, who had succeeded Pitt as Prime Minister. Nelson spoke alone with the Prince and Lindholm, both of whom knew English. He was sure that they were politically well disposed towards Britain, but that fear of Russia was "the preponderating consideration".

Having gone over the principles behind the Armed Neutrality, the Prince suddenly asked: "Lord Nelson—Pray answer me a question: for what is the British fleet come into the Baltic? My answer—to crush a most formidable and unprovoked Coalition against Great Britain." The Prince declared that his ships should never join any Power against England, "but," said Nelson, "it required not much argument to satisfy him that he could not help it."

Nelson next explained that what Britain wanted was that Denmark should join her, or that she should disarm. When pressed to define disarmament, Nelson would not commit himself too closely. He then suggested "a free entry of the

British Fleet into Copenhagen, and the free use of everything we may want from it. Before I could get on, the Prince replied quick, '*That* you shall have with pleasure.' " Nelson's next demand was, "whilst this explanation is going on, a total suspension of your Treaties with Russia". "I will venture to say", wrote Hardy afterwards, "that his Royal Highness never had so much plain *trooth* spoken to him in his life."

In spite of that, Nelson felt "my reception was such as I have always found it, far beyond my deserts". Hardy added that he had "as much acclamation as when we went to the Lord *Mare's* Show". In a later letter, while pointing out— far too modestly—that "a negociator is certainly out of my line", Nelson set forth various points for Addington's consideration. "1st. We had beat the Danes. 2nd. We wish to make them feel that we are their real friends, therefore have spared their Town. 3rd. They understand perfectly that we are at War with them for their Treaty of Armed Neutrality made last year. 4th. We have made them suspend the operations of that Treaty. 5th. It has given our Fleet scope to act against Russia and Sweden. 6th which we never should have done, although Copenhagen would have been burnt, for Sir Hyde Parker was determined not to have Denmark hostile in his rear 7th. Every reinforcement, even a cutter, can join us without molestation, and also provisions, stores etc. 8th. Great Britain is left with the stake of all the Danish property in her hands, her Colonies &c, if she refuses Peace. 9th. the hands of Denmark are tied up; ours are free to act against her confederate Allies. 10th. Although we might have burnt the City, I have my doubts whether we could their Ships." Nelson meant those in the inner harbour, protected as they still were by the Trekroner Battery.

Further conferences resulted in an armistice, formally ratified. It was made securer by the fact that belated news arrived of the murder of the Czar of Russia, on 24th March. Had this come sooner, the battle itself might have proved unnecessary, for Paul's successor soon reversed the pro-French policy of his Government, and as his liberal views were already known in Denmark, it was likely that the Danes would have temporised until a reorientation of Baltic affairs had been agreed.

Stewart was ordered home with news of the negotiations, and with official despatches. He carried a letter from Nelson in which all the principal officers engaged found honourable mention, no blame whatever being fastened upon the captains of the ships which had grounded.[1] Words from Sir Hyde Parker were equally generous. "Was it possible for me to add anything to the well-earned renown of Lord Nelson," said the Commander-in-Chief, "it would be by asserting that his exertions, great as they have heretofore been, never were carried to a higher pitch of zeal for his Country's service."

No one was better able to spread Nelson's praises than Stewart; England soon resounded with them. "I never saw a man in our Profession," wrote the First Lord a few weeks later, "excepting yourself and Troubridge, who possessed the magic art of infusing the same spirit into others, which inspired their own actions, exclusive of other talents and habits of business not common to Naval characters. Your Lordships whole conduct, from your first appointment to this hour, is the subject of our constant admiration. It does not become me to make comparisons: all agree there is but one Nelson. That he may long continue the pride of his Country is the fervent wish of your Lordship's truly affectionate St Vincent."

Praise was balm to Nelson, but tangible rewards were meagre, for the prizes were mostly burnt or sunk in shallow water, and the step in the peerage which Nelson received for his newest service was pleasing chiefly to his family, and in particular to his prospective heir, his parson brother William. To Nelson the promotion was blemished by the fact that, although he later enjoyed the privilege of investing Admiral Graves with the knighthood of the Bath on the King's behalf for his services as tactical second-in-command, yet the sovereign's gold medal, such as he himself already wore for St Vincent and the Nile, and which he thought worth a Dukedom, was withheld in this instance from both him and

[1] Lieutenant Southey told his brother that in fact the grounding of the *Bellona* was the captain's own fault. As for the dangerous condition of her guns, "Were you not saying as you pulled the trigger," asked Nelson's biographer, "here goes the death of six!" Six men made up a gun's crew.

his captains. Nor had they any special mark of thanks from the City of London.

The lack of recognition in the highest, and in City quarters, was the subject of prolonged and increasingly bitter protests on Nelson's part. To his dying hour he hoped that honour would be paid by authority to those who had shared in what he considered to be his professional master-piece, and what was by any standard one of the most testing actions of his life.

In advising that official medals should not be awarded, the Admiralty were acting with deliberation. The difficulty was twofold: first, England had not, strictly speaking, been at war with Denmark at the time of the engagement, which was "preventative"; again, on the precedent of Troubridge at the Nile, medals would need to have been given to the Commander-in-Chief and the captains of the larger ships with him. One such eccentricity was, in the view of St Vincent and others, quite enough. Only unofficial awards, and Nelson's viscounty, would commemorate Copenhagen among contemporaries. So the ruling went, and so it re-mained until the institution of a Naval General Service Medal for all ranks in 1848, long after any survivors who might have been entitled to the "Copenhagen" clasp had ceased to worry whether it was bestowed or not.

How little the King was interested personally in the matter was shown in a remark recorded by Lady Elizabeth Foster, "Lord Nelson," said George III, when the victor paid his respects after his return, "do you get out?" "And," said Nelson, "I was tempted to say 'Sir, I have been out and am come in again. Your Majesty perhaps has not heard of the Battle of Copenhagen!'"

v

"I am tired to death," wrote Nelson to St Vincent on 9th April. "No man but those who are on the spot can tell what I have gone through, and do suffer. I make no scruple in saying, that I would have been at Reval fourteen days ago; that without this Armistice the Fleet would never have gone but by order of the Admiralty; and with it, I daresay, we shall not go this week. I wanted Sir Hyde to let me at least go and cruise off Carlscrona," from which it was expected that the Swedes would make a sortie, "to prevent the Reval ships from getting in to join them. I said I would not go to Reval to take any of those laurels which I was sure he would reap there. Think for me, my dear Lord, and if I have deserved well, let me retire; if ill, for heaven's sake supersede me, for I cannot exist in this state."

Reval, then as earlier, was Nelson's great object, for, as he wrote to Addington: "I look upon the Northern League to be like a tree, of which Paul was the trunk, and Sweden and Denmark the branches. If I can get at the trunk, and hew it down, the branches fall of course; but I may lop the branches and yet not be able to fell the tree, and my power must be weaker when its greatest strength is required. If we could have cut up the Russian fleet, that was my object. Denmark and Sweden deserved whipping, but Paul deserved punishment."

However self-effacing Nelson expressed himself to be in offering Sir Hyde the opportunity to gather laurels, Sir Hyde's own reluctance was insuperable. Reporting to Emma that he had been left behind to conduct the battle-damaged ships into the Baltic, Nelson added, "—but if there is any work to do, I dare say they will wait for me. *Nelson will be first.* Who can stop him?"

When reports came back that the Swedish fleet were active, Nelson entered words in his Journal which proved his letter true. "April 15. At 6 o'clock received a note from Sir Hyde Parker to say that the Swedish fleet was at sea and that I might hoist my flag in the *Elephant* . . . at 11 o'clock got on board her."

"All our fellows are longing to be at them," he told Emma "and so do I, as great a boy as any of them, for I consider this as being at school, and going to England as going home for the holidays, therefore I really long to finish my task." So alarmed was he at the thought of missing a battle that the five-hour pull to the *Elephant* against wind and current on a bitter day in an open boat was made without a cloak. His servant Allen had forgotten to provide this in the scurry of departure. Nelson did not go back for it, and refused the offer of a greatcoat from a lieutenant, saying, "No, I am not

cold; my anxiety for my Country will keep me warm."
But when the immediate excitement was over, he paid for
his temerity with a long spell of what he called influenza,
which kept him many days wretchedly confined to his cabin.

"Pray God we may get up with them," wrote Nelson
anxiously, but the Swedes were in no mood to fight. When
they saw the fleet approaching, they took shelter under the
Carlscrona batteries. Parker sent in a flag of truce with
details of the armistice with Denmark, and to require that
Sweden would abandon her hostile measures against Britain.
Answer came that while Sweden would not fail to honour her
obligations, she "would not refuse to listen to equitable pro-
posals made by deputies furnished with proper authority by
the King of Great Britain to the United Northern Powers".

Satisfied, from this temporising answer, and from his
experience in his passage through the waters past Elsinore
that this particular northern Court did not mean business,
Parker continued towards the Gulf of Finland. There he
had news that the new Emperor, Alexander, had accepted
the offer to terminate the dispute by Convention. Even so,
Nelson would have continued active. "We are very lazy," he
complained to Emma. "We Mediterranean people are not
used to it." He would have placed the fleet between Reval
and Cronstadt, to ensure no junction of Russian squadrons,
for it was his view that it was best to negotiate with well-
disposed forces close at hand. Parker thought otherwise. He
returned to the coast of Denmark, and anchored in Kioge
Bay, there to await patiently whatever might happen.

It was there, most suitably, that news arrived of a change.
Nelson entered in his Journal on April 29th: "Colonel
Stewart arrived with an order for me to command-in-chief
and for Sir Hyde to return home; at 4 o'clock the *Blanche*
sailed and left me the Command, to my great sorrow."
Domett agreed to remain as Captain of the Fleet.

On receiving full reports of Copenhagen, the Admiralty
acted at once, and their alacrity was equalled by the way in
which Parker, for once, flew to obey. He was no man for the
Baltic and, whatever might have been the state of Nelson's
health, he and he alone could see things through. Charitable
to Parker to the last, he added a secret postscript to a letter

to Davison, sent later in the year. "They are not Sir Hyde Parker's real friends who wish for an enquiry," he said. "His friends in the Fleet wish everything to be forgot, for we all respect and love Sir Hyde; but the dearer his friends, the more uneasy they have been at his *idleness*, for that is the truth—no criminality. I believe Sir H. P. to be as good a subject as his Majesty has." By criminality, Nelson meant cowardice; no one who knew him suspected Parker of that.

How the public, or at any rate those who knew Nelson's character best, felt about affairs in the Baltic is amusingly illustrated by an entry in the Betting Book at Brooks' Club, made at a time when the outcome of the actual fighting was still unknown. *"Mr Coke bets Sir Thomas Miller 50 guineas that Nelson is neither taken prisoner or capitulated."* The great Mr Coke of Holkham had complete assurance that wherever Nelson sailed, victory would attend him.

VI

Tired as he then was, and longing to return, Nelson was incapable of inactivity. "The keeping of his Fleet continually on the alert, and amply furnishing it with fresh water and provisions, were the objects of his Lordship's unremitted care," said Stewart, "and to this may be in a great measure ascribed the uniform good health and discipline which prevailed. Another point to which he gave nearly equal attention was his economy of the resources of the Fleet in regard to stores; their consumption was as remarkable for its smallness in the Baltic as it was in the Fleet that was afterwards under his command in the Mediterranean."

Of the Admiral's own habits at this time, when well enough to leave his cot, Stewart said, "his hour of rising was four or five o'clock, and of going to rest about ten; breakfast was never later than six, and generally nearer to five o'clock. A midshipman or two were always of the party; and I have known him send during the middle watch to invite the little fellows to breakfast with him, when relieved. At table with them he would enter into the boyish jokes, and be the most youthful of the party. At dinner he invariably had every Officer of his Ship in their turn, and was both a polite and hospitable host. The whole ordinary business of the Fleet was invariably despatched, as it had been by Earl St Vincent, before eight o'clock. The great command of time which Lord Nelson thus gave himself, and the alertness which this example imparted throughout the Fleet, can only be understood by those who witnessed it, or who know the value of those early hours."

In this vignette, Stewart hit upon the secret of much of Nelson's prodigies, for his written output, despite all handicaps, was enormous, and his actions would have afforded honour enough for a dozen lesser men. Habit, training, zeal and an acute awareness of the passing hour—these were what mattered. Henceforward, whatever happened in the Baltic, there would be no anchoring in Kioge Bay to wait upon events.

Part of the fleet was left at Bornholm to watch the Swedes, from whom Nelson required and obtained an assurance that British trade in the Cattegat and the Baltic should not be molested. Meanwhile he himself, with ten sail of the line and smaller vessels, headed once more into the Gulf of Finland. Paul, in one of his freaks of tyranny, had seized upon all British ships and property in Russia. "I will have all restored," said Nelson, "but I will do nothing violently."

Within four days he was in Reval Roads, but the port was empty. The Russians had cut through the last of the ice and sailed away to Cronstadt while Parker had been at anchor. "Nothing," said Nelson, "if it had been right to make the attack, could have saved one ship of them in two hours after our entering the Bay."

On 12th May Nelson sent on shore to say that he came in a friendly spirit, and was ready to return a salute. On the Russian part the courtesy referred to was delayed not by ill-will but through the inefficiency of the artillery officer, who was promptly put under arrest. Nelson next wrote to the Emperor, proposing to wait on him personally, and urging the release of any British subjects or property which might still be under detention.

An answer came within four days. Alexander's ministers expressed surprise at the arrival of the fleet in a Russian port, and anxiety that it should withdraw. They proposed the most friendly disposition towards Great Britain, but declined a personal visit on Nelson's part, unless he should come in a single ship, for news from Copenhagen had travelled. Having got his way, Nelson stood out to sea, leaving a brig to bring off the provisions he had bought in Reval. "I hope all is right," he wrote to the ambassador in Berlin, "but seamen are but bad negociators; for we put to issue in five minutes what diplomatic forms would be five months doing."

On his way down the Baltic, Nelson met the Russian admiral Tchitchagof, whom Alexander had sent to communicate personally with the British. Amiabilities were exchanged, and a further communication invited Nelson to St Petersburg "in whatever mode might be most agreeable to himself". Nelson sent Fremantle as his deputy, and that gallant officer was received with every attention. At Rostock, the Duke of Mecklenburg-Strelitz, brother of the Queen of England, arrived on board the *St George* with a suite of nearly a hundred, on a visit of curiosity. Nelson managed to get rid of him quicker than Court etiquette warranted, though without offence. He also received many German deputations, who waited upon him in the flattering way which recalled experiences on the journey across the Continent the year before.

At Rostock, too, Nelson had news of the death of his brother Maurice, which left William and himself sole survivors out of eight sons. Maurice had died as First Clerk in the Navy Office and Secretary to the Committee of Accounts. St Vincent wrote to say that he had been working for his interest at the time of his last illness. Maurice was about to be appointed Commissioner of Customs and Excise, until there should be a vacancy on the Navy Board.

Maurice Nelson had always been good to Horatio, and the affection was warmly returned. It was continued to the poor blind woman, Sarah Ford, with whom Maurice, it was supposed out of pity, had lived for many years. In a long letter to Emma, begun on 24th May, Nelson wrote: "Will you have the goodness to . . . say every kind thing for me. She shall be fixed where she pleases and with every comfort in this world, and ever be considered as my honoured sister-in-law. I feel my dear brother's confidence, and she shall feel he has not mistaken me."

Nelson repeated this assurance of protection over and over again, to Emma, Davison and others, and he was as good as his word. Four years later he was still attending to small debts incurred by a man whose way of life had never been extravagant, and he did not fail to see that "poor Blindy's" little pension was faithfully paid, whatever the state of his own finances. Emma was equally kind, long after Nelson could do no more for Sarah. Irregular unions were no bar to sympathy; Nelson had been familiar with one in the Suckling family, and in his own experience it was the heart rather than the marriage lines that mattered.

It was partly because he could rely on her kindness, partly from relief that Emma had not and would not succumb to the charm of princes, which led him to say, in the course of his letter, ". . . . a saint you are if ever there was one in this world, for what makes a saint—the being so much better than the rest of the human race; therefore as truly as I believe in God I believe you are a saint, and in this age of wickedness you set an example of real virtue and goodness which, if we are not too far sunk in luxury and infamy ought to raise up almost forgot Virtue: and may God's curse alight upon those who want to draw you my dearest Emma from a quiet house into the company of men and women of bad character, and I am one of those who believe that in England the higher the class the worse the company. I speak generally. I will not think so bad of any class but there may be some good individuals in it. How can I thank you sufficiently for all your goodness and kindness to me, a forlorn outcast except in your generous soul."

Glancing in his spontaneous way at the circumstances around him, he added, "the Baltic folks will never fight me if it is to be avoided. In my humble opinion we shall have peace with the Northern Powers, if we are *just* in our desires." He ended: "I want not to conquer any heart: if that which I have conquered is happy in its lot, I am content for the Conqueror to become the *conquered*. I want but one true heart, there can be but one *love* although many well-wishers. Ever for ever your dear and truly affectionate friend *Nelson and Brontë*." He added, at the bottom of the letter: "Best regards to Sir William."

This significant letter, which is very little known, is strange in several ways. Emma was an odd person to consider as a "saint", whatever her attributes and qualities; again, from whom had Nelson been an "outcast"? Certainly not from the world in general, only perhaps from his more tranquil self and—of his own free-will—from his wife. The truth may well be that he craved a living aspiration as well as a disembodied one in the form of a patriotic idea, and that, when one failed or seemed to fail, he must needs quickly find another.

This would certainly account for his more familiar letter, sent earlier in the year from the *San Josef*, in which he said to Emma: "It is your sex that make us go forth; and seem to tell us—'None but the Brave deserve the Fair!' and, if we fall, we still live in the hearts of those females who are dear to us; it is your sex who cherish our memories; and you, my dear, honoured friend, are, believe me, the *first*, the best of your sex. I have been the world around, and never yet saw your equal, or even one which could be put in comparison with you. You know how to reward virtue, honour and courage."

If Emma was difficult in her special ways, if she fed on flattery as much as Nelson, she yet had the power of evoking, not merely from him but from other men of stature, expressions of admiration far beyond those given to most women. That she could equally arouse dislike, even execration, is merely to say that where she impinged, she did so to some purpose.

On 11th June Nelson wrote: "This day, twenty-two years, I was made a Post-Captain by Sir Peter Parker. If you meet him again, say that I shall drink his health in a bumper, for I do not forget that I owe my present exalted rank to his partiality, although I feel, if I had been in an humbler sphere, that Nelson would have been Nelson still."

VII

If the Baltic Powers showed natural reluctance to fight, now that Nelson commanded-in-chief, he himself was far from satisfied at the turn which affairs in Denmark seemed to have taken during his brief absence. "In this nation," he said truly, "we shall not be forgiven for having the upper hand of them: I only thank God we have, or they would try to humble us to the dust."

He observed that a French officer was the companion and counsellor of the Prince, and that things were done in such open violation of the armistice that he thought a second display of force might be necessary. "I see everything which is dirty and mean going on, and the Prince-Royal at the head of it. Ships have been masted, guns taken on board, floating batteries prepared, and except hauling out and completing their rigging, everything is done in defiance of the treaty."

The judgment was well founded. Bonaparte himself told Admiral Cockburn, many years later, that the Danes were supplying France with masts soon after the battle; and it was not many years before another expedition was necessary, leading to further damage to Copenhagen and suppression of the Danish fleet. Among the soldiers who then took part was the future Duke of Wellington.

In June, Nelson's repeated pleas for relief were attended to. Sir Morice Pole, an old acquaintance and a fellow-pupil with Nelson of Captain Locker, arrived to take command. Pole signalised his Baltic service by passing the Great Belt for the first time with British sail of the line, working through the channels against contrary winds. The tradition of Lord Hawke, transmitted through Locker, was indeed still active in the navy.

Nelson returned to England in a brig, declining to accept a frigate. It was an act of which few admirals would have been capable, particularly if, like Nelson, they always suffered from sickness in small ships. On his arrival at Yarmouth, his first thought was to attend the hospital, where he had a cheerful word with all who had been wounded in the battle.

There had been a space of nearly twenty years between Nelson's two appearances in Danish waters. He had visited the northern region in the *Albemarle* in the winter of 1781, serving for a time under an uncle of his new friend Colonel Stewart. He had then, as he told Locker, "almost been froze on the other side". He was equally glad to see Yarmouth on 1st July 1801. It was his last recorded visit to the region of his birth.

LORD NELSON
by John Hoppner, R.A.

Hoppner's portrait, which, like Beechey's, was probably painted
in 1801, hangs in *St James's Palace*

Chapter 9

ENGLAND, HOME AND BEAUTY

I

THE two portraits for which Nelson gave sittings soon after his return home are the only full-scale representations from the life which date from his later years. They are of particular interest as emphasising the masculine and feminine side of his nature. They also show a marked advance in maturity. In the Baltic, Nelson gained in self-mastery, and the fact was apparent.

Norwich, eager for a canvas to memorialise both the hero and the sword which he had presented to the City after St Vincent, chose Sir William Beechey as executant. The artist had worked in Norwich, had married a Norfolk wife, and had already painted old Edmund Nelson. It was a happy decision.

Nelson and Beechey got on famously. Nelson stood sponsor for one of Beechey's children, and gave him the hat which he had worn at the Nile, parting with it, he said, "as an old and tried friend, for he had worn it in many battles". He was delighted to hear that Beechey had been asked to paint the Nile captains for Lord St Vincent. Nelson proved an excellent sitter, and Beechey showed a virile, confident, even masterful man worthy of the elaborate frame of trophies by which the finished picture was surrounded. Beechey was at work on facsimiles and variations for some years after Nelson's death.

Hoppner, the principal version of whose picture was designed for the Royal Collection, showed a face full of suffering and sensibility, delicate, sympathetic and vivid. His rendering was chosen, after Trafalgar, as the basis for the effigy now in the Norman Undercroft at Westminster Abbey. In this case the modeller, Catherine Andras, actually had sittings at some time from Nelson himself, but Hoppner's conception, it was thought, would capture the public fancy. Again the decision was right. Emma, who knew Nelson best, had nothing but praise for the interpretation (though she readjusted the hair to hide the Nile scar, as had been Nelson's own habit), and the Duchess of Devonshire said, "it was as if he was standing there", so exact was the likeness. Nelson could stimulate artists to their best; it was sad that he never sat as a young man to Gainsborough, or as an older one to Lawrence.

In both the Beechey and the Hoppner pictures Nelson wore his stars of the Bath, Ferdinand and Merit of Naples, and the Turkish Crescent, together with the badge and ribbon of the first two orders, and the king's gold medals for St Vincent and the Nile. One star remained to be added, that of the Equestrian Order of St Joachim of Leiningen. This came to him in the year 1802, and completed his decorations.

Meanwhile, he was allowed but the briefest holiday before he was recalled to service. Part of this he spent at Box Hill, part in fishing excursions with the Hamiltons from the Bush Inn, Staines. A young friend, Edward Parker, to whom he had taken a great fancy in the Baltic, was with them, as were the William Nelsons and their daughter Charlotte. A visit was made to Laleham near by, to see "poor Blindy", Maurice Nelson's lady. Parker, a commander, had been among Nelson's retinue, and had sat next the admiral at table, cutting his meat when necessary. "I feel not a little interested and indeed enthusiastic at accompanying the Hero of Aboukir and Copenhagen to England," he had written to Emma: and a few months later, when wounded in battle, "to call me a *Nelsonite* is more to me than making me a Duke —oh God! how is it possible ever to be sufficiently thankful for all his attentions. . . . I would lose a dozen limbs to serve him."

Nelson's new appointment, though important in its way, was half political, in the sense that it was designed to show the government was aware of its responsibility to use his services to the best advantage. Although war had ceased on the Continent after the Treaty of Lunéville, signed by France and Austria in February, Great Britain was not yet ready for peace, except on her own terms. There was reason to expect that these would be conceded, for if Europe was at Bonaparte's feet, yet where sea power was concerned he had everywhere been frustrated. Malta had fallen; the Baltic Neutrality dissolved; and the army of Egypt was at its last gasp. Bonaparte, believing, like Nelson, that negotiation could be quickened by a display of force, now actively revived his project of assembling large invasion forces on the coast opposite Britain, within distant sight of her citizens, the headquarters at Boulogne.

Professional opinion, in the navy at any rate, held to the view that the enemy project was chimerical. St Vincent wittily summed the matter up in the phrase: "I do not say that the French cannot come. I only say that they cannot come by sea," and Nelson wrote categorically to Sir Edward Berry: "I do not believe that the French army will embark from Boulogne," though he was less sure about Flanders. But public opinion was alarmed, and Nelson's name carried reassurance. Negotiations for peace were in a delicate state, "and I need not add," said St Vincent in a letter from which there was no appeal, "how very important it is that the enemy should know that *you* are constantly opposed to him".

Before the end of July Nelson wrote to the Duke of Clarence to say that he had received his "commission as Commander-in-Chief of a Squadron of Ships and Vessels employed on a particular service. My command is to extend from Orfordness to Beachy Head . . . but without interfering with either the Nore or Downs command. I assure your Royal Highness that I feel my ability to render service . . . only in my zeal; in many other respects I am sensible of much deficiency, and require that great allowance should be made for me."

The duties, which consisted of the raising of Sea Fencibles, for which employment there was little enthusiasm, work with small craft flotillas of defence, shore fortifications and so on, scarcely gave scope to an officer who had made his reputation in command of big ships; but if his presence was deemed necessary, he intended, as usual, to do his utmost, and his sympathetic tact, where senior officers in home commands were concerned, ensured that there would be no ruffled feelings. No one could be more punctilious than

Nelson where trespass was in question. It was not until later, when he experienced the frustrations of his post, that he came to suspect that one of the true reasons behind the appointment might have been to keep him away from Lady Hamilton.

"Everything, my dear Lord, must have a beginning," he wrote to St Vincent the day after he had hoisted his flag at Sheerness, "and we are literally at the foundation of our fabric of defence." Arguing that passive measures were inadequate, he added, "I perfectly agree with you, that we must keep the enemy as far from our coasts as possible, and be able to attack them the moment they come out of their ports." Preparations were made against a raid in force, with the supposition that the principal objective would be London. In 1667 the Dutch had entered the Medway led by Jan van Brakel, had taken or destroyed sixteen English ships of war, and dominated the approaches to the capital. The disgrace had never been forgotten. Although no seaman over-estimated French capabilities, no Board of Admiralty could neglect any reasonable precaution.

On 1st August, the third anniversary of the Nile, Nelson, who had by then taken up his headquarters in the frigate *Medusa*, and was in the Downs, stood over for the coast of France to "look into Boulogne". He got some information of the enemy's dispositions, lobbed a few shells into the place with little apparent effect, had one of his artillery officers and three seamen wounded by the return fire, and withdrew, satisfied at showing the French "that they could not, with impunity, come outside their ports". Longer term results were less fortunate.

In the middle of the month an attack was mounted in force, Nelson's intention being to destroy the whole Boulogne Flotilla. An extract from his orders ran: ". . . when any Boats have taken one Vessel, the business is not to be considered as finished, but a sufficient number being left to guard the prize, the others are immediately to pursue the object by proceeding on to the next, and so on until the whole of the Flottilla be either taken or totally annihilated, for there must not be the smallest cessation until their destruction is completely finished. . . ."

The intention was illustrative of Nelson's invariable tactical intentions, and of his dislike of a half-hearted business. But this time the French were ready. They had secured their vessels so well, chaining many to the shore, that it was impossible to cut them out, and the four British divisions of what were known as flat boats, forerunners of modern landing-craft, some armed with 8-inch howitzers, some with 24-pounder carronades, manned by seamen with pikes, cutlasses and tomahawks, and marines with muskets and bayonets, met with a bloody repulse. The boats, as at Teneriffe, did not arrive simultaneously, and although all parties fought stubbornly, they were driven off with negligible damage to the enemy. It was the last of Nelson's failures, and a tonic to the French army ashore. It also brought great sorrow, for Parker, who had commanded one of the divisions, was dangerously wounded in the leg and spent agonised weeks ashore in sick-quarters, constantly attended by Nelson, who was almost as much attached to him as if the young man had been his own son. Late in September, after alternating hope and despair, death gave him release. "I beg his hair may be cut off and given to me," wrote Nelson to Dr Baird: "It shall remain and be buried with me." The admiral's flag-lieutenant, Langford, had also been wounded, though less seriously, and a long casualty list showed no compensating military advantage.

Nelson, who was downcast at the set-back, attributed it to the fact that he had not commanded in person. His only consolation lay in the thought of the spirit in which the sortie had been made, and in the fact that no English boat had been lost. St Vincent, always responsive to zeal, wrote in his kindest vein: "It is not given us to command success. Your lordship, and the gallant men under your orders, certainly deserve it: and I cannot sufficiently express my admiration of the persevering courage with which this enterprise was followed up." In his message to those he had commanded, Nelson, praising their fortitude, added: "the Vice-Admiral begs to assure them, that the enemy will not have long to boast of their security; for he trusts, ere long, to assist them in person, in a way which will completely annihilate the whole of them. . . ."

The failure had one curious result. Early in September Nelson received a paper containing severe strictures on his conduct of the operation. "Should Lord Nelson wish the enclosed not to be inserted in the newspapers," wrote a man who believed the admiral knew the value of publicity, "he will please to enclose by return of post a bank-note of £100, to Mr Hill, to be left at the Post Office till called for."

Nelson reacted vigorously to this blackmail. He sent the paper itself, and a copy of his answer, to Nepean at the Admiralty, suggesting that he might be "pleased to send proper people to take up whoever comes for Mr Hill's letter". To the sender he replied: "Very likely I am unfit for my present command, and whenever Government change me, I hope they will find no difficulty in selecting an Officer of greater abilities; but you will, I trust, be punished for threatening my character. But I have not been brought up in the school of fear, and therefore care not what you do. I defy you and your malice."

Hill, who was one of several who voiced dissatisfaction at the conduct of the affair against the Flotillas, did in fact publish his letter.

II

In August 1801 there were two official announcements respecting Nelson's dignities. His peerage was newly gazetted as "of the Nile and of Hilborough in the County of Norfolk", the succession being remaindered on his father and his heirs male, and, in default, to the heirs male of his sisters. Future holders of the title were charged to use the surname of Nelson only, "in consideration", so the notice ran, "of the great and important services that renowned man, Horatio Nelson, hath rendered to his King and Country, and in order to perpetuate to the latest posterity the remembrance of his glorious actions, and to incite others to imitate his example". Addington told Nelson that the King had been particularly gracious in approving the new arrangement of the peerage. It was also announced that he had been given leave, by warrant dated the previous January, "to adopt, for himself and heirs, the title of Duke of Brontë, with the fief of the Duchy annexed thereto". Henceforward the signature he had used with variations for some two years had full official sanction.

Hardy, writing from the *Isis* in the Downs, told a relative, "Lord Nelson has given me one hundred acres in any part of his estate at Brontë that I choose to point out, with apartments in his House, a knife and fork etc., (he being determined to reside there in Peace). The former part I certainly have accepted and intend to keep, but the latter I have not yet determined on, nor shall I till I know the company that will attend him there." For all his fondness for Nelson, Hardy still thought Fanny "one of the best women in the world"—and sometimes made bold to say so.

At Nelson's pressing request, Sir William and Lady Hamilton paid a visit to Deal, in September, to help look after the wounded from Boulogne. Their presence so cheered Nelson, who had been chagrined by refusal of the Admiralty to allow him leave of absence, that when they left, shortly before Parker's death and funeral, he suffered a sharp reaction. As was his way, he gave vent to all the loneliness and misery he felt. Addressing his letter to "Mrs Thomson, care of Lady Hamilton," he said: "I came on board, but no Emma. No, no, my heart will break! I am in silent distraction. The four pictures of Lady Hn. are hung up, but alas! I have lost the original. But we part only to meet again very soon; it must be, it *shall* be." On the other side of the sheet he wrote: "My dearest wife, how can I bear our separation? Good God, what a change! I am so low I cannot hold up my head. When I reflect on the many happy scenes we have passed together, the being separated is terrible, but better times *will* come, *shall* come if it pleases God. And to make one worse, the fate of poor Parker! But God's will be done. Love my Horatia, and prepare for me the farm. . . ."

The "farm" referred to was the estate which Nelson had long wished for, as the "stake in the country" which Roundwood had not proved to be. He felt it appropriate that, as a peer, he should have landed property; and, as a sailor, he liked the novelty of ordering things in an unfamiliar element. The place was at Merton, then a quiet village close to

Wimbledon, and about eight miles from Westminster. It was exactly an hour's carriage drive from London, rather less by road than it is today in times of congested traffic, the route crossing the newly laid Surrey Iron Railway, whose horse-drawn trucks were to carry merchandise from Wandsworth to Croydon. The house and grounds cost £9,000, a sum which Nelson found difficulty in raising, so generous were his commitments. He had, indeed, as he told Emma, a soul too big for his purse.

Merton had once belonged to Sir Richard Hotham, and the principal building was about a century old. A nephew by marriage of Captain Cook lived on the property, and the great explorer's widow was a frequent visitor. There was a moat and pond—called the Canal—for Sir William to fish in, farmland which was soon extended by purchase, and the house itself was large enough for the joint household which Nelson proposed. "You are to be Lady Paramount of all the territories and waters of Merton," he wrote to Emma, "and we are all to be your guests, and to obey all lawful commands."

On 13th October Pitt visited Nelson off Deal. "He thinks it very hard to keep me now all is over," said the admiral. By this, Nelson meant that the preliminaries to the Peace of Amiens had been arranged, and that the first phase of the long war had virtually ended. Next day, Nelson wrote to the Admiralty: "Their Lordships appointment for my particular service being now done away with by the preliminary Articles of Peace, viz. to prevent the invasion of this country, which service I have not only, by Their Lordships appointing so large a force to serve under my command, been enabled effectively to perform, but also to be able to acquaint you that not one boat belonging to this country has been captured by the enemy; and as my state of health requires repose on shore, I have, therefore, to request that Their Lordships will, when they think the service will admit of it, allow me permission to go on shore." The leave was soon obtained, though Nelson was ordered to keep his flag flying afloat until further notice. The effect of this qualified permission was that he remained in pay, and at immediate call, but was allowed to live ashore, preferably within easy distance of the Admiralty. Merton suited the requirements admirably.

As for the Peace, Nelson did not much like it. He thought that any Englishman worth his salt should be damned rather than show himself elated. He did not share the wave of enthusiasm which spread over the country. It was, in truth, much more disadvantageous than could have been looked for. Great Britain restored all her oversea conquests to France, Spain and Holland, with the exception of Ceylon and Trinidad. She agreed to give back Malta to the Knights of St John, and George III renounced the empty title "King of France" which had been borne by the Sovereigns of England since 1340. On her part, France agreed to withdraw from the Papal States and from Naples, acknowledged the independence of the Ionian Islands, and restored Egypt to the Porte. She could scarcely have done less, after the victory near Alexandria by troops under Sir Ralph Abercrombie, which was an augury of what British land forces would achieve when, in due time, they were fully deployed against those of Bonaparte.

On 16th October a letter from Sir William Hamilton greatly cheered the newly landed proprietor. "We have now inhabited Your Lordships premises some days," he wrote, "& I can now speak with some certainty. I have lived with our dear Emma several years. I know her merit, have a great opinion of the head & heart that God Almighty has been pleased to give her; but a seaman alone could have given a fine woman full power to chuse and fit up a residence for him without seeing it himself. You are in luck, for in my conscience I verily believe that a place so suitable to your views could not have been found, & at so cheap a rate, for if you stay away 3 days longer I do not think you can have any wish but you will find it completed here & then the bargain was fortunately struck 3 days before an idea of peace got abroad. Now every estate in this neighbourhood has increased in value, and you might get a thousand pounds [more] tomorrow for your bargain. The proximity to the capital, and the perfect retirement of this place, are, for your Lordship, two points beyond estimation. You have nothing but to come and enjoy immediately; you have a good mile of pleasant dry walk around your own farm. It would make you laugh to see Emma & her mother fitting up pig-sties and hen-coops, & already the Canal is enlivened with ducks, & the cock is strutting with his hens about the walks."

Early on 22nd October Nelson went ashore from the *Amazon*, which was then flying his flag, and set off at once for Merton. "On his arriving at this small village," so Emma told James Harrison, "it is a singular fact that, being asked by the post-boy which was the house, his Lordship could not reply. It was, however, soon found, and never was man more delighted at beholding his new residence. Every glowing feature of his amiable friends spoke the welcome which was felt by each heart, as the various beauties of this little spot were pointed out to his inquisitive eye. He viewed all with admiration and astonishment, so greatly did it surpass every idea which he had formed. 'Is this, too, mine?' he repeatedly asked, as he was shown different parts of the estate; the house, the gardens, the dairy &c. He was particularly charmed with the admirable contrivance of a commodious subterranean passage, formed beneath the high road, and leading to the beautiful and extensive plantation walks with which the fields and kitchen gardens, on that side, are so agreeably environed." Harrison may have been wrong in this particular, since other accounts date the passage as a later improvement: indeed a myth is not yet quite dead at Merton that Nelson went to the church (over a mile away) by an underground route!

However complete or incomplete were the new dispensations planned to embellish the property, the owner himself was enchanted. Harrison records him as being in ecstasy. "Oh, Sir William!" exclaimed his lordship, embracing his most worthy friend when he had seen the whole, "the longest liver shall possess it all!"

III

The year and a half between October 1801, when he first felt the enchantment of Merton, and May 1803, when war re-engrossed him, were the most enjoyable which Nelson ever spent ashore. The months were not inactive, for he was incapable of idling, and his health was variable, but they were passed in company with those he loved, largely on a property whose care and improvement became an absorbing interest. Merton and Emma were the reward of those years of ardours, exiles and responsibilities which he endured so long. Every moment had its pleasure, every meeting its value.

The first weeks were slightly clouded by the fact that Edmund Nelson seemed still unable to reconcile his son's attitude to his wife with what he believed to be his fundamental goodness. "If Lady Nelson is in a hired house," Edmund had written early in October, "and by herself, gratitude requires that I should sometimes be with her, if it is likely to be of any comfort to *her*." Yet Emma, determined that nothing should be lacking to the comfort of the man who loved her, made such successful efforts to win the old man's heart that he consented to visit Merton as early as November. There he found a "Mansion of Peace", adding, "I must become one of the inhabitants. Sir William and I are both old men, and we will witness the hero's felicity in retirement." In Lord Minto's view the Mansion of Peace was too much like a Nelson museum of trophies: he found "an excess of vanity which counteracts its own purpose".

For all Edmund Nelson's approbation of his new surroundings, he could not easily wean himself from his old routine of sheltering from the rigours of the winter in Bath, though it was arranged that he should return in May, and live under his son's roof. But fate intervened. Edmund Nelson died at the spa on 26th April 1802, aged nearly eighty. Horatio was too indisposed to attend him, though he said that he would have flown to do so had it been found necessary. Fanny, who truly loved her father-in-law, offered her services, though she was convinced that her intentions would not be appreciated by the rest of the family, most of whom were now Emma's partisans. "Even supposing his lordship resided in Italy, the offence would be the same"— so Fanny wrote to Mrs Matcham from the depths of bitter experience. Catherine Matcham disagreed, adding that her brother knew that "no one can attend to my father as you do".

The sudden loss of his father's society enhanced Nelson's pleasure in that of Sir William. As a regular visitor at the offices of learned institutions, Hamilton kept on his house in Piccadilly for the convenience of himself and his friend, no doubt with some persuasion from Emma. He also took a lively interest in the Welsh estates he had inherited from his first wife, though these were managed by his heir, Charles Greville. There is evidence that Nelson himself shared in Hamilton's pursuits, at least in a small way. A letter written from sea in 1803 to Sir Joseph Banks, President of the Royal Society, after a British frigate had captured a French corvette laden with works of art from Greece, showed a keen sense of the value of antiquities, and a personal regard for Banks which certainly derived from direct acquaintance.

Like Nelson, Sir William was not free from money difficulties, for the style of living which gave Emma scope for her prodigal hospitality and love of show would have strained a larger income than he commanded. "It is but reasonable," he wrote to Greville on 24th January 1802, "after having fagged all my life, that my last days should pass off comfortably & quietly. Nothing at present disturbs me but my debt, and the nonsense I am obliged to submit to here without coming to an explosion, which would be attended with many disagreeable effects, and would totally destroy the comfort of the best man and the best friend I have in the world."

A letter such as this gives the lie to any idea of Sir William's senility, and to any notion that he was not aware of what was going on between Nelson and Emma—and no one knew Emma's character better than the man he was addressing, whose mistress she had long been, and who was, indeed, responsible for much of the success Emma had had in society. "I am determined that my quiet shall not be disturbed," added Hamilton philosophically, "let the nonsensical world go on as it will."

If Sir William was employed in reaping enjoyment from years spent in the rediscovery of antiquity, Nelson, for his part, did not fail in his duties in the House of Lords, to which he had been introduced as a Viscount soon after his return from sea. He was no debater, but two of his most pointed speeches in Parliament were in honour of men with whom he was not always in great sympathy, and the occasions seemed to give emphasis to his words. He had paid high tribute to Sir James Saumarez for his recovery from near-disaster in the summer of 1801, when he had defeated a superior Spanish squadron in a night action off Algeciras. He also bestowed formal though sincere compliments on Lord Keith for the naval part in the recent victory in Egypt, which had crowned his own endeavours of 1798 in Aboukir Bay. "I see by almost every paper that Lord Nelson has been speaking in the House," grumbled Hardy. "I am sorry for it, and I am fully convinced that sailors should not talk too much."

Towards the end of July both Sir William Hamilton and Nelson felt well enough for a protracted excursion to the West Country. This resolved itself into a triumphant progress in honour of the admiral, and it gave hope to Sir William that Milford Haven, where his financial interests were centred, might one day be developed into a port of consequence. Nelson's elder brother, his wife and son were of the party.

At Oxford, on 21st July, the two Matchams and their eldest boy were among an assembly which had the pleasure of seeing Nelson given the freedom of the city in a gold box. Upon Sir William Hamilton was bestowed a law degree, and William Nelson, who had already taken his Doctorship of Divinity at Cambridge, received a like mark of distinction from the sister university. The clerical William gloried in his new title, though he did not cease to plague his brother when Deaneries fell vacant, and a year later he owed a Prebend's stall at Canterbury to Nelson's importunity.

Then, as later, a visit to Blenheim was part of the pleasures of an Oxford excursion, but the reigning Duke of Marlborough, although in residence, did not appear in person to welcome the visitors. They were offered instead a cold collation, which was coldly refused.

There was a warmer welcome at Gloucester, where Nelson visited both cathedral and jail, and at Ross-on-Wye. From there the tourists proceeded to Monmouth by water. They were attended by a vast number of people," wrote Harrison, "who decorated the boat provided for his lordship and friends with laurels, and exhibited every other demonstration of respect and joy."

At Monmouth was a Naval Temple, the Kymin, which was a fit object of curiosity. Here the Corporation turned out in force. A formal address was presented, and the bands of the Monmouth and Brecon Militia played popular tunes. Nelson and his party were pressed to return on their way home. Many years later an abiding memorial of the visit was established, with the foundation, by Lady Llangattock, of a Nelson Museum to house the relics which her enthusiasm assembled.

At Milford, where Sir William shared some of the lime-light, Charles Greville had arranged every kind of festivity. There was a rowing-match, a cattle-show and a fair. Sir William presented one of the Guzzardi portraits of his friend to the proprietor of the New Inn, with an elaborate inscription in Italian. Thomas Bolton, Nelson's less well-endowed brother-in-law, determined not to be left out of the progress, joined the party from far away Norfolk, and as Captain Foley, hero of many battles, had a brother living in South Wales, Nelson was able to propose a companion-in-arms in a fitting toast, saying truly that there was not a braver or a better man in the King's service.

Nelson made a careful survey of the possibilities of Milford, and declared that he considered it to possess one of the finest harbours he had ever seen. Despite his opinion, the port had long to wait before reaping the advantages of natural situation, and neither Sir William nor Charles Greville lived to see their hopes fulfilled.

Swansea and its porcelain factory were next visited, and by the evening of 18th August the party, tired but gratified, returned to loyal Monmouth, where they were received with renewed attention. There, as Harrison recorded, Emma sang two songs at an evening reception. These, rendered "with her usual scientific taste and superior vocal excellence, enraptured the whole company".

Ross had by now been given time to erect a triumphal arch, ornamented with oak and laurel, under which the party drove to suitable cheering. At Rudhall, during the course of a private visit, Nelson heard that the corporation of Hereford wished to do him honour. In this town, as so often elsewhere, the horses were taken from the carriage, which was drawn by the people. The Freedom was presented in a box cut from an apple tree, symbolic of a cider county.

The next visit was to Richard Payne Knight, at Downton Castle, near Ludlow. Payne Knight and Sir William Hamilton were old friends, with many interests in common. The host was a famous numismatist, a lover of the classical antique, and he had known Goethe well in Italy. He was an arbiter of taste, a lover of the picturesque, and a discerning patron of artists of the best period of the English water-colour.

From Ludlow the way led to Worcester, where bells rang out, cannon roared, and crowds cheered wherever Nelson went. Messrs Chamberlain's china factory was an obvious attraction, and Nelson found it irresistible to place a large order for services, embellished with his armorial achievements. Worcester's freedom was appropriately tendered in "an elegant china vase", and on this occasion he made one of his longer speeches.

At Worcester an invitation arrived from Birmingham. The party departed for that place "in two post-coaches and four, with the drivers in blue jackets, wearing ribbons of the same colour in their hats". Birmingham was then known as the Toy-Shop of Europe. Nelson rejoiced at the phrase. "The French have always, in ridicule, called us a Nation of Shopkeepers," he had written a few months before to the Mayor of Yarmouth, "—so, I hope, we shall always remain, and, like other shopkeepers, if our goods are better than those of any other country, and we can afford to sell them cheaper, we must depend on our shop being well resorted to."

Entertainment at Birmingham included the theatre. On the entrance of the party " 'Rule Britannia' was played in full orchestra, and the whole audience, respectfully standing up, instantly testified to the happiness which they experienced at thus seeing the renowned hero of the Nile".

A crowded day was spent in visiting places of employment, the first being the swordsmith's establishment belonging to the High Bailiff, James Woolley, which had been in existence nearly twenty years. Then followed a button factory, a buckle-and-ring factory, a patent-sash factory, and a stained-glass establishment at Handworth, "where they were received by a party of beautiful young ladies, dressed in white, who strewed the hero's way with flowers". Boulton's Soho mint was not neglected, and medals were struck in Nelson's presence, the great engineer himself, who was indisposed, receiving the visitors in his bedroom.

After seeing Warwick and Coventry, and paying a call on Lord Spencer at Althorp, a return was made direct to Merton. The journey, so far from fatiguing Nelson, "not only established his health", so Harrison recorded, "but exhilarated his feeling mind, and freed it from every depression". It affected Sir William rather less favourably, and it was, in fact, his last protracted jaunt. It had also been costly. The full bill has been preserved, and the outlay was £481, 3s. 10d.

In August, Joseph Farington noted that Nelson's old acquaintance Edridge, the artist who had drawn the admiral and his lady in 1797, had been at Merton to attempt a second portrait. Edridge had not been wholly impressed. "The only circumstance from which he could judge that Lord Nelson was capable of great actions," so he told the diarist, "was an apparent decision about him, which is very observable and must be of great effect in action when supported by courage. He appeared to be possessed of religious sentiments", added Edridge, "and said that a time should be appropriated by each man to settle his business with futurity." If accurately recorded, this was perhaps the most Johnsonian of Nelson's remarks.

An important address from Sir William to his wife probably dates from soon after his return from the tour. "I have passed the last 40 years of my life in the hurry & bustle that must necessarily be attendant on a publick character," he wrote, feelingly. "I am arrived at an age when some repose is really necessary, & I promised myself a quiet home, & altho' I was sensible, & said so when I married, that I should be superannuated when my wife would be in her full beauty and vigour of youth. That time is arrived, and we must make the best of it for the comfort of both parties.

LORD NELSON
by Sir William Beechey

Beechey's portrait, in its frame of trophies, was
commissioned for the City of Norwich

"Unfortunately our tastes as to the manner of living are very different. I by no means wish to live in solitary retreat, but to have seldom less than 12 to 14 at table, & those varying continually, is coming back to what was become so irksome to me in Italy during the latter years of my residence in that country. I have no connections out of my own family. I have no complaint to make, but I feel that the whole attention of my wife is given to Lord N. and his interest at Merton. I well know the purity of Ld N's friendship for Emma and me, and I know how very uncomfortable it would make his Lp. our best friend, if a separation should take place, & am therefore determined to do all in my power to prevent such an extremity, which would be essentially detrimental to all parties, but would be more sensibly felt by our dear friend than by us. Provided that our expenses in housekeeping do not increase beyond all measure (of which I must own I see some danger), I am willing to go upon our present footing; but as I cannot expect to live many years, every moment to me is precious, & I hope I may be allowed sometimes to be my own master, & pass my time according to my own inclination, either by going my fishing parties on the Thames or by going to London to attend the Museum, the R. Society, the Tuesday Club & Auctions of Pictures. This is my plan, & we might go on very well, but I am fully determined not to have more of the very silly altercations that happen too often between us and embitter the present moments exceedingly. . . . There is no time for nonsense or trifling. I know and admire your talents & many excellent qualities but I am not blind to your defects & confess having many myself; therefore let us bear and forbear for God's sake."

It was characteristic of Emma—whether of her faults or virtues it is difficult to say—that she kept this letter from her husband among all the varied and compromising documents which emanated from Nelson. It is doubtful whether it was ever actually posted, though the undated draft exists, an odd mixture of detachment, as if Hamilton were addressing his nephew, and the closer touch of husband to wife.

What the altercations were about it is not now possible to say, but the whole letter is a cogent and rather pathetic plea for liberty on the part of a man who knows he has little longer in a world once brimming with pleasures, and which is not yet a weariness.

IV

Sir William was indeed right to savour every hour, for his end was approaching. It was characteristic of his thoughtfulness for his wife and his friend that when, in the spring of 1803, he felt the onset of an illness from which he was unlikely to recover, "with a calmness which he was unable to communicate to his lady," so Emma told Harrison, "he announced the solemn certainty; and declared his resolution immediately to leave Merton Place lest he should, by dying there, render it an insupportable future abode to the feelings of his tender and illustrious friend". At the end of March he moved to Piccadilly, and on the 29th of the month composed his will, in which the sentence occurred, quite unequivocal in its sentiment: "the copy of Madame le Brun's picture of Emma, in enamel, by Bone, I give to my dearest friend, Lord Nelson, Duke of Brontë: a small token of the great regard I have for his lordship; the most virtuous, loyal and truly brave character I have ever met with. God bless him, and shame fall on those who do not say—Amen".

When once he knew that the illness was mortal, Nelson scarcely quitted his friend's side. Sir William died in his wife's arms, with Nelson's hand in his, on 6th April 1803.

With that care for superficial appearances which was characteristic of a curious *menage*, Nelson at once took lodgings in another house. He shared expenses with Charles Greville, Emma's earlier lover. A sheet enumerating their housekeeping bills has survived, and the sum total must have been a shock to Greville's cheese-paring way of thought. In eleven days, from 7th to 18th April 1803, the pair laid out no less than £71, 19s. 5d., of which £20, 6s. 1d. went to a butcher, presumably for the funeral meats. Only some £8 represented amounts carried over from Merton.

SIR WILLIAM HAMILTON
by David Allan

Sir William wears the insignia of the Order of the Bath

Chapter 10

THE LONG WATCH

I

EVEN had Sir William Hamilton not died when he did, Nelson's life would soon have changed its direction. He was marked for the Mediterranean command, which, so St Vincent once pronounced, required "an officer of splendour". Keith had hoped to return there, but was given the North Sea. To Nelson fell the task of ceaseless watch upon an enemy whose intentions, apart from the long-contemplated invasion of Great Britain, were a matter of speculation.

Emma had been widowed little more than a month when war with France was resumed. The Declaration was made on 18th May 1803. Nelson's appointment had been announced two days earlier, and he hoisted his flag as a Vice-Admiral of the Blue in the very hour when hostilities began.

He was an altered man since his Baltic adventure, and the fact was apparent not merely in his own reflections. During the later months of 1800 St Vincent, when in command of the Channel fleet, had expressed the view in a letter to Nepean that Nelson never could "become an officer fit to be placed where I am". But Nelson's conduct before Copenhagen had so transformed the old warrior's opinion of one whom he had conceived to be a brilliant eccentric, that it caused him to remark (after he had himself been appointed First Lord) that when Nelson in due time came to occupy that high office, he would realise the impossibility of meeting every claim upon his favour. The change was none the less remarkable for being quite unconscious on the part of St Vincent—and there was no shrewder judge. Nelson had shown himself supremely responsible, and would henceforward be trusted accordingly.

His spell ashore had given him leisure to take thought upon the European scene, and his position as a member of the House of Lords had given him access to information which did not come the way of every sea officer: he had, moreover, been enabled to sharpen his mind in the company of men in other spheres of activity. "I am the friend of Peace without fearing war," he wrote; but if war came, he would again seek glory. This was illustrated by an amusing glimpse recorded, some years later, by Benjamin West, the historical painter.

The pair found themselves neighbours at dinner. The admiral, by way of making conversation, said how much he regretted that he had not acquired a taste for art in his youth, as well as some discrimination. "But," he added, "there is one picture whose power I *do* feel. I never pass a print shop where your *Death of Wolfe* is in the window without being stopped by it." He asked why West had done no more like it. "Because, my lord, there are no more subjects," said the painter simply. "Damn it," said Nelson, "I didn't think of that!" He then asked West to take a glass of champagne, the wine he favoured. "My lord," continued West, "I fear that your intrepidity may yet furnish me with another such scene, and if it should, I shall certainly avail myself of it." "Will you?" asked Nelson, pouring out bumpers. "*Will* you, Mr West? Then I hope I shall die in the next battle!"

If Nelson's thoughts on the Peace of Amiens came to be somewhat like Alexander Ball's, who told Coleridge that he considered "our conduct was not much wiser than that of the weary traveller who, having proceeded half-way on his journey, procured a short rest for himself by getting up behind a chaise which was going the contrary road", it was largely because his opinion of Bonaparte was unaltered. The First Consul of France was soon to become the Emperor Napoleon, an exaltation which caused Beethoven, irately disillusioned, to change the original dedication of his Eroica Symphony to "the *memory* of a great man". Nelson, with none of Beethoven's irony, remarked to Addington that it did not matter how you placed a poker on the hearth, but that if Bonaparte said that it should be *this* way, it was England's duty to insist that it be done in another. There could be no sustained amity with a man of such consuming ambition, and by sending Nelson to the Mediterranean the

Government knew that they were giving the direction of affairs in that important area to one who, though he no longer pined for battles, would assure the enemy that business was intended, and one who would make the utmost use of limited resources. Bonaparte's counter was to post Admiral La Touche-Tréville at Toulon. La Touche-Tréville was perhaps the ablest officer in the French naval service. It was he who had repulsed Nelson's attack on Boulogne.

Although, for a man of his temperament, Nelson's duty was likely to be taxing, it would complete his equipment in his profession. The essence of the matter was put by George Monck, who had exercised the admiral's art in earlier days. Describing the qualities needed in the perfect *"Souldier"*, a matter of which he also knew much, Monck wrote, a century and a half before Nelson's coming years of ceaseless watch, words which applied perfectly to them. "Let a Souldier's Resolution be never so great, and his Courage invincible in the day of Battel, yet if he faint under the burthen of such tediousness as usually attendeth upon warlike designments, he is in no way fit for enterprise: because the two chief parts of a Souldier are *Valour* and *Sufferance*; and there is as much Honour gained by suffering Wants patiently in War, as by fighting Valiantly; and as great achievements effected by the one, as by the other. It is no virtue, but a weakness of the mind, not to be able to endure want a little while: and yet it is an easier matter to find men that will offer themselves willingly to death, than such as will endure Labour with patience."

Monck's *Observations* were not among Nelson's recorded reading; had they been so, it is likely that he would have savoured the passage. He had long proved his Valour; now was the turn for Sufferance. "If the enemy venture out," wrote a correspondent to Lady Hamilton, "we are sure of a victory over them. If they continue in port, we may expect the continuance of his victory over himself, the hardest victory of all! For a high heart like his to endure a destiny where there is nothing to display but the melancholy miracles of passive valour!"

Before leaving England, Nelson would have been glad enough to improve two very mundane matters, the first of which never ceased to occupy him. Emma Hamilton, had been left an income of £800 a year by her husband, but Hamilton's efforts to secure her the reversion of his own pension of £1,200, in recognition of her services at Naples, had met with no response whatever. Nelson, in pressing Emma's claims in any and every quarter which might be expected to listen, and in others where no flicker of optimism would have been justified, assumed yet another burden. Emma took up the tale herself in her last years, and found how true was the saying that there are none so deaf as those who won't hear. Had her habits and generosity been other than they were, she need never have approached penury, but her ideas were large, she had been long used to gay society, and she retained that charitable outlook which had made her write to Greville many years before, "you must know I send my grandmother every Christmas twenty pounds, and so I ought. I have two hundred a year for nonsense, and it would be hard if I could not give her twenty pounds, when she has so often given me her last shilling."

As for Nelson himself, he told Emma: "I have known the pinch, and shall endeavour never to know it again"— and he put his case before Addington, in the March of 1803, in frank detail. He pointed out that both Lords St Vincent and Duncan enjoyed pensions of £3,000 a year for their victories, which were certainly not on the scale of the Nile, much less of the Nile and Copenhagen together. One-third of these pensions came from the Irish Establishment, and in this respect Nelson was unfortunate, for by the time the question of his reward came before the House for detailed consideration, the Irish Parliament was about to be merged, by the Act of Union, with that at Westminster, and the question of an Irish share was never followed up. Nelson was £1,000 a year poorer than his fellow-victors, who had moreover done well with prize-money, and he very pertinently put the question to the Minister: "Was it, or not, the intention of His Majesty's Government to place my rewards for services lower than Lord St Vincent or Lord Duncan? I had the happiness to be a sharer of the glory of the 14th of February (St Vincent); and I had the honour to command the Fleet that gained the Victory of the Nile, which, till that of Copenhagen, was, I believe, the most complete one ever obtained."

Nelson set out his affairs in business-like fashion.

"LORD NELSON'S INCOME AND PROPERTY

My Exchequer Pension for the Nile . .	£2,000	0 0
Navy Pension for loss of one arm and one eye	923	0 0
Half-pay as Vice-Admiral	465	0 0
Interest of £1,000 3 per Cents . . .	30	0 0
	£3,418	0 0

OUTGOINGS OF LORD NELSON

To Lady Nelson	£1,800	0 0
Interest on money owing	500	0 0
Pension to my Brother's Widow . .	200	0 0
To assisting in educating my Nephews .	150	0 0
Expenditure	£2,650	0 0
Income	3,418	0 0
For Lord Nelson	£768	0 0

Therefore, Lord Nelson is *free* of House-rent, but has to pay charities necessary for his station in life, taxes, repairs, servants, and to live upon £768 per annum.

PROPERTY OF LORD NELSON

Merton House, land, plate, and furniture .	£20,000	0 0

In 3 per Cents, £1,000 Stock.

DEBTS

By Mortgage on Merton, to assist in the purchase	6,000	0 0
Fitting out for the Baltic, and again for my command on the Coast, in Summer 1801 .	4,000	0 0
	£10,000	0 0

Real Property of Lord Nelson £10,000.
In Three per Cents, £1,000 Stock."

Upon this statement there were obvious comments, though they did not alter what was in fact an anomaly of reward in Nelson's disfavour. The first was that it was not necessary for Lady Nelson to have a separate establishment, in fact this was still a grief to most of Nelson's older friends. The second was that, according to surviving statements of his account with his bankers, Marsh, Page and Creed, dated 1802, it was £400, not £450 that he paid to Fanny every quarter, though he may have increased an already generous provision by the time he forwarded his reluctant plea. Again, he made no mention of any revenue from Brontë, and did not include the value of the Sicilian estate, presumably because both revenue and value were uncertain. Addington, usually sympathetic, and always ready to listen to Nelson's views on affairs in general, for which indeed he sometimes asked, was unable to help him.

If his own finances, and those of Emma, were one cause of anxiety, another was that the proprieties should not merely be observed, but sustained. Nelson went to extreme lengths to ensure this. One of his first enquiries, after he had bought Merton, had been to ask Emma if there was a "nice church" near by, for, he said, "we will set an example of goodness to the under-parishioners"; a wish which he fulfilled in many acts of charity. Lady Spencer's mother, who seems to have been persuaded of the innocence of Nelson's relationship with Emma, recalled being told that he took the Sacrament in private before leaving Merton. After the service, taking Emma's hand and facing the priest, he said: "Emma, I have taken the Sacrament with you this day to prove to the world that our friendship is most pure and innocent, and of this I call God to witness!" The authorities for this incident, which is recorded in the Diary of Lady Frances Shelley, would have been Emma or the priest who administered the rite, and it bears evidence of Emma's more dramatic style.

Nelson was concerned with the appearances of his own spiritual health, even with the gross hypocrisy implied in the incident, and he continued mindful of that of his men. He wrote from his new flagship, soon after he had joined her, to ask the Society for the Promotion of Christian Knowledge to send a supply of Bibles and Prayer Books for the use of the Ship's Company, "consisting of 874 men". By this time the diligent Secretary had grown so used to his requests, and the Society were so warm in their response, that it could have been no surprise to them to have received a letter, a few months after the first, assuring them that "Divine Service is regularly performed; that the men are by far more regular and decent than when it is not; and that in that Ship only two Men have been punish'd for upwards of two months."

Soon after Nelson's departure for foreign service, Emma visited an old acquaintance, the French painter Vigée-Lebrun, who was then in London. Madame Lebrun described her caller as "wearing the deepest mourning. An immense black veil surrounded her." The painter also noticed that "she had had beautiful hair cut short in order to have her head dressed according to the fashion of the day. I found this Andromache huge," continued a trained observer, "for she had become dreadfully stout. She said to me, with tears in her eyes, that she was deeply to be pitied; that she had lost in Sir William a friend and father, and that she would never be able to console herself. I admit that her grief made little impression on me, for I could see she was acting a part. How little I deceived myself was shown a few minutes later when, having seen some pieces of music on my piano, she began to sing one of the airs which she found there."

Emma and the Frenchwoman understood one another pretty well, though Madame Lebrun did not yet know the full range of her friend's accomplishments, and she was astonished at a party where they met a second time, given by the painter in honour of the Dukes of Berri and Bourbon, to notice how much porter Emma could enjoy without the slightest effect on her stability. "*Il fallait qu'elle y fût bien accoutumée,*" was her comment. Later still, going to call on her one morning in London, she found Emma "radiant with happiness; more than that, she had put a rose in her hair". Madame Lebrun could not refrain from asking what the flower implied. "It means," said Emma proudly, "that I have just had a letter from Lord Nelson."

II

Merton, as the seat of a famous man, was modest in scale, but Nelson's more enduring activities were afloat, and in his new flagship, the *Victory*, he had one of the stateliest three-deckers ever built, a vessel in every way worthy to receive him. She had been laid down when he was still in his cradle, had been launched at Chatham in 1765, and had worn the flags of Keppel, Kempenfelt, Howe, Hood, St Vincent and other, lesser, admirals. She had just undergone a large repair which was practically a rebuilding, and was capable of a surprising turn of speed. Had Nelson been offered his choice, he could not have proposed a finer or a lovelier ship. But his tenure was at first uncertain. His orders were to rendezvous with Cornwallis, then commanding off Brest, and to offer the *Victory* as a reinforcement. If, as was expected, Cornwallis had no need of her, she was to convey Nelson to the Mediterranean.

Cornwallis could not readily be found, and, eager to reach his new command, Nelson transferred his entire retinue, together with that of Hugh Elliot, whom he was taking to the Court of Naples, to the cramped quarters of a frigate, rather than lose an unnecessary moment, or disobey his instructions. It entailed sacrifice of comfort for all concerned, the officers being crowded six or seven to a cabin. It was an incident that Nelson no doubt remembered, though he never openly recalled it, when, just before Trafalgar, Sir Robert Calder, an officer whom he had no reason to love, was so reluctant to obey official directions that he sought to cling to his powerful flagship rather than diminish his personal dignity in the eyes of the fleet—and this at a time when the enemy were almost within sight, and every vessel needed.

In one way, the change from the *Victory* to the *Amphion* was not unwelcome, for it was Hardy who had charge of the frigate, and Nelson could conceive no better captain. He was equally happy in his personal staff. John Scott, his secretary, recorded later that Nelson's "political, able and ready decisions astonish me beyond measure, indeed, all his public business is transacted with a degree of correctness peculiar to himself, nor does the most trifling circumstance escape his penetrating eye; from a knowledge of his private and secret correspondence I am led to consider him the greatest character I am met with, in fact he is a wonderful great man, as good as great. Lord Nelson will certainly *think* more in a *minute* than *most* men will do in an *hour*. . . ." The enthusiastic italics, the result of close knowledge, served to show that familiarity bred content. Adding to the portrait in a letter to Lady Hamilton, Scott said that, in company, Nelson did not "appear to bear any weight in his mind" and was "so cheerful and pleasant, that it is a happiness to be about his hand". Most enthusiastically would Scott have endorsed the words of one of the Matcham nephews, who said that Nelson was "anxious to give pleasure to everyone about him, distinguishing each in turn by some act of kindness, and chiefly those who seemed to require it most."

Another character, ambling, absent-minded and talkative, was the eccentric Doctor Scott, Nelson's Secretary for foreign correspondence, always designated by his learned title to distinguish him from his lay colleague. The reverend Doctor was skilled in languages, and had impressed Nelson while serving in a similar capacity with Sir Hyde Parker. During the Peace, he had travelled to the West Indies, where he had been injured by lightning. Nelson attended him constantly on his return, and inspired in Scott's mind lasting, almost dog-like devotion, wholly unaffected by Nelson's chaff in saying that he preferred practical men, wise in the school not of books but of experience.

Another acquisition resulting from the Baltic was George Murray, the Captain of the Fleet. Murray had won praise from Nelson by his conduct at Copenhagen, but had been reluctant to accept his new appointment, saying, what was true enough, that the nature of the office "often led to disagreements between the Admiral and First Captain, and that he should be very unwilling to risk a diminution of the regard and respect which he entertained for his lordship". Nelson persuaded him by replying that under no circumstances would he forget the bond between them, "and that even should anything go contrary to his wishes, he would waive the rank of Admiral, and explain or expostulate with him as his *friend*". Murray was the only Captain of the Fleet Nelson ever had. As, for private reasons, he could not sail on the Trafalgar voyage, Nelson fought the battle without him, Hardy acting in his place.

On 28th June 1803, writing from the *Amphion* between Sardinia and Naples, Nelson sent a long letter to Addington describing the aspect of affairs as it then appeared to him from the sea which he knew so well. Gibraltar, he thought, should be garrisoned with British troops, not entrusted, as it then was, to regiments recruited from foreigners.

It was only a few months since two outbreaks of mutiny had occurred at the Rock under the Governorship of the Duke of Kent, and the incident would still have been fresh in Nelson's mind. As for Algiers, that nest of piracy, Nelson begged that if matters were left to him, "our demands for satisfaction be fixed; for if we give way in the smallest thing, the insolence of the Dey will but increase". Malta he had already visited; his views upon its value were well known. It had been the nominal cause of the renewal of war, Britain refusing to leave it while France still effectually occupied Holland and Switzerland, but it was useless for a watch upon French arsenals, Sardinia being preferable for the purpose. "The Fleet," he said, "can never go there if I can find any other corner to put them in; but having said this, I now declare that I consider Malta as a most important outwork to India, that it will ever give us great influence in the Levant, and indeed all the Southern parts of Italy. In this view, I hope we shall never give it up."

As for Sicily, the seat of his Dukedom, he thought that its state was "almost as bad as a civilized country can be. There are no Troops fit to be called such, with a scarcity of corn never known, and of course bread so dear that the lower class of people are discontented. The Nobles are oppressors, and the middle rank wish for a change; and although they would prefer us to the French, yet I believe they would receive the French, rather than not change from the oppression."

Nelson was already in correspondence with the Court of Naples, both directly and via Hugh Elliot and Sir John

Acton. He hoped it would still be Great Britain's wish to make the Neapolitans "feel that we were true friends". He had already told Acton that "a Ship of War—and, generally, of the Line—shall, on some pretence or other, always be in the Bay of Naples, to prevent that worst of all accidents, the loss of the Royal Family". Acton must indeed have felt that old times had come again, particularly as Nelson had been able to add the detail, "I do assure you that the last words of Mr Addington to me were: 'Take care of their Sicilian Majesties, for the King considers them as the most faithful allies that he has ever had!'"

Sardinia, Rome and Tuscany he considered would be allowed by the French to remain neutral, though Leghorn, a centre of French influence and traffic, had been declared by Bonaparte to be in a state of siege. Nelson thought that the British Government should place it in a state of blockade so long as an enemy garrison remained in the town. "Everything in Genoa is French," he added, recommending an immediate declaration of blockade, and he saw new signs of French activity in the Morea. He considered that there were some 13,000 French troops in the kingdom of Naples, occupying the useful ports of Brindisi and Taranto and spread about elsewhere: 8,000 were in Leghorn, and about 6,000 destined for other parts of Italy. As for the enemy fleet, he added in a postscript that he thought they had nine ships of the line to oppose the seven upon which he himself could usually rely as being on station. "We are in hopes that Bonaparte may be angry, and order them out," he added, "which I have no doubt, will put our Ships in high feather; for I never knew any wants after a Victory, although we are always full of them before." He added later: "My first object must be to keep the French fleet in check: and, if they put to sea, to have force enough with me to *annihilate* them."

By 8th July 1803 the *Amphion* had joined the squadron then on watch off Toulon—nine sail of the line and three frigates. Well disciplined, perfect in war training, they were finding mounting difficulty in supply, and several ships needed repair if they were to sustain a winter of cruising. But the dockyards at Malta and Gibraltar were almost empty of stores, and in writing to him that "with the resources of your mind you will do very well", St Vincent was saying in effect that he relied upon Nelson's ingenuity to make good the drastic economies for which he, St Vincent, had himself been responsible during the brief Peace.

Incapable of working by half measures, St Vincent had determined to eradicate corruption and waste in the naval yards and ports. But such was the incrustation of vested interest, traditional methods, and what the modern world knows as the principle of the closed shop, that he had set himself a hopeless task. His efforts, vigorous though they were, merely had the result of uniting almost all the dock-yard suppliers against him, and they found powerful support in Parliament itself. The First Lord's reformatory drive, together with the laying up of the major part of the fleet, as was the custom in peace, meant that, when war was resumed, while the French arsenals had been replenished from every quarter, the Royal Navy was denuded of resources to an extent which it had not known for decades, and this at a time when they would be needed as never before in history.

If Nelson had known the pinch in his pocket, he now knew it in his command, and he had need of all his qualities of contrivance, forethought and optimism to keep increasingly crazy ships afloat. The measure of his success was that after nearly two years' incessant blockade, exercised in all weathers, he was able to lead them four thousand miles on a chase to the West Indies. No one else could have done as much, and it is an indication of the difference between the old naval warfare and the new that Nelson could think in terms of months and even years consecutively at sea, while today, even with all the resources of a Fleet-Train, no large force could be expected to keep efficient for such a stretch.

By the end of July the *Victory*, released from her short spell under Cornwallis, was able to resume her rôle as Nelson's headquarters. The admiral and Hardy removed into their ampler quarters, and quickly settled down to the routine in which both men found professional satisfaction, and which, with only one brief interval, was to continue for the rest of Nelson's life.

Impressive as the *Victory* still is, in her meticulously pre-served condition at Portsmouth, she is now but a shell of the

H.M.S. *VICTORY*

Nelson's stately home. The second row of windows belonged
to his quarters. Hardy lived above

sea fortress which then dominated the Mediterranean. Her immense spread of sail, which gave her speed, has gone for ever; her eight hundred and fifty men, who gave her power, are no more than memories. Such a ship was "tall" indeed, for her main-mast, with its top-mast and top-gallant, rose 175 feet above her deck. She was over 200 feet long, with a 52-foot beam and of a tonnage well over 2,000. She mounted 104 guns, and with all her size and capacity there was not a corner wasted, from the depths of her hold with its ordered stores and well-stowed ammunition to the skid-beams on the spar-deck where the boats—the admiral's Barge, pulling 14 oars, the Pinnace, the Launch, pulling 16 oars double-banked, and the handy Cutter, were ready for hoisting out by tackle at the word of command.

Hardy's cabins, immediately beneath the poop, were, like all cabins of the time, scant in head-room for a man of six foot: but the Georgian navy was under-sized by modern standards, and surviving records of a typical ship of Nelson's time reveal the fact that sixty-one of her men were less than five foot tall, and only three could have ranged themselves beside Hardy. His own inconvenience of a constant stoop was not a general discomfort. He had a day-cabin aft, leading into a dining-cabin, with sleeping-quarters adjoining, on the starboard side. Nelson's accommodation was on the deck below, and was still more spacious, for his dining-cabin was twice the size of Hardy's, occupying most of the width of the ship. There were rooms adjoining his sleeping-quarters for a small retinue of personal attendants, in charge of Chevalier, his Italian steward, who had pantries and facilities for cooking. The admiral apart, the ship's company relied for their heated meals on the huge iron stove on the deck below, level with the ward-room though a long way forward, with its chain-turned spits for roasting, its ovens for baking the duff the sailors loved, and its funnel emerging through the top deck not far from the ship's bell.

From Nelson's day-cabin, with its spacious outlook from stern and quarter galleries, its elegant furnishings, desks, sofa and chairs, bookshelves, its portraits of Emma and its silver bowl of fruit, the orders for the fleet went forth by the hand of his two secretaries, the clerical and multi-lingual

Scott, so clever with the foreign intelligence, and his name-sake, who dealt with the routine orders and despatches. Nelson soon established his methods. His was to be a distant watch rather than a close blockade, a fact which he was at pains to make clear whenever he was congratulated on his vigilance, for his interest was to draw the enemy out, not to keep him in. He kept a frigate inshore, but stood away with his bigger ships, hoping to tempt an adventure.

In the storms which made his cruising-ground miserable at times, he either ran to the southward, or "furled all sails and made the ships as easy as possible". His usual stretch of sea was bounded on the west by the coast of Spain, on the south by the Balearics and on the east by Corsica and Sardinia. Northward, France barred the way.

The Emperor at Boulogne, Cornwallis, Nelson, Keith and others on their several stations, all were praying for the chance to deal a decisive blow to their seemingly inaccessible adversaries. Power grew; more and more forces completed training; plans were drafted and improved. So far as the two greatest protagonists were concerned, while Napoleon was meditating his long-proposed invasion, Nelson, in Mahan's well-remembered phrases, was "before Toulon, wearing away the last two years of his glorious but suffering life, fighting the fierce north-westers of the Gulf of Lyon and questioning, questioning continually with feverish anxiety, whether Napoleon's object was Egypt again or Great Britain. They were dull, weary, eventless months, those months of watching and waiting of the big ships before the French arsenals. Purposeless they surely seemed to many, but they saved England. The world has never seen a more impressive demonstration of the influence of sea power upon its history. Those far-distant, storm-beaten ships, upon which the Grand Army never looked, stood between it and the dominion of the world."

III

It was upon Sardinia that Nelson came to rely as a base and a source of refreshment. During the Peace, Keith had

stationed a ship at the Maddalena Islands, off its north-east
coast, to forestall French occupation. Nelson reaped the
benefit of his foresight, for although the King of Sardinia,
who had lost his mainland possessions to the French, and
who had been promised compensation elsewhere, maintained neutrality, the northern parts of his wild and moun-
tainous island afforded the British fleet some of its recurrent
needs. The Maddalenas themselves offered wood, water and
an anchorage which Nelson put to constant use. Small
bullocks, goats, sheep, chestnuts, olives and fruit in season
could be had at times, and there was fishing to supplement
the uncertain provender, for the waters were the haunt of the
tunny, the sardine and the anchovy. The goat-herds on the
rocky shore grew used to seeing the weather-worn ships
with their chequered sides swinging to anchor, the men
filling their water-casks, the shore parties glad of a brief spell
with land beneath their feet, their nostrils freshened with the
scent of myrtle, broom and juniper.

But with all its consolations, Sardinia was a bleak place.
Snow was visible on the peak of Gennargento for nine
months of the year; strong winds were seasonal, the north-
westerly *maestrale*, the north-easterly *greco*, and the *sirocco*
from the south-west; it was scourged with malaria; but it
was the nearest the sailors knew to home, and there grew up
friendship and understanding between them and the peas-
ants of the littoral, who no longer went armed night and day,
as they had done for generations past, against the attacks of
Algerine raiders. Nelson came so to rely upon his island
anchorage that he said that if he lost Sardinia, he lost the
French fleet. There were in fact other amenities than those
of the Maddalenas: for instance, at Pula, on the southern
shore Nelson noted that "the river is of the very finest water
I ever tasted: it is called by the natives Aqua Dulce and it
runs all the year in the greatest abundance. Twenty ships
can water at one time . . . the river runs for several hundred
yards parallel to the Beach".

"The great thing in all military service is health," he
wrote to Dr Moseley, his friend of Nicaraguan days, "and
you will agree with me that it is easier for an officer to keep
men healthy, than for a physician to cure them. Situated as

this fleet has been, without a friendly port where we could get the things so necessary for us, yet I have, by changing the cruising ground, not allowed the sameness of prospect to satiate the mind—sometimes by looking at Toulon, Ville Franche, Barcelona and Rosas; then running round Minorca, Majorca, Sardinia and Corsica; and two or three times anchoring for a few days, and sending a ship to the last place for *onions*, which I find the best thing that can be given to seamen; having always good mutton for the sick & cattle when we can get them, and plenty of fresh water." Occasionally, so Nelson discovered with amusement, his supplies were drawn indirectly from the enemy.

Not the most trivial administrative detail missed his attention; not the smallest chance of diversion. There were few sick (despite the compensation of a mutton diet), and the male world which Nelson ruled grew into such unity as had distinguished the squadron he had led to Aboukir. As always, he believed his men invincible, though the chance to prove it seemed long in coming. "La Touche," he wrote grimly, "was sent for on purpose, as he *beat me* at Boulogne, to beat me again; but he seems very loath to try."

Colonel Stewart had been impressed in the Baltic by Nelson's principle of keeping all hands employed, "no matter how and no matter where". It was a sound plan in that more mischief was likely to arise through idleness than any other single cause, and, in a fleet in which mutiny had become a factor to be reckoned with, trouble of any kind was to be avoided like the plague. Under Nelson, and indeed any commander with imagination or the ability to inspire devotion, continual employment helped the efficiency and even the harmony of ship's companies in time of war. Hardened to a dogma, and applied in peace-time without the spur of danger, the practice led to shocking excesses, as is apparent in more than one description of the fleet of the post-Nelson age.

Of himself he was, as always, unsparing. It was a saying well known to him that, once past Gibraltar, every officer assumed the habits of a bachelor, and although his letters to Emma flowed ceaselessly on their uncertain way to Merton, as fond in their expressions as ever, yet he welcomed the idea of seeing her in his fleet—a prospect she dangled before him

—as little as he had that of Fanny joining him in Italy. "Imagine what a cruise off Toulon is," he told her. "Even in summer-time we have a hard gale every week, and two days' heavy swell. It would kill you; and myself to see you. . . . And I, that have given orders to carry no women to sea in the *Victory*, to be the first to break them!"

Despite this sharp warning, the life of a commander-in-chief was not without its amenities, as was right and proper. Dr Gillespie, one of the retinue, wrote a detailed account of a typical day. "At 6 o'clock my servant brings a light, and informs me of the hour, wind, weather and course of the ship, when I immediately dress and generally repair to the deck," he said. "Breakfast is announced in the Admiral's cabin, where Lord Nelson, Rear-Admiral Murray (the Captain of the Fleet), Captain Hardy, commander of the *Victory*, the chaplain, secretary, one or two officers of the ship, and your humble servant assemble and breakfast on tea, hot rolls, toast, cold tongue, etc., which when finished we repair upon deck to enjoy the majestic sight of the rising sun (scarcely ever obscured by clouds in this fine climate) surmounting the smooth and placid waves of the Mediterranean, which supports the lofty and tremendous bulwarks of Britain, following in regular train their Admiral in the *Victory*." Gillespie chose one of the better days for his set-piece.

"Between the hours of 7 and 2 there is plenty of time for business, study, writing and exercise. At 2 o'clock a band of music plays till within a quarter of 3, when the drum beats the tune called 'The Roast Beef of Old England', to announce the Admiral's dinner, which is served up exactly at three o'clock, and which generally consists of three courses and a dessert of the choicest fruit, together with three or four of the best wines, champagne and claret not excepted. If a person does not feel himself perfectly at his ease it must be his own fault, such is the urbanity and hospitality which reign here. . . .

"Coffee and liqueurs close the dinner about half-past 4 or 5 o'clock, after which the company generally walk the deck, where the band of music plays for nearly an hour. At 6 o'clock tea is announced, when the company again assemble in the Admiral's cabin, where tea is served up before 7 o'clock, and, as we are inclined, the party continue to converse with his lordship, who at this time generally unbends himself, though he is at all times as free from stiffness and pomp as a regard to proper dignity will admit, and is very communicative. At 8 o'clock a rummer of punch with cake or biscuit is served up, soon after which we wish the Admiral a good night (who is generally in bed before 9 o'clock). Such is the journal of a day at sea in fine or at least moderate weather, in which this floating castle goes through the water with the greatest imaginable steadiness."

Nelson was always noted for a generous table, and Dr Gillespie's account must be read as of a time when action was not expected, and when a visit to Sardinia or elsewhere had enabled the stores to be replenished, the "choicest fruit" being proof of this. That Nelson's own thoughts did not always picture things so rosily is shown by his letter to Emma, dated 27th June 1804, when he heard first of a change of Ministry, Lord Melville replacing St Vincent at the Admiralty, and then that his friend Davison had been confined for bribery at an Election. "He would only consult Lord Moira and such clever folks," wrote Nelson, "but an ignoramus like me could only warn him not to touch Boroughs. . . . I am most sincerely sorry for him, but a year will soon pass away. Have I not been shut up in a ship without any one comfort? He is ashore with his friends round him, and even you go to see him. I would change with him with much pleasure."

William Beatty, another doctor, who later wrote the best account of Nelson's last hours, recorded other details of his life. At one time Nelson suffered from gout, which he cured permanently by abstaining from meat, wine and all fermented drink for two whole years, living on vegetables, milk and water. Quite early in life, when he first went to sea, he had left off the use of salt, and never afterwards took it with his food. "His lordship used a great deal of exercise," said Beatty, "generally walking on deck six or seven hours in the day. . . . He ate very sparingly, the liver and wing of a fowl and a small plate of macaroni in general composing his meal, during which he occasionally took a glass of champagne. He never exceeded four glasses of wine after dinner, and seldom drank three; and even those were diluted with Bristol or common water.

"Few men subject to the vicissitudes of a Naval life equalled his lordship in an habitual systematic mode of living. He possessed such a wonderful activity of mind, as even prevented him from taking ordinary repose, seldom enjoying two hours of uninterrupted sleep; and on several occasions he did not quit the deck the whole night. At these times he took no pains to protect himself from the wet, or the night air; wearing only a thin great coat; and he has frequently, after having his clothes wet through with rain, refused to have them changed, saying that the leather waistcoat which he wore over his flannel one would secure him from complaint. He seldom wore boots, and was consequently very liable to have his feet wet. When this occurred he has often been known to go down to his cabin, throw off his clothes, and walk on the carpet in his stockings for the purpose of drying the feet of them. He chose to adopt this uncomfortable expedient, rather than to give his servants the trouble of assisting him to put on fresh stockings, which, from his having only one hand, he could not himself conveniently affect."

Another characteristic recorded by Beatty was well known to all who sailed with Nelson; it was "a slight rheumatic affection of the stump of his amputated arm on any sudden variation in the state of the weather. His Lordship usually predicted an alteration in the weather with as much certainty from feeling transient pains in his stump as he could by his marine barometer, from the indications of which latter he kept a diary of the atmospheric changes, which was written with his own hand."

In addition to the routine cares of his post, which he could and did mitigate by forethought and by living, so far as he could, the life of an "officer of splendour" and a peer of the realm, Nelson had two private anxieties, one of which he could not share. Emma was expecting another child, and a girl was born to her during the early days of 1804. The infant did not live long, and Nelson never saw her. The references to the event in a letter dated 18th March lack the ecstasy attendant upon the arrival of his first-born, as was perhaps not surprising in the altered pattern of Emma's life. "Kiss dear Horatia for me," he said, "and the other. Call him what you please, if a girl, Emma. . . ."

The other matter was his sight. The two Scotts, zealous secretaries, could indeed take upon themselves, with increasing confidence and pleasure, much of the reading and writing required from their chief, but even Doctor Beatty, who took an optimistic view of Nelson's health in general, never doubted the seriousness of the condition which Nelson himself felt most keenly. "My eyesight fails me most dreadfully," he told the now troubled Davison. "I firmly believe that, in a very few years, I shall be stone blind. It is this only, of all my maladies, that makes me unhappy; but God's will be done."

IV

Nelson kept a series of notebooks, some in marbled covers and some in plain, in which he entered the day-to-day events of his Mediterranean command. They record the actions of a single-minded man in time of war, writing for himself. He invariably noted the wind, the state of the sea, and—if inshore—important soundings. He would then state the bare happenings of the day—ships detached, ships sighted, ships spoken. An occasional note (always at the top of a day's entry), "*Wrote Ly Hm.*", meant that there was chance of conveying a packet to Emma in England.

Rarely there was a more general observation, as, for instance, on the fifth anniversary of the Nile, when he wrote: "Had the pleasure of rewarding merit in the person of Mr Hindmarsh Gunner's son of the *Bellerophon*, for his conduct this day five years." Mr Hindmarsh became a lieutenant, but whether the merit was his own or his father's appears neither from the ambiguous note itself nor from a reference to the matter in a letter home. In the back of the fifth volume he wrote out a list of young officers he wished to note or promote, "a very good young man" being a favourite remark entered after a name. Of one of these young men, Peter

Parker, then a lieutenant in the *Victory*, Nelson allowed himself to say that he was "to get both the steps as fast as possible—his grandfather made me everything that I am".

The case of Peter Parker is notable on general grounds, showing once again the valuable favour which could be given to those who were indeed the Children of the Service. The young man's grandfather, Nelson's early patron, had by the end of the eighteenth century become Admiral of the Fleet, and was the senior officer in the Navy List. His father, since dead, had also reached flag rank, and Peter Parker himself had been on a ship's books since the age of eight. At sixteen he had been made lieutenant, being then officially reported as "upwards of twenty-one". Nelson was able to get him the first of the two "steps", the rank of commander, in May 1804. Collingwood, another beneficiary of old Admiral Parker's, got him the second, immediately after Trafalgar. It needs to be added that Parker deserved every possible encouragement for his brilliance and zest for the service. He did not live long to enjoy post rank, for he was killed in action at the age of twenty-six, in America, his death occasioning verse from his cousin, Lord Byron.

Less good fortune attended Nelson's efforts on behalf of two other young officers. One was William Layman, who had first attracted his notice in the Baltic; the other was his kinsman, William Bolton. Layman was a dashing fellow who, so Nelson told Emma, talked too much and wrote too fast. But he was keen and active, and it was sheer misfortune that, through the negligence of a subordinate, he lost his fine sloop, the *Raven*, on the rocks off Cadiz, early in 1805, having won golden opinions in the earlier months of Nelson's cruise. Layman was court-martialled. The resultant reprimand, which ruined his career, was felt by Nelson to be partly his fault, since he had persuaded Layman to suppress a severe reflection on the officer of the watch, saying that if he did not do so, the man would be hanged!

The sentence, which involved relegation to the bottom of the commander's list, and brought with it an inevitable black mark from the Admiralty, upset Nelson so much that he wrote to Lord Melville "to recommend Captain Layman to your kind protection; for, notwithstanding the Court Martial has thought him deserving of censure for his running in with the land, yet, my Lord, allow me to say, that Captain Layman's misfortune was, perhaps, conceiving that other people's abilities were equal to his own, which, indeed, very few people's are.

"I own myself one of those who do not fear the shore, for hardly any great things are done in a small Ship by a man that is; therefore, I make very great allowances for him. Indeed, his station was intended never to be from the shore in the Straits: and if he did not every day risk his Sloop, he would be useless upon that Station. Captain Layman has served with me in three ships, and I am well acquainted with his bravery, zeal, judgment and activity; nor do I regret the loss of the *Raven* compared to the value of Captain Layman's services, which are a National loss.

"You must, my dear Lord, forgive the warmth which I express for Captain Layman; but he is in adversity, and, therefore, has the more claim to my attention and regard. If I had been censured every time I have run my Ship, or Fleets under my command, into great danger, I should long ago have been *out* of the Service, and never *in* the House of Peers."

Extraordinarily enough, this letter was of no avail, nor was a later plea made to Lord Barham. The episode had, however, one memorable result. The "generous and characteristic" terms in which Nelson spoke of Layman, and his realisation that a man may sometimes be of more value to the country than a ship, so warmed the heart of Sir Harris Nicolas that it inspired him to the collection of Nelson's letters and despatches, a labour of affection and scholarship for which posterity has reason to be grateful.

The case of William Bolton was very different. "Billy" Bolton, who married his cousin, Nelson's niece, had been knighted when he stood proxy for Nelson at the Installation of the Knights Elect of the Order of the Bath, at Westminster Abbey, which was a ceremony of splendour. Soon afterwards he was given command of a sloop and sent to the Mediterranean station. Nelson, with that attention to his family's interest which was so characteristic of his career, gave the young knight chance after chance of distinction and prize-money, for he liked him and longed to put him in the way of a fortune. Alas, Billy Bolton, charming as he was, was inactive and uncertain, and in the end he exhausted even Nelson's patience by being unable to turn to the best use whatever opportunities were put in his way. To be pleasant was all very well, but in a sea officer it was not enough: such was Nelson's view, and certainly, had Layman been given Bolton's chances, he would not have failed to profit by them.

Such asides as concerned the future career of hopeful young officers were rare in Nelson's notebook series. The general impression given by the entries, often laconic though never obscure, is one of stern attention to matters in hand. Nothing was put down for other eyes; nothing was casual; and the writing itself was indicative of every variation due to stress of weather, state of health, and anxiety. The earlier months reflect the tedium of events, for the more dramatic incidents were concentrated, as they were in Nelson's life as a whole, towards the end. He could be vivid enough in his letters, even in his speech, but what he recorded in this series were the sober professional memoranda of a sea officer. Only the clarity and flow of words, with scarcely a correction, betokened the swift, exceptional mind.

In the early months of 1804, La Touche-Tréville at last began to exercise his ships beyond sheltered waters. "My friend," said Nelson, "sometimes plays bo-peep in and out of Toulon, like a mouse at the edge of her hole." On 5th April there was a bigger sortie than any made before, and on the 9th Nelson reported that "a rear admiral and seven sail, including frigates, put their nose outside the harbour. If they go on playing this game, some day we shall lay salt upon their tails, and so end the campaign."

"I have taken a method of making Mr La Touche-Tréville angry," he explained. "I have left Sir Richard Bickerton, with part of the fleet, twenty leagues from hence, and, with five of the line, am preventing his cutting capers, which he has done for some time past, off Cape Sicie." His idea was that "the Frenchman might be tempted by my keeping so great an inferiority close to him". Bickerton's orders were to remain due south from Port Cros, at a distance such that, with their upper sails furled, his ships could not be seen from the Hyères islands, but could keep the main fleet in sight from their mast heads. "I am perfectly prepared how to act with either a superior or an inferior force," Nelson added. "My mind is as firm as a rock, and my plans for every event fixed in my mind." He depended only for the final touches on the inspiration of the moment; no admiral ever made himself better prepared for every condition of engagement.

On St Georges Day, 1804, in a general promotion, Nelson became Vice-Admiral of the White, the highest position he ever attained in the navy. "As I rise in rank," he said with perfect truth, "so do my exertions." About the time when the news reached him, he was greatly upset as a result of an encounter with his old adversary. On 13th June two French frigates and a brig were seen off Hyères, where they had been sent on a report that there were British ships cruising in the neighbourhood. Nelson sent two frigates after them, but, owing to light winds, they could not get near until the next day, when the Frenchmen were observed to be under the shelter of shore batteries. The *Excellent*, a 74, was sent to their support, upon which La Touche himself got under way, and about 5 p.m. came out of harbour with eight of the line. Nelson recalled the *Excellent*, reduced his own canvas, and hauled to the wind in line of battle. As the wind then was, the ship's heads were offshore. They remained hove-to until the next morning, offering the French the challenge they had seemed to look for. "I did not believe anything was meant," wrote Nelson to Lord Minto, "but merely a gasconade." Next day, the French were chased back into Toulon. Great was Nelson's wrath when, weeks later, he read La Touche's account of how he had caused Nelson to run away.

"You will have seen Monsieur La Touche's letter of how he chased me and how I *ran*," he wrote to his brother in fury. "I keep it; and by God, if I take him, he shall *eat* it!" To Davison he added: "If my character for *not* running away is not fixed by this time, and if any Englishman believed for one moment the story, I may to my friend say, without fear of being thought arrogant, that they do not deserve to have me serve them."

Things had gone exactly to plan, so far as Nelson's dispositions were concerned. He did not intend to engage the

French so close to their own sanctuary that their damaged ships could find shelter, while his own could not; but, given the necessary sea room, he felt no doubt that, even with dilapidated ships, he could successfully meet odds. But if reasonable odds were one thing, rashness was another. No better indication of Nelson's sense of proportion in this matter exists than the letter he wrote to Rear-Admiral George Campbell, a flag-officer recently joined, just a month after La Touche-Tréville's sortie, after hearing that Campbell had refused an engagement on thoroughly disadvantageous terms. "I am more obliged to you than I can express," wrote Nelson, "for your not allowing the very superior force of the Enemy to bring you to action. Whatever credit would have accrued to your own and your gallant Companions' exertions no sound advantage could have arisen to our Country; for so close to their own harbour, they could always have returned, and left your ships unfit, probably, to keep the sea. I again, my dear Admiral, thank you for your conduct. Some day, very soon, I have no doubt but an opportunity will offer of giving them fair battle."

It was no wonder that, with such understanding sympathy, Nelson attracted the devotion of subordinates; and if confidence, discipline and training were the keynote of his relationship with Bickerton, Campbell and the captains of the ships of the line, it was much the same with the frigates. One of Nelson's captains recorded a conversation held with Capel, his former signal lieutenant, and with William Parker a nephew of St Vincent—two young men of promise—in case they ever had the chance of attacking two French frigates with two of their own. Nelson's advice was that they should not take an opponent apiece, but that both should concentrate on capturing a single enemy. "If successful, chase the other," he added, "but if you do not take the second, still you have won a victory, and your country will gain a frigate." Then, half laughing and half snappishly, remembering he had once been young himself, he added kindly, as he wished them good-bye, "I daresay you consider yourselves a couple of fine fellows, and when you get away from me you will do nothing of the sort, but think yourselves wiser than I am!" Actually, no more sensible advice was ever given. Had it been remembered more often, during the course of the Napoleonic War, fewer indecisive actions would have resulted. It illustrated the principle of concentration, enjoined by every experienced tactician.

La Touche-Tréville and Nelson were never again to measure swords, for the Frenchman died in August 1804. His place was taken by Villeneuve, who had fled from Aboukir Bay with searing memories of the havoc wrought by British gunfire. "He has given me the slip," wrote Nelson of his adversary: "the French papers say he died of walking so often up to the signal-post to watch us: I always pronounced that would be his death." Villeneuve also showed his skill in eluding Nelson, but if he feared his opponent, he was yet able to cause him many months of anxiety.

v

By August 1804 Nelson felt his health had so deteriorated that he asked leave to go home. "Another winter such as the last, I feel myself unable to stand against," he wrote to the Admiralty. "No officer could be placed in a more enviable Command," he added, to make plain his regret at taking such a course, "and no Command ever produced so much happiness to a Commander-in-Chief."

Besides his failing sight, Nelson felt the seven-year-old wound from St Vincent, slight as it had then seemed. "My cough is very bad," he told Davison, "and it brings back the effect of my blow of the 14th February." He hoped that Lord Melville, who had recently been appointed First Lord, would allow Sir Richard Bickerton to remain in temporary charge, for it was Nelson's wish to return to the Mediterranean as soon as recovery permitted.

Within a year, Melville was to get into a serious scrape over malversation of funds, a matter which Hardy said "makes us all stare, and to say truth I am sorry for him, for I believe it was much his wish to befriend the Navy, in spite of his being a Scotchman". But whatever his shortcomings, the new First Lord was eager enough to please Nelson.

Home leave was reluctantly granted, and Bickerton was authorised to take over in his absence. The decision did not reach Nelson until December, and in the meanwhile much had happened in the wider field of strategy.

The most important event was that, before the year was out, indeed in the very month when Nelson heard that his wish was obtained, Napoleon dragged Spain into renewal of war with Great Britain, his intention being to make use of her fleet in a new design of invasion. The *casus belli* was an act of stupidity on the part of Great Britain. Four Spanish treasure ships, their cargoes destined for French coffers, were intercepted by an equal number of frigates. Had bigger ships been sent, the Spaniards could have submitted honourably to search. As it was, resistance was inevitable, and in the resultant action, one of the Spaniards blew up with the loss of all on board, women included.

On learning the news, Nelson deduced the probable result, and decided to stay on at his post. But he was cut to the quick that the Admiralty (quite reasonably, in view of his expected return) made a separate command west of Gibraltar. They gave this to Sir John Orde, an admiral who, already rich, thereby gained a splendid opportunity for amassing prize-money.

Nelson felt bitterly that it should have been Orde of all men who had obtained this plum. Although he was above Nelson in the flag-list, he could have had no expectations whatever from Melville's predecessor, the Earl of St Vincent, with whom he had quarrelled so small-mindedly about Nelson's appointment to independent command in the Mediterranean. That Sir John now stood between Nelson and prize-money was a hurt in a tender place. As might have been expected, friction soon grew between the squadrons.

Orde's tenure of command was in point of fact one long grumble. Gout rarely permitted him to leave his cabin; but there he was, squarely blocking Nelson's hopes of lawful gain, and enabled to intercept all north-bound ships. "Surely," said Nelson, quoting his familiar Shakespeare, "I have dreamed that I have 'done the State some service'. But never mind, I am superior to those who could treat me so. . . . I believe I attend more to the French fleet than making captures, but what I have, I can say as old Haddock[1] said, 'it never cost a sailor a tear, nor the nation a farthing'. This thought is far better than prize-money, not that I despise money, quite the contrary. I wish I had one hundred thousand pounds this moment." "Whatever happens," he told Minto with unself-conscious pride, "I have run a glorious race." "If I know my own thoughts," he said, "it is not for myself, or on my own account chiefly, that I feel the sting and the disappointment. No! It is for my brave officers; for my noble minded friends and comrades. Such a gallant set of fellows! Such a band of brothers! My heart swells at the thought of them."

The situation led to odd adventures. Once, wishing to send despatches to Lisbon quickly and without interference, Nelson summoned St Vincent's nephew, William Parker, to the *Victory*. "Sir John Orde takes my frigates from me," said the Commander-in-Chief, "and sends them away in some other direction from what I wish. I cannot even get my despatches home. You must contrive to get to the westward and avoid his ships. . . . Take your orders, and goodbye, and remember, Parker, if you cannot weather that fellow, I shall think you have not a drop of your old uncle's blood in your veins!"

Parker succeeded—narrowly. Leaving Gibraltar in the *Amazon* with a north wind, he passed Cape Spartel as directed, and then saw Orde's squadron in the distance, by moonlight, under easy sail. Unluckily, one of the outlying frigates also saw him, and gave chase. Her captain came aboard, and was about to give orders not to proceed when Parker brusquely stopped him from speaking on the quarter-deck within earshot of others, and took him into the cabin. The stranger was none other than William Hoste, devoted pupil of Nelson, and now a rising officer. "Captain Hoste," said Parker solemnly, "I believe you owe all your advancement in the service to my uncle, Lord St Vincent, and to Lord Nelson. I am avoiding Sir John Orde's squadron by desire of Lord Nelson; you know his handwriting; *I must go on*."

As Parker was senior to Hoste, the latter could not

[1] Admiral Sir Richard Haddock; *temp*. William III.

detain him by his own authority, and he understood that if Sir John's orders were actually produced, they would become a matter of record, would be disobeyed, and entail a court-martial. "Do you not think," said Parker quietly, "it would be better if you were not to meet the *Amazon* this night?" After a little thought, Hoste left the ship without presenting his admiral's instructions.

With the fleets of Spain, France and Holland united against the blockading power of Britain, the general disposition of force was as follows. Sixty ships of the line, sometimes more, sometimes fewer, contained the enemy in the Texel, at Brest, Rochefort, Ferrol, Cadiz, Cartagena and Toulon. As Minorca (incredibly enough, in view of its naval value), had been returned to Spain at the Peace of Amiens, Gibraltar was the only available base, to the south of the British Isles, upon which the blockaders could depend in their struggle against the western Continent. Malta was too far away for the immediate purpose, as Nelson was never tired of repeating; Lisbon was no longer hospitable as a British headquarters, as it had been in the earlier stages of the war with France.

Seeing himself, at least from the evidence of the map, so advantageously placed, Napoleon devised a plan of strategy, seemingly admirable in its breadth and simplicity. His scattered naval squadrons were to escape, to unite, to fall upon the British at their focal area off Ushant, to secure temporary command of the Channel, and to free the flotillas at Boulogne for their descent upon the enemy coast. His admirals were ordered to rendezvous in the West Indies, which manœuvre would itself be a shrewd blow to British interests, and then sweep back into northern waters, carrying all before them. It took a great deal for granted.

The conception was logical: how could it fail, when the winds should serve to drive the British from their stations? Even if the commanders could not get away simultaneously, yet if the Toulon and Rochefort squadrons could unite, preferably at Martinique, they could return, and by their superior force free others from the unceasing British watch. To Admiral Missiessy fell the task of getting away from Rochefort, and on New Year's Day 1805 he succeeded, actually for the second time in his tenure of command. He got clean away to the West Indies, though only with a small force. Just over a fortnight later, Villeneuve's ships left Toulon, and caused Nelson the most acute anxiety he had had since the summer of 1798.

It was 19th January before he knew for certain that he had missed them. His frigates had kept touch as long as they could, but storm and the dark had helped Villeneuve, whose destination was unknown. Nelson had with him, besides the *Victory*, the *Donegal*, *Superb*, *Canopus*, *Spencer*, *Tigre*, *Royal Sovereign*, *Leviathan*, *Belle Isle*, *Conqueror* and *Swiftsure*, together with the frigates *Active* and *Seahorse*. One of these ships, the *Swiftsure*, he had already made famous at the Nile; others would add to their honours before the year was out.

By 20th January the squadron was off the southern end of Sardinia, at battle stations, "If Cagliari is their object," wrote Nelson in his diary, "if the Sardes will but defend their capital, we shall be in time to save them. Pray God it may be so."

When it appeared that Sardinia was not the French goal, even a secondary one, Nelson at length sailed eastwards, in the direction he had taken nearly seven years before. By 7th February he was off Alexandria, which was found in the usual state of unpreparedness and decrepitude. It was Hallowell who was chosen, appropriately enough from his earlier services, to go ashore to seek what information was to be had. He reported the Turks "very surprised and shocked, and in no condition to beat off five hundred men". Having no firm news whatever, Nelson had no choice but to return westwards. On 19th February, at Malta, he heard that Villeneuve had returned to Toulon, having been driven back by weather, a fact which excited contempt in a fleet which had endured so many Gulf of Lyons gales.

"I have consulted no man," wrote Nelson to the Admiralty, "therefore, the whole blame of ignorance in forming my judgment must rest with me. I would allow no man to take from me an atom of my glory had I fallen in with the French fleet; nor do I desire any man to partake any of the responsibility. All is mine, right or wrong. . . . At this moment of sorrow, I still feel that I have acted right." To Ball he added, "When I call to remembrance all the circumstances I approve, if nobody else does, of my own conduct."

If Nelson was chagrined, so indeed was his opponent. "My fleet looked well at Toulon," wrote the unhappy Villeneuve to Decrés, the French Minister of Marine, "but when the storm came on, things changed at once. The sailors were not used to storms; they were lost among the mass of soldiers: these from seasickness lay in heaps about the decks: it was impossible to work the ships: hence yardarms were broken and sails were carried away: our losses resulted as much from clumsiness and inexperience as from defects in the materials delivered by the arsenals." When Nelson heard what had happened to the French, he wrote to Collingwood, "Bonaparte has often made his boast that our fleet would be worn out by keeping the sea, and that his was kept in order and increasing by staying in port; but he now finds, I fancy, if Emperors hear truth, that his fleet suffers more in a night than ours in a year." But for all his misadventure, Villeneuve had still a few months' wry enjoyment of the Emperor's belief in his luck. Within a few weeks he was ordered to try again, and again he succeeded in leaving Toulon without his destination being discovered.

Napoleon's latest plans envisaged that Villeneuve would join the Brest squadron, led out by Ganteaume, away in Martinique. Ganteaume would release the ships at Ferrol, while Villeneuve would pick up Spaniards from Cadiz under their own admiral, Gravina. At the rendezvous, Ganteaume was to take supreme command, and to sail for Ushant and Boulogne. It was expected that Villeneuve would arrive first, and he was to wait for Ganteaume forty days.

Nelson was at Palma when Villeneuve escaped, on 30th March. When told the news, he still thought that his opponent's destination was eastwards, for he had heard that the French had taken many saddles and muskets on board. This time, he made no precipitate move towards Alexandria. "I shall neither go to the eastward of Sicily nor to the westward of Sardinia until I know something positive," he said. He was at Ustica, an island north of Palermo, when Villeneuve looked into Cartagena, far to the westward. On

18th April, off Toro, he learnt that the French fleet had passed Gibraltar ten days before. This time Villeneuve had outwitted both Nelson and the weather. By 9th April the French admiral was off Cadiz. He signalled Gravina to join him. Fearing that Nelson was many miles nearer than in fact he was, Villeneuve would not wait for his allies. They straggled out alone, to begin their long voyage across the Atlantic to the rendezvous.

Sir Richard Strachan, who had seen the French coming through the Straits, immediately warned Orde, stationed off Cadiz. Orde, who had only four sail of the line with him, and who had no obsession about expeditions to the Orient, guessed the enemy plan. He stood away to join the main British fleet off Ushant. This was traditional strategy when the enemy intentions were unknown, the idea being to concentrate the maximum force where it would be most effective, at the western approaches of the English Channel.

Nelson had at first decided to shape course for a position west of the Scilly Isles, but he was baffled by foul winds. "My good fortune, my dear Ball, seems flown away," he wrote despairingly. "I cannot get a fair wind, or even a side wind. Dead foul! . . . I believe this ill luck will go near to kill me." "By this wind," he wrote in his diary on the last day of April, "I am locked up in the Mediterranean." Then, on 6th May, he had news from Commodore Donald Campbell, a British officer in the Portuguese service, that the French destination was the West Indies. It was the second time that Campbell had given the British good intelligence, and it cost him his lucrative post, for he had no business— except as a patriot—to give away the French plans, and they put pressure on the Portuguese to dismiss him. Nelson decided, in spite of the long French start, to go in pursuit.

His first decision to steer north was, strategically, wiser, for Lord Barham, who had succeeded Melville at the Admiralty that very month, and who was an experienced manager of fleets, had already ordered eleven ships under Collingwood to the West Indies. Luckily Collingwood fell in with Bickerton, who knew of Nelson's decision, so that only Nelson's squadron actually went on what proved to be a wild goose chase, Collingwood remaining off the Spanish coast.

Considering the state of his ships, Nelson made a creditable passage to Barbados. He had with him the same
squadron that had sailed in January to Alexandria, except
that the *Royal Sovereign* was detached, and the frigates were
now the *Amphion*, *Amazon* and *Diana*. But the whole fleet
badly needed docking, and the condition of the *Superb*,
about which Nelson sent more than one compassionate and
encouraging message to her captain, Richard Keats, was
lamentable. Rear-Admiral Cochrane joined him with two
more of the line on the far side of the Atlantic, and with
twelve big ships under his orders Nelson felt perfect confidence in his ability to face the combined squadrons of
France and Spain, even though Villeneuve eventually had at
his disposal twenty ships of the line, eight frigates and four
lighter vessels. "Take you a Frenchman apiece," said Nelson
to his captains, "and leave me the Spaniards. When I haul
down my colours, I expect you to do the same; and not till
then. We shall not part without a battle," he promised, but
it would be fought on the most advantageous terms he could
contrive.

When Villeneuve reached Martinique on 14th May he
found that Missiessy had returned to Rochefort, and that
Ganteaume had not arrived from Brest. Ganteaume had in
fact been punched back by Cornwallis on the first sign of his
appearance outside sheltered waters. Napoleon's latest orders
were that Villeneuve should stay for thirty-five days in the
West Indies. If Ganteaume had not joined him by then, he
was to sail for Ferrol, pick up the ships blockaded in that
port, then release the twenty-one at Brest, and make for the
Channel and Boulogne. A vessel arrived at Martinique with
these orders, on 4th June. Three days later Villeneuve heard
that Nelson, with his inferior numbers, was within striking
distance. Villeneuve's fear of Nelson was greater even than
his reverence for the soldier who ruled France. Four days
later still, against orders, he sailed for Europe.

Nelson, but for faulty information, might have fought a
battle in the same waters off Dominica which had brought
Rodney his peerage in 1782; but when in Carlisle Bay,
Barbados, he was given what appeared to be unimpeachable
news that the enemy had made for Tobago and Trinidad. In

Nelson's private opinion, this seemed unlikely, but he could not go counter to what seemed good evidence. He embarked 2,000 troops for shore service, reached Tobago on the 6th June, discovered nothing, and anchored in the Gulf of Paria, Trinidad.

Two accidents seemed to support the false report. A merchant at Tobago, not knowing whether Nelson's fleet was friend or foe, sent out a schooner to reconnoitre, and to acquaint him of the facts by signal. The signal chosen happened to be the very one which had been arranged by the local colonel of engineers to signify that the French were at Trinidad. It was picked up by the officers, and as night was falling there was no opportunity of discovering the mistake. The garrison was alerted. Moreover, the captain of an American brig, met with about the same time, told Nelson that he had been boarded by the French off Grenada a few days before, and that they were standing south. The information was false, but it removed all remaining doubts, and Nelson entered the Gulf of Paria, on 7th June, cleared for action and expecting another Aboukir.

There followed a small comedy. Sir Thomas Hislop, lieutenant-governor of Trinidad, was a zealous soldier, an old comrade-in-arms of days in Corsica and, incidentally, a future son-in-law of Hugh Elliot. He had everything in a state of readiness for defence. When Nelson's ships were sighted, they were the same in number as those expected from the enemy. The lieutenant in charge of the signal post at Galera Point, acting in accordance with orders, set fire to the buildings, spiked his few guns, and retreated to the Port of Spain. From his action Nelson concluded that the island was already in French hands. When, in due time, boats approached the shore, and English hails were answered in the same tongue by men of the 37th Regiment who had been prepared to die at their posts, surprise, relief and disappointment were felt in the squadron.

Nelson lost no time in beating back to Grenada. There he learnt that Villeneuve's ships had captured an assembled convoy which had ventured beyond shore protection, but Nelson's very presence in the area had saved the great majority of the shipping. He disembarked the troops at

Antigua, which he had last seen as a young bridegroom eighteen years before, picked up the *Spartiate* of 74 guns, and sailed impatiently for Europe. "June 21, midnight— nearly calm," he wrote. "Saw three planks, which I think came from the French fleet. Very miserable, which is very foolish." "It appears hard," he added on 4th July, "but as it pleases God, he knows what is best for us poor weak mortals." By 8th July he was due south of the Azores, and on 18th July he recorded: "Cape Spartel in sight, but no French fleet, nor any information about them. How sorrowful this makes me, but I cannot help myself."

On Saturday, 20th July, he made an entry in his Diary momentous for what it implies in sustained dedication of service: "Employ'd completing the Fleet with provisions and stores: went on shore for the first time since June 16th, 1803 and from having my foot out of the *Victory*, two years wanting ten days." He was at Gibraltar.

VI

"I am the child of opinion," Nelson once wrote, meaning that his reputation, if not his inner serenity, was shaped by what others thought and said about him. As he paid his call on the Governor of the Rock that busy July Saturday, he was as perplexed and disappointed as he had been ever since the year opened, and he surmised that he might have lost the good opinion of his countrymen.

He had exchanged messages with Collingwood off Cadiz. Like Orde, this friend of earlier days in Antigua had no easterly fixations. His view was that the enemy design was towards Ireland, and that Villeneuve's route would be by way of Ferrol, Rochefort and Ushant. "Their flight to the West Indies," he wrote percipiently, "was to take off the naval force, which proved the great impediment to their undertaking."

Early in August Nelson received orders that his squadron should join Cornwallis off Ushant, but before these arrived he knew at least a little more of Villeneuve's course, for the brig *Curieux* sent him news that she had seen the French and Spaniards on the 19th, standing to the northward. It seemed that Collingwood had been right. It was this same brig that Nelson speeded home in advance of his squadron to give the Admiralty the latest information. She had actually sighted the French fleet on her way, and her captain was able to relay news of their course and number to an anxious administration before he rejoining Nelson.

While off St Vincent, Nelson showed a glimpse of powers which would have been creditable in another profession. One of his frigates spoke with an American who, when a little to west of the Azores, had fallen in with an armed vessel, a partly wrecked and dismasted privateer deserted by her crew. She had been set on fire after an encounter, but the fire had gone out. A log-book, and a few seamen's jackets, were found in a cabin and were brought to Nelson.

The log ended with the words "two large vessels in the W.N.W.". This led Nelson to hazard that the vessel had been a British privateer cruising off the western islands. But he also noticed in the book a scrap of dirty paper filled with figures. Nelson observed that the figures were written by a Frenchman. "I can explain the whole," he said thoughtfully. "The jackets are of French manufacture, and prove that the privateer was in possession of the enemy. She had been chased and taken by the two ships that were seen in the W.N.W. The prize-master, going on board in a hurry, forgot to take with him his reckoning; there is none on the log-book; and the dirty paper contains her work for the number of days since the privateer last left Corvo; with an unaccounted-for run, which I take to have been the chase. . . . By some mismanagement, I conclude, she was run on board of by one of the enemy's ships, and dismasted. Not liking delay (for I am satisfied that those two ships were the advanced ones of the French squadron), and fancying we were close at their heels, they set fire to the vessel, and abandoned her in a hurry. If this explanation be correct, I infer from it that they are gone more to the northward, and more to the northward I will look for them."

Luck was still against him. It was not Nelson who was then destined to encounter the French fleet. It was his old acquaintance, Sir Robert Calder, the man who had noted his disobedience at the Battle of St Vincent. Nevertheless, Nelson's achievement had been much. "Either the distances between the distant quarters of the globe are diminished," wrote Hugh Elliot from Naples, "or you have extended the powers of human action. After an unremitting cruise of two long years in the stormy Gulf of Lyons, to have proceeded without going into port to Alexandria, from Alexandria to the West Indies, from the West Indies back again to Gibraltar; to have kept your ships afloat, your rigging standing, and your crews in health and spirits is an effort such as never was realised in former times, nor, I doubt, will ever again be repeated by any other admiral. You have protected us for two long years, and you saved the West Indies by only a few days." As a summing up of resolute endeavour, uncrowned with a general action, Elliot's words could scarcely be bettered.

The general action which might have ensured the immediate overthrow of Napoleon's grand design came about exactly as Barham had planned, though its results were disappointing. On having news of Villeneuve's movements through the *Curieux*, the First Lord ordered the ships then watching Rochefort to move south, to reinforce Calder off Ferrol. Calder was then told to cruise off Finisterre. The decision meant that although all the enemy ports were unguarded except Brest and Cadiz, a force was at sea which, in the hands of an able commander, should have been strong enough to ensure such damage to the enemy, even if met with in superior numbers, that the squadron would be useless for immediate further operations.

On 22nd July Calder duly met Villeneuve off Finisterre, in misty weather. He had with him fifteen ships of the line, five less than Villeneuve, and he managed to capture two Spaniards. But, in securing his prizes, he missed the essential point of the operation, which was to cling to and maul the enemy, or at the very worst to keep him in sight. After the inconclusive engagement, Calder fell back upon Cornwallis, pleased with his captures, and feeling proud that he had won a victory against odds. He was astonished at the outcry which soon reverberated throughout the United Kingdom that he had not done enough. The fact was that Nelson, ever since his conduct at St Vincent, had set a new standard, and even a layman could perceive the sort of battle Barham hoped for. "You have put us out of conceit with all other admirals," wrote Richard Bulkeley to his friend, and it was the general feeling that had Nelson been in the place of Calder, a very different result must have followed.

By mid-August Nelson joined Cornwallis. He was excused any formal visitation by his old friend, and was allowed to proceed at once to Spithead, in company with the worn *Superb*. He had heard news of Calder's encounter whilst off Ushant, and wrote about it to Fremantle, in his most generous frame of mind. "I could not last night sit down to thank you for your truly kind letter," he told him on 16th August, "and for your large packet of newspapers, for I was in truth bewildered by the account of Sir Robert Calder's Victory, and the joy of the event; together with the hearing that John Bull was not content, which I am sorry for. Who can, my dear Fremantle, command all the success which our Country may wish? We have fought together, and therefore well know what it is. I have had the best disposed Fleet of friends, but who can say what will be the event of a Battle: and it most sincerely grieves me, that in any of the papers it should be insinuated, that Lord Nelson could have done better. I should have fought the enemy; so did my friend Calder; but who can say that he will be more successful than another? I only wish to stand upon my own merits, and not by comparison, one way or the other, upon the conduct of a brother officer. . . ." To William Nelson he added next day: "We must not talk of Sir Robert Calder's battle: I might not have done so much with my small force. If I had fallen in with them, you would probably have been a Lord before I wished; for I know they meant to make a dead set at the *Victory*."

At long last, on Sunday, 18th August, his cruise came to an end. "Just two years and three months from my arrival at Portsmouth," he noted in his diary. "At daylight weighed, working up to Spithead: at nine anchored at Spithead." Cheers from the shore, as his barge approached, told him the kind of welcome he would receive in England.

Chapter 11

FAREWELL TO ENGLAND

I

"SWEET was the intelligence that my dearest Brother was arrived," wrote Mrs Bolton to Emma. "What a Paradise he must think Merton, to say nothing of the Eve it contains. I need not give you joy, for I am *sure* you have it." She herself was soon to add to it by her presence.

Fremantle had been right in his statement, made in a letter which had accompanied the newspapers he had sent to Nelson. "You will on your arrival in England find everyone disposed to do you entire credit, and at no period, according to my judgment, did you ever stand higher in the estimation of the public."

These were courageous words to use about a man who seemed to have failed in his mission. An opposite view was that of Lord Radstock, who remarked that, admire him as he did, he scarcely felt that, after Nelson's protracted ill luck, those in office would do much to support him. The truth was that there had been general anxiety over the Mediterranean squadron after it had disappeared to the West Indies, and there was happy relief at news that all was well, even if victory seemed elusive. The ardour of Nelson's long watch had not gone unrealised; a new aspect of his genius was appreciated at its real worth. Fremantle had judged well.

The feeling of warmth was shown in countless private letters. "Never was there a man come back so enthusiastically revered," wrote Emma's cousin, Sarah Connor. "Timid spinsters and widows are terrified at his foot being on shore; yet this is the man that is to have a Sir R. Calder and a Sir J. Orde sent to intercept his well-earned advantages. I hope he may never quit his own house again! This was my thundering reply last night to a set of cowardly women." Sarah's sentiments were reinforced, in more pompous terms, by a delegation of merchants concerned with the West India trade, who sought to express their thanks at Nelson's speed and address in safeguarding their interests.

Having paid his respects to the Admiral commanding at Portsmouth, Nelson drove all through the summer night to Merton, where he arrived at six o'clock on the morning of 20th August, for the first of five and twenty crowded days at home. His Atlantic foray had actually done him good, so he told William: certainly he was seldom busier in his life. His days were of ceaseless bustle, and Merton itself was never quiet. The voices with which its rooms soon echoed included those of most of his immediate family; at one time or another William, his wife and children, the Bolton and Matcham sisters, with appropriate nephews and nieces, helped to make the party gay, while naval and civilian friends were sure of a welcome in a household ably though lavishly managed by Emma and her mother. Twenty men worked in the grounds: and an appropriate indoor staff included several foreigners, among them Chevalier, the steward who helped to make life in the *Victory* agreeable to his master.

According to a tradition long current among his relations, Captain Hardy, who was among the fortunates in the flagship to enjoy a spell of shore leave, actually called upon Fanny, with Nelson's knowledge. If true, it was a kindly and befitting gesture on the part of one who had long been her friend. Hardy certainly waited upon the King, who was spending the summer at Weymouth. He had a long audience one morning, early in September, after George III had returned from a ride.

If the talk was upon public events, much was then engaging the royal attention. Pitt was in office once again, and a fresh coalition against France and Spain was five months old. Britain's allies were Russia, Prussia and Austria, a familiar though scarcely a proven combination. Britain engaged to pay £1,250,000 for each 100,000 soldiers placed in arms against the enemy, with a limit of 400,000. It was a system which had the sanction of history: it had been employed in the days of Frederick the Great and the Seven Years War, though it gave rise to the persistent gibe that Britain would fight to the last drop of her allies' blood.

The Coalition did not in fact impress Napoleon, who soon proved, as he had so often done before, what French veterans could do against tired troops and old-world commanders. Meanwhile, the aspect of affairs at sea was of more immediate interest to the European Paymaster. Upon that element, it was his own blood that was in jeopardy.

After his encounter with Calder, Villeneuve had kept his force together, first in Vigo Bay and then off Ferrol. There he received orders from Paris to proceed south, to Cadiz, always presuming that he could not effect his over-riding task of making a junction with the squadrons of Rochefort and Brest and attaining superiority in the Channel. Leaving three damaged ships at Ferrol, Villeneuve proceeded to Corunna, where he was joined by fourteen further vessels. A bolder man would instantly have headed north, for he now had a truly formidable concentration. It might have been overwhelming if French staff work had been better. For on 17th August, when the *Victory* and *Superb* were sailing up-Channel, Allemand, who had replaced Missiessy in the Rochefort command, got away, and would have joined Villeneuve had Napoleon warned the combined fleet to expect him. As it was, the affair was bungled. Its failure meant postponement of the great scheme of invasion.

Never had the French navy been better placed for success, for at the time when Allemand might have combined with Villeneuve, Cornwallis had split his forces. Such a great fleet as Villeneuve would have commanded should have been able to release the squadron penned in at Brest and have ensured the essential moves preliminary to the movement of the Boulogne flotillas.

As it was, by taking his alternative station in a southerly Spanish port, Villeneuve had baulked Napoleon's highest hopes for the year. The season was advancing, the weather was unseasonably inclement, and the golden chance was vanishing.

By 20th August, the day Nelson reached Merton, Villeneuve was in Cadiz. He was watched by Collingwood, whose small shadowing force was soon increased by Sir Richard Bickerton and Sir Robert Calder. At the end of the month twenty-five British ships guarded Villeneuve's thirty-four,

and the likelihood of successful French aggression seemed
to be well and truly gone.

Early in September, despairing of his navy, and in particular of Villeneuve, Napoleon began to break up his camp
at Boulogne. His troops would employ their energies in the
direction of the Rhine, not contemplating the Channel. On
2nd September 1805, the day of the Emperor's final decision,
Captain Henry Blackwood, once of the frigate *Penelope*, and
now commanding the equally smart *Euryalus*, brought
Nelson news at Merton that Villeneuve was at Cadiz.
Although the intention to invade was henceforth dead, and
Napoleon's plans for his fleet shifted to the Mediterranean
(thus justifying Nelson's persisting obsession), news of the
change in strategy was not at once heard in England.

It was five in the morning when Blackwood's carriage
swung into the Merton drive. The captain was on his way
to the Admiralty, and had interrupted his journey to call
upon the man under whose orders he had first made a name
for himself; he knew it was not a late-riser he would be
disturbing, and he was certain of his welcome. Nelson realised that an immediate personal crisis was at hand. "I am
sure you bring me news of the French and Spanish fleets,"
he said at once, on seeing the frigate officer, "and I think I
shall yet have to beat them."

When Nelson followed Blackwood to London, he was
requested to resume his command forthwith, old Lord
Barham giving him *carte blanche* to choose his own officers.
The parting from Merton and its guests was made easier by
Emma's generous acceptance of his decision, once she had
seen that Nelson was set on going. She told Harrison she
had said: "Nelson, however we may lament your absence,
offer your services immediately, to go off to Cadiz; they will
be accepted, and you will gain a quiet heart by it. You will
have a glorious victory, and then, you may come here, and
be happy." Nelson looked at Emma for some moments and
then, with tears in his eyes, exclaimed—"Brave Emma!
Good Emma! if there were more Emmas, there would be
more Nelsons; you have penetrated my thoughts. I wish all
you say, but was afraid to trust even myself with reflecting
on the subject. However, I will go to Town."

Nelson felt flattered that Pitt himself should have been so eager for his services, for he had long admired the statesman who had been in power for so much of his life, and who had shown him much personal kindness, even when he was unhappily employed on Channel defence. The First Minister, after a momentous interview, attended Nelson to his carriage, a compliment which the admiral did not think he would have accorded even to a Prince of the Blood.

When the news was known that Nelson, despite indifferent health and the shortness of his spell ashore, would once more take up his station, there was universal enthusiasm. "I met Nelson in a mob in Piccadilly," recorded Lord Minto, who saw much of him both in London and at Merton, "and got hold of his arm, so that I was mobbed too. It is really quite affecting to see the wonder and admiration, and love and respect, of the whole world; and the genuine expression of all these sentiments at once, from gentle and simple, the moment he is seen. It is beyond anything represented in a play or a poem of fame." Minto flattered himself that his affection for Nelson was as great as that of Emma—and more sincere.

Nelson had the advantage—it would have seemed so to him—of being the most easily recognisable of great men. If in uniform, his medals, and his four stars of chivalry proclaimed his renown in an age when it was rare to have decorations of any sort. If in plain clothes, his empty sleeve, his slight build and his eye-shade quickly betrayed him to the observant. As for his character, while it was evident, at any rate to Lord Minto, that Nelson's passion for Emma was as constant as ever, he was forced to admit that Emma was "a clever being, after all", and had contrived to make him happy. General acceptance of a relationship in which the proprieties were still kept up almost silenced criticism. Even the gossips and cartoonists showed no unkindness, at this time at any rate, to a man and woman whom no feeling heart would censure.

"All the pomps and vanities of the world retained their power over him," wrote Sir James Mackintosh in considering Nelson's character as a public man. "Neither pleasantry, nor speculation, nor the familiarity of rank or wealth had weakened the force of these illusions. He had not lived in that society where wit makes the gratifications of vanity ridiculous, or where reason proves their emptiness, or where satiety rejects them with disgust; he came forth from the most humble privacy. Fame, with all her marks, and praise from every source, worked with irresistible efficacy on his fresh and simple mind. The love of glory, and even of praise and honours, the indignant contempt of money, the sincerity and ardour of his character, and the simplicity and energy of his sayings, give him more the appearance of an ancient than a modern hero."

If Sir James's estimate was borne out by Nelson's conduct in a wider sphere, Sir Alexander Ball told Coleridge the secret of his success within his profession. "Lord Nelson was an admiral every inch of him," wrote the poet from the fullness of Ball's knowledge. "He looked at everything, not merely in its possible relation to the naval service in general, but in its immediate bearings on his own squadron; to his officers, his men, to the particular ships themselves, his affections were as steady and ardent as those of a lover. Hence, though his temper was constitutionally irritable and uneven, yet never was a commander so enthusiastically loved by men of all ranks, from the captain of the fleet to the youngest ship-boy. Hence too the unexampled harmony which reigned in his fleet year after year, under circumstances that might well have undermined the patience of the best balanced dispositions, much more of men with the impetuous character of British sailors."

It is not inappropriate to quote a writer's reflection on Nelson, for he was one of those rare commanders prepared and even eager to acknowledge critical statements and ideas whenever presented with them—even by scribbling laymen. He had the touching belief that no one ever put pen to paper without something useful to say, and there is Hardy's word for it that he was a student of the work of Clark of Eldin, a Scots merchant and amateur strategist who addressed his mind to answering the question why, for all their bravery in battle, admirals throughout the eighteenth century had rarely been able to obtain *decision*. Clark's view was that deadlock arose from the awe with which the old, formal line of battle was regarded, and he suggested certain lines of attack which seemed to assure success, if only from novelty. The line must be broken.

Nelson, pondering how best to use his "grey geese", as he sometimes called his beloved ships of the line, agreed much with Clark, and did not add the scornful words so often on the lips of other admirals, that his ideas were splendidly adapted for use with models on the dining-room table at Eldin. Both Nelson's best-known tactical memoranda, one of which was probably drafted on the way to the West Indies, and the other which took final shape just before Trafalgar, envisaged something new in battle, and a total disregard of rules which had bemused so many predecessors.

Nelson summed up his ideas in a conversation with Captain Keats at Merton shortly before he left England for the last time. In essence, the talk was as clear as any more elaborate document, and, except for the important fact that he was then without the fast squadron for which he had provided, it was strikingly prophetic of Trafalgar.

"One morning," so Keats told Edward Hawke Locker, son of Nelson's old captain, "in the grounds of Merton, talking of naval matters, Nelson said to me: 'No day can be long enough to arrange a couple of Fleets, and fight a decisive Battle, according to the old system. When *we* meet them' (I was to have been with him) 'for meet them we shall, I'll tell you how I shall fight them. I shall form the Fleet into three Divisions in three Lines. One Division shall be composed of twelve or fourteen of the fastest two-decked Ships, which I shall keep always to windward, or in a situation of advantage; and I shall put them under an Officer who, I am sure, will employ them in the manner I wish, if possible. I consider it will always be in my power to throw them into Battle in any part I may choose; but if circumstances prevent their being carried against the Enemy where I desire, I shall feel certain he will employ them effectually and, perhaps, in a more advantageous manner than if he could have followed my orders.' He continued: 'With the remaining part of the Fleet formed in two lines, I shall go at them at once, if I can, about one-third of their Line from their leading Ship.'

"He then said: 'What do you think of it?' Such a question I felt required consideration, I paused. Seeing it he said: 'But I'll tell you what *I* think of it. I think it will surprise and confound the Enemy! They won't know what I am about. It will bring forward a pell-mell Battle, and that is what I want.' " It was the "Nelson touch".

Nelson held a similar conversation with his old friend Addington, now Lord Sidmouth, and even Emma was soon ready to expound the Admiral's ideas at the dinner-table. Indeed, the openness with which Nelson communicated his thoughts had the result that they were actually known to Villeneuve before the day of battle. Confound the enemy he well might, but surprise was forfeit. As his plan disregarded every earlier rule of naval practice, in that he deliberately incurred the risk of drawing such a devastating fire on the leading ships of the principal lines as to invite their destruction, Nelson may be said to have been working to the lowest factor of safety even in his own unique career. His more knowledgeable listeners must have wondered at his enthusiasm, certainty and unorthodoxy, and been reassured only by knowledge of his incomparable experience.

How dearly that experience had been bought, his person plainly showed. Yet, undeterred by reverses, ill fortune or increasing years, Nelson remained of Chatham's opinion that the boldest measures were the safest, and that victory was his duty. By victory he meant, as always, annihilation. He had enjoyed it at the Nile, he had missed it at Boulogne and Copenhagen: it would not elude him, he was determined, if at last he should cross swords with Villeneuve.

II

The sense of veneration, almost of worship, that swept the country when it was generally realised that Nelson was home was unlike the excitement which had greeted his return five years earlier. People had then acclaimed the victor of the Nile. Now it was a different achievement they respected, one which they could realise but not easily define.

There had never been another admiral to compare with him in capturing the public imagination. Even those who, like Charles Lamb, had once been prejudiced, now succumbed to his attraction. Friends were, as ever, lyrical in his praise, and Lady Elizabeth Foster, who was ardent among them, confirmed in her Journal Lord Minto's statement that whenever he appeared he "electrified the cold English character", and that rapture and applause followed all his steps. She added, "sometimes a poor woman asks to touch his coat . . . the very children learn to bless him, and doors and windows are crowded".

Nelson was in some degree surprised at this manifestation. He had already shown himself aware of how fleeting was favour. "Pray don't," he said to Emma in a low voice at the dinner-table one day, when she referred to the mobbing he had had that morning in the City, "but," he said, "I own I have been gratified and touched with the kindness shown to me, because this time I have done nothing. It is all kindness to me personally."

Not that he ceased to boast, particularly with strangers. Lady Elizabeth was inclined to excuse this on the ground that it was partly his love of praise that had led him to such glorious actions. For this reason she felt that his vanity, as well as his love for Emma, should be generously looked upon by the society he protected with such devotion.

"Emma was beautiful when I first knew her," reflected one whose own looks would remain with her, and she added that she believed her to be so inextricably bound up in Nelson's mind with his aspiration to glory that he could not see her for what she then was, an ageing Juno who sometimes over-acted her part. "She fed his vanity with every art that could gratify it," added the diarist. "She sat by him and said, 'I would wish with all my heart to die in two hours, so that I might be your wife for one.' Nelson, delighted, kissed her hand, and it is by this enthusiasm that she keeps up his love and his vanity."

With all his enjoyment of adulation, Nelson wrote to George Rose of his remembrance that self was out of the question when there was work to be done, either for the country or for a friend. To be beloved was sweet, but victory

FIVE SIGNATURES

The first, right-handed, dates from 1777; the second from nearly twenty years later. The third was written on 1st September 1797, left-handed, shortly after the loss of Nelson's right arm. The fourth was signed in 1800 after he had been made a peer. The last, after he was confirmed Duke of Brontë, was the regular signature of his final years.

remained his purpose—that, and attention to those under his care, both at home and at sea. Service in his fleet was a stern schooling, yet he enchanted parents whose lads were afloat with him by his obvious delight when they showed promise. Who could have resisted a Commander-in-Chief who, asked by a fond mother to deliver a last minute note to a midshipman, requested her to kiss it, so that "he might take the kiss to him too"?

Nor was he always boastful. His old friend the Duke of Clarence, driving over from Bushey, where he lived with an increasing tribe of offspring, to another irregular household at Merton, listened to Nelson's professional opinions, modestly expressed, with the deference he had shown when pacing the sun-lit quarter-deck of the *Boreas* in the West Indies eighteen years before. A Matcham nephew, who thought the Duke very like his father King George, noted the talk, and recorded later that in general his illustrious uncle "delighted in quiet conversation, through which occasionally ran an undercurrent of pleasantry not unmixed with caustic wit. At his table he was the least heard among the company, and so far from being the hero of his own tale, I never heard him allude voluntarily to any of the great actions of his life."

It was where he was not known that Nelson wished to impress. The classic instance occurred during his chance meeting with the future Duke of Wellington, then Sir Arthur Wellesley. This took place between 11th and 13th September 1805, immediately before Nelson left England for the last time. It was an appropriate occasion on which the soldier and the sailor whose names were, for their own times, to epitomise valour and achievement by British arms came together, for it was one of state business. Sir Arthur Wellesley was eleven years younger than Nelson, but even at the age of thirty-six he had a splendid career in India behind him. Ahead was a succession of triumphs on the Continent of Europe unapproached since the days of Marlborough.

"Lord Nelson was, in different circumstances, two quite different men," so Wellington told John Wilson Croker, many years later, vouching for the fact from direct observation. "I only saw him once in my life, and for, perhaps, an hour. It was soon after I returned from India. I went to the Colonial Office in Downing Street, and there I was shown into the little waiting-room on the right hand, where I found also waiting to see the Secretary of State, a gentleman, whom from his likeness to his pictures and the loss of an arm, I immediately recognised as Lord Nelson. He could not know who I was, but he entered at once into conversation with me, if I can call it conversation, for it was almost all on his side and all about himself, and in, really, a style so vain and so silly as to surprise and almost disgust me.

"I suppose something that I happened to say may have made him guess that I was *somebody*, and he went out of the room for a moment, I have no doubt to ask the office-keeper who I was, for when he came back he was altogether a different man, both in manner and matter. All that I had thought a charlatan style had vanished, and he talked of the state of the country and of the aspect and probabilities of affairs on the Continent with a good sense, and a knowledge of subjects both at home and abroad, that surprised me equally and more agreeably than the first part of our interview had done; in fact, he talked like an officer and a statesman.

"The Secretary of State kept us long waiting, and certainly, for the last half or three-quarters of an hour, I don't know that I ever had a conversation that interested me more. Now, if the Secretary of State had been punctual, and admitted Lord Nelson in the first quarter of an hour, I should have had the same impression of a light and trivial character that other people have had, but luckily I saw enough to be satisfied that he was really a very superior man; but certainly a more sudden and complete metamorphosis I never saw."

It was Castlereagh with whom their business lay—he was then Secretary for War and for the Colonies, and it is notable that the statesman said afterwards of the soldier, "I never met any military officer with whom it was so satisfactory to converse. He states every difficulty before he undertakes any service, but none after he has undertaken it."

A very different and unfamiliar Nelson was recorded in a privately printed memoir by Sir John Theophilus Lee. The writer had gone to sea as a child, had been present at the battle of St Vincent at the age of nine, had served with Hallowell in the *Swiftsure* at the battle of the Nile when still not quite eleven, and had later taken up a civil post. His patron, Lord St Vincent, did not approve this course: Nelson thought otherwise, rightly, for Lee made a fortune.

Nelson called to see the young man a day or two before he left London, "and asked him to walk with him down the Strand, as far as Salter's shop,[1] which he was proud to do. The crowd, which waited outside Somerset House till the noble viscount came out, was very great. He was then very ill," wrote Lee, "and neither in look nor dress betokened the naval hero, having on a pair of drab green breeches, and high black gaiters, a yellow waistcoat, and a plain blue coat, with a cocked hat, quite square, a large green shade over the eye, and a gold-headed stick in his hand, yet the crowd ran before him and gave his lordship repeated and hearty cheers; indeed the two pedestrians could hardly get to Salter's shop, so dense was the crowd. Lord Nelson said to our narrator, 'does not this remind you of former days at Naples, when the crowd thus pressed on me?' On arriving at Salter's shop, the door was closed, and his Lordship inspected all his swords which had been presented at different periods, the diamond aigrette, numerous snuff-boxes, etc."

Sir Thomas Thompson, the officer who had lost a leg in the *Bellona* at Copenhagen, then came in, but before Nelson said good-bye to Lee he told him that he still had the coffin given him by his old captain, and was intending to use it. Lee's is one of the very rare glimpses of Nelson out of uniform.

One of the most touching farewells was recorded by Lady Elizabeth Foster. Nelson had been long closeted with Pitt, and had arrived late at a party at which she was present with various other friends. He was obviously tired, and Lady Elizabeth in kindness soon rose and took leave of him, saying only "God Bless you" in a quiet voice. Nelson took her hand, and Emma told him to embrace her. "I consented with great pleasure," recorded Lady Elizabeth, "and hurried

[1] John Salter, Nelson's sword-cutler and jeweller, who then occupied premises at No. 35 Strand.

away. Lady Hamilton told him also to embrace Lady
Percival. When we were in the carriage my son, who had not
seen Nelson embrace me, said 'Are you not jealous?' 'No,' I
said, 'for he embraced me also.' 'Do you think,' said Lady
Percival with some humour, 'that I should otherwise have
got into the same carriage?' "

III

More than two years earlier, writing to Emma from sea
soon after leaving for the long cruise, Nelson had said: "I
assure you . . . that I feel a thorough conviction that we shall
meet again, with honour, riches and health, and remain
together to a good old age." Whatever his inward feelings in
September 1805, he did not allow Emma to be shadowed
by any sense of fatality, for she recorded later that although
he had taken a particularly affectionate farewell of Horatia,
now established happily under his roof, and had come back
four times to say good-bye, he had felt no premonition that
it would be for the last time.

Rather a different story was told among the family by
Nelson's sister Catherine Matcham. Meeting her one day in
London, where they had both gone from Merton on their
separate businesses, Nelson had said to her, with inexpress-
ible sadness: "Ah Katty! Katty, that Gipsy," reminding her
of the creature who, long ago in the West Indies, had told
him she could see as far as the year they were then in, ending
with the words: "I can see no further."

Certainly everything conspired to make the parting memorable. "Friday Night at half-past Ten drove from dear,
dear Merton," wrote Nelson on 13th September in his
private Diary, "where I left all which I hold dear in this
World, to go to serve my King & Country. May the Great
God Whom I adore enable me to fulfill the expectations of
my Country, and if it is His good pleasure that I should
return, my thanks will never cease being offered up to the
Throne of His Mercy. If it is His good providence to cut
short my days upon Earth, I bow with the greatest sub-

mission, relying that He will protect those so dear to me that I may leave behind.

"His Will be done. Amen. Amen. Amen."

Early next day he arrived at Portsmouth, where, having despatched his shore business, he embarked with his friend George Rose, then Vice-President of the Board of Trade, and with George Canning, the Treasurer of the Navy; the two statesmen dined with him in the *Victory*.

"Nelson," said Southey, "endeavoured to elude the populace by taking a bye-way to the beach; but a crowd collected in his train, pressing forward to obtain sight of his face; many were in tears, and many knelt down before him, and blessed him as he passed. England has had many heroes; but never one who so entirely possessed the love of his fellow-countrymen as Nelson. All men knew that his heart was as humane as it was fearless: that there was not in his nature the slightest alloy of selfishness or cupidity; but that, with perfect and entire devotion, he served his country with all his heart, and with all his soul, and with all his strength; and, therefore, they loved him as truly and as fervently as he loved England."

If Nelson felt excitement or premonition when the shrill note of the boatswain's call piped him aboard for the last time, no indication whatever was betrayed by the entries in his Diary. This was resumed in its practical, laconic manner as if the events of the long watch had been unbroken. "*Sunday, Sept.* 15*th*, 1805.—At day weighed with light airs Northerly. At 6 was obliged to anchor. At 8 weighed. All day light breezes. At sun sett off Christ Church. At night light Breezes & very foggy. *Euryalus* in company."

Nelson was away, and Blackwood was with him. Having such a frigate captain, the eyes of the fleet would this time miss little.

Chapter 12

TRAFALGAR

I

A NAMESAKE of her captain, writing ninety years later in *The Trumpet Major* of the majestic three-decker as she made her way down Channel, described how, from a vantage point on Portland Bill, Anne Garland saw "the courses of the *Victory* absorbed into the main, then her top-sails went, and then her top-gallants. She was now no more than a dead fly's wing on a sheet of spider's web; and even this fragment diminished. . . . The admiral's flag sank behind the watery line, and in a minute the very truck of the top-mast stole away. The *Victory* was gone."

Nelson's own thoughts off Portland, expressed in a letter to Emma written on 16th September, were less poetical. "We are standing near Weymouth," he said, "the place of all others I should wish to avoid, but if it continues moderate I hope to escape without anchoring, but, should I be forced, I shall act as a man and your Nelson, neither courting nor ashamed to hold up my head before the greatest monarch in the world. I have, thank God, nothing to be ashamed of. . . ."

Nelson was less eager than had been his flag-captain to pay his duty in person to a sovereign who, over several years, had shown himself disapproving of the admiral's way of life, and who would not readily be forgiven for refusing to receive the wife of the Minister to Naples on her return from Italy. George III could scarcely criticise the professional abilities of his most devoted seaman, but he had a stickler's memory for conjugal transgression, and his Queen's was the same. Fortunately, any likelihood of having to anchor in Weymouth Bay, and within the vision of the royal telescope, soon passed. "All night standing to the Westward," Nelson noted in his Diary next day. He was soon out of sight of England, this time for ever. "I had their huzzas before," he had said to Hardy of the crowds at Portsmouth: "I have their hearts now."

Blackwood was sent into Plymouth on 17th September to summon the *Ajax* and *Thunderer*, which were to join the fleet. Three days later, well into the Atlantic, the frigate *Decade* was met with. She was flying the flag of Sir Richard Bickerton, who was on his way home, sick. Her captain came on board the *Victory* to receive orders, Bickerton himself being too ill to do so. He had the latest news of the ships before Cadiz, and was given letters for home.

On 25th September the Rock of Lisbon was distantly sighted. That day, Nelson had word from the captain of the *Constance* which greatly cheered him. "The Enemy's Fleet had not left Cadiz the 18th of this month," he noted, "therefore I yet hope they may wait my arrival." He was luckier than he knew. Villeneuve had just been sent orders from Napoleon to proceed with all his forces to the Mediterranean, picking up the Cartagena squadron on the way. He was to land troops before returning to his familiar Toulon. "Our intention is that wherever you meet the enemy in inferior force," said the Emperor, "you will attack them without hesitation and obtain a decision against them." Two days later he nominated Rosily to take Villeneuve's place. He had ceased to believe either in Villeneuve's luck or his abilities; it was high time for a change. It was just the stimulus which would drive Villeneuve out.

On 26th September, at 4 o'clock, Nelson sent the *Euryalus* ahead to "join Vice-Admiral Collingwood, with my orders to put himself under my Command". His old friend was enjoined not to salute the *Victory* when she herself arrived. Security in London was one thing—tactical and strategical notions were bandied round club-room and dining-table, war and peace alike: in the face of the enemy it was quite another matter to give your presence away unnecessarily.

Two days later Nelson was once again in immediate control of the fleet, and in the evening he had his first glimpse of the enemy at Cadiz. They amounted to thirty-six sail of the line, and the scene was fairly set.

Although Collingwood was a friend upon whom Nelson could depend, the fleet itself was neither united nor happy.

Collingwood's best nature emerged from his graceful letters to his family, but his outward aspect, rigid, reserved, punctilious, was not winning to subordinates, though its nobler side was lastingly described by Alfred de Vigny in his *Servitude et Grandeur Militaires*. He exercised a discipline as stern as that of St Vincent at his harshest, but without that great man's humour. Captains were restive. His second-in-command, Sir Robert Calder, was in no state to afford him relaxation and was, in fact, soon under the need to proceed home for an enquiry into the circumstances of his summer action.

Calder, who had been so sure he had won a great victory that he had written to Lord Barham to ask him to remember his nephew when the appropriate honours were considered, would have deserved more sympathy, as an officer whose standards belonged to an era before Nelson enlarged them, had he not pressed Nelson for leave to return home in his invaluable 90-gun ship, the *Prince of Wales*, rather than in a frigate, as the Admiralty intended. Nelson, ever kindly to distress, at first asked him to stay until the enemy came out, and to share in the glory of encounter, but this Calder was unwilling to do, and as soon as another three-decker, the *Royal Sovereign*, arrived from England, Nelson, against orders and even common prudence, allowed him to have his way. It was the last time he ever disobeyed instructions, and it was sad that the cause was not a better one. "He has an ordeal to pass through which I fear he little expects," he wrote to Collingwood, adding that Calder seemed "too wise" to apprehend the feeling against him at home. "He is in adversity," he added, "and if he has ever been my enemy, he now feels the pang of it, and finds me one of his best friends." Calder took home with him the captains of the newly joined *Ajax* and *Thunderer*, who had been in the July action, to give evidence at the enquiry. They thus missed Trafalgar, which was fortunate for their first lieutenants, who were promoted to post rank and received the coveted King's gold medal.

Nelson's arrival off Cadiz, on the eve of the forty-seventh anniversary of his birthday, transformed the fleet. "For Charity's sake, send us Lord Nelson, ye men of power!" So Codrington of the *Orion* had written, before the *Victory*'s appearance, and for once the men of power had responded. "Nelson was the man to *love*," wrote Malcolm of the *Donegal*, who knew both him and Wellington. "He is so good and pleasant that we all wish to do what he likes, without any kind of orders," said Duff of the *Mars*. "Exalt! the word seems to be created for the man"—such was Conrad's summing up.

Nelson noted the relief and joy at his arrival, and wrote to a friend that "the reception I met with on joining the Fleet caused the sweetest sensation of my life. The Officers who came on board to welcome my return forgot my rank as Commander-in-Chief in the enthusiasm with which they greeted me. As soon as these emotions were passed, I laid before them the Plan I had previously arranged for attacking the Enemy; and it was not only my pleasure to find it generally approved, but clearly perceived and understood." The ideas which he had outlined to Keats at Merton were soon eager talk among the captains, and were the subject of a tactical memorandum, issued from the *Victory* on 10th October. This assumed that Nelson, on the day of battle, would have enough ships to provide the three columns of which he had spoken. It included the sentence, a splendid echo of one by Lord Hawke: "Captains are to look to their particular line as their rallying point, but in case signals cannot be seen, or clearly understood, no captain can do very wrong if he places his ship alongside that of an enemy." Decision was his aim, and decision he would achieve.

In expounding his plan, he had a rapt audience. Fifteen commanding officers dined with him on his birthday, and as many on the succeeding day. "I believe my arrival was most welcome, not only to the Commanders of the Fleet, but to almost every individual in it; and when I came to explain to them the '*Nelson touch*' "—his idea for bringing on a mêlée —"it was like an electric shock. Some shed tears, all approved —'It was new—it was singular—it was simple!' and, from Admirals downwards it was repeated—'It must succeed, if ever they will allow us to get at them. You are, my Lord, surrounded by friends, whom you inspire with confidence.' " There was a general desire to avoid an inconclusive engagement, of which the navy had already had too many.

If the spirit of a new "Band of Brothers" was in embryo before Cadiz, much needed doing before the captains could achieve that perfection of training and fullness of understanding which Nelson looked for. There was a nucleus of senior officers whom he knew well—Collingwood and Fremantle, his old friends, dined with him alone on 1st October, but no one of rank except Hardy had served with him in all his battles, and the fleet was made up of Calder's squadron from the Channel fleet, a few survivors from the ships which had made the long journey to the West Indies, and reinforcements from home. Of the twenty-seven of the line which Nelson led at Trafalgar, the captains of only eight had served with him before, and only five had commanded a big ship in battle. An electric shock was just what was required to give the fleet a sense of purpose, activity, determination.

On 2nd October Nelson made a sad but necessary decision. Admiral Louis in the *Canopus*, Captain Hallowell in the *Tigre*, together with the *Spencer*, *Queen* and *Zealous*, ships and friends which had taken part in the long watch, were ordered to Gibraltar and Tetuan to water and provision. They were also to cover a convoy passing through the Straits. This carried supplies for Sir James Craig and a small military force which was destined for Naples and Sicily; and in fact it was British, not Napoleonic troops which arrived in Ferdinand's kingdom that fateful year. Louis begged to be detained, short as he was of necessities, till after the battle, but Nelson explained that he sent him away first because he hoped to have him back at the decisive moment. Fate willed it otherwise, and those whom Nelson would have delighted to have had with him missed Trafalgar, to their lifelong sorrow.

II

While Nelson was appraising his command, and working out the tactics for his clash with Villeneuve, Emma was staying with the William Nelsons at Canterbury. "My most dear Nelson," she wrote on 4th October, in the first of two letters which her correspondent never received (and so could not afterwards destroy), "Lord Douglas has just call'd; he would have given much to have seen you when you was in England; he looks upon you as the sweetest of all human beings. The Dr has invited him to dinner tomorrow. The poor old Duke [Queensberry] must have a letter every day from me. I had begun to fret at not having letters from you. I send you a letter of Miss Connor's [Horatia's governess], for there is much in it about our dear girl, you will like it. I also had one from my mother, who doats on her, she says she could not live without her. What a blessing for her parents to have such a child, so sweet, altho' so young, so amiable! God spare her to them, and be assured, my life, my soul, of your own Emma's fondest affections. You are my all of good. Heaven bless you."

Four days later she wrote: "My dearest life, we are just come from church, for I am so fond of the Church Service and the cannons are so civil; we have every day a fine Anthem for me. Yesterday, Mr Mrs and Miss Harrison, Mrs Bridges, Marquis of Douglas, and General Thornton, and Mr Baker the Member, dined with us. The Dr gave a good dinner, and Mariana dressed the macaroni and curry, so all went off well. Our Julia is very ill yet, but not brought to bed, as she is only seven months. I do not mean to keep Julia after she gets well.

"I was obliged to send for Mariana down, & my mother can ill spare her; she gives me such an amiable account of our dearest Horatia. She now reads very well, & is learning her notes, & French, & Italian, & my mother doats on her. The other day she said at table, 'Mrs Candogging, I wonder Julia did not run out of the church when she went to be married, for I should, seeing my squinting husband come in, for, my God! how ugly he is, and how he looks cross-eyed; why, as my lady says, he looks 2 ways for Sunday!'

"Now Julia's husband is the ugliest man you ever saw, but how that little thing cou'd observe him; but she is clever, is she not, Nelson? We go tomorrow for 2 days to Ramsgate to see an old friend, poor Lady Dunmore, who is there, in great affliction for the loss of her son, Captain John Murry. Today we dine alone, to eat up all the scraps, & drink tea with old Mrs Percy. Charlotte hates Canterbury, it is so *dull*; so it is.

"My dear girl writes every day in Miss Conner's letter & I am so pleased with her. My heart is broke away from her, but I have now had her so long at Merton that my heart cannot bear to be without her. You will be even fonder of her when you return. She says, 'I love my dear, dear godpapa, but Mrs Gibson told me he kill'd all the people, and I was afraid'. Dearest angel that she is! Oh, Nelson, how I love her, but how do I idolize you—the dearest husband of my heart, you are all in this world to your Emma. May God send you victory, and home to your *Emma, Horatia and paradise Merton*, for when you are there it will be paradise. My own Nelson, may God prosper & preserve you, for the sake of your affectionate Emma."

III

It was too much to be hoped that the difficulties in the fleet which had exercised Nelson would disappear overnight. They did not do so. Collingwood at first disliked his new flagship, the *Royal Sovereign*. She had once been a dull sailer: newly coppered, she steadily improved with acquaintance. Nelson hoped this would also be so with Rotherham, her flag-captain, with whom Collingwood soon had differences, needing to be reminded from the *Victory* that "in the presence of the Enemy, all men should be as brothers". "We are one," said Nelson on another occasion, "and I hope always shall be." Blackwood also needed soothing, in his trying task of inshore watch. "Do not, my dear Blackwood, be angry with anyone," begged his friend. Another recalcitrant was enjoined to remember "in our several stations . . . we must all put our shoulders to the wheel, and make the great machine of the Fleet, entrusted to our charge, go on smoothly."

Reinforcements began to arrive in ones and twos, though Nelson still needed more "eyes". There never were enough. "The last Fleet was lost to me for want of Frigates," he wrote to those in office: "God forbid this should." On Sunday, 13th October, a tall ship was made out, and she proved a portent. "Fine weather," noted Nelson. "*Aga-*

memnon join'd from England having fallen in with the French Squadron off Cape Finistre, consisting of 1 Three decker and 5 Two deck'd ships, and had a narrow escape from capture." The frigate *L'Aimable* was with her.

No reinforcement could have been more welcome than the ship in which, long ago, Nelson had made his name as a Mediterranean man. In the *Agamemnon* was none other than Sir Edward Berry. He had been chased and all but taken by the Rochefort squadron when eight days out from Plymouth, and had needed all his seamanship to get away.

"Here comes that damned fool Berry! *Now* we shall have a battle," exclaimed Nelson, rubbing his "fin". It was typical of Berry's luck that, having long and restlessly awaited a new ship, he should have been given the *Agamemnon* (and one of the scares of his life) before having the infinite happiness of joining Nelson on the eve of his greatest battle.

Nelson's chief remaining anxiety was Hardy. His health had long been poorly, and he was not yet recovered. Being without Murray, his Captain of the Fleet, Nelson had hoped that Hardy would take upon his broad shoulders much administrative work, but in fact this now fell wholly upon Nelson, who also missed his captain at table. Hardy was accustomed to cut up Nelson's meat for him at sea, and in his absence Nelson fell back on a macaroni diet, and sometimes pettishly refused to eat at all.

On the 14th October the enemy were seen at the harbour's mouth, and Nelson knew that the battle could not be long delayed. "Placed *Defence* and *Agamemnon* from seven to ten leagues West of Cadiz," he wrote, "and *Mars* and *Colossus* five leagues East from the Fleet, whose station will be from 15 leagues to twenty West of Cadiz, and by this chain I hope to have a constant communication with the Frigates off Cadiz." Every inducement was intended for Villeneuve to come out.

Knowing the value of concealment of strength, Nelson had disposed his forces with that purpose. Blackwood with his frigates would see everything in Cadiz; the linking ships of the line would give him speedy notice by signal of any important enemy movement, while Nelson himself, with the bulk of his fleet, stood away, well out of sight, between forty-five and fifty miles to the westward.

He did not like to be quite so far from Cadiz, but he was conditioned by the elements. For if a westerly gale sprang up and caught the British too near the shoals of Trafalgar to enable them to keep to windward, they would be driven through the Straits of Gibraltar. It would then only need a timely shift of wind to the south or east to give Villeneuve a clear run into the Atlantic.

Again, if Villeneuve was in fact bound for the Mediterranean he might come out at night, when a land-breeze served his purpose, then catch the sea breeze at the Straits' mouth, and be far on an eastward course with the British out of reach. In order to guard against such happenings, Blackwood was told that, in easterly breezes, Nelson would beat up towards Cadiz, and that if Villeneuve's fleet came out he would carry a press of sail towards Gibraltar, assuming the enemy intention to be to make for the Mediterranean.

By 14th October Nelson had under his immediate command all the ships which were to serve with him in the day of battle—twenty-seven of the line, four frigates, a schooner and a cutter. His written instructions were discussed with the captains newly joined from home, and the points were emphasised. The order of sailing was to be the order of battle; no time was to be wasted if, at the crucial hour, ships were not in the formation which Nelson had previously arranged. It was a provision suitable for a chase. The second-in-command, after Nelson's intentions had been made known by signal, would have entire direction of his line. If possible he was to cut through the enemy about the twelfth ship from the rear. The remainder of the combined fleet was to be left to the management of the Commander-in-Chief, whose endeavour would be to see that, while the rear was pulverised by Collingwood, no interference should be encountered from the van.

Villeneuve knew well enough that his opponent would not wait to form line parallel with his own, slogging it out with the distant gun in the old manner. He had already committed this opinion to paper for the benefit of his staff. "He will try to double our rear, cut through the line, and bring against the ships thus isolated groups of his own, to surround and capture them," he wrote. "Captains must rely upon their courage and love of glory, rather than upon the signals of the admiral, who may already be engaged and wrapped in smoke. The Captain who is not in action is not at his post." This was indeed a discerning appreciation, supported no doubt by good intelligence and by memories of the Nile.

On 18th October, Villeneuve heard that four British ships were on their way eastwards from Gibraltar, and that there were two more in the port itself. He knew that his successor had already reached Madrid. The wind had turned southerly, which was favourable to him, and if he was to reach the Mediterranean, he must act quickly. There might never be a better chance.

That same day Nelson wrote: "My dearest beloved Emma, the dear friend of my bosom, the signal has been made that the Enemy's combined fleet are coming out of Port. We have very little wind, so that I have no hopes of seeing them before tomorrow. May the God of Battles crown my endeavours with success. At all events I will take care that my name shall ever be most dear to you and Horatia, both of whom I love as much as my own life; and as my last writing before the battle will be to you, so I hope in God that I shall live to finish my letter after the Battle. May heaven bless you, prays your *Nelson and Brontë*."

Next day he jotted down some particulars of the enemy's dispositions, but expressed his belief that they might get back into Harbour before night. "May God Almighty give us success over these fellows," he concluded, "and enable us to get a Peace." They were the last words he ever wrote to the woman he loved. A note to his Dearest Angel, Horatia, enjoined her to "love dear Lady Hamilton, who most dearly loves you. Give her a kiss for me."

In conversation at dinner Nelson said he thought he might lose a leg in action. If he should be killed, he added, he felt sure that such glory would reflect on the naval profession that there would be a general wish to emulate his example. He added that he hoped he might be buried in St Paul's, not Westminster Abbey. Someone had told him that, as the Abbey had originally been built on marshy ground, it would one day disappear, while St Paul's, on its slight eminence, would be safe for ever. But for all this talk of lost limbs and public funerals, the admiral was noticed to be as cheerful as he always was when action was in prospect.

Soon after daylight on 20th October, twenty-four hours after his preliminary movement, Villeneuve ordered the rest of his fleet to leave Cadiz. He commanded thirty-three of the line—eighteen French and fifteen Spanish, with five French frigates and two brigs. At first he stood to the westward. As his ships cleared the Bay the wind began to freshen; there were strong gusts, with rain. Some of the Spaniards split their sails in reefing, falling to leeward. Towards midday Villeneuve made the signal to form in three columns. Admiral Gravina had the windward station. It became his duty to keep a look-out to the westward, and, if he could, to drive off Blackwood's shadowing frigates.

At about four o'clock the weather cleared, and the wind flew round to west. The change took the Combined Fleet aback, throwing it into disorder. Villeneuve ordered it to re-form in the original three columns on a course of south-south-west—that is, heading slightly away from the Straits. His ships were still taking up position when darkness fell. At half-past seven the brig *Argus* came under the stern of the *Bucentaure*, the French flagship, with news that eighteen British vessels had been sighted ahead.

As Villeneuve was then in a situation where only one of his three squadrons could fire without risk to friends, he made a signal to form a single line of battle. Confusion resulted, and this continued throughout the night. Daylight found the Combined Fleet in several straggling groups. It was apparent to Villeneuve that he could not rely on his captains to execute commands with speed or precision.

At eight o'clock on the morning of 20th October, while Villeneuve was clearing Cadiz, the *Victory* hove-to, and Collingwood was signalled to "Close nearer to the Admiral." Nelson wished for a word with his friend. He still feared that the enemy might return to port, but word soon came that the whole Combined Fleet was at sea, and appeared to be setting a westerly course. At four o'clock, Nelson made sail and stood away in the two columns in which he would give battle. The enemy was only twenty miles distant, and a

frigate reported that Villeneuve was standing to the southward. Nelson continued to close with the enemy, but signalled that the fleet would come to the wind on the starboard
tack at nightfall. It would then be about ten miles to windward of Villeneuve and ready to act on any further information from the frigates. These were to burn two blue lights
every hour, "in order to make the greater blaze", if Villeneuve held his course. If he altered westward, "three guns,
quick, every hour," would be the sign.

There is no reason to believe that Nelson contemplated
a night action. In the mêlée he intended to bring about,
friend and foe would be inextricably mingled, and daylight
was essential to full success. The circumstances were utterly
different from those at the Nile, when Brueys had been at
anchor. By waiting until dawn before making his final
dispositions, Nelson ensured that the Combined Fleet would
be too far south to make an easy retreat upon Cadiz.

At 8.40 p.m. Nelson wore the fleet to the south-south-
west, heading it in the same direction as Villeneuve. He was
marking time. The *Africa* missed the signal and continued
standing to the north. At daylight she was some eight miles
from the *Victory*, and Henry Digby, her captain, received one
of Nelson's final signals. At four o'clock in the morning
Nelson wore again, and held a course north by east. This
movement placed him nine miles to windward of his enemy,
a good disposition for a commander set upon battle. By half-
past five it was light enough to see the French and Spanish
ships, silhouetted against the dawn. So far as preparation was
concerned, another masterpiece had been achieved. Manœuvre as he might, Villeneuve could not now avoid battle.

IV

The morning was clear, the westerly wind light, and there
was a swell which increased all day, heralding a gale. Just
after six o'clock, when it was bright enough to distinguish
flags, Nelson hoisted the signal to form order of sailing in
two columns. Only the ships at the head of the line got even

roughly into proper station. The rest scrambled into battle as best they could, some of the slow sailers being left so far behind that they could take no protracted part in the fighting. Even so, the pace was stately, never exceeding that of a walk. The leisured approach, conditioned by the strength of the wind, enabled much to be said and done before the fleets came within range of one another.

Nelson remembered it was a happy anniversary in the annals of his family, that of his uncle Suckling's most successful engagement; it was also the day of the Fair at Burnham Thorpe. Collingwood, dressing and shaving meticulously for his third full-scale battle in the Atlantic (he had memories of service with Howe at the Glorious First of June as well as of St Vincent three years later), recommended the first lieutenant of the *Royal Sovereign* to follow his example and change his boots for shoes and silk-stockings. "They were," he explained, "so much more manageable for the surgeon."

Owing to disadvantage in position, Villeneuve was about ten minutes later than Nelson in getting a clear view of his opponents. When he did so, the British appeared to be in no discernible order. Then they divided into two groups, steering, it seemed, for the centre and rear of the French and Spanish. Villeneuve's immediate care was to get his ships into line, and then to reverse their direction. As early as seven o'clock Nelson thought that the enemy were wearing in succession in an attempt to run for Cadiz, as he had fully expected they would do on sighting the British fleet; in fact, it was not until eight that Villeneuve was able to turn his ships together to the northward. Even as the signal flags went up, Commodore Churruca, commanding the *San Juan Nepomucino*, now the rear ship, turned to a subordinate with the words: "This fleet is doomed. The French admiral does not know his business. He has compromised us all!" Soon afterwards, he summoned his crew to prayers.

It was, in fact, nearly two hours before the Combined Fleet was in anything approaching orderly disposition. Collingwood, in his despatch, described it as forming "a crescent, convexing to leeward", stretching from north to south.

Soon after dawn, Nelson was seen to be pacing the
Victory's quarter-deck, wearing the undress uniform with its
four stars that he had commonly used since he left Portsmouth. He was without his sword, which was lying on a
table below. Blackwood was summoned aboard, and he was
followed, at about eight o'clock, by the three junior frigate
captains, Dundas of the *Naiad*, Capel of the *Phoebe*, who
had been Nelson's signal lieutenant at the Nile, and Prowse
of the *Sirius*. They had all done well, but their business was
not yet over. "I mean today to bleed the captains of the
frigates," said Nelson briskly, "as I shall keep you on board
until the very last."

Blackwood and Hardy, after a few minutes given to professional conversation, were invited below to the admiral's
quarters. There they were asked to witness a document,
written by Nelson earlier that day, giving an account of the
services to the nation of Emma Hamilton, and leaving her
as a legacy to her King and Country "that they will give her
an ample provision to maintain her rank in life". He also
left "to the beneficence of my Country my adopted daughter,
Horatia Nelson Thompson; and I desire she will use in
future the name of Nelson only.

"These are the only favours I ask of my King and Country
at this moment when I am going to fight their Battle. May
God Bless my King and Country, and all those who I hold
dear. My relations it is needless to mention; they will of
course be amply provided for. Nelson and Brontë."

The only attention which was ever paid to this document
in official quarters was in respect of Nelson's relations, whom
he knew would be generously treated. He had already
bequeathed Merton to Emma, in fulfilment of his wish that
"the longest liver" of the trio who had so enjoyed the
property "should possess it all". She also benefited from an
annuity chargeable upon the Brontë estate. There was
£4,000 in trust for Horatia, and an income for his wife.
Nelson could go into battle assured that he had left nothing
undone for the comfort of those to whom he was bound by
affection or by duty. It was the final example of his practic-
ality, for it would have been impossible to engage in battle
with that singleness of mind demanded of a responsible

commander without first ensuring that his personal affairs were arranged as he intended. For battle, the supreme test for all who took part in it, admitted no distraction, though the admiral's prevision had been so thorough that part at least of the long and otherwise intolerably tense hours before gunfire opened could be given over to private matters. Such conditions would never occur again with an enemy in sight. They belonged essentially to the days of sail.

No one remarked Nelson's blithe assumption that the *Victory* would not suffer irreparable damage, or be sunk. Blackwood never even asked whether he should take charge of the precious document until after the battle. He did, however, venture to suggest that the Commander-in-Chief should shift his flag to the *Euryalus* and conduct affairs from a safe distance, Nelson could not hear of such a plan, giving force of example as his reason. He next made a round of the quarters of the flagship, praising Hardy's arrangements, and exchanging cheerful words with the men, who included Americans, Frenchmen, Spaniards, Germans, Dutch and Swiss.

Blackwood, having failed to persuade Nelson to transfer to his frigate, next suggested that he should allow one or two ships to precede the *Victory* into action. He and Hardy both felt that it might be of advantage to the fleet if the admiral kept out of battle as long as possible. Nelson consented, and the three-decked *Temeraire*, was ordered to go ahead. But it was a half-hearted assent, for the *Victory* did not give way, and when the *Temeraire* at last ranged upon the flagship's quarter Nelson hailed her with the words: "I'll thank you, Captain Harvey, to keep in your proper station, which is astern of the *Victory*."

In fact, Harvey got into action so close upon his admiral that, in his own words "the *Temeraire* almost touched the stern of the *Victory*". Nelson, in placing three great ships at the head of his line, had packed his punch, for Fremantle in the *Neptune* was not far behind. It happened that in Harvey he had a man whose reckless gallantry—he was a great gambler—was exactly what was needed in the ordeal to which Nelson was deliberately subjecting the leading ships. "They put a good face upon it," he said from time to time, observing his opponents, and impatient that, even with a press of sail, the speed of advance was actually diminishing. A little before eleven, he went below for the last time.

In his cabin he added words to the entry under the date of "*Monday, Octr. 21st, 1805,*" made in his private Diary, which have passed into the treasury of the language. "*May the Great God whom I worship Grant to my Country and for the benefit of Europe in General a great and Glorious Victory, and may no misconduct in anyone tarnish it, and may humanity after Victory be the predominant feature in the British Fleet. For myself individually I commit my life to Him Who made me, and may His blessing light upon my endeavours for serving my Country faithfully. To Him I resign myself and the just cause which is entrusted me to Defend. Amen, Amen, Amen.*"

John Pasco, who was acting as Signal Lieutenant, though his seniority entitled him to be executive officer, then entered, to request Nelson to allow him to assume his proper duties. He found the admiral on his knees, and forbore to make his plea, thus losing promotion to post rank after the battle. He could not, he felt, trouble the admiral with any grievance of his own. Nelson soon followed him to the deck. The time was a quarter to twelve, and on the poop of the *Victory* a band was playing.

Nelson said to Pasco that he would amuse the fleet with a signal. "I wish to say . . . '*England Confides that Every Man will do his Duty*'. You must be quick," he added, "for I have one more to make, which is for Close Action." Pasco suggested the substitution of "expects" for "confides", for "expects" was already in the signal book and would save various alphabetical hoists. "That will do, Pasco," said Nelson, "make it directly." The response was unexpected. "What is Nelson signalling about?" muttered the austere Collingwood. "We all know what we have to do." Between decks the feeling was much the same. A lieutenant of Marines, sent below to deliver the message to those who would be working the guns, found the sailors stripped to the waist, handkerchiefs round their heads and ears to deaden the noise of shot, sharpening cutlasses and giving their pieces last minute attention. A few, he noticed, were actually dancing a hornpipe.

The lieutenant repeated the signal which was now fluttering from the halyards. "Jack, however, did not appreciate it," he noted, "for there were murmurs from some, whilst others in an audible whisper murmured 'Do your duty! Of course we'll do our duty. I've always done mine, haven't you?' Still they cheered," he added, "more, I believe, from love and admiration for their admiral than from an appreciation of this well known signal." It was not, however, made in vain. Some weeks later, when Napoleon heard that Nelson had flown it in battle, he ordered that ships of his navy should be embellished with an inscription, placed in a prominent place: *"La France Compte que chacun fera son Devoir."*

v

"See how that noble fellow Collingwood takes his ship into action," said Nelson just before noon: "how I envy him!" "What would Nelson give to be here!" Such was Collingwood's remark.

The *Royal Sovereign* had, in fact, got into action far ahead of her squadron, which was advancing upon the enemy in line of bearing, in a formation resembling an echelon. For twenty minutes, so Collingwood reckoned, he fought without close support, and it was as well that his gunnery was the most effectual in the fleet. He broke the enemy line astern of the Spanish three-decker *Santa Anna*, wearing the flag of Admiral Alava. Battle was fairly joined, and it was not many minutes before the *Victory* herself came under distant fire.

The first shot at the flagship fell short, the second alongside and the third over. At this point Nelson bade the frigate captains hurry away to their own ships, and told them that their duty, as they went down the column was to bid the captains of all ships of the line to get into action immediately. "They might adopt whatever course they thought best, provided it led them quickly and closely alongside an enemy," he said. "God bless you, Blackwood," were his words to the Captain of *Euryalus* as he went over the side. "I shall never speak to you again."

Firing now increased, and a round shot, flying across the quarter-deck of the *Victory*, almost tore in half an officer then engaged in speech with Hardy. Captain Adair of the Marines called up a seaman to cast overboard, without ceremony or delay, the body of the Admiral's official secretary. Nelson had noticed. "Is that poor Scott?" he asked, as the corpse was committed to the deep.

Those of Adair's men who were stationed on the poop were soon suffering heavily. Nelson gave orders that they should be dispersed around the ship. Then the wheel was knocked to pieces, but the tiller was manned, and the ship was steered from the lower gun-deck, the first lieutenant, Quilliam, and Atkinson, the Master, taking turns at supervising this duty, which required the strength of forty men.

Nelson and Hardy, though differing greatly in size, had long adjusted their pace to one another for the walk along the quarter-deck, which they now took together. Soon a shot hit the forebrace bitts, its blast whistling so close to them that they looked at each other questioningly. The only damage was to the buckle of Hardy's shoe. Nelson said: "This is too warm work to last long," and congratulated his companion on the steady behaviour of the ship's company under a fire which they could not yet return. The *Victory* was standing towards the enemy van, a feint which, it was intended, should relieve Collingwood from all possibility that his line would be doubled. Nelson at last gave the order to port the helm, and the *Victory* opened with her effective guns. She passed close under the stern of a French three-decker and poured shot into the cabin windows of what was later known to be Villeneuve's *Bucentaure*. Close to her was a 74, the *Redoubtable*, Captain Lucas, the best-fought ship in the Combined Fleet. Near at hand was the towering *Santissima Trinidad*, the Spanish four-decker which, had things gone right, should have been captured at St Vincent eight years before. It was from this ship, so Harvey observed from the *Temeraire*, that the first shots had been fired at Nelson's squadron. By pure chance, Nelson had pierced the allied line at the exact place he would have wished. "Oft did the little man himself, with his remaining eye, cast an anxious glance towards the Franco Spanish line in search of

the ship he meant the *Victory* first to grapple with," so ran
the account in James's *Naval History*, "and so lightly did
Lord Nelson value personal risk, that although urged
more than once on the subject, he would not suffer those
barriers from the Enemy's grape and musketry, the
hammocks, to be placed one inch higher than, to facilitate
his view of objects around him, they were accustomed to be
placed."

The mêlée had been well and truly brought about. Henceforward it would be close fighting. The *Victory* and *Temeraire*
were soon locked in death-grips with opponents, muzzles
touching—"so nearly engaged," as Harvey said after the
battle, "that I can give you no other account of this part of
the most glorious day's work".

At one time, fire from the *Redoubtable*'s fighting tops
almost cleared the decks of the *Victory*, and there was some
danger that she would be boarded. After the battle, French
survivors said that more than two hundred grenades had
been thrown on board, and that the British forecastle and
poop were heaped with dead. Cadet Yon and four sailors
actually reached the deck by means of an anchor; Captain
Adair was killed in directing a repulse. Before the French
intruders could be supported by a larger party, the *Temeraire*
ranged up on the starboard side and battered the *Redoubtable*
so severely that she sank next day. She had, in fact, by far the
heaviest casualties of the battle. Nearly five hundred killed,
and over eighty wounded, was a devastating number even
compared with the losses of the *Victory*, whose fifty-seven
dead was the highest among the British ships.

At about a quarter-past one, when the flagship had been
in action a full hour, Hardy, turning in his walk, suddenly
saw the admiral on his knees, the finger tips of his left hand
touching the deck. Then his arm gave way, and he fell on
his left side, just where Scott had been killed in the opening
moments of the battle. Sergeant-Major Secker of the
Marines, together with two seamen, was soon on the spot,
tenderly raising the wounded man. "They have done for me
at last, Hardy," said Nelson. "I hope not," answered his
friend. "Yes," said Nelson, "my backbone is shot through."

VI

Hardy told the three men to carry the admiral down to the cockpit, which was below the water-line. On the way, Nelson, as he reached the middle deck, thought that the tiller ropes should be re-rove, and told the midshipman stationed there to ask Hardy to see to this. Having given the order, he took his handkerchief from his pocket and covered his face with it, so that he might not be seen by the men.

The surgeon, who wrote the most circumstantial account of Nelson's last hours, had then over forty under his care, wounded and dying. It was not long before someone drew his attention by saying: "Mr Beatty, Lord Nelson is here: Mr Beatty, the Admiral is wounded." On looking round, Beatty saw the handkerchief fall from Nelson's face. Mr Burke, the Purser, relieved the seamen of their burden, and when Beatty went over to attend to his chief his first words were, "Ah, Mr Beatty! You can do nothing for me. I have but a short time to live: my back is shot through."

Dr Scott, the chaplain, was present in the cockpit, though he would never afterwards speak of a scene which, he thought, resembled a butcher's shambles. The admiral was put on a bed, stripped of his clothes, and covered with a sheet. While this was being done he said to Scott repeatedly: "Doctor, I told you so. Doctor, I am gone." After a pause he added in a hurried, agitated manner, though with pauses: "Remember me to Lady Hamilton! Remember me to Horatia! Remember me to all my friends. Doctor, remember me to Mr Rose; tell him I have left a will, and left Lady Hamilton and Horatia to my Country." He repeated his remembrances to Lady Hamilton several times, and told Scott to mind what he said.

Gradually he became less agitated, and at last was calm enough to ask questions about what was going on. This led him to think of Hardy, for whom he now sent, exclaiming that he would not believe he was alive unless he saw him. He grew anxious when Hardy did not come, and doubted every assurance of his being safe.

Beatty examined the wound, saying he would not put his patient to much pain in trying to trace the course which the ball had taken. Fired from above, from a fighting top in the *Redoubtable*, it had penetrated deep into Nelson's chest, and had lodged in his spine. Nelson was meticulous in describing his symptoms, telling Beatty that he felt a gush of blood every minute within his breast; that he had no feeling in the lower part of his body, that his breathing was difficult, and gave him severe pain about that part of the spine where he was sure the bullet had struck, "for," he said, "I felt it break my back". All the signs, not least the state of Nelson's pulse, showed Beatty the hopeless nature of the case, but its gravity was kept from all but Hardy, Scott, Burke and the assistant surgeons.

The *Victory*'s men cheered whenever they saw through the open ports the surrender of an enemy ship. Nelson asked the cause of the noise and Pasco, who lay wounded some distance from the admiral, raised himself up and told him, glad to see Nelson's satisfaction at the news. Nelson then felt an ardent thirst, and called for drink, being given lemonade or wine and water. "Fan, fan, drink drink," was his repeated expression.

At last he said: "Will no one bring Hardy to me? He must be killed: he is surely destroyed." Bulkeley, a midshipman, son of an old friend, then came below and explained that the management of the fleet still required Hardy's presence on deck, but that he would go below as soon as possible. Nelson recognised Bulkeley's voice, and told him to remember him to his father.

At about half-past two Hardy arrived, shook hands with his chief, and was asked how went the battle. "Very well, my Lord," Hardy answered. "We have got twelve or fourteen of the Enemy's ships in our possession, but five of their van have tacked, and show an intention of bearing down on the *Victory*. I have therefore called two or three of our fresh ships around us, and have no doubt of giving them a drubbing." "I hope none of our ships have struck," said Nelson. "No, my lord," answered Hardy, "there is no fear of that." "I am a dead man, Hardy," Nelson then said. "I am going fast: it will all be over with me soon. Come nearer to me. Pray let my dear Lady Hamilton have my hair, and all other things belonging to me." "Is your pain great?" asked Hardy.

"Yes, but I shall live half an hour longer yet," was the reply. Soon afterwards, Hardy returned to the deck.

Beatty had been attending a midshipman who had lost a leg, but he returned to the admiral after Hardy had gone. Nelson told him to look after the others. "You can do nothing for me," he added. The pain continued so severe that he wished he were dead, "Yet," he added, "one would like to live a little longer too. God be praised," he said again and again, "I have done my duty."

Presently, the *Victory* fired a broadside at the enemy van, whose attempt to redeem the day was ineffectual. "Oh *Victory, Victory*! how you distract my poor brain," said Nelson when the concussion shook the cockpit and everyone in it. He added: "How dear is life to all men."

About fifty minutes after his first visit, Hardy descended to the cockpit a second time. He had now sent a message to Collingwood to let him know the gravity of Nelson's wound. The two men again shook hands: "And," said Beatty, "while the Captain retained his Lordship's, he congratulated him even in the arms of death, on his brilliant victory; 'which,' he said, 'was complete; though he did not know how many of the Enemy were captured, as it was impossible to perceive every Ship distinctly. He was certain however of fourteen or fifteen having surrendered.' His Lordship answered, 'That is well, but I bargained for twenty': and then emphatically exclaimed, 'Anchor, Hardy, anchor!' To this the Captain replied: 'I suppose, my Lord, Admiral Collingwood will now take upon himself the direction of affairs.' 'Not while I live, I hope, Hardy!' cried the dying Chief; and at that moment endeavoured ineffectually to raise himself from the bed. 'No,' added he; 'do *you* anchor, Hardy.'

"He then told Hardy, 'he felt that in a few minutes he should be no more'; adding in a low tone, 'Don't throw me overboard, Hardy.' The Captain answered: 'Oh! no, certainly not.' 'Then,' replied his Lordship, 'you know what to do': and, continued he, 'take care of my dear Lady Hamilton, Hardy: take care of poor Lady Hamilton. Kiss me, Hardy.' The Captain now knelt down, and kissed his cheek; when his Lordship said: 'Now I am satisfied. Thank God, I have done my duty.' Captain Hardy stood for a minute or two in silent contemplation: he knelt down again, and kissed his Lordship's forehead. His Lordship said: 'Who is that?' The Captain answered: 'It is Hardy,' to which his Lordship replied, 'God bless you, Hardy!' After this affecting scene Captain Hardy withdrew, and returned to the quarter-deck, having spent about eight minutes in this his last interview with his dying friend.

"Lord Nelson now desired Mr Chevalier, his Steward, to turn him upon his right side; which being effected, his Lordship said: 'I wish I had not left the deck, for I shall soon be gone.' He afterwards became very low; his breathing was oppressed, and his voice faint. He said to Doctor Scott, 'Doctor, I have *not* been a *great* sinner,' and after a short pause, '*Remember*, that I leave Lady Hamilton and my Daughter Horatia as a legacy to my Country: and,' added he, 'never forget Horatia.' His thirst now increased; and he called for 'drink, drink', 'fan, fan', and 'rub, rub', addressing himself in the last case to Doctor Scott, who had been rubbing his Lordship's breast with his hand, from which he found some relief.

"His Lordship became speechless in about fifteen minutes after Captain Hardy left him. Dr Scott and Mr Burke, who had all along sustained the bed under his shoulders (which raised him in nearly a semi-recumbent posture, the only one that was supportable to him), forbore to disturb him by speaking to him; and when he had remained speechless about five minutes, his Lordship's Steward went to the Surgeon, who had been a short time occupied with the wounded in another part of the cockpit, and stated his apprehensions that his Lordship was dying. The Surgeon immediately repaired to him, and found him on the verge of dissolution. He knelt down by his side, and took up his hand; which was cold, and the pulse gone from the wrist. On the Surgeon's feeling his forehead, which was likewise cold, his Lordship opened his eyes, looked up, and shut them again. The Surgeon again left him, and returned to the wounded who required his assistance; but was not absent five minutes before the Steward announced to him that 'he believed his Lordship had expired'. The Surgeon returned, and found that the report was but too well founded: his Lordship had

October, may heaven bless you prays
your Nelson Bronte, Oct 20ᵗʰ in the
morning we were near the mouth of the
Straights but the Wind had not come far
enough to the Westward to allow the Combined
fleets to Weather the Shoals off Trafalgar but
they were counted as far as forty Sail of ships
of War which I suppose to be 34 of the Line
and six frigates, a group of them was
seen off the lighthouse of Cadiz this morning
but it blows so very fresh & thick weather
that I rather believe they will wait within
the Harbour before his part, May God
Almighty give us success over these fellows
and enable us to get a Peace

*This letter was found open on
his desk & brought to
Lady Hamilton by
Capt. Hardy*

*at Merton — 1805)
Emma*

in glorious & happy by Nelson

NELSON'S LAST LETTER TO EMMA HAMILTON

breathed his last, at thirty minutes past four o'clock; at which period Doctor Scott was in the act of rubbing his Lordship's breast, and Mr Burke supporting the bed upon his shoulders."

The Combined Fleet had been broken and scattered; Villeneuve was a prisoner; no British ship was lost; but there was little elation. "I am a dying man," said the Spanish admiral, Gravina, "but I hope and trust that I am going to join Nelson." "I never set eyes on him," wrote a sailor in his letter home, "for which I am both sorry and glad, for to be sure I should like to have seen him, but then, all the men in our ship who have seen him are such soft toads, they have done nothing but Blast their Eyes and cry ever since he was killed. God bless you! chaps that fought like the Devil sit down and cry like a wench."

Surely no admiral ever had a more genuine tribute from men who had nothing to gain from their devotion. Nelson had won glory enough, through his enduring courage and the art of war, to ensure himself a place as one of the foremost heroes of his country, but what was the secret that caused men who had known all the leaders of a great age to say, as they did so emphatically, that he was the man to *love*?

Partly, no doubt, it was his imperfections. It is seldom that model characters arouse that mixture of sympathy, wonder and affectionate forbearance which drew men and women of every rank to Nelson. He was human, vital, warm —and he remembered kindnesses. These are not characteristics always found with genius.

Some of Nelson's magic died with him: his leadership, and his pervading charm, which affected all with whom he came into contact. His detractors, mostly contemporaries jealous of his success and scornful of his vanity, were few. His superiors, with rare exceptions, valued him properly, and showed it. As for his family, his friends, his officers and men, he was beloved by one and all. In life, he retained his hold upon their hearts, and his memory was never over-shadowed.

Of the three Nelsons which have been transmitted to posterity—the subject of a legion of biographers, the writer of letters and despatches, and the author of the sometimes frenzied and always intimate notes to Emma Hamilton, it is

the letter-writer who impresses most—by his unfailing
clarity, his range of understanding, and his response to every
appeal with even a shred of claim behind it. He made duty
more than a pious word, and he never expected more of
others than he would do himself.

Nelson was, pre-eminently, a generous man, and if any
biographer leaves his readers in a shadow of doubt as to why
he inspired devotion, the fault is his. It was Oliver Cromwell
who enjoined his limner to render his countenance "warts
and all", and the picture gained from unsparing truth, as
portraits will: but no one has ever surrendered to the seven
great volumes of Nelson's printed correspondence without
feeling the assurance that Nelson's character and activities
were infinitely rewarding. They will remain an inspiration to
all who share his eternal eagerness to serve his country, and
to those who—in the words of his beloved Emma—"can
never be a lukewarm friend".

Coleridge was at Naples, of all cities, when the news of
Trafalgar reached Italy, on his way home from his service
with Sir Alexander Ball. "When Nelson died," he wrote, "it
seemed as if no man was a stranger to another: for all were
made acquaintances in the rights of a common anguish.
Never can I forget the sorrow and consternation that lay on
every countenance. . . . Numbers stopped and shook hands
with me, because they had seen the tears on my cheek, and
conjectured that I was an Englishman; and some, as they
held my hand, burst, themselves, into tears."

"This letter," wrote the recipient upon the note addressed
to her by Nelson on 19th October 1805, "was found open
on his desk and brought to Lady Hamilton by Capt. Hardy."

"*My dearest beloved Emma,*" she re-read, "*the dear friend
of my bosom, the Signal has been made that the Enemy's combined fleet are coming out of port . . . May God Almighty give us
success over these fellows and enable us to get a Peace.*" Then,
where the sheet was still un-filled, she wrote, in a handwriting whose distraction is apparent to the most casual
glance:

> "*Oh miserable wretched Emma*
> *Oh glorious and happy Nelson.*"

2 A

Epilogue

NELSON'S call to Hardy "do *you* anchor" was not carried out generally in the fleet. The westerly sea rose after Trafalgar, as Nelson feared it would, and the victorious ships rode the storm with the utmost difficulty. Although the battle itself was annihilating, only four prizes were safely brought in to Gibraltar. Many foundered; and even the *Victory* herself, battered and leaking, was in some danger. She reached the shelter of the Rock on 28th October, with Nelson's body preserved in a cask of spirits. She was then put into a fit state for the journey home. She made Spithead on 4th December 1805, and sailed a week later for the Nore.

On 23rd December Nelson's body was conveyed up the Thames to Greenwich, where it lay in state in Wren's magnificent Painted Hall. Dr Scott, that devoted chaplain, watched by it continuously until the day—8th January 1806 —when the river journey was continued to Whitehall. The body was then taken to the Admiralty, and on the 9th the funeral procession, the most elaborate within memory, attended by royalty, officers of state, representatives of both services, including men from the *Victory*, and a vast concourse of people, watched the black car on its way through the winter streets to St Paul's.

The coffin, made from the wood of the French *L'Orient*, was at length placed within a black marble sarcophagus, originally designed by Benedetto da Rovezzano for Cardinal Wolsey. Surmounted by a viscount's coronet, the tomb became one of the hallowed sights of London. It is befitting that it is now surrounded by others, enclosing the mortal remains of those who carried on Nelson's sea tradition.

As the admiral had expected, his relations were generously remembered. His brother William, that worldly cleric, was made an earl, and a pension of £5,000 a year was settled with the title ("for ever", so the Act said: it was actually given for not quite a century and a half); and the sum of £99,000 was also granted by Parliament towards the pur-

NELSON'S TOMB AT ST PAUL'S and his EFFIGY AT WESTMINSTER ABBEY

Nelson's tomb at St Paul's, exactly beneath the centre of Wren's dome

His effigy at Westminster Abbey, made by Catherine Andras

chase of an estate, which remained in the family until after the Second World War. Nelson's sisters each received a gift of £15,000, and it was to the heir of one of them, Mrs Bolton that the title eventually descended. Fanny was given a pension of £2,000 a year for life.

Emma Hamilton survived Nelson by more than nine years, dying in January 1815, a few months before Waterloo. Her affairs, never well managed, became increasingly confused after the death of her mother, and her last days were spent as an exile in Calais, not in actual want, but in debt, and in humble circumstances. Horatia was with her at the last, and was later cared for by her aunt, Mrs Matcham, Nelson's favourite sister. Horatia became the wife of a Victorian clergyman, the mother of many children, and lived to a ripe old age.

All Nelson's principal officers continued their careers with distinction. Collingwood was made a peer, and died on active service in 1810. Hardy became a baronet, and lived to be Governor of Greenwich Hospital, his pleasure being to watch over the interests of the pensioners who had given their best years in the service of the navy. As for Fanny, the "little viscountess" as the family called her, despite her delicate health—or perhaps because of the care she took of it—she outlived her own son, Josiah Nisbet, and some of his children. She died, greatly respected, in 1831, and was buried in the quiet Devonshire village of Littleham.

Once repaired, the *Victory* continued operational during the remainder of the war with Napoleon. She carried the flag of Saumarez in the Baltic, and later served off Spain. Since it was unthinkable to Nelson's countrymen that she should be broken up in her old age, her timbers scattered, she remained at Portsmouth throughout the latter part of the nineteenth century, the flagship of successive Commanders-in-Chief. In the reign of George V she was restored with affectionate care to her condition at Trafalgar, and in March 1941 she survived a direct hit by an enemy bomb. She continues to be the most eagerly visited memorial to the admiral who lived so long in her, and who fought her so valiantly. She will ever be an object of pilgrimage for those of every nation who see in the sailing ship one of the noblest structures devised by man's hand.

Appendix

CONTEMPORARY PORTRAITS OF NELSON

"THAT foolish little fellow Nelson has sat to every painter in London," said Lord St Vincent to Lady Elizabeth Foster on Valentine's Day 1801. Alas, it was a gross exaggeration, and the following list of contemporary versions, most of which were made from the life, includes all of which I have been able to find reliable record, together with others which are undocumented and upon which information would be welcome. Further discovery is always possible, but one or two items, purporting to be of the admiral, have been excluded, since the evidence does not seem to me conclusive.

Groups and action pictures are excluded, and as regards pure portraits, perhaps the most notable omission is the picture at Norwich Castle by an unknown artist which, by tradition, shows Nelson when captain of the *Albemarle*. I should like to think that this was a right attribution, since it would help to span the gap between Collingwood's amateur rendering of about 1785 and the miniature painted by Leghorn in 1795 for Lady Nelson—but I am not convinced. Posthumous versions abound. The good ones must all derive from one or other of those made from the living man.

By J. F. Rigaud, R.A. (1742-1810)
Canvas, 49" × 42". Three-quarter length. Begun in 1777, when Nelson was a lieutenant: altered 1781 (to show insignia of a post-captain and details of Fort San Juan), and possibly again later. *National Maritime Museum.*
> Print by R. Shipster, 1797.
> Nicolas: *Dispatches and Letters*, Vol. I, pp. 38n, 39, 41.

By Cuthbert Collingwood (1750-1810)
Coloured profile drawn in the West Indies, *c.* 1785, by the officer who afterwards became Vice-Admiral Lord Collingwood. Nelson returned the compliment in monochrome. *National Maritime Museum.*

By a Miniaturist Unknown
Miniature painted at Leghorn, 1795. Uniform of a post-captain. *National Maritime Museum.*
> Print by R. Laurie, 1797.
> E. M. Keate: *Nelson's Wife* (1939), p. 265.
> Mahan: *Life of Nelson* (ed. of 1899), p. 451.

By Henry Edridge, A.R.A. (1769-1821)
Pencil and Indian Ink, 12"×8¾". Full length. 1797. The earlier of two separate portraits by this artist. *Royal Hospital School, Holbrook.*
Print by W. Evans, 1798.
Nelson and Hamilton Papers (1893-94), Vol. II, p. 181.

By L. F. Abbott (1769-1821)
Canvas, 30"×25". 1797. *National Portrait Gallery.* Other versions, including several at the *National Maritime Museum*, show important variations.
Prints by W. Barnard, 1798 and 1799; R. Earlom, 1798 and 1801; R. Shipster, 1798; J. Chapman, 1798; V. Green, 1799; W. Ridley, 1801 and 1805; R. S. Syer, 1801, and many later versions.
Nicolas: *Dispatches and Letters*, Vol. III, p. 125.

By L. Gahagan (1756-1820)
Bust, bronze gilt. 1798. *Lord Cottesloe.* The first of several versions by Gahagan, recorded in 1801, 1804 and later.
Print by W. Barnard, 1805.
Notes and Queries, 7th Series, IX (1890), p. 107.

By H. Singleton (1766-1839)
Pencil Drawing. Half length. 1798. *National Maritime Museum.*
Fine mezzotint in colour by G. Keating, 1798.
The Times, 26.4.1955.

By D. Orme (1766-1822)
Miniature. 1798. Whereabouts unknown. Orme also painted a series illustrating some of Nelson's exploits, now at Greenwich.
Print by the artist 1798.

By Charles Grignion (1754-1804)
Drawing. February 1799, Palermo. *Royal United Services Institution.*
Lithographed, n.d.
The notes to W. T. Whitley's *Artists and Their Friends in England* (2 vols. 1928) in the British Museum Print Room establish the date, sometimes wrongly given as "Naples 1797."
Country Life, 2.8.1956.

By L. Guzzardi(fl. 1799)

Canvas. Full length. 1799. *National Maritime Museum.* Versions at the Admiralty, National Portrait Gallery and elsewhere.
Prints by J. Young, 1800 (after a copy by Keymer), and by C. Argento.
The Times, 21.10.1930.
Notes and Queries, 7th Series, IV (1887), p. 367.

By an Artist Unknown

Red and Black Chalk, and Water Colour, oval, $9\frac{1}{4}'' \times 7\frac{1}{4}''$. *Lord Mackintosh of Halifax.* A hatted version (miniature) is at the *Nelson Museum, Monmouth.* A miniature signed E. Nash 1800, based on these portraits, which were made in 1799 at Palermo, is in private possession.
Print by T. Burke.
Broadley and Bartelot: *Three Dorset Captains at Trafalgar* (1906), p. 60.

By H. Füger (1751-1818)

Canvas, $19'' \times 15\frac{1}{2}''$. Half length. 1800. *National Portrait Gallery* (unfinished). The only representation of Nelson in plain clothes.

By Matthias Ranson and Franz Thaller (1759-1817)

Bust, 1800. Another by D. Cardossi (*National Portrait Gallery*) seems to derive from this, as does one by Flaxman in the United Services Club, and another by Turnerelli in the Town Hall, Lewes. There is a version in coloured plaster at the Nelson Museum, Monmouth. Flaxman's statue in St Paul's (1809) seems to be based on another model. He met Nelson, but does not appear to have had sittings.

By J. H. Schmidt (1749-1829)

Pastel touched with gold. Half length. 1800. *National Maritime Museum.* A replica dated 1801 is in the same collection.

By S. de Koster (1761-1831)

Canvas, $24'' \times 21''$. 1800. *National Maritime Museum.*
Prints by T. Burke, 1800; J. Stow, 1801; S. I. Neale, 1820.

By an Artist Unknown

Canvas, $32'' \times 25''$, "Nelson Wounded at the Nile". *National Maritime Museum.* A dramatic picture of Nelson in his shirt, with bandaged head, wearing the medal for St Vincent. Given by him to Lady Parker.

By Anne Damer (1749-1828)
Bust, 1801. *London: Guildhall.* Mrs Damer made later versions, varying in scale.
> Prints: Anonymous, 1805; C. Knight, 1806; J. Godby, 1806.
> *Mariner's Mirror* (1922), p. 35; (1949), p. 342.

By Matthew Keymer
Canvas. Head and shoulders. 1801. *Town Hall, Great Yarmouth.* Keymer copied Guzzardi's portrait for Sir William Hamilton and painted an original in March 1801. Other versions exist.
> *The Times*, 21.10.1950.

By J. Rising (1756-1815)
Canvas, 36" × 26". Full length. 1801. *National Maritime Museum.*
> Print by J. Young, 1801.

By J. Hoppner, R.A. (1758-1810)
Canvas, 92" × 58". Full length. 1801. *St James's Palace.* Other versions exist.
> Prints by H. Meyer, 1805; Charles Turner, 1806; and others later.
> Enamels by Henry Bone, 1805 and 1808.
> Farington's *Diary*, 24.3.1802.
> Mackay and Roberts: *John Hoppner* (2 vols. 1909-14).

By Sir William Beechey, R.A. (1753-1835)
Canvas. Full length. 1801. *St Andrew's Hall, Norwich.* Other versions exist.
> Prints by R. Earlom, W. Say, H. R. Cook and E. Bell, 1806.
> Roberts: *Sir William Beechey* (1907).

By Henry Edridge, A.R.A. (1769-1821)
Drawing, 12" × 8¾". Full length. *National Portrait Gallery.* Edridge's second version.
> Print by A. Cardon, 1802.
> *Nelson and Hamilton Papers* (1893-94), Vol. II, p. 181.
> Farington's *Diary*, 6.8.1802.

By B. Papera
Plaster Bust, 18". 1802. Executed for Wedgwood and now at Barlaston, as is a wax model by John de Vaere, 1798, for medallion.

By J. Downman, A.R.A. (1750-1824)
Black Chalk and Stump, 12" × 9½". Half length. 1802. *Agnew and Son.*

By J. Whichelo

Pastel, oval, 20" × 15". *Sir William Parker*. Sketched at Merton in September 1805.

By R. Bowyer (1758-1834)

Miniature. Whereabouts unknown.
Print by W. Bromley, 1809.

By A. W. Devis (1763-1822)

Canvas. Head and shoulders. 1805. *National Maritime Museum*. Versions elsewhere. This is posthumous, but it was sketched in the *Victory* before Nelson's burial.
Print by E. Scriven, 1806.

By an Artist Unknown

Canvas, 27" × 23½". Hat without shade. No decorations. *National Maritime Museum*. Probably by Keymer.

By an Unknown Sculptor

Terra Cotta Bust, 15" high. *National Maritime Museum*. There is a bronze version of this outstanding representation in the same collection. It is probably not earlier than 1802. Certain medals struck in memory of Nelson, e.g. those by T. Webb and T. Wyon of 1805, seem to be based on this likeness.

By C. Andras

Effigy. Life size. 1806. *Westminster Abbey*. Based on Hoppner's portrait, but the sculptress is believed to have had sittings from life, for she showed a wax of Nelson at the Royal Academy in 1801.
Quarterly Review, February 1810.
Archaeologia, 85, VII, p. 169.
The Times, 8.12.1932.
Mariner's Mirror (1941), pp. 307-13.

A useful general reference is an article by Commander C. N. Robinson in *The Print Collector's Quarterly*, Vol. 17, No. 4. "The Engraved Portraits of Nelson": and I acknowledge with pleasure the collaboration of Mr Michael Robinson of the National Maritime Museum, Greenwich. See also *Mariner's Mirror*, Vol. 42, No. 4.

Index

Edinburgh : Printed by T. and A. CONSTABLE LTD.

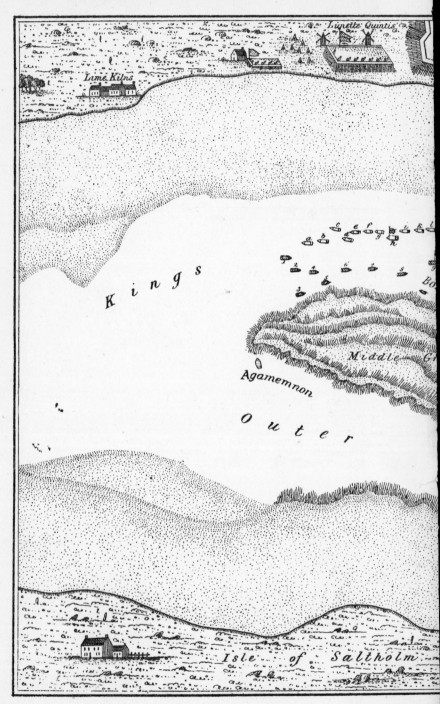

A PLAN OF THE BATTLE

Lime Kilns

Trinette Quintis

Kings

Agamemnon

Outer

Middle G

Bo

Isle of Saltholm